THE GREATEST PROBLEM
AND OTHER ESSAYS

Also by F. L. LUCAS

THE WORKS OF JOHN WEBSTER

AUTHORS DEAD AND LIVING
TRAGEDY
TEN VICTORIAN POETS
THE DECLINE AND FALL OF THE ROMANTIC IDEAL
STUDIES FRENCH AND ENGLISH
LITERATURE AND PSYCHOLOGY
STYLE
THE SEARCH FOR GOOD SENSE
THE ART OF LIVING

BEDDOES
CRABBE
D. G. ROSSETTI
TENNYSON

FROM OLYMPUS TO THE STYX

JOURNAL UNDER THE TERROR, 1938

CÉCILE
DOCTOR DIDO
THE WOMAN CLOTHED WITH THE SUN

THE BEAR DANCES
FOUR PLAYS

POEMS 1935
ARIADNE
GILGAMESH
HERO AND LEANDER
APHRODITE
A GREEK GARLAND
GREEK POETRY FOR EVERYMAN
GREEK DRAMA FOR EVERYMAN
FROM MANY TIMES AND LANDS

THE GREATEST
PROBLEM

AND OTHER ESSAYS

BY

F. L. LUCAS

Fellow of King's College, Cambridge
University Reader in English

New York   THE MACMILLAN COMPANY   1961

First Printing

Excerpts of Housman's poetry from *Complete Poems
of A. E. Housman,* Copyright, 1940, © 1959, by
Henry Holt and Company, Inc. By permission of
Holt, Rinehart and Winston, Inc.

Printed in the United States of America

Library of Congress catalog card number: 61-6162

TO
DESMOND FLOWER

Acknowledgements

I should like to express my thanks to Professor Kenneth Harrison and Professor Richard Stone for helpful comments on the last of these essays, dealing with world-population. Also to Messrs. J. M. Dent and Sons for permission to quote from my *Greek Poetry for Everyman;* and to the Society of Authors (as literary representatives of the Trustees of the late A. E. Housman's Estate) and Messrs. Jonathan Cape, publishers of his *Collected Poems,* for leave to include some of these in the essay upon him. Most of the sketch of Berlin during the Air-lift appeared in the *Manchester Guardian* during October 1948; and 'The Literature of Greek Travel' in the *Transactions* of the Royal Society of Literature for 1938. Some parts of 'Happiness' appeared in the August, 1960, issue of *Holiday.* I should like also to record my indebtedness to Mr. T. F. Higham's stimulating introduction to *The Oxford Book of Greek Verse in Translation.*

Contents

	Page
A Purpose in Life: the Tragedy of Tolstoy	1
A Glimpse of History: Berlin of the Air-lift, 1948	37
Translation	45
The Literature of Greek Travel	79
Testtuberculosis: the Menace of Science to the Humanities	99
Of Books	125
'Fool's-errand to the Grave': the Personality and Poetry of Housman	179
Happiness	235
The Greatest Problem of To-day	299

THE GREATEST PROBLEM
AND OTHER ESSAYS

A Purpose in Life:
the Tragedy of Tolstoy

I saw the body of Wisdom, and of shifting guise was she wrought,
And I stretched out my hands to hold her, and a mote of the dust
they caught.

MORRIS, *Sigurd the Volsung*

THERE come moments when a Western reader of Russian
fiction may find himself asking whether most Russians are not
intermittently drunk or mad.

'Absurd!' it may be answered. 'Your complaint probably springs
from an overdose of Dostoievsky. You mistake the nightmares of that
terrible imagination for realities. But, after all, Dostoievsky was an
epileptic genius, portentously exceptional. Why, the scientific precision
of Dr Tchyj has computed twenty-five per cent of Dostoievsky's
characters to be neuropaths—two in *The Brothers Karamazov*, four in
The Idiot, six in *Crime and Punishment*, and six in *The Possessed*.
Genius can create abnormal worlds of its own. You might as well imagine Americans in general to be sadistic necrophilists, just because you
have read Edgar Allan Poe!'

Yet this baffling Russian oddity is not confined to Dostoievsky
alone—think, for example, of Gogol and parts of Tolstoy. The suspicion persists that there really *is* some strange gap between the ordinary mentality of the West and certain qualities in the Russian character
at large.

Maurice Baring, indeed, claimed that the essential qualities of the
Russian mind were realism, matter-of-factness, and freedom from all
affectation or artifice. In illustration he cited the Russian folk-tale of
The Fool.

An old man left three sons: two clever, one a fool. The fool inherited
only a bony ox. This he forthwith sold, for twenty roubles, to an old
birch tree. He tied the ox to the tree; and that night the poor beast was
devoured by wolves. The next day, and the next, the fool came back
for payment. But as the old birch could only sigh and moan in the
forest-wind, in fury he hit it with his axe. Its trunk split, and revealed a

treasure. His brothers, when he told them, started eagerly carrying the gold to their home; but on the way there they met a deacon, to whom, naturally, the fool blabbed the secret. The deacon began grabbing his share of the gold, and was promptly axed by the fool. His anxious brothers first hid the corpse in a cellar; then, feeling still unsafe, buried it elsewhere, flinging a dead goat into the cellar in its stead. When the neighbours began searching for their lost deacon, the fool again blurted out the truth, confessed his murder, and was dragged to the cellar, into which they made him descend. 'Was your deacon black?' he asked them, as they stood above. 'Yes.' 'Had he a beard?' 'Yes.' 'And horns?' 'What sort of horns, fool!' Then the fool tossed up the goat's head; the people spat at him, as a hopeless idiot, and went home.

In this not very engaging story there is, it may be granted, 'realism' of a sort. But 'realism' seems somewhat to change its meaning east of the Niemen. No doubt, the story contains details realistic enough. No doubt, its underlying idea—that the naïve sometimes succeed better than the cunning, simpletons than wiseacres—contains also a real truth (though this curious moral might not have appealed much to the deacon, or to the ox). But such a tale, which for Baring typified Russian 'realism', may be felt by others to show also a fantasy and extravagance equally Russian. Indeed, it is not wholly unlike the curious blend of realism, farce, and reckless fantasy which meets us in Gogol's *Government-Inspector*; or in his narrative of the nose that absconded from an official's face to lead an official life of its own; or in Goncharov's Oblomov, a creature sunk in such depths of sloth and inertia, doubt and indecision, that beside him even Hamlet seems a very Fortinbras.

Again, the fool-hero of this folk-tale may be seen also as a remote foreshadowing of Dostoievsky's Idiot. Russian fiction in general, it has been said, is fond of two recurrent types—the simple soul that yet proves wiser than the children of this world; and, in contrast, the sinner with a pride as stark as Lucifer's. Now both these types are extremes. And while not denying that Russian gift for realistic vividness admired by Baring, one may feel that the Russian mind—whether or no it has been influenced by the extremes of Russian climate—tends often to a fantastic passion for the vast, the violent, the unrestrained, and the extreme. In the words of Bryúsov (1873-1924): 'Beautiful in the splendour of his power is the Oriental King Assarhaddon, and beautiful the ocean of a people's wrath beating to pieces a tottering throne. But *hateful are half-measures*.'

In thus generalizing, of course, it remains important not to become extreme ourselves. Most generalizations are, at best, like small-scale maps; even if accurate, there is an infinity of detail that they must omit; whole cities, full of hopes and fears, joys and tragedies, are reduced to black dots. Yet such maps remain useful.

Further one must admit that, take what nation you will, its successful imaginative writers are bound to be in many ways exceptional people; and so the imaginary characters they create are likely to be often highly exceptional too. If Soloviev, mystically pursuing the quest of the Divine Wisdom, could have a vision in the British Museum Reading Room (of all places) bidding him go at once to Egypt—where in the desert he had a further vision of the said Sophia, still, you may argue, the same might have happened to our English Blake (though I have some doubts whether Blake would actually have taken ship for Cairo). If the message of Andreyev was 'horror and madness', so to some extent was Leopardi's or Baudelaire's. (And as for the twentieth century, a good deal of its literature seems mad, all the world over.) If Gogol, again, could conduct his comic burlesque in *Dead Souls*, like his own life, to its typically Russian conclusion of conversion, repentance, and redemption (which seems, at first sight, almost as queer as if Mr Micawber and Charles Dickens had both ended as Methodist missionaries), yet Gogol's master, Pushkin, though his life was Byronic and his death quixotic, does not, I own, give any such impression of mental abnormality. If Dostoievsky becomes often like a man possessed, yet Turgenev seems sane enough—indeed, when confronted with some fantastic absurdity, Turgenev would merely observe, 'C'est du Dostoievsky.' And if Tolstoy at times, as in *The Kreutzer Sonata*, appears fantastic and perverse, yet the letters of Chekhov, on the other hand, wake instant sympathy just because they are so fundamentally sane, or so penetratingly prophetic. 'My Holy of Holies is the human body, health, mind, talent, inspiration, love, and the most absolute freedom—freedom from violence and falsehood, in whatever they may be manifested. This is the programme I would follow if I were a great artist.' And again—'Under the flag of science, art, and freedom of thought, we shall have such toads and crocodiles ruling Russia as were unknown even in Spain at the time of the Inquisition.'

To-day, after half a century, neither of those passages has lost its wisdom or its force. Prince Mirsky in his interesting history of Russian Literature was rather disparaging towards Chekhov; but perhaps Prince Mirsky knew his countrymen less well; he was rash enough to return to the Soviet Union—and duly disappeared.

And yet even in Turgenev and Chekhov there remains much that to Western eyes may seem bizarre. Even Turgenev, in a moment of spleen, is related to have stood himself in a corner with a fool's cap on his head, made out of a window-blind. And even through *his* pages, as through Chekhov's, there creep the queer shapes of what Chekhov called 'the wood-lice and molluscs—the drowsy, apathetic, lazily philosophizing, cold intelligentzia'. The English reader has by now come to accept them—'Yes, apparently intelligent Russians of the time could be like that.' Yet they interest him precisely because they *are* so odd. He can seldom conceive becoming like that himself.

* * *

And it is not only the fiction of Russia that gives this recurrent sense of bewildering oddity—of action, passion, or passivity all carried to extraordinary extremes. Russian history and biography show the same queer combination of megalomania and masochism, patience and impatience, violence and acceptance, ardour and apathy.

No doubt the history of all European lands is full enough of folly, wickedness, anguish. And it might be fanciful to urge it as specially characteristic that Russian Christianity should have begun with so bizarre and unrestrained a Saint as Vladímir, who is credited with two wives, three mistresses, and three large harems of eight hundred concubines; and is related to have preferred Christianity to Islam for the not very saintly reason that 'we Russians cannot live without drinking'.

But when, in the sixteenth century, the West began to make contact with Muscovy, it reacted, even then, with considerable astonishment, and some horror, to what it saw there; tough and unsqueamish though the sixteenth century was. 'It remains in doubt', wrote Freiherr von Herberstein, 'whether such a people requires such grievous government, or whether it is such cruel government that makes such a good-for-nothing people.' We think of Queen Elizabeth as sufficiently domineering; but even Elizabethans gasped at the Muscovy of Ivan the Terrible. 'Slave-born Muscovite', writes Sidney; 'slave-born Muscovite', echoes Webster. And the disgust was mutual. 'I thought', wrote the angry Ivan to Elizabeth, anglophil though he had been, and anxious perhaps to make her his fifth or sixth wife, 'that you were mistress at home, and free to command your wishes; now I perceive that you let yourself be ruled by men. And by what men! Mere moujiks! You are yourself but a common wench, and act like one. I therefore renounce relations with you. Moscow can do without English moujiks.' So a Russian poet has written, of his countrywomen's destiny—

> Fate has three ordeals in store.
> The first is to be married to a slave;
> The second is to be mother to the slave's son;
> The third to obey the slave till death.
> All these grim ordeals
> Await the woman of the Russian land.

Even to-day, when we should have learnt to be surprised by nothing in human nature, the imagination staggers at the fantastic barbarism of this Tsar Ivan, who, it is said, while eager to turn to the West and learn from it, yet murdered his own son; wedded the Archbishop of Novgorod in mockery to a pregnant white mare; or played monk himself in the Slobodá of Alexandrov, defended by a ditch too wide for demons to leap, and a rampart too slippery for them to climb—his days spent partly in beating his forehead, till it bled, against the floor of the church; partly in torturing prisoners; and partly in listening, childlike, to the fairy-tales told him in the evenings by three blind men.

And what successors! There is Peter the Great, who was still keener than Ivan to modernize and westernize Russia, yet demonstrated his passion for progress by clamouring, when shown an executioner's wheel in Brandenburg, for a criminal to experiment with; by commanding members of his suite in Boerhaave's Dutch laboratory, when they muttered disgust at a dissection, to bite the corpse; by pulling out his own subjects' teeth[1] on his return, or tapping a woman for dropsy, then graciously attending her funeral when she died.

There is that militarist maniac, Peter III, holding in full uniform an officers' court martial at Oranienbaum on a rat which had impertinently eaten a papier-mâché sentry from his castle of toy soldiers (it was sentenced to be hanged, and solemnly executed); or drilling his wife Catherine, one day to become 'the Great', in the palace of Peterhof,

---

[1] A bag of these was preserved in the Art Museum at St Petersburg.

until, in her own words, 'thanks to his pains I can shoulder arms to-day as well as the best-drilled grenadier. For hours at a time I had to stand on guard, at the door of the room between his and mine, with a musket on my shoulder.'

There is her son Paul, who forbade the accursed word 'revolution' to be uttered even by astronomers talking of heavenly bodies; and, when the French Ambassador rashly referred to some Russian as 'important', coldly replied, 'In *my* Empire there is no one "important" except the man to whom I happen to be speaking; and he is "important" only so long as I speak to him.'

There is *his* son the mystical Alexander, whose minister Arakchéev created a collective Paradise, hardly equalled for thoroughness even by modern China. Part of the province of Novgorod was turned into a military district; its peasants were shaved, dressed in uniform, and formed into military units. They even did their cultivation in uniform, singing at a given signal, and advancing their ploughs at the word of command. A strict time-table decided their hours for drill, agriculture, rest, and procreation. For even their marriages were militarily regulated, sometimes by drawing lots; and wives were fined if they failed to give birth to the proper quota of infant-recruits. The population was housed in symmetrical villages of two-roomed dwellings, painted blue or pink. From May to mid-September, cooking had to be done out of doors, whatever the weather; to ensure this, their stoves were sealed. For some reason, however, this Utopia was neither happy nor successful; not even though Alexander wrote: 'The military colonies shall go on, even if I have to cover the road with corpses from Petersburg to Chudov.' And, in fact, two hundred and seventy-five of the refractory were made to run the gauntlet of a thousand men twelve times. From which, it is said, one hundred and sixty died.

Similarly with the strange sects that have at times emerged from Russian religion—the Khlysty with their orgies of flagellation and fornication; the Skoptsy castrating themselves; the Fire-Baptists burning themselves alive.

But there is no need to multiply examples of this Russian tendency to the most violent extremes, often to contradictory extremes—to tenacious, unconquerable vitality, but also to nerveless resignation; to delightful gaiety, but also to morbid love of suffering; to brilliant energy, but also to feckless incompetence; to grim asceticism, but also to reckless sensuality; to great sincerity, but also to gross self-deception; to the microscopic realism of psychological novels, but also to fantastic day-dreaming and fanatical obsessions.

*   *   *

These are not merely the impressions of the foreigner. In the words of Dostoievsky himself—'As for me, I have done nothing in life but push towards the extreme what you dared push only half-way. . . . And so perhaps I am more alive than you.' And again—'The Russian people tastes a sort of pleasure in suffering. . . . I believe that the spiritual need most deeply inrooted in the Russian is a need for inexhaustible suffering—at every instant, everywhere, in everything.' Even when translating *Eugénie Grandet*, it is typical that Dostoievsky felt impelled to exaggerate what Balzac merely calls 'souffrances' into 'profound and terrible torments'. (And Balzac himself was hardly a type of moderation.)

Chekhov, again, speaks of that 'excessive excitability' which leaves a Russian emotionally bankrupt, whereas a German, he says, is not excitable (after Hitler, this seems highly dubious), and a Frenchman generally keeps his excitement at a less excessive level. Perhaps one may see significance even in the Russian saying, 'The goose is a stupid bird, because it is not enough for two, yet disgraceful to consume alone'—not a problem that would worry most Western stomachs.

Hence 'holy Russia' and 'the Russian soul' have often astonished and perplexed the West. The very phrases are significant. 'La belle France'—yes. 'Merry England'—perhaps. But 'holy France', 'holy England' would sound curiously incongruous.[1] 'French logic'— 'English commonsense'; but we do not debate the French or the English 'soul'.

In his *Government-Inspector* Gogol describes the hero Khlestakov as a man 'without a Tsar in his head'. For Khlestakov's brain is an unruly chaos of anarchy. The description seems to fit many of his race. Through the ages the Russian has been crushed under a tyrannous climate and tyrannous autocrats; yet, paradoxically enough, he appears to have often kept a strange, even excessive freedom of spirit. External oppression, inward liberty—even inward licence.

[1] True, Western monarchs have called themselves 'Defender of the Faith', or 'Most Christian King', or 'Most Catholic Majesty'; but this pomp of royal titles does not seem really analogous. A closer parallel would be 'Holy Ireland'; but Ireland has often stood apart, in spirit as well as in geography, from Western Europe.

7

All this makes a glaring contrast with the traditions of Western Europe. The Egyptian priest called the Greeks 'eternal children'; yet even the Homeric Greeks of perhaps the ninth century B.C. seem already riper in wisdom—more grown-up—than many Russians of the nineteenth A.D. For the Greeks learnt early to recognize the power of Necessity—*Ananke*—and the limitations of mortality; the need to think soberly, and to feel in moderation. No doubt they often failed to practise it; but perhaps we owe even more, though we talk of it far less, to Greek sanity than to Greek art. *They* first taught to men the ceaseless aspiration towards reason and balance—the 'dry light' of Heraclitus, the ironic scepticism of Socrates. 'Know thyself'— 'nothing too much'.

The Roman of the best type and time, less intellectual, was yet trained to value that self-disciplined 'gravitas' which respected alike its own dignity and the liberty of others, and would have found merely Scythian and barbarous the unrestraint of Russia.

Moribus antiquis stat res Romana virisque.

Rome's commonweal stands steady on the ways, and the men, of old.

In the stoic disillusion of Lucretius, the melancholy of Virgil, or the proud bitterness of Tacitus, in the Roman heroes of Plutarch, or the grave faces of the Ara Pacis, in the massive arches of the Pont du Gard, or the great monuments of Roman law, there endures a combination of dignity and discipline that the world has hardly found again.

France, in her turn, developed the ideals of 'bon sens', 'bon goût', 'bon ton', till life was at times in danger of being stifled artificially under these three excellent things. True, they have all at times been swept away by the revolutions of French politics or French literature. Still there remains something typical in that motto of Madame Geoffrin's salon, 'Rien en relief'; or in that maxim of Talleyrand's, 'Surtout point de zèle!' From Montaigne to Racine, from Fontenelle to Anatole France, some of the most characteristic monuments of the French mind, as of the Greek, are marked, above all, by their sense of measure.

The English, again, have also tended to pursue moderation; in different ways from the French, but perhaps with greater persistence and more practical success. No doubt the French have sometimes found our imaginations 'déréglées'; no doubt we have produced extra-ordinary eccentrics, like George Fox, or Beckford, or Bentham; no doubt our history has its full share of follies and horrors. And yet if it

8

has fewer of these to blush for, over the space of a thousand years, than the history of any other nation that I know, a main cause for this may lie in the rooted English distrust and dislike for all extremists, doctrinaires, and fanatics. When Marx raged that a certain Comrade Odgers was 'possessed with a mania for compromise, and a thirst for respectability', he was in effect merely complaining because an Englishman was typically English.

Naturally foreigners do not find this restraint an unmixed blessing. The very Russian Princess Lieven, who plunged so eagerly into English society, was yet driven to lament: 'This beautiful England is always the same . . . but when one has seen everything and grown tired of admiring, one wishes to feel, and England is not the country of emotions.' She was wrong. The emotions were there. But they were not things that one talked of; they might even be things one did not admit to oneself. Similarly a foreign psycho-analyst once complained to me that we were, as a nation, uniquely difficult to analyse, because of all this inhibition and repression. Indeed it has sometimes seemed to other races that we live embedded in what Milyukov, like Maurice Baring, praised the Russian mind for avoiding—'a cement of hypocrisy'.

Perhaps a combination of the Russian kind of realism and the English, of their uninhibited spontaneity and our practical sense of where to stop, would be ideal. But certainly it would not be easy. One may feel that no race has been better than the Russians at depicting reality on paper, yet more hopeless at coping with it in life. But, disastrous as their history has for this reason been, it often adds to their charm as individuals, or as writers, that Russians can strike us as so much nearer to the child, or to the primitive, unsophisticated man. They tend to be less bottled up, to see life more with a child's vividness and naïveté and naturalness. Is a character, for example, wildly inconsistent in his moods? 'Why not?' they answer. 'It is only human.' Has he cherished insane or criminal impulses? 'It is only human.' Has he even committed crimes ? 'That, too, is only human. Perhaps he will expiate them by suffering. He is not untouchable; merely unfortunate.'

> To sin shamelessly and uninterruptedly,
> To lose count of days and nights,
> And with a head heavy with drunkenness
> To insinuate oneself into God's temple

9

—so Alexander Blok wrote of the Russian temperament; and, after picturing its worst degradations, he adds—

> Yes, and even in this form, my Russia,
> You are dearer to me than all the world.

Dostoievsky went still further. Because the Russian people has this sympathy, this understanding, this acceptance of crime and anguish, it alone, he proclaimed, is destined to comprehend the other nations of the earth, and bring them all at last to unity.

But at this point the sceptical Westerner begins to smile; especially when this apocalypse is combined by Dostoievsky with a brusquely practical demand for the annexation of Constantinople.

Once more one feels that Russians can be fascinating to contemplate or listen to; but perilous to follow or obey. No people has combined more strikingly in its history both invincible energy and yet tragic frustration. No wonder that its nineteenth-century intellectuals came constantly to cry 'What is it all for? What is the purpose of life?' It is hard to imagine a Russian Johnson, or a Russian Hume. And I own that after a bout of Russian literature I come back with a sigh of relief to the clear commonsense and tranquil irony of our own eighteenth century.

But much though I prefer our ways of thinking and feeling, it would be a loss to know nothing of theirs. And if we wish to ask what is life's purpose (supposing it has one), and to see what comes of asking that eternal question too persistently, then it becomes of special interest to watch what the Russian mind has made of it; not only because their writers have been so often salvationist; but also because they are so different from ourselves—so natural and intense—that in their hands these hackneyed questions grow new and young again. Further, if the Russians are often temperamental extremists, yet it is precisely such extreme cases that are often the most interesting and instructive. One may tire at times of daemonic characters, who tear passions to tatters; but at least they reveal the human spirit at its most naked.

*   *   *

Now even in Russia it would not be easy to find a man who pursued 'the meaning of life' with more persistent singleness of purpose, even into extreme old age, than Leo Tolstoy. Not even *his* genius, I think, ever conceived a novel so strange and tragic as his own life; a character so mysterious and tormented as his own; or a household so fantastic as the Yasnaya Polyana of his last years.

At the heart of his life's drama lay his marriage. Had he lived a hermit, as in his last dying effort he set out to do, he might still not have been happy; but he would at least have escaped the endless frustrations, heart-burnings, and humiliations that tortured his old age.

Marriage, Tolstoy once said, is either heaven or downright hell—it has no purgatory. As so often, he generalized wildly. Though his own marriage proved no heaven, yet the love of this tragic pair, who could be happy neither together nor apart, was never wholly killed by all the growing quarrels and embitterments of forty-eight years. Merely to call it 'hell' would show, I think, too much imagination, or too little, or both.

Tolstoy, like most geniuses, had never been an easy husband. Then in 1879, just after he was fifty, came his 'conversion'. In 1883 he gave up control of his property. In 1891 he divided it, like another Lear, between his wife and his nine children. But this resignation brought him no peace. More and more his home became divided against itself; and he found, like Christian in the City of Destruction, his worst enemies beside his own hearth.

There on one side of the house white-gloved lackeys hand ices to counts and princes, who chalk their distinguished names on the table-cloth, to be immortalized in embroidery; on the other side, by a different door, the 'dark people' detested by the Countess file into the poor quarters where the Count lives in peasant dress and peasant simplicity, cobbling his own shoes, emptying his own slops. And queer indeed some of these visitors are, as depicted in the Countess's exasperated diary—'a miserable, disappointed, disgruntled-looking in-dividual'; 'a dark, skinny, gloomy, exalted idealist'; 'miserable abor-tions of human society, aimless babblers, uneducated loafers'. One is a mad peasant, who thinks himself Christ, and Tolstoy God; another is a blind peasant, who screams that Tolstoy's Christianity, though bet-ter than the Christianity of priests, is yet a lie; that his disciples are scoundrels and bandits; and that Tolstoy himself is the worst of all. The concourse is swelled by half-mad ne'er-do-wells, by inquisitive foreigners, by violent young revolutionaries, scornful of the Master's non-resistance, yet met by this once violent and overbearing man with gentleness and humility; though at times even *his* patience with disciples wore thin. 'He is "a Tolstoyan",' he growled to Golden-veizer about one of them, 'that is, a man of convictions utterly opposed to mine.'

If these seekers cannot come personally on pilgrimage, they deluge him with letters (till the greatest writer of his country wastes time and energy scribbling up to twenty-five replies a day)—letters begging for money (though Tolstoy has now no property), in order that they may buy, perhaps, a camera, or a trousseau; letters begging his advice about life, or his judgement of the writer's manuscripts; letters denouncing him as traitor, heretic, corrupter; even a parcel from an indignant 'Russian Mother' with a halter neatly coiled inside.

And beyond the walls of this 'Heartbreak House' the rift spreads wider into the outer world. The Count feels, now, that a writer who takes money for his books is on a level with the woman who takes money for her body; yet the Countess prosecutes infringers of the copyrights that have now become hers. She prosecutes, too, the thievish peasants who steal her timber, or her cabbages; while he feels miserably guilty and begs for their acquittal. She demands armed police from the Governor of Tula; he clamours for their odious presence to be removed. And all these domestic broils and scandals wake malignant laughter in the clerical or reactionary press.

Further and further the conflict extends, till it fills Russia. Tolstoy is excommunicated. He is denounced by the Bishop of Saratov as a damned blasphemer, a Russian Judas. When he brings famine-relief, the Church sends its emissaries to warn the starving peasants against taking the bread of 'Antichrist'; when he seems dying, it sends priests to haunt his neighbourhood, ready to proclaim that he died recanting. His followers are imprisoned in fortresses, or exiled; yet the Government dares not touch their Master, though he publicly denounces the tyranny of the Russian state, the brutalities of Russian law, the wicked-ness of military service and of the Russian war against Japan. The Russian censorship may ban his articles or books; but they slip across the frontier to be printed in the foreign press, to be published abroad in translation or in Russian, and so flood back into Russia itself. He writes to the Ministers of Justice and of the Interior demanding to be arrested like his followers. But still the Government dares not make a martyr of this national saint. For the Tsars were children at autocracy compared with the Communists; and their Russia a land of free speech beside the U.S.S.R.

Naturally, all these external conflicts only deepen the conflicts within the home. The younger sons side with their mother. One of them, Andrei, flouts his father by deserting his own wife and children, to elope with the wife of the Governor of Tula, herself the mother of six. Another, Leo, directly attacks him in a novel, and in the press—Tolstoy, he says, is 'a baneful influence' in Russia, and to blame for the menacing drift towards revolution.

And now appears the unpleasing figure of one Chertkov, since 1883 a leading disciple of Tolstoy's, and at moments unpleasantly recalling the moral immaculacies of Mr Chadband. He had been an exile in England; but now, from 1907 onwards, he rouses to frenzy the dread and hatred of the Countess by haunting the neighbourhood of Yasnaya Polyana. She sees herself driven to a battle without quarter for those copyrights of her husband's which she regards as the rightful heritage of her twenty-three children and grandchildren; a battle for her husband's too intimate diaries, which have passed into Chertkov's hands; a battle for her husband's very heart and soul.

And since the Count cannot now have long to live, this frenzied struggle extends also into the future beyond his grave. Chertkov persuades Tolstoy to will his works surreptitiously away from this wife who can only think, like a she-bear, of her own whelps. The old man makes stealthy testaments, which turn out to be invalid; then more testaments, in the privacy of his room, or in the silence of the woods round Yasnaya Polyana. Yet there is no privacy in this house where war has bred espionage, where the Countess lives in conflict not only with her husband, but also with her youngest daughter, and with other Tolstoyans of Chertkov's faction. At last the Countess finds, hidden in her husband's boot, a part of the last of his fatal diaries; it confirms her suspicions of a secret will.

So now the conflicts of this thirty years' war reach new heights of bitterness, of tears and anger and menaces of suicide. Tolstoy had once threatened to shoot himself; now such attempts grow ever more frequent on the Countess's part—poison, pistols, scissors, the railway (like Anna Karénina), or half-clad exposure to the Russian night. Chertkov has become, for her, as devilish as his name.[1] She calls in a priest to exorcise from Tolstoy's room, with incense and holy water, Chertkov's evil spirit. She tries denouncing Chertkov to the Government, to get him removed. She even taxes her husband of eighty-one

[1] *Chert* in Russian means 'devil'.

13

with a homosexual passion for his disciple of fifty-six. Imagination fails before the spectacle of this Bedlam of scenes and whisperings, conspiracies and hysterics, while beneath its roof actors and supers sit scribbling no less than eight of those eternal diaries.[1] 'And a man's foes shall be they of his own household.'

The end is familiar. On October 28th, 1910, the old Tolstoy did at last what for years he had threatened to do—fled. Not, however, to any peaceful hermitage where he could rest forgotten by the world— only to lie gasping (but still keeping a diary) in the stationmaster's house at Astapovo, while, amid the humming of the world's telegraph-wires, officials, police, journalists, doctors, desperate relatives, and prowling ecclesiastics tumbled over one another on that obscure station which bears to-day the name of 'Leo Tolstoy'.

At length, when he was no longer conscious, the sobbing Countess, who after his flight had flung herself into the lake at Yasnaya Polyana, was allowed to kneel by the deathbed of the husband she had passionately loved and, often, passionately hated, for nearly half a century.

And so that weary body, which had warred so long with the soul that possessed it, found peace at last, with no religious rites, in the stillness of the Zakaz woods. When Tolstoy was only five, his eldest brother Nikolai, aged eleven, had once told the three younger boys that in those woods he had buried a little green stick, on which he had written the secret of all human happiness—of a Golden Age without sickness or sorrow or hate, when all men would love one another. They would become, said Nikolai, like 'Ant Brothers';[2] and the four small boys used to play at ant-brotherhood, cuddling together in the dark, under rug-draped chairs. But the little green stick lies hidden still.

Tolstoy's was a very different funeral, there in the quiet of the woodland, from that imposing procession of seventy-two delegations and thirty thousand mourners which had borne Dostoievsky to his rest in the Alexander Nevsky monastery thirty years before. For Dostoievsky, the one-time Siberian exile, had become in the end a pillar of

[1] The Count and the Countess, at this time, each kept two; one more secret than the other. A gruesome picture of the madhouse that Yasnaya Polyana had now become, with a cranky old husband and a crazy wife maddened by love-hatred for each other, will be found in *The Last Struggle* (the Countess's diaries for 1910, and extracts from her husband's, translated by Aylmer Maude). No wonder they found each other unendurable; at this stage few ordinary persons could have endured to live with either.

[2] '*Muraveinye bratya*'—perhaps because Nikolai had heard of *Moravskiye bratya*, Moravian Brothers.

church and throne, with his strange visions of a Russia redeemed by the pure orthodoxy of the moujik, and a world redeemed by the disinterested benevolence of Russia. But Tolstoy the heretic would have felt no envy for such splendours; and he had little cause.

Nine years later, after a World-war and a Communist revolution, such as Tolstoy had foreseen and dreaded, his Countess too died at Yasnaya Polyana, in that new Russia which holds her husband, as an artist, supreme; but, as a thinker, pernicious.

*   *   *

And yet what ended so tragically had begun, fifty years before, in passionate romance.

As a boy of nine, Tolstoy one day pushed down the stairs at home a neighbour's daughter of eleven, because she was neglecting him. She was his future mother-in-law. Five years later, at sixteen, she married Dr Behrs, twenty years her senior and one day to become Court Physician to the Tsar. Fourteen years later still, Tolstoy's diary records a visit to her and her family—'What dear, merry little girls! We walked and played leapfrog.'

Next year the 'merry little girls' seemed no longer quite so little—'If Sonya', said Tolstoy to a friend, 'were sixteen and not fourteen, I would propose at once.' And on her side, Sonya, the second of the three sisters, with her dark, intense eyes, had already begun a childish adoration of the famous writer; wearing a passage from his *Youth* next her heart, and decking with ribbons the chair he used. But this hero-worship did not prevent her from feeling also a more normal fondness for a young cadet, Polivanov. And, in her feeling for Tolstoy, Sonya herself had a rival—her elder sister Liza, who began to be backed by her parents and by Tolstoy's own sister Marya.

In 1862 the Behrs family visited Yasnaya Polyana; beds were too few, and with his own hands Tolstoy made Sonya's in a large armchair. Next day the two rode out together. When the guests departed for their next place of stay, forty miles off, Tolstoy soon followed them on his white horse. When they returned to Moscow, he drove with them. All that August saw him racked with indecision. He was now a man of thirty-four, with experience of many brief mistresses and several love-affairs; though the love-affairs suggest a character who, at heart, fled from marriage, like Gogol, almost as anxiously as he pursued it.

Sonya now showed her faint-heart lover a story she had written, where one Dublitsky, middle-aged, unattractive in appearance,[1] and unstable in his opinions, was loved by the young Elena; who in the end, however, married a lover of her own age, and resigned Dublitsky to her elder sister. Tolstoy did not much relish seeing himself as Dublitsky. But his agonies of vacillation continued. He wrote Sonya a letter of renunciation; but he renounced sending it. He wrote a letter of hesitating proposal; but for three days he dared not give it. Finally, on the third evening, September 16th, 1862, he called and played a waltz, while Sonya's younger sister Tanya sang. Then Tolstoy took a sudden resolve (he had long been a gambler, so desperate and unlucky that some of his fellow-officers refused to play with him)—if Tanya managed the last high note, he would give the letter. Tanya took the high note easily; and so there began a marriage whose last notes were to be far from high. Sonya fled with the letter to her room; Liza's anguished voice came through the door—'What has the Count written? Speak! What has the Count written?' 'He has proposed.' 'Refuse! Refuse at once!' Sonya went back and accepted.

But this fatal love was never to run smooth for long. Sonya's parents were ill pleased. Next day her mother announced to gathered relatives and friends that Tolstoy was to wed her daughter. But she failed (perhaps from unconscious reluctance) to say *which* daughter; and congratulations poured on the wincing Liza. Polivanov, too, was there.

Tolstoy insisted on marriage within a week. But even so he found time—with incredible folly, for a skilled analyst of the human heart[2]— to hand his betrothed the diary of his past amours. Honest frankness between lovers is one thing; elaborate details another. Tolstoy could be at times as disastrously fat-fisted with truth as Ibsen's Gregers Werle. The girl of eighteen was horrified. 'If only', she wrote in her own journal three months later, 'I could burn his diary and his whole past!'[3]

---

[1] In later portraits Tolstoy looks more and more like a typical moujik; but a likeness of about 1855, in uniform, shows a not unhandsome, though rather heavy, ruthless face. His physical strength was such that at Sevastopol, lying flat, he could life a heavy man off the ground with the palm of each hand.

[2] Cf. the comment of the critic Druzhinin, who complained that Tolstoy carried psychological subtlety *too* far—'You are sometimes on the point of saying that so-and-so's thigh indicated a wish to travel in India.'

[3] One may recall how Strindberg vainly made his second and third wives promise not to read his bitter account of his first wife—*A Fool's Defence*; a similar Bluebeard's cupboard. Journals are often safety-valves; but often, also, dynamite. They should be kept under lock and key.

On the very morning of the wedding, against all Russian etiquette, Tolstoy rushed round to the bride's home; there he poured out to her his doubts and misgivings, till her mother found her in tears, and hunted him away. In the evening he failed to appear at the Court Church in the Kremlin. By mistake his dress-shirts had all been packed and sent round with his luggage to the bride's house. (Again the unconscious uttered its vain warning.) Finally, the ceremony was performed and his six-horsed *dormeuse* drove him and the sobbing Sonya away through the autumn night towards Yasnaya Polyana.

'It is better', said the Apostle, 'to marry than to burn.' Yet celibate saints and sages have often been over-ready with their matrimonial counsels. Those who rush into marriage as a lesser evil may find they have made an evil marriage. Tolstoy's curious behaviour makes one wonder whether he should ever have married at all—whether he would not have been happier, or at least less unhappy, had he chosen instead that solitude into which, with the last dying strength of his old age, he finally tried to flee. Sonya on her side had possibly found in him a father-substitute; but father-substitutes tend to prove in the end poor substitutes for more normal husbands.

Yet for a moment all seemed bliss. 'I did not realize', Tolstoy wrote, 'that one can love so much and be so happy.' 'No one has had, or will have, such happiness.' But those of whom happiness makes such fools, are likely to play the fool with their happiness. Quarrels came quickly. Again the accursed diaries played their part. Both husband and wife poured out their feelings in journals which, with fantastic idiocy, the other was allowed to read.[1] Everyone has petty moods and irritations. The only sensible course is to forget them. But, recorded on paper, they become less easy to forget; recorded and read by a lover, they may rankle for life. How far such a marriage of fevers and frenzies seems from the grave humanity of the terse old Chinese adage—'In bed, man and wife; out of bed, guests'!

But even these accursed diaries were not enough; not enough that Sonya was maddened by seeing still about the house the peasant-mistress of her husband's journal, Aksinya.[2] Sonya (it will surprise no psychologist) was also frigid; and Tolstoy now wrote a story, *The*

---

[1] An entry in hers is prophetic. 'He likes to torture me and see me weep. . . . Gradually I shall retreat into myself and shall poison his life.'

[2] Tolstoy's memories of her reappear in his story *The Devil*.

Porcelain Doll, the point of which, though she pretended not to see it, was hardly mistakable, even for her.

And yet the two were devoted; despite the quarrels, despite the lack of physical passion on one side and the excess of it on the other, despite the recklessly crowded succession of pregnancies, there seems to have been plenty of sunshine between the storms, for some seventeen years —that great period which produced *War and Peace* and *Anna Karénina*. But about 1879, soon after he was fifty, came Tolstoy's conversion. Even before this, at moments, he had been gripped by an unspeakable horror of inevitable death. What was the meaning, the purpose of life? He removed a cord from his room lest he use it as a halter; he stopped hunting, lest he be tempted to shoot himself.

In earlier years, the author of *War and Peace* (finished in 1869) had been accused of indifference to the social questions of the hour; and he had himself denied that a true artist should bother his head with such things.

> If I were told that I could write a novel in which I could irrefutably prove my own views on every social question, I would not devote two hours to it; but were I told that my writing would be read twenty years hence by those now children—that they would laugh over it and fall in love with the life of it, then I would spend on it all my existence and my powers.

But now, in place of Tolstoy the artist, there rose up Tolstoy the prophet. This not only sharpened the tension in his home, where he became more and more like a John the Baptist married to a Martha, and vainly struggling to reconcile luxury with locusts, fine raiment with camel's hair; it deepened the discords with himself as well.

For the plot of this most complex tragedy involved most complex characters. The one essential thing in Tolstoy's final doctrine was universal love; yet Turgenev doubted, as the Countess sometimes doubted, whether Tolstoy had ever in his life really loved anyone. Again, he preached passive non-resistance; yet he was by nature a pugnacious, resentful, rebellious person. He was, for example, unpleasantly cantankerous with Turgenev;[1] and when he clashed in 1872 with a local magistrate about a bull of his that had killed its herdsman, he became so

---

[1] Tolstoy at this period could carry dialectical browbeating to lengths that even Dr Johnson might have thought immoderate. 'I can stand no more,' cried the outraged Turgenev in the middle of some furious discussion, 'I have bronchitis.' 'Bronchitis!' snorted his scornful opponent. 'Bronchitis is a *metal*!'

furious that he thought of migrating to England—'Away to England for only there is personal freedom protected from every kind of outrage.' His creed was self-effacement; and yet, 'whatever I do', he writes, with characteristic and disarming candour, 'I at heart always feel convinced that forty centuries gaze down on me from the heights of the pyramids, and that the world will perish if ever I stand still'. He told Gorky that he had not had a fortnight's happiness in life, 'because I have never lived—I cannot live for my own self; I live for show, for people' (an accusation echoed, less graciously, by the Countess). And finally, throughout his wife's diaries there recurs, with growing bitterness, the reproach that this preacher of purity and asceticism—even though it should involve the extinction of the human race—was here too in practice the very opposite of what he preached. 'At his wish I have been pregnant sixteen times—thirteen children born and three miscarriages. In those days he suggested to me, a young woman, that he could not work or write or be healthy if I refused to cohabit with him.' And twelve years after Tolstoy's 'conversion', in 1891, she still records: 'Tanya' (her daughter) 'has just gone past and said that Lyovochka had asked her to tell me that he had gone to bed and put out the light. Her innocent lips have brought me a message that is far from innocent: I know what it means, and I am annoyed.' Always, she complained, he was tender only at such moments of desire; at other times, cold, callous, and indifferent.

No doubt the Countess herself grew into an unbalanced, neurotic woman—feverishly busy (no doubt to avoid thinking of her unhappiness); jealously suspicious; hysterically clutching at her husband, at her children, at the family possessions. Yet it was not mere self-seeking on her part. If the money she battled for so desperately, often went in the end only to subsidize idle, wasteful, and tippling sons, it was still a mother's natural instinct. And when one thinks of her endless copying and recopying of her husband's endlessly corrected manuscripts (*War and Peace*, it is said, she wrote out half a dozen times), of her endless corrections of his proofs, besides the cares of thirteen children, of business dealings with publishers, and of running the estate, it becomes difficult not to feel that if she grew warped and embittered, the poor woman had at least some excuse.

> Thus piteously Love closed what he begat:
> The union of this ever-diverse pair.

*   *   *

It is rash to pass judgements on the living; still rasher, to pass them on the dead. One never really knows enough. Their long anguish is over; there remains only the pity of it, the human interest. But, as in the art of war, though it is foolish to be too ready with praise for one commander, and blame for another, yet it remains possible, and useful, to consider what kinds of strategy or tactics do *tend* to succeed, and what do not—so with the art of life.[1] Few inner lives have ever been so amply documented as these; is there anything to learn from them?

Two typical incidents, one from Tolstoy's childhood, one from his old age, perhaps illumine the whole course of his career. As a child, he fancied that by shutting his eyes, squatting on his heels, and clasping his arms round his knees, he would be able to fly. (A curious pose for flight, and intriguing to the psychologist.) Intense as always, he put his dream into practice, like the crazy hero of Browning's *Turf and Towers*; and, having thus soared out of a window, was found unconscious with concussion. Highly symbolic.

Again, as an old man, when visited by some of his devotees, he picked up his almanac of wise sayings and read: 'A man standing on tiptoe cannot stand long.' And he laughed delightedly (his humour remains one of his most redeeming and endearing qualities) at its appropriateness to himself.

It may indeed be said that Tolstoy spent much of his later years in urging mankind to live on tiptoe, and to fly blind, without wings.

His crisis had come when dread of death forced on him the whole question of the meaning of life. He thought he had found the answer; and towards that answer he felt called to lead mankind. The motive was noble. And yet such assumptions of leadership show, surely, something of the *hubris* of Prometheus; who was punished by agelong laceration on that Caucasus so loved by Tolstoy in his youth.

God, for Tolstoy in the end, became impersonal. (Tolstoy's attitude to God reminded Gorky of two rather surly bears sharing the same den.) Christ became a man, who had taught the essential message of *all* the best religions—human brotherhood and human love, universal

---

[1] Nothing is more exasperating in *War and Peace* than Tolstoy's fixed idea that generalship is a chimera, and that it no more mattered if Napoleon had a cold than if it had been the humblest private in his army. It is only human that front-line soldiers should be implacably prejudiced against the staff-mind. But I have seen enough of both to respect both. And so long as armies exist, their officers will rightly have to study the art and theory of war, as things that really do exist.

sympathy, and ascetic simplicity. Violence was evil; war was evil; government was evil; sex was evil. The only hope for humanity was a change of heart.

And yet, had it not been for Tolstoy's own artistic genius and personality, one may doubt if this strangely over-simple creed of his would ever have made many converts. Little in it was new; and little, I think, true. He wanted all men to love one another. But I do not really know what this means. For most of us, 'love' signifies a strong personal affection. Romeo had it for Juliet (but Tolstoy disapproved of *that*); or David for Absalom. But those who really have it, can have it only for a few. When, in Hardy's *Dynasts*, the Prince Regent appears, 'surrounded by a hundred and forty of his particular friends', we smile. And we are meant to smile. If I am asked to love all mankind from China to Peru, I can only confess that I do not feel equal to it. It takes long arms to embrace the globe. And indeed to use the word 'love' so promiscuously seems to me only to profane it. It does not often, in the long run, make men become better: it merely makes the word 'love' become weaker. Further, the innate aggressiveness of human nature is apt, sometimes, to take grim revenges for such exaggerated idealism. Turn over these volumes filled with 'love', and you come to the crude and cruel absurdities of Tolstoy's *Kreutzer Sonata*.[1] Overstrained benevolence is too apt to bring unpleasant compensations. Christianity could bring rack and faggot. On the lips of Christ himself, in Dostoievsky's tale, falls the ruthless kiss of the Grand Inquisitor.

Though Tolstoy preached love to the world, he could not create it by his own fireside even. Might it not have been better to leave men to love only those few they find truly lovable? Better to work simply for that slow increase of goodwill, justice, sympathy, and tolerance which, despite hideous setbacks, the last three centuries have seen? Towards *that* thinkers and writers *can* contribute; though often they prefer to do the exact opposite.

Again, Tolstoy wanted men to renounce all violence, all resistance;

[1] Novels have a nasty way of turning out prophetic; sometimes because they reveal subconscious trends working in the writer; sometimes because they have great powers of suggestion. *The Kreutzer Sonata* (finished 1889) relates the jealousy felt by a husband for a musician, which drives him brutally to stab his wife. Half a dozen years later Tolstoy's own wife was seized by an infatuation for a musician, which, though platonic, for years caused the old writer poignant jealousy.

even towards the drunkard or the maniac. And no doubt passive resistance can sometimes be powerful; as Tolstoy's most important disciple, Gandhi, was to demonstrate in India. But a good deal depends on what is being resisted—a state like modern England where, whatever its hypocrisies, public opinion has at times a conscience; or some more ruthless power. It is not so long since millions of non-resisting Jews filed in miserable procession towards the death-camps and gas-chambers of Hitler's Reich. Much good their non-resistance did for *them*!

Thirdly, Tolstoy wanted to abolish governments. In his eyes they were based on four accursed expedients—terror, bribery, hypnotism, militarism. They all committed 'the sin of organization'. And yet revolutionaries, he thought, were no remedy. For revolutionaries neither knew the people nor loved them. Communism would only breed a new caste of tyrants; commit still worse 'sins of organization'; and infringe the sanctity of the home. As for Western democracy— 'To ask me what I think of parliamentary government is just like asking—I won't say the Pope—but some monk his opinion how prostitution should be run.'[1]

One may grant that all governments are a curse. Unfortunately they remain a necessary curse. Some, indeed, may hymn democracy; but that seems to me excessive rapture. Democracy is not, I think, a good form of government. There are no good forms of government. Democracy seems merely the least evil form, by far, for nations with enough good sense and good humour to play its complicated game. Since no succession of men and no body of men in history, so far as I know, have ever held uncontrolled power for generations without rotting, it becomes essential for a country to be able at least to change its masters peaceably. There has never been less social injustice in England than now, however much remains still to be done; and this has come about, not because we have learnt to love one another (we do not); nor because we have abolished government (we never had so much); but because, after a century, the workers have finally learned how to use their votes. They have at last applied political power to redress the balance of economic power, in 'a revolution by due course of law'. Needless to add that this has been possible only because the English

---

[1] A type of the somewhat crude imagery for which Tolstoy had a significant fondness; compare his likening of railway travel to brothels—convenient, but inhumanly mechanical and monotonous.

in general have an unusual respect for law, for playing the game according to the rules, and for fundamental decency. To-day no party proposes to abolish the Welfare State; partly because it would be impracticable, but partly also because many of the once rich (who, despite Marx's prediction, have grown poorer while the poor grew richer) recognize that things are fairer so. But this change in economic status has not come just by a change of heart; it might be truer to say that a change of heart has accompanied the change in economic status.

Again, Tolstoy wanted to abolish sex—even though mankind should in the end become extinct. He forgot the bitter laughter of Aphrodite above the doomed Hippolytus.

Finally, Tolstoy wanted to abolish most art, as immoral. '*Fiat justitia, pereat cultura.*' Similarly he wanted to abolish most science—even to abandon railways and electricity, and go back to the horse and to tilling the ground with sticks. I suppose, thinking only of agrarian Russia, he failed even to realize that without science many of the most civilized parts of Europe would starve. He jeered at the folly of scientists in classifying seven thousand kinds of flies. He refused to believe in heredity. Once he had jested about the spread of books being the most effective means of disseminating ignorance; but he came to wonder if it were not actually true. When his wife had a dangerous internal growth, he objected, though only passively, to an operation, as interfering with 'the great and magnificent act of death'. 'The Kaffirs', he said once to Goldenveizer, 'are the only hope left.' And yet he was embarrassed when Verigin, the leader of the Dukhobors, logically carried these crotchets into yet wilder fantasies—that one should make one's own boots, but without metal (since the miners are enslaved); that one should set free all horses and cattle; that men should live naked, off fruit and nuts.

But perhaps the unhappiest part of Tolstoy's creed was his sense of sin, that carefully cultivated feeling of guilt (perhaps the deadliest legacy of medieval Christendom) which, even after he discarded the dogmas of the Orthodox Church, he could never discard.

Even at twenty-two his diary grows grotesque with its fantastic searchings of heart.

March 10th, 1851. Again did not rise till late. Spoke amiss to Ozerov, and pressed on him a horse. *Meanness*. Poiret. *Deception and hastiness*. Lied to Begichev that I knew the Siberian Gorchakovs. Left my fur coat behind (*hastiness and lack of solidity*). At the Council showed *diffidence*; at gymnastics, *vanity*; at the Lvovs', *presumption and affectation*. Omitted to make any transcriptions, *sloth*. Even my journal of failings I am writing hastily and without care.[1]

Little wonder that, even at twenty-six, he grew ambitious to found a new religion. When one's 'worm of conscience' grows so uppish, it would be wiser to bottle it in good spirits at once. Better even Falstaff and the Wife of Bath, than Malvolio and Zeal-of-the-Land Busy.

Curiously medieval, too, is Tolstoy's reflection during his Caucasus days, when he feared having caught syphilis—'At the thought that my nose might fall in, I imagined what an immense and beneficial impulse this would give towards moral growth.'

With similar self-persecution, though of a humaner kind, he dwelt through his last thirty years on the tormenting thought that, while he lived in comfort at Yasnaya Polyana, peasants were starving in their hovels. If peasants did manual labour and grew their own food, should not all men do manual labour and grow their own food? If peasants were lousy, was it not perhaps a sinful luxury to be clean? (And indeed among the trials of the poor Countess was the harsh fact that her husband was at times far from clean, or pleasant to be near.)

Tolstoy was a far more honest character than Shaw (whom Tolstoy, perhaps with some justice, thought a trivial person, with more brains than were good for him); but he lacked the element of good sense which made Shaw argue that, though the just man should try to change the rules of the economic game, even to his own disadvantage, still, while those rules remain in force, he is quite right to observe them; and not in the least bound to start a private revolution on his own, and attempt to live fifty years ahead of his age on fifty shillings a week.

A large part of the human dilemma, I suppose, is due to our being at the same time highly individual and highly gregarious creatures. These two sides of man's nature perpetually develop inner conflicts that can drive him to the borders of madness, or beyond. The ego pursues its own advantage; but the gregarious side—conscience—cannot forget the claims of fellowship. Even if the egoistic side stifles the

---

[1] One is reminded of the seventeenth-century diary of Lord Wariston, in which he describes himself, with singular satisfaction, as 'the unworthyest, filthiest, passionatest, deceitfullest, crookedest, backslydingest, rebelliousest, perjurest, unaiblest' of all God's servants. So Plato saw the pride of Antisthenes peeping through the holes in his rags.

gregarious, there may still survive an accusing ghost that poisons, perhaps from a hiding-place in the Unconscious, all the joy of life; or, on the contrary, the gregarious side may nag and bully the tyrannized ego into morbid extremes of abnegation. 'Be not righteous over much; . . . why shouldest thou destroy thyself?'

It may indeed be wondered if, with all his stress on love, Tolstoy did not come in the end to hate life itself. The burden of this split personality grew too heavy. And so he ended by preaching that in this world one should lose oneself in the mass; while, beyond the grave, he abandoned personal immortality. He even played with the idea of annihilating the human race. Let it attain perfection by sexlessness, and fulfil its function, and die out. Men harsh to themselves easily grow harsh also to others.

No wonder Tolstoy was attracted by the pessimist Schopenhauer, and by the final peace of the Buddhist Nirvana. No mystic by temperament, he yet came to have some of the mystic's craving for return to the happy quiet of the womb. That is what, in childhood, the little Ant-brothers had been unconsciously enacting in the darkness beneath their rug-covered chairs. And at seventy-two he wrote: 'Dull, miserable state the whole day. . . . If I could be little again and snuggle up to my mother, as I imagine her to myself . . . my highest image of pure love; not cold divine love, but earthly, warm, motherly.' This does not seem to me a healthy or a happy type of mind for facing life; nor was it likely to bring happiness in marriage.

*   *   *   *

For Tolstoy's tragedy there seem to me two main causes. With his temperament, they may have been unavoidable; but that need not lessen their general interest. First, there was his overpowering compulsion, under the horror of coming death, to seek life's purpose; second, the compulsion, when he thought he had discovered that purpose, to preach it, as a prophet, to the world.

First, then, this question of life's meaning. Is it really, one may wonder, so imperative to ask it? The answer may be unknowable. Or there may be no answer, the very question being absurd. There may be no purpose, and no meaning. What is the purpose of an earthquake? The meaning of a comet? Once men thought they knew—these were portents meant to warn us of evil to come. But they were wrong. The meaning of 'hippopotamus' is in the dictionary: the meaning of *a* hippopotamus, no one knows. There may be none. The purpose of the Universe? 'Pour nous enrager', was the answer of Voltaire's Martin. That seems unduly pessimistic. I should have thought it wiser to be content with choosing a purpose of one's own. The rest is silence.

When I think of those long years spent by Tolstoy in anguished pursuit of the 'meaning of life', my memory goes back to the men, most of them long dead, whom I learnt to know on Salisbury Plain and by the Somme. They were not noble peasants from Holy Russia; but I suppose they were the nearest counterpart produced by saner, more civilized, less mystical and emotional England. Little more than boys, most of them, they were living closer to death, at twenty, than Tolstoy even at eighty. But they were not, like him, overmastered by the horror of death; nor did they groan about the meaning of life. Life was something hard to lose, that yet had to be risked—for the sake of self-respect, for the sake of loyalty to their fellows and their battalion, for the sake of keeping untrampled the England symbolized for them by some village of the Kentish Weald, or by the dingy street-fronts of the Old Kent Road.

That sufficed. Unlike some of their officers, they hardly bothered their heads about the wider, political issues—about the necessity of keeping a certain kind of beastliness from dominating the world. They had not needed even this motive to volunteer in 1914, as soon as the War began. They were fuddled with no follies about military glory; on the march they sang ribald mockeries of *that*. They did not chant Hymns of Hate; they did not hiss the name of 'Boche'; they merely talked with good-humoured irony of 'Jerry', and tossed him a cigarette when he was taken prisoner. Quite spontaneously, in their brief lives they were living up to that unassuming, unhating, yet unyielding tradition of the English, which speaks so typically in the recorded comment of a gunner in the *Goliath* off Cape Saint Vincent on St Valentine's Day, 1797, a century and a half ago—'We gave them their Valentines in style; not that we loved fighting, but we all wished to be free to return to our homes and follow our own pursuits. "The hotter war, the sooner peace", we said.'

Few of them were sustained by religion—from censoring their letters, I should say only two or three out of the thirty in my platoon. Church Parade was particularly cursed and damned. 'Will you come and put up some barbed wire to-night, Whiting?' 'Well, sir, one can only die once.' Those half-dozen words cling in my memory after forty

years, where so many millions of other words have left not a trace.
How simple! Yet a hundred philosophers could have taught Whiting
no more. 'One can only die once.' And most of them died.

> Life, to be sure, is nothing much to lose;
> But young men think it is, and we were young.

Unimaginative generals killed them by the hundred thousand; well-
intentioned politicians squandered what they had died for, till a new
generation had all their work to do again; fools between the Wars
jeered that they had died like fools. But they had done the job that
called them. The dead of the Somme had nothing to blush for, had the
power to blush still been theirs.

But, since then, my sympathy is not wholly warm towards comparatively comfortable persons who torment themselves and others
with frantic questions about 'the purpose of life'; and with still more
fantastic answers.

However, having found his solution of the problem in universal
love, non-violence, and the simple life of poverty, Tolstoy very naturally felt it his duty to preach this gospel to the world.

Tolstoy's great predecessor Pushkin has left a flaming vision of the
prophet's calling (which has lost none of its force since the triumph
of Communism in Russia).

> With fainting soul athirst for Grace,
> I wandered in a desert place,
> And at the crossing of the ways
> I saw a sixfold Seraph blaze;
> He touched mine eyes with fingers light
> As sleep that cometh in the night:
> And like a frighted eagle's eyes
> They opened wide with prophecies.
> He touched mine ears, and they were drowned
> With tumult and a roaring sound:
> I heard convulsion in the sky
> And flight of angel hosts on high,
> And beasts that move beneath the sea,
> And the sap creeping in the tree.
> And bending to my mouth he wrung
> From out of it my sinful tongue,
> And all its lies and idle rust,
> And 'twixt my lips a-perishing

A subtle serpent's forkéd sting
With right hand wet with blood he thrust.
And with his sword my breast he cleft,
My quaking heart thereout he reft,
And in the yawning of my breast
A coal of living fire he pressed.
Then in the desert I lay dead,
And God called unto me and said:
'Arise, and let My voice be heard,
Charged with My will go forth and span
The land and sea, and let My word
Lay waste with fire the heart of man.'

(Translated by Maurice Baring)

This is a poet's magnificent imagining, magnificently translated; but it does not appear ever to have tempted Pushkin himself to play prophet. Nor is it, after all, a very beneficent vision—with its 'subtle serpent's forkéd sting', its utterance that 'lays waste the heart of man'. 'Sixfold Seraphs' are capable of a good deal of duplicity; and no one will ever number the countless hearts that have agonized or broken as a result of such prophets' dreams.

It seems, indeed, remarkable that, from age to age, prophets should be found to rise up and confidently proclaim that *they* can lead humanity from the wilderness to the Promised Land, if only men will wholly change their ways. For the resulting benefits have proved less remarkable. Mankind seems to me to owe far more to those more modest leaders who have *not* promised the conquest, for eternity, of some New Jerusalem, but have been content to lead their fellows, if they could, through the urgent difficulties or dangers of the present hour—such figures as Solon the Athenian or Joan of Arc, Abraham Lincoln or Winston Churchill.

But such more limited achievement does not suffice the prophets. They must legislate for *all* mankind, for *all* posterity. There may have been more excuse for such pretensions in simpler ages, before men had realized the infinite complexities of existence, the infinite uncertainties of the future, the infinite intricacies of the human mind; and before society itself had grown so crushingly complex. Plato could dream of a static Utopia amid the eternal transience; but we have learnt that such immutability is not for human things. No aristocracy of 'Guardians' remains incorruptible. Too often the Rule of the Saints, whether in

28

Calvin's Geneva, or Cromwell's England, or, still more, in Stalin's Russia, becomes a reign of human decadence or diabolism.

In Tolstoy's lifetime there arose two other prophets destined to have more practical influence than he, in directions exactly opposite to his. Nietzsche (who praised violence and the proud individual as passionately as Tolstoy denounced them, and condemned humanitarianism as fervidly as Tolstoy preached it) had a considerable practical effect, though of a kind he had by no means intended, in encouraging German arrogance on its road to ruin. And a peevish, fanatical Jew in London, as fervid in advocating revolution and dictatorship as Tolstoy in rejecting them, was to change the whole face of the twentieth century; which remembers Tolstoy only as a story-teller of genius, and cares nothing for the faith that made him condemn, in the end, even his own stories.

Yet both these more successful prophets were likewise to become the playthings of time's irony. Nietzsche scorned the Second Reich, and he would have loathed the Third; but even he could hardly have laughed more bitterly over the ruins of Berlin than Marx would over the modern Kremlin—if Marx was sincere in his vision of that happy future where both classes and the state should wither away.

Johnson was no doubt a Tory reactionary. But I know no picture more eloquent, in its melancholy, of the dangerous folly of Utopian legislation than he drew in *Rasselas*.

'Hear, Imlac,' says the mad astronomer in *Rasselas*, 'what thou wilt not without difficulty credit. I have possessed for five years the regulation of the weather, and the distribution of the seasons; the sun has listened to my dictates, and passed from tropick to tropick by my direction; the clouds, at my call, have poured their waters, and the Nile has overflowed at my command; I have restrained the rage of the dog-star, and mitigated the fervours of the crab. . . .'

The prince heard the narration with very serious regard; but the princess smiled, and Pekuah convulsed herself with laughter. 'Ladies,' said Imlac, 'to mock the heaviest of human afflictions is neither charitable nor wise. Few can attain this man's knowledge, and few practise his virtues; but all may suffer his calamity. Of the uncertainties of our present state, the most dreadful and alarming is the uncertain continuance of reason. . . .

'No man will be found in whose mind airy notions do not sometimes tyrannize, and force him to hope or fear beyond the limits of sober probability. . . . In time, some particular train of ideas fixes the attention, all other intellectual gratifications are rejected, the mind, in weariness or leisure, recurs constantly to the favourite conception, and feasts on the luscious falsehood, whenever she is offended by the bitterness of truth. By degrees the reign of fancy is confirmed; she grows first imperious, and in time despotick. Then fictions begin to operate as realities, false opinions fasten upon the mind, and life passes in dreams of rapture or anguish. . . .'

'I will no more,' said the favourite,[1] 'imagine myself the queen of Abissinia. I have often spent the hours which the princess gave to my own disposal, in adjusting ceremonies and regulating the court; I have repressed the pride of the powerful, and granted the petitions of the poor; I have built new palaces in more happy situations, planted groves upon the tops of mountains, and have exulted in the beneficence of royalty, till, when the princess entered, I had almost forgotten to bow down before her.'

'And I,' said the princess, 'will not allow myself any more to play the shepherdess in my waking dreams. I have often soothed my thoughts with the quiet and innocence of pastoral employments, till I have in my chamber heard the winds whistle, and the sheep bleat; sometimes freed the lamb entangled in the thicket, and sometimes with my crook encountered the wolf. . . .'

'I will confess,' said the prince, 'an indulgence of fantastick delight more dangerous than yours. I have frequently endeavoured to image the possibility of a perfect government, by which all wrong should be restrained, all vice reformed, and all the subjects preserved in tranquillity and innocence. . . .'

'Such,' says Imlac, 'are the effects of visionary schemes: when we first form them we know them to be absurd, but familiarize them by degrees, and in time lose sight of their folly.'

Rasselas is not a popular book; and yet how fine this passage is—in its wisdom, its sonorous eloquence, its comic, yet tragic irony! (Tolstoy was, doubtless, a greater writer; but I doubt if he ever wrote anything so wise.) New? No. But deeply true, and superbly put. In that same year 1759 was born a twin to *Rasselas*—not less disillusioned, but far more gay—*Candide*. Yet in his story's end the puckish Voltaire showed, I think, a deeper wisdom even than the sombre Johnson. Voltaire saw that it is fatal to ask too much what life in this world is for. Whatever, if any, the purpose of this curious Universe, the vital thing is to have a purpose of one's own. Rasselas, in the end, merely goes back disillusioned to the boring idleness of the Happy Valley: but Candide by the Bosphorus learns at last that familiar, but far saner, conclusion—'Il faut cultiver son jardin.'

[1] Pekuah.

There in that garden, if anywhere, grows Tolstoy's little green stick. The garden of Candide is unlikely ever to become the Garden of Eden; we must expect that there will always be weeds and thorns and tares in it, evil and pain and unhappiness. To try cultivating it with the dynamite of revolutionaries does not seem ever to succeed as well as the patient work of the spade. The agelong, desperate cry of prophets for a change of heart only shows how little they know the human heart, and how little the human heart can really change—in anything less than the slow lapse of centuries. Even if our earthly garden blossoms at last like the rose, even that cannot efface the abominations of the past, nor abolish the self-tormentings of the soul, nor evade that ultimate future when all gardens go back to desert in the end, under the impassive gaze of the galaxies across the burning cold of space. To be frightened, like Pascal, of their infinite and eternal silence is to be no better than a scared child. Pascal lacked nerve—a real fault, to my mind; unlike those imaginary sins which tormented him with neurotic nightmares unworthy of his genius. Better, indeed, for its possessor (though not, very often, for the world), the temperament of a healthy ploughman than a genius that is three parts disease.

The prophets, indeed, seem to me to fall by the same sin as Lucifer —pride. Even when they proclaim that the secret of life is meekness and humility. Were they content merely to suggest their views, well and good. But the prophets are not content to suggest. They proclaim. They speak with authority. And by what authority? I have never understood the virtue of faith. Faith consists in believing things without adequate logical or experimental reasons. The very mention of faith implies that the reasons are logically and experimentally inadequate. It may be retorted that the coldest rationalist holds an irrational faith in reason. But I believe that the most reasonable minds are cautiously distrustful even of reason itself; remembering that tower at Montaigne and the prudent mottoes inscribed upon its rafters— οὐδὲν ὁρίζω (I take no definite view)—ἐπέχω (I suspend judgement)—ἀκαταλήπτω (I do not commit myself)—*vae qui sapientes estis in oculis vestris* (woe to you that are wise in your own eyes!). The best that can be said for reason is that it seems to work better than most other methods of understanding the past, of controlling the present, and of preparing the future.

In short, it seems wiser to confess our inevitable blindness, and to limit our objectives. Indeed one of the striking things in Tolstoy's own life is how much better he succeeded when he too was content with some definite, limited task, instead of straining for the stars with the uncompromising fanaticism of Ibsen's Brand. In the same way Voltaire filled a splendid rôle in his defence of Calas, Sirven, or the Chevalier de la Barre—for these were particular outrages, about which few will doubt him right; while, on the other hand, had he lived another fifteen years, he might well have regretted that general over-confidence in human reasonableness which led him too rashly and widely to undermine the foundations of the eighteenth-century world.

Thus Tolstoy's great novels were written before he became a prophet at all. His personal experiment of educating little peasants with a system of liberty recalling modern schools like Summerhill was also a striking success; though there one suspects that the success of such a system, or lack of system, depends mainly on the unusual personality of the teacher. So too with the persecution of the Dukhobors, of which *The Times* published Tolstoy's denunciation in 1895, to the intense annoyance of the Russian Government and Church. In 1898 he further aided these unfortunates by helping to raise the money for twelve thousand Dukhobors to migrate to Canada.

The same success with definitely limited objectives reappears in his relief-work for the famine of 1891 in central and south-east Russia. The Tsar's Government, ruthless as Stalin's, belittled the emergency, because it cared for official prestige far more than for human lives. 'In Russia', said Alexander III, 'there is no famine; but there *are* localities suffering from a failure of crops.' But here Tolstoy showed himself at his indomitable best. When the Russian Government barred the news from appearing in Russian papers, Tolstoy saw to it that the truth emerged in the English press. When the Russian Government refused to take steps, he took his own. By July 1892 he had set up three hundred and ninety kitchens, feeding thirteen thousand adults and three thousand children. The practical Sonya could see the point of *this*; and for a while their own marriage-relations became far happier. But even here Tolstoy's fantastic conscience troubled him: he had preached that charity was debasing—therefore his relief-work must be morally wrong. Fortunately, he was better than his principles; and this crazy pedantry did not prevail. But the emergency passed; Tolstoy resumed the burden of his prophet's mantle, and of his frustrating unhappiness. He could not be content to cultivate any garden; he must go gathering the stars.

Vain to blame him for lacking the calm doubt of Socrates or Montaigne. He could not change his nature for theirs; just as a Wesley cannot become a Hume. Many will add 'And so much the better'. But I am not so sure. Faith, no doubt, can move mountains; but too often in the wrong direction—and on the heads of luckless multitudes. Heavens taken by storm too often turn out Hells. Sceptics need not become Hamlets—Hamlet was a sickened soul. In war, success is more likely to go, not to the soldier who fools himself that the chances are ten to one in his favour, when they are really ten to one against, but to the soldier who accepts the odds, however menacing, and calmly does his best. 'Dutch courage' (a libel on the Dutch) does not seem to me the best kind of courage.

*　*　*

One may distrust certain aspects of the scientific mind; one may find in it at times a tendency to aridity, even to naïveté; but when it becomes a question of changing anything so tangled as the world, I am afraid that the only chance lies, not with prophets who have a devastating trust in that perilous thing, intuition, but with men who mingle good sense, scepticism, and science. Turgenev wrote an essay preferring Don Quixote, who acts, even if blindly and madly, to Hamlet, the intellectual who cannot act at all. But I should not have thought it very wise to follow either. Don Quixote in rusty armour may do little harm; Don Quixote in prophet's garb can be calamitous. Indeed I doubt if in all history there have been many prophets apart from Confucius (who was hardly one) that have not done more harm than good. For one thing they are usually so drastic in their haste to turn life upside down. Deluges and eruptions may sometimes fertilize; but as agricultural implements they are inferior to dams and tractors.

As for the artists, seeing science encroach each year more and more upon our lives, they have two choices—to take refuge in the irrational, or to become more rational themselves. Many in our century have preferred the irrational; the results appear to me dismal. The artist's prime object is to make men feel, as well as see, life's values. But, as psychology becomes a science, it becomes more and more a *scientific* question what states of mind really are valuable and healthy. That seems to me one reason why everyone, artists included, should aim at thinking more scientifically. Another reason is that really scientific thinking is cautiously sceptical; and the more complex our life becomes, the less we can jump to conclusions.

To some, such a conclusion will itself seem intolerably bleak. Men have clung so hard and so long, like Tennyson, to the faith that there *is*—

> one far-off divine event
> To which the whole creation moves;

to the hope that—

> somehow good
> Will be the final goal of ill.

And yet. . . .

Suppose a purpose to exist, what is it? That all should at last be happy? Then why such misery meanwhile? That only a chosen few should at last be happy? Then better, one might think, if things had not begun at all.

Or perhaps there is a conflict of purposes—Good against Evil, Ormuzd against Ahriman? Were I religious, I should perhaps choose as least improbable this creed of Zoroastrian and Manichee. Yet, as Hume pointed out long since, one would expect such a conflict to rock the Universe; whereas the course of natural events seems to flow on its way changeless and imperturbable.

Or again there is the view that life at large has only now begun to acquire, or will some day acquire, what we might call a purpose. Some, for example, have conceived a Life-force, a sort of blind-worm, conducting its education, as was said of George Moore, in public. For this transcendental Blind-worm, dear to Bernard Shaw and entertained at times by Thomas Hardy, I can neither see much evidence nor feel much enthusiasm. No future millennium seems to me capable of redeeming the tragic, irreparable chaos of the past.

Or there is the complementary view that the world, instead of acquiring a purpose it previously had not, has lost a purpose it once had—like a vast factory whose constructor has died or disappeared, leaving it to grind blindly on with multiplying faults and disasters. But all such ideas seem mere fantasies of analogy.

Then again it has been suggested that the nature of things for some reason tends towards ever greater complexity; and towards this we are, for some reason, enthusiastically invited to collaborate. But I see no reason for this yearning after more and more complexity. Many things in the modern world appear to me badly in need of a little healthy simplification. Why this indiscriminate admiration for complexity? The married life of Solomon must surely have been much more complex than that of Odysseus and Penelope; but more valuable?

And now there are those who, seeing the growing powers of science, hope that Man may at last impose a steady and beneficent purpose on at least his local fragment of the Universe. They may hope. But those who read history, or psychology, may doubt if any trust in human wisdom is very wise. Too many Utopian thinkers, from Plato to Marx, seem to have come to grief that way.

To sum up, the search for a general purpose in existence seems to me to serve no purpose at all. We know too little. And we can foreknow even less. Better, I should have thought, to be frankly and boldly individualist—content to pursue a purpose of one's own—the very simple purpose of making the best of things, and of making things, if possible, a little better. 'Travaillons sans raisonner, dit Martin, c'est le seul moyen de rendre la vie supportable.' 'Without reasoning', indeed, seems excessive. Martin was a too splenetic pessimist. For to reason is often amusing—sometimes useful. But to reason like Tolstoy, racking his brains and breaking his heart, seems void of use and amusement alike. To his metaphysical problems the only answer may be 'Wait and see'; though one must be prepared to wait and never see. Work and affection; courage and, if possible, a gaily ironic resignation—these, for some temperaments, though perhaps only for a few, may be safer guides than the faith and hope of the Apostle, that through the centuries have so often and disastrously deceived.

So, after all, some of us come back to no better answer than that of *Candide*. This may seem a very small, very grey mouse, in which no maternal mountain could feel any particular pride. But it is not a 'ridiculous mouse'. And it seems a very tough and tenacious one. In practice, whatever their theories, a large part of mankind has always followed it. It has not merely 9 lives, but 9^n.

A Glimpse of History:
Berlin of the Air-lift, 1948

BELOW, London sinks into the grimy vapours of the October morning, like a city drowning in a grey tidal-wave; and above its submerging streets the cloud-wisps swimming from the west mass thicker and thicker, like shoals of dirty-white jellyfish. Then suddenly (as one sees the snows of the Oberland, sixty miles away, from the ridge of the Weissenstein) to eastward a mountain-range of cumulus, golden from an unseen sun, against a sky of turquoise and emerald like a great window opened on infinity. Beneath, through cracks in the grey cloud-floor, the wrinkled face of the North Sea; then Holland—a great green floating leaf, veined with silvery canals; then a bumpy plunge from the upper sunlight into another world of pewter-coloured mist. There Hamburg lay, under a sky as drab and low-roofed as London's, beside the long sweep of the Elbe, livid as some river of the dead, where the frontier of Asia now begins.

Above the airfield buildings, the Union Jack; within, British Frontier Control Officers, and girls in dark-blue uniform, working beside green-clad German customs officials with as friendly unconcern as if Western Europe had been federated twenty years.

After an hour, airborne again for Berlin, the romantic traveller found his first disillusionment, if he expected a sky flickering with Russian Yaks, or roads black with Russian columns scowling upward. In fact, all seemed emptiness—highways without cars, railways without trains, and indeed, where they had been double-tracked, stripped of one set of rails. Little, indeed, but great void stretches of forest, ploughland and pasture, lifeless except for occasional cows; till at last the circling swoop on Berlin-Gatow, with its coveys of parked aircraft, its gangs of German labourers busily extending the runways that were now their last link with civilization.

Within a mile or two of Gatow the ruins thickened; till one found oneself in the heart of that wilderness which was once Berlin.

> Mile on mile on mile of desolation,
> League on league on league without a change.

One had heard of it, read of it, seen pictures of it; but still the reality staggered and appalled. The eye, scanning street after street of shambles, rested with relief on some exceptionally fortunate house that remained habitable above its ground-floor. Among these endless rows of gaunt, hollow-eyed façades, one felt like a mouse wandering amid the skulls of some vast catacomb. Still towering walls of naked brickwork took the memory back to Roman ruins like the Baths of Caracalla; but from the ruins of Rome time has swept away the cheap, pitiful débris, the hideous shards of twisted and corroding iron, and left only the superb Roman vaulting which has defied the tempests of two thousand years. The wreckage of a modern city has no such tragic pride. Here a broken, rusty cistern jutted grotesquely into vacancy, like a Mahomet's coffin between earth and heaven, from the top of some gutted building that seemed waiting for the next squall to topple it. (Only a few days before, a cinema had collapsed upon its audience.) There the skeleton of a bank still ironically flaunted in large letters the word 'Versicherung'—though all it had 'insured' was long since blown to the winds. Above the hollow shell of a theatre a bronze horse, beautifully patinaed, still lifted its maimed wings to the skies. Church-towers still raised to heaven crosses that could not save. The gilt hands of clocks recorded the hour when their final doom had struck. On the approach to Hitler's Olympic Stadium the flagstaffs rose flagless, their red paint faded with wind and rain. Above the sweep of the East-West Axis there towered still the Siegessäule of 1873, with its golden Victory; but over her head fluttered, mocking, the tricolour of France. On her left, the Tiergarten had become a waste, backed by a wilderness of wrecked houses— imagine a desolated Hyde Park, ringed with ruins. Wild grasses climbed round the white-marble potentates of the Siegesallee. To the east the Hammer and Sickle floated above the broken Doric columns of the Brandenburger Tor, now the gate of Tartary; and just to north of that there towered a grimmer monument to Nemesis than the pompous Russian war-memorial in front—the burnt skeleton of the Reichstag. Little had Hermann Goering dreamed, on the night he set fire to the seat of German democratic government, that before a dozen years were gone, round it would lie the cinder-heap of all Berlin.

But beyond the Brandenburger Tor, past the shattered pomp of the Wilhelmstrasse, rose the most significant ruin of all—Hitler's Reichs-kanzlei; hardly more frigid and funereal in its downfall than it must have looked even in its prime; so grim and cold and lifeless seemed the lines of this mountain of brick and marble which Berlin wit had derided as 'the Pompeian goods-station'. Now its marble casing was being stripped for a vast Soviet war-memorial—the new tyranny donning with unconscious irony the marmoreal mantle of the old. 'Amurath to Amurath succeeds.'

The first reaction of the stranger dropped straight from London into this world of nightmare was sickened horror—and a sense of infinite gratitude to Winston Churchill and Fighter Command, who alone saved England from a fate as horrible. And yet, within two or three days, one was astonished—and slightly appalled—to observe what was happening in one's own mind. One was growing used to it! As if ruins were a recognized modern style of architecture; as if it were almost normal and natural to walk down a street containing one habitable house. And this bewildering adaptability of the human mind seemed both merciful and yet frightful—merciful, because without it whole populations in our time must have gone mad; but frightful, also, because it suggests that there is nothing of which we are not capable, under pressure sufficiently crushing. The civilized man of to-day, it seems, could become the complacent cannibal of to-morrow. Of all the discoveries of our too inventive century this is perhaps the most ghastly—that the civilized standards which our grandfathers thought founded on rock, are really built on a flimsy crust above a bottomless abyss.

As with the city, so with its people. At first one sickened at all the grey faces, tightened mouths, and haggard eyes. Only childhood seemed to keep some of its marvellous resilience; though, even so, its pallor contrasted pitifully with the red-cheeked gaiety that bursts laughing from an English school. But life for the old was clearly terrible. I climbed, with a parcel I had been asked to bring from England, up the gaunt stairs to a fifth floor, where on the door of half a flat was the name I sought. A knock—a louder knock—a frightened voice 'Wer ist da?'—as if I might have been the Gestapo. Then the door opened on a dim-lit room, and from the doorway peered a pallid, ghastly face with elf-locks trailing to the shoulders, that made one think of Hecuba among the ruins of Troy. Behind her, an old husband as pathetic. The anxiety in their eyes changed to a miserable delight—but how long would one parcel last, when each year had 365 crawling, snake-like days?

And yet after a day or two one came to see deeper. This battered people was not dead, nor sleep-walking. There was an extraordinary friendliness, which was not servility; a touching eagerness, as of year-long prisoners, for the ideas of the West; an admirable determination to lift out of lethargy their own intellectual life. They would flock to evening lectures at the British Information Centre, undeterred by the lack of transport, the lightless S-Bahn, the Stygian darkness of the streets. Young women with a dozen holes in each silk stocking could still talk with smiling humour and vivacity of the trials and strains of Berlin life. And passing from the wreckage of the streets into the Städtische Oper one was suddenly transported into a different world by the still brilliant setting, and buoyant verve, of a performance of *The Barber of Seville*.

Yet this too was only one face of the truth. Behind this brighter side lurked in its turn a grimmer reality. Berlin might seem strangely calm, after England, under the menace of Russia. In streets without soldiers, or sandbags, or wire-entanglements, English and Germans alike might go about their business in apparent tranquillity. But it was the tranquillity of dwellers on a volcano. You might stroll from the British to the Russian sector without a barrier or a sentry in sight, except the Russian soldier with fixed bayonet at the war-memorial; or be freely visited by people from East Berlin. And yet it was the hush of a jungle; and through its darkness pulsed relentlessly from the distance the steady roar of the air-lift. The Berliner who had once made himself obnoxious to Moscow could vanish without trace; the absent-minded German who took West-marks in his pocket across the Russian boundary was liable to return no more. For he had committed 'a currency offence'.

You asked if the charming, clever woman in black whom you met at lunch, had lost her husband—'Yes, he was hanged. By the Nazis. After the July conspiracy.' Or another woman would say, quite quietly, 'Yes, I have been raped once.'

Russian propaganda, often so successful elsewhere—among those with no experience of Russian deeds—had clearly no success in West Berlin. One felt the fortitude of this long-tormented people. Whatever their past guilt, their courage was not cheap. Often fireless, often light-less, they were not resisting for amusement. At moments one saw Berlin living like a diver who feels the slimy tentacles of cold monsters groping, now here, now there, at the slender life-line that alone con-nects him with the upper air of freely breathing men. And among those deserts of shattered masonry there would recur to memory the words of the Greek poet: 'It is not its walls that make a city—it is its men.'

In England it had seemed easy enough to take some sort of view like this—'The position is impossible. Roosevelt, already a sick man, gave the game away, from the moment he was gullible enough to trust the word of a Russian, and agree that we should occupy sectors in Berlin with communications as hopelessly vulnerable as the neck of a giraffe under the blade of a guillotine. Now Berlin is as untenable as the Channel Isles in 1940. The air-lift may be magnificent; but it is not war—not even cold war. We must fall back to our real line—the line of the Elbe.'

But when one turned from looking at maps of Germany to talking with people in Berlin, the shape of things grew different. For there thinking men and women—alike English and German—were feeling passionately that Berlin had become for Europe what Khartoum once was for Gordon, or Verdun for France. The idea that the hauling down of the Western flags in Berlin would be followed by the hoisting of the Hammer and Sickle in Frankfurt, Paris, Rome, and Madrid might, or might not, be exaggerated. But Berlin—as *they* saw it—was not only a breakwater for the West; it was also a beacon for the East. With its surrender a still deeper gloom would fall on all decent men in Poland, in Czechoslovakia, in all the other lands in the Valley of the Shadow of the Kremlin. Time could no longer be gained by selling space—only by holding it. Bargains with Moscow were useless. Reasoning with Moscow was useless. One must hold.

When such an attitude was taken by people who stood themselves in the front line, it impressed. For, if things did come to violence, it was they themselves that would be the very first to pay. But there in contact with the enemy, they had learnt to face, apparently, what the faint-hearts and the idealists further west consistently refused to see.

The intolerable thing about Moscow is not that it is Communist; it is that it is *not* Communist. Genuine Communism, while one might disagree with it, one could respect. But this pseudo-Communism of the Kremlin is perhaps the most gigantic sham in history. It has waded through seas of blood, oceans of tears bitterer, often, than death—for what? That a régime where the rich were powerful might be replaced by a régime where the powerful are rich. The Soviet system soon turned into an aquarium of crabs battling for power, whose first idea about using that power has been to keep it; and their second, to extend it till their pincers have grasped the world.

We have seen enough of that; in Berlin they had seen more than enough. This is by no means to say that they showed no blindnesses of their own. I gained the impression that the Germans still often failed to realize the horror of the world at what Germans had done. It was too easy to put it all off on the Nazis; but after all the Nazis too were Germans. This need not mean that one adopts the twaddle of Sartre about everyone being guiltily responsible for everything that is done evilly in our hideous world. Even supposing human free-will not to be an illusion, the ordinary man in a modern giant-state remains as helpless as a wet straw in Niagara. But though there may usually be little health or profit in senses of guilt, there are times when a decent person can, and should, blush for his country. I felt, rationally or not, that many Germans still blushed too little. It was not for Germans to talk, as one of them did to me, of French 'Militarismus' and the need for an Anglo-German rapprochement against it. And I could only gasp when another Berliner blandly remarked, because the Poles had maltreated Germans in Silesia, 'Now we and the Poles can cry quits.' It will be long before *that* occurs.[1] Above all, one felt no confidence that this gifted, but too docile race might not again cry 'Hail, Barabbas!' to some new dictator. Much hangs on what can be done to unite Western Europe. But one thing at a time. It is Russia we now have to face.

And so one left Berlin having seen so much, and felt so much, that a week seemed to have been a month. It had been easy enough to gather applause from people starving, in their islet encompassed with barbarism, for a little contact with the traditions of civilized Europe. But as the aircraft lifted her wings from the runway of Gatow towards the freedom of the West, one's admiration went out to the human courage and devotion that remained behind in the bleak isolation of this besieged city; and to the young American and British airmen who carried on day after day, night after night, with no publicity and no applause—only the thin, disembodied voices calling through the darkness from the control-towers of Templehof or Gatow.

*　　　*　　　*

[1] Only the other day (1959) in Norway, a Norwegian told me of German tourists there singing, with incredible crassness, *Deutschland über alles*, in a country where the memory of Nazi iniquities still stank to heaven.

So Berlin seemed a dozen years ago. Now, so hectic is the rush of the modern world, it all seems ancient history; but perhaps, for that very reason, of some historic interest. And yet, though Berlin has risen from its ashes, in other ways things remain ironically the same, as a new storm blackens above this city which has become, like fifteenth-century Byzantium, an outpost of the West completely encircled by the East. One still longs to know the inner details of the debates that could ever bring the leaders of the Western Allies to accept this strange decision— to put back the frontier of Slavdom where it stood in the days of Charlemagne, upon the Elbe—to be lured into occupying half a capital with all its communications in such faithless hands. Stalin made many mistakes; but he must surely have smiled to himself with some reason the day he duped us into taking this wolf by the ears, in equal peril whether we held on or let go.[1] For the peril was plain enough from the very first; long before the fall of Berlin, I remember the dismay with which I saw a confidential map of the German areas we had agreed to leave in Russian hands.

Napoleon too made blunders enough; but one may doubt if he would have made this one. It is curious to read now what he said at Saint Helena, a century and a half ago: 'Qu'il se trouve, disait-il, un Empereur de Russie, vaillant, impétueux, capable, en un mot un Czar qui ait de la barbe au menton (ce qu'il exprimait, du reste, beaucoup plus énergiquement), et l'Europe est à lui. Il peut commencer ses opérations sur le sol allemand même, à cent lieues des deux capitales, Berlin et Vienne. . . . Assurément, moi, dans une telle situation, j'arriverais à Calais à temps fixe et par journées d'étape, et je m'y trouverais le maître et l'arbitre de l'Europe.'[2]

But for the atom bomb, that might by now have made more remarkable reading still. One can, presumably, only play for time. Time in the end has blunted the teeth and claws of the most tigerishly aggressive fanaticisms. But the process is deadly slow. More than two hundred years after the fall of Byzantium the Turk was still strong enough to besiege Vienna. 'The mills of God grind slowly'; and one may be excused for not much liking the flour.

Twice in my lifetime, after infinite struggle, suffering, and slaughter, we have at last battled through to a victory that proved, not the

---

[1] Imagine the inward thoughts of this Machiavelli when remarking at Yalta: 'I, as a naïve man, think it best not to deceive my ally even if he is a fool'!

[2] Las Cases, *Mémorial de Sainte-Hélène*.

longed-for bed of roses, but a bed of snakes. And yet what use lamenting? What does one know? Gibbon thought the happiest period in civilized history to have been the Age of the Antonines. Yet after nearly a century of such beneficent rulers, the civilized world had become an apple with many a maggot in it, rotten-ripe for its fall. It seems hard for men to keep through years of felicity the robust qualities by which that felicity was gained.

Perhaps we should remember the catfish. I have been told that the captured cod carried in ships' tanks from the fishing-grounds were apt to reach port flabby and out of condition; until some ingenious soul had the idea of putting in with the cod a nasty and ferocious creature called a catfish. That kept them splendidly fit. The story may be a myth; but it is true enough of human nature. Too often the activities of mankind, when they cease to be fatal, decline to the futile and the frivolous. So perhaps, after all, we should be grateful to the rulers of Russia. But *that* they do not make very easy.

Translation

Quince. Bless thee, Bottom, bless thee; thou art translated.
Bottom. I see their knavery; this is to make an asse of me.
SHAKESPEARE, *A Midsummer Night's Dream*

Translation is a traffique of high price;
It brings all learning in one Paradise.
JOHN WEBSTER

RANSLATORS have become dogs with a bad name. 'Traduttori—traditori' runs the Italian adage; 'translators are traitors', or 'versions are perversions'. 'Everything suffers by translation,' observed Lord Chesterfield, 'except a bishop.'

Then there is the gibe of his contemporary Voltaire—'How does one translate music?' There is the remark made by someone I have forgotten, to a lifelong translator—'Have you not thought for twenty years!'

'Translation,' growled Mark Pattison, 'is the laziest of all modes of dealing with the classics.' 'Never translate,' said Moritz Haupt, 'translation is the death of the understanding.' Would he have had us read the Bible in Hebrew? He would have been disappointed.

In fine, some have seemed to think translation quite useless except as an instrument of torture for schoolboys, such as that young innocent who is said to have transformed 'le peuple, ému, répondit' into 'the purple emu laid another egg'.

Then, more reasonable, there is Anatole France—'Il y a de belles traductions, peut-être; il n'y en a pas de fidèles.' And to one that said translation was impossible, he replied: 'Precisely, my friend. The realization of that truth is a necessary preliminary to success in that art.' Yet this is at least a little more hopeful; for it admits some sort of success to be conceivable.

No doubt, there have been translators who justified this chorus of contempt. For instance, the title of Cibber's play *Love's Last Shift* once found itself rendered *La Dernière Chemise de l'Amour*. Victor Hugo himself is said to have converted 'the Firth of Forth' into the more mystical form—'Le Premier du Quatrième'. Or again there is the warning example of the late Humbert Wolfe (a graceful poet, now unduly forgotten), who, translating Ronsard's Sonnets, with Hamlet's father too much in his head, rendered 'un jeune poulain' as 'a young Polack'. Ronsard's 'young horse' becomes surprisingly transformed into 'a young Pole'. Poetry needs enchantment; but not this kind. There is, too, Mr Ezra Pound who improves the cry of Charles d'Orléans about his mistress's beauty—'Dieu qu'il fait bon la re-garder!' into 'God! that mad'st her well regard her' (in place of 'God! how good she is to look on!'—'Dieu qu'il fait bon la regarder').[1] To invite the deity Himself to gaze on this adored damsel may be more dramatic. It might have occurred to John Donne. But it had not occurred to Charles d'Orléans.

Evidently not all translators are so honest as the good French Abbé, Marolles, who would put here and there in the margin of his versions— 'I have not translated this passage, because it is very difficult, and in truth I could never understand it.'

Yet there have been times when translation was better esteemed. Eustache Deschamps considered it a high compliment to salute Chaucer as 'grand translateur'. What was done for the Bible by Wycliffe and his scholars, then by Tyndale, Coverdale, and Luther, was done for secular literature in the sixteenth and seventeenth centuries by poets like Wyat, Surrey, Ronsard, Marlowe, Chapman, Harington, Fairfax, and Dryden; and by prose versions such as Amyot's *Plutarch*, North's *Plutarch*, Philemon Holland's[2] *Livy* and *Pliny*, Adlington's *Apuleius*, Florio's and Cotton's *Montaigne*, Shel-ton's *Don Quixote*, and Urquhart's *Rabelais*.

In those good days men rushed to plunder the wealth of Greece and Rome as eagerly as their barbarian ancestors fifteen centuries before. When Dryden produced his Virgil, 'the nation', says Johnson, 'con-sidered its honour as interested in the event'. Still greater was the renown of Pope's *Homer*; perhaps, with Gibbon's *Roman Empire*, the nearest thing to a living epic produced by our eighteenth century. The *Iliad* alone brought Pope £5,320 4s.; the equivalent of many times that sum in our impoverished days.

---

[1] First published in 1912, this reappeared still unabashed after forty years, in 1952.

[2] Called by the admiring Fuller, 'the Translator General of his age, so that those bookes alone of his turning into English will make a country gentleman a competent library for Historians, insomuch that one saith

> Holland with translations so doth fill us
> He will not let Suetonius be Tranquillus.'

Since then, however, the prestige of translators has gradually declined; though the nineteenth century brought, for example, Fitz-Gerald and Rossetti; the twentieth, Gilbert Murray and Arthur Waley, and the admirable *Arabian Nights* in French by Mardrus.

None the less we continue to translate; perhaps more eagerly than ever. We must. For the world grows smaller and, perforce, more international. Less and less can we afford insularity and isolationism. At the same time, the crushing increase of knowledge, especially scientific, leaves less and less time for learning foreign tongues, especially dead ones. Yet the classics refuse to die. The most successful volume of the Penguin series is said, astonishingly enough, to be Homer's *Odyssey*. Dr Rieu's version, I gather, had sold by 1954 no fewer than 750,000 copies. What a tribute to Homer's power of sheer story-telling! For his poetry cannot be expected to take effect in a prose rendering; especially in one that deliberately—for me, too deliberately—renounces all attempts at the poetic.

*   *   *

Translation is sometimes a craft, sometimes an art. I call it a craft when it is applied to utilitarian ends, where content matters rather than form—such as interpreting international conferences, translating diplomatic documents, or rendering works of science. One does not look primarily for beauty in a monograph on beetles (though there may be beauty even there).

Obviously this kind of translation is far less difficult—though even here it is only too easy to underestimate the difficulty. For all handling of words is difficult. It is like the croquet-match in *Alice* played with living hedgehogs and flamingoes. For words too are living, wriggling things, perpetually showing a bewildering wilfulness of their own, perpetually wandering off into thickets of obscurity, ambiguity, or verbosity. However, hopes are held out to us that this type of utility translation may soon be accomplished by machines; though it would probably be merciful if it could also be left to machines to read the products that result.

But with translation as an art—the translation of works of art—the traps and pitfalls multiply many-fold. So do the disagreements.

My purpose here is merely to hazard a few suggestions on things to aim at, and things to avoid. And since the classical languages, by their greater remoteness in structure, are the most difficult of all to render, it is with these that I shall chiefly deal.

In discussing such a problem there are two main methods. One can give conclusions first, then support them by examples; or one can give examples first, then draw conclusions. This second way seems to me often the better.

The detective examines his pieces of evidence, then draws his conclusions; the barrister urges his conclusions by adducing his evidence. Now I notice that detective stories are much more read than law-reports. If the evidence comes first, readers or audience are led to draw their own inferences. That they find more exciting. They become themselves more active, less inert. Besides, if the evidence is only brought in afterwards to support the conclusions, one may acquire uneasy suspicions that the evidence is cooked. Therefore I shall give my examples first.

*　　　*　　　*

Let us begin with one of the best-loved stanzas of FitzGerald's *Omar*.

> A Book of Verses underneath the Bough,
> A Jug of Wine, a Loaf of Bread and thou
> 　Beside me singing in the Wilderness—
> Oh, Wilderness were Paradise enow.

Now what did Omar Khayyám really say, in those years when William the Conqueror was firmly grinding down his newly conquered England? Turn to Professor Arberry. Omar, it appears, really said something like this—

> Let me have a loaf of fine wheaten flour,
> A flagon of wine, and a thigh of mutton,
> And beside me, amid the desolation, a comely youth—
> This is happiness no sultan's palace holds.

Here FitzGerald has boldly inserted the 'Book of Verses'; whereas a cultured Persian would have carried his verses with him in his head.

He has added the 'Bough', in a wilderness that was probably treeless.

He has cautiously omitted that prosaic leg of mutton; and also the fine wheaten flour—characteristic of an Epicurean poet, who prized comfort even on picnics.

He has turned the lad into a lass; and also, perhaps in consideration for his respectably Victorian audience, omitted certain verbal echoes of an improper kind, on which Professor Arberry discreetly does not dwell.

Here is another example from FitzGerald.

> And lately, by the Tavern Door agape,
> Came stealing through the Dusk an Angel shape
>   Bearing a Vessel on his shoulder; and
> He bid me taste of it; and 'twas the Grape!

But Omar had really written something to this effect—

> Last night I passed drunken by the tavern,
> And I saw an old man, jug on shoulder, drunk.
> I said: 'Art thou not ashamed before God?'
> 'God,' he answered, 'is indulgent. Drink!'

This disreputable old gentleman, who, instead of rebuking the equally drunken young one, dares to defend drunkenness with impudent impiety, has been transformed by FitzGerald into an 'Angel shape'! I must say I do not like being so totally misled.

It would, I think, be thankless to wish FitzGerald's poem other than it is. It may be sneered at by literary snobs, who long always to feel themselves in a select minority; cannot enjoy anything if many others enjoy it; and would vomit at caviar itself if it ever became popular. But for minds less pernickety FitzGerald's *Omar* remains a lasting possession.

Yet—and this is my first conclusion—it seems misleading to call this kind of work 'translation'. FitzGerald should not, I feel, have put on his title-page the word 'rendered'. For Omar is not 'rendered'—on the contrary, much of him is surrendered. And a sensible reader likes to know where he is.

'To translate', said Johnson, 'is to change into another language, *retaining the sense*.' Use 'sense' in a very wide sense, and this seems to me a reasonable definition. Translation should faithfully convey, as far as possible, the meaning of what Omar said; and not only the meaning, but also the tone and overtones of what he said; even, so far as practicable, the general rhythm of what he said. But it should never interpolate, nor omit, nor distort, nor transpose.[1]

---

[1] An amusing example of the irresponsible heedlessness of some translation, without even the least aesthetic excuse, is provided by Ervine's life of Shaw (p. 299) from the obituary Shaw wrote on Irving for the Vienna *Neue Freie Presse*

Therefore to call FitzGerald's poem a 'translation' seems muddling.
(And mental muddle appears to me one of the few things in this world
that are wholly and invariably bad.) I would suggest that, instead, we
call FitzGerald's work 'adaptation'; and rest at that, and be thankful
for it. 'Adaptation' can be an excellent thing; but 'translation' in any
real sense, it is not. Never mind. Chaucer adapted Boccaccio; and we
are the richer. Called by another name, this Persian rose still smells as
sweet. Only it seems to me important to know that it is not exactly
Omar's rose, but a much modified variety, grafted upon an English
stock. Its beauty is often perfect; but its truth is not. Real translation
should be true; adaptation need not be. But the two things, I think,
should be kept quite distinct. Otherwise the simple reader is deceived.

* * *

Take another example from another famous English translation—
Pope's *Homer*. The Trojans, in *Iliad*, VIII, have forced the Greeks back
to their ships, and are camping triumphant out on the Trojan plain.
And in one of his loveliest similes Homer compares their countless
campfires to the countless stars of night.

Pope—

> As when the moon, refulgent lamp of night,
> O'er heaven's pure azure spreads her sacred light,
> When not a breath disturbs the deep serene,
> And not a cloud o'ercasts the solemn scene,
> Around her throne the vivid planets roll,
> And stars unnumber'd gild the glowing pole,
> O'er the dark trees a yellower verdure shed,
> And tip with silver every mountain's head:
> Then shine the vales, the rocks in prospect rise,
> A flood of glory bursts from all the skies:
> The conscious swains, rejoicing in the sight,
> Eye the blue vault, and bless the useful light.
>
> (*Iliad*, VIII, 555–9)

Pope has here expanded five lines of Homer into twelve of his own.

in 1905. 'The truth is,' wrote G.B.S., 'Irving was interested in nothing but himself; and the self he was interested in was an imaginary self in an imaginary
world. He lived in a dream.' This was translated into German; and one can
imagine its author's delight when it reappeared, translated back into English by
a London paper, as follows: 'He was a narrow-minded egoist, devoid of culture,
and living on the dream of his own greatness.' Legitimate criticism had been
garbled into vulgar scurrility.

He has added, wholly out of his own head, 'lamp of night', 'And not a cloud o'ercasts the solemn scene', 'Around her throne the vivid planets roll', 'O'er the dark trees a yellower verdure shed, And tip with silver every mountain's head'. More than four whole lines in a passage of twelve.

Further, in addition to this 'yellower verdure' and the 'silver' light on the mountain-tops, Pope has also splashed in other colours of his own—'pure azure', 'gild', 'blue vault'.

Why? Probably because he had been taking lessons in painting from the artist Jervas. But, for a translator, this reason seems to me inadequate. The simple reader is deceived.

Finally, Pope's 'conscious swains', with their horribly self-conscious air, suggesting a moonlit opera, replace what was in Homer a single solitary shepherd; contrasted, almost Wordsworthianly, in his happy loneliness with the serried bonfires of that grimly crowded battlefield. Nor had Homer made any drably Benthamite suggestion about the moonlight being 'useful'.

This same Homeric passage has also been translated in a fragment by Tennyson.

> As when in heaven the stars about the moon
> Look beautiful, when all the winds are laid,
> And every height comes out, and jutting peak
> And valley, and the immeasurable heavens
> Break open to their highest, and all the stars
> Shine, and the Shepherd gladdens in his heart.

That I call real translation. Tennyson has only six lines to Pope's twelve. Homer himself, indeed, has only five lines; but his lines have six feet to Tennyson's five, so that both Homer and Tennyson have done their picture in exactly thirty feet. Trivial arithmetic; but it helps to illuminate how Tennyson has kept his eye on his original, neither adding nor dropping a single idea or image. I am not quite happy over 'the stars about the moon look beautiful'. It seems a trifle too aesthetic. Homer had simply said (with a deliberate repetition of 'shining') 'the stars round the shining moon shine sharp and clear'. But, apart from that, Tennyson has kept faith with Homer's sense. I do not, indeed, think that he is as faithful as one would wish to Homer's sound and rhythm. Blank verse walks in state; the hexameter gallops. But of that aspect more later.

Pope, in short, while less free than FitzGerald, remains far more free than Tennyson. It might perhaps be excessive to say that Pope has 'adapted' Homer, rather than translated him; but it might be fair to say that Pope's Homer is not so much a 'translation' as a 'paraphrase'.

I am not denying or decrying Pope's achievement. He had some grounds for the licences he took. If Tennyson had lived in Pope's age, he might often have written like Pope; for both had meticulous ears (though Tennyson seems to me a far finer person). If Pope had lived in Tennyson's age, he might have written at times like Tennyson; for Pope too had in him a definite vein of romance. But, living when he did, if Pope had not thus classicized Homer, and polished him, and barbered him, his polite audience would have fidgeted and taken snuff; as Chesterfield did over the later books of the *Aeneid*. A translator may fail if he produces an original in a form too strange for native stomachs; just as Wesley failed at Holyhead in 1750 before an audience comprising, he says, 'some eminently wicked men', 'daubed with gold and silver'—'I delivered my soul; but they could in no wise bear it.' So, if Pope had delivered Homer's soul too nakedly, his age could in no wise have borne it.

Bentley's 'pretty . . . but not Homer' was a just criticism of Pope; still, had Pope given his age something more like Homer, they would not have thought it 'pretty' at all.

As Pope himself complains in his preface, in words quite as relevant to-day—'a mere modern wit can like nothing that is not modern, and a pedant nothing that is not Greek'. A translator has always to steer halfway between the pedants and the 'modern wits'.

All this amounts to saying that Queen Anne's time (like ours) provided an unfavourable climate for translating Homer. The 'modern wits' were too strong; and they had not yet acquired a romantic taste for ages more primitive. 'Homer', says Johnson, 'doubtless owes his translator many Ovidian graces not exactly suitable to his character; but to have added is no great crime if nothing be taken away. Elegance is surely to be desired if it be not gained at the expense of dignity.' I dislike disagreeing with Johnson. But here I must disagree. A true translator should *not* 'add'. By adding elegance, Pope *has* taken something away. He has taken away Homer's simple directness.

These two Homeric versions, by Pope and Tennyson, suggest two further conclusions. First, the Tennyson shows that poetry can sometimes be translated, even in verse, with strict fidelity, without thereby ceasing to be poetry. The excessive liberties still taken by so many modern translators are, to my mind, often sheer laziness, or lack of ingenuity, or both.

Secondly, Pope's version is not only *literally* untruthful to the letter of the Greek. It is also *historically* untruthful; in that its pictorial phrases and colour-epithets are quite anachronistic for Homer's age. But a good translation should, I think, remain *historically*, as well as verbally, true. In rendering Homer, as in editing Shakespeare, Pope took liberties that seem to me wrong-headed. For the simple reader is deceived.

In justice I should add that if you would see Pope's *Homer* at its best, you must turn from its narrative to its passages of oratory. Pope was pre-eminently an oratorical—a rhetorical poet; and Homer, with Shakespeare, is the greatest orator I know. But, even here, Pope allows himself licences that make me tremble.

Take, for example, Poseidon's rebuke to the fleeing Greeks, as he comes in human shape to rally them—

> Prevent this evil, and your country save:
> Small thought retrieves the spirits of the brave.
> Think and subdue! on dastards dead to fame
> I waste no anger, for they feel no shame:
> But you, the pride, the flower of all our host,
> My heart weeps blood to see your glory lost!
> Nor deem this day, this battle, all you lose;
> A day more black, a fate more vile, ensues.
> Let each reflect, who prizes fame or breath,
> On endless infamy, on instant death.
> For lo! the fated time, the appointed shore:
> Hark! the gates burst, the brazen barriers roar!
> Impetuous Hector thunders at the wall;
> The hour, the spot, to conquer or to fall.
> (*Iliad*, XIII, 115–24)

The last eight lines seem to me eloquence not unworthy the lips of a god. Pope here fulfils at least one requisite—that a translation of fine literature must itself be fine.

Unfortunately Pope has here too been recklessly free; a lot of the passage comes not from the Greek, but from Pope's own head. Compare the same passage in Chapman's version—you can hardly believe that he and Pope are rendering the same original. Further, in Chapman the thing becomes blankly incomprehensible.

> We must not cease t'assist ourselves. Forgive our Gen'ral then,
> And quickly too. Apt to forgive are all good-minded men.
> Yet you, quite void of their good minds, give good, in you quite lost,
> For ill in others, though ye be the worthiest of your host.
> As old as I am, I would scorn to fight with one that flies,
> Or leaves the fight as you do now. The Gen'ral slothful lies,
> And you, though slothful too, maintain with him a fight of spleen.
> Out, out, I hate ye from my heart. Ye rotten-minded men,
> In this ye add an ill that's worse than all your sloth's dislikes.
> But as I know to all your hearts my reprehension strikes,
> So thither let just shame strike too; for while you still stand here
> A mighty fight swarms at your fleet, great Hector rageth there,
> Hath burst the long bar and the gates. Thus Neptune rous'd these men.

Pope I understand; Chapman I do not. I doubt if Chapman understood himself.[1] His translation is often abject gibberish; though he retains his reputation, by not being read. The sonnet of Keats on Chapman's *Homer* would be hard to overpraise for its own beauty—but it wildly overpraises Chapman.

Now one may like or dislike these liberties taken by FitzGerald, Pope, or Chapman. That is a matter of taste; and all taste, I believe, is relative and subjective. But, to avoid muddle, I repeat that it would be better at least to use words more carefully, and draw a clear distinction, in ascending order of freedom, between (1) 'translation'; (2) 'paraphrase'; (3) 'adaptation'. Fourth, with still freer licence, one might add 'imitation'—such as Johnson's *London*. Attempt whichever you please; but at least make it clear to the poor reader what you are attempting.

* * *

Here is another example of licence that seems yet more extreme:

> For this there's no mood-lofty man over earth's midst,
> Not though he be given his good, but will have in his youth greed;
> Nor his deed to the daring, nor his king to the faithful,
> But shall have his sorrow for sea-fare
> Whatever his lord will.

[1] The reader may well be curious to know what Homer really said. Here is a prose version: 'Come, let us heal the ill that is done—as noble hearts are quick to do. This is no hour to forget your warlike valour—you that are mightiest in all our host. I would not quarrel if there shrank back from battle some mere dastard: but *you*—you fill my soul with rage. Ah, my comrades, your weakness will bring worse ills behind it. Think of your honour, and of others' scorn. For grim indeed is the struggle risen now. It is by our *ships* that Hector of the mighty war-cry battles hard; it is through our *gates*, and the bolt that barred them, that he has broken now.'

Do you understand? Then you are cleverer than I. What on earth is the meaning of 'Nor his deed to the daring, nor his king to the faithful, But shall have his sorrow for sea-fare'?

I know no Anglo-Saxon. But it appears from Professor Sisam[1] that the original text of *The Seafarer* here translated by Mr Ezra Pound means, quite simply, something utterly different—'There is no man on earth so high-hearted, or so generous in his gifts, or so venturous in his youth, or so glorious in his deeds, or so secure in his lord's favour, that he is not always anxious about his sea-faring.'

Perfectly plain, perfectly straightforward. But some people hate clear light as frantically as bats.

After Professor Sisam had pointed out blunder on blunder, I assumed that Mr Pound's *Seafarer* was finally torpedoed. But not a bit of it. Such is the odd mentality of our truth-indifferent age that indignant voices were at once raised protesting that they did not care in the least how many times Mr Pound howled; because he howled so melodiously.

Now if Mr Pound had published his piece as an *original* poem, with some such title as *After reading The Seafarer* or *Lines suggested by The Seafarer*, I should still hate it; but it would at least not be a humbug and a sham.

Even with translators who do possess some literary conscience, it is still seldom realized how hard it remains to be really faithful. Take, for example, a passage picked out for praise by the *Times Literary Supplement* in a recent American version of *Oedipus the King*:

> Phoibos Apollo, stretch *the sun's* bowstring,
> That golden cord until it sings for us,
> Flashing arrows in heaven!
>   ARTEMIS, *Huntress*,
> Race with flaring lights upon *our* mountains!
> O *scarlet* god, O golden-banded brow,
> O Theban Bacchus *in a storm* of Maenads,
> Whirl upon *Death*, that all the Undying hate!
> Come with *blinding* torches, come in joy!
>   (204–15)

Here, to begin with, the words italicized are additions, or modifications, by the two translators, with no warrant whatever in the

---

[1] *Times Literary Supplement*, 25 June 1954.

original Greek. For 'paraphrase' such licence may be legitimate; but if offered to the trusting reader as 'translation', such freedoms seem to me unpardonable. What the Greek does say is something like this (I have italicized ideas *omitted* in the previous rendering):

'Lycēan King, I would too that from thy gold-twisted bowstring thy arrows might be showered *invincibly* in our *defence*; and, with them, the fiery torches of Artemis, with which she leaps across the *Lycian* hills. And I *call on him* whose locks are girt with gold, the ruddy Bacchus *of the Bacchic cry*, to come with his company of Maenads to our aid, blazing with his *gay* torchlight against that god dishonoured among the gods.'

Further, it should be noted that the translators have identified Apollo with the sun. But there is no reason to suppose that Sophocles was thinking of this identification; which, in fact, seems comparatively late in Greek literature, and does not occur, so far as I know, in Greek tragedy at all, apart from a fragment of the *Phaethon* of Euripides. Artemis, again, should leap over the mountains of remote Lycia, not of Thebes—a considerable difference. To call Bacchus 'scarlet', instead of 'ruddy' (as wine is red), seems to me misleading, and indeed incomprehensible. Imagine the Bible saying of David—'Now he was scarlet and withal of a beautiful countenance'! The god 'dishonoured among the gods' is not Death at all, but Ares, bringer of war and (as here) of pestilence. The Immortals might hate Death; but a Greek could hardly have imagined them 'dishonouring' that solemn figure who bears Sarpedon to his last rest in Lycia, or stands beside Alcestis on the temple-column of Ephesus. The bullying Ares, on the other hand, is already in Homer one of the least loved and honoured of the Olympians.

Further, having substituted Death for Ares, the translators have imported into their text a neat little antithesis between 'Death' and 'the Undying', the Olympians, which had never occurred to Sophocles. Repeatedly the Greekless reader is led astray. And this sort of thing is happening more and more in the modern world, as such versions, purporting to be faithful, multiply. Call them 'paraphrases', and we should at least know a little better where we stood.

*　　　*　　　*

But there are other forms of excess in translation, besides over-freedom. Here is an example of the opposite extreme:

CHOROS

Alas for mortal matters! Happy-fortuned—
Why, any shade would turn them: if unhappy
By throws the wetting sponge has spoiled the picture!
And more by much in mortals this I pity.
The being well-to-do—
Insatiate a desire of this
Born with all mortals is,
Nor any is there who
Well-being forces off, aroints
From roofs whereat a finger points,
'No more come in!' exclaiming.[1]

This may sound very up-to-date. For it is so unintelligible that, instead of the English helping one to understand the Greek, one needs the Greek to understand the English.

Actually, however, the piece is eighty years old. It comes from the *Agamemnon* of Browning. Browning was here straining after that exact and unvarnished truthfulness which is so conspicuously absent in Pope or FitzGerald (to say nothing of Mr Pound). But Browning seems to me to have fallen into an opposite exaggeration that is yet worse. He has become so servilely literal as to be gibberish. To turn beautiful writing into ugly is itself one of the worst forms of untruthfulness. Browning should have remembered that line of his great rival, Tennyson—

Faith unfaithful kept him falsely true.

It was Carlyle who inspired Browning to this catastrophe, by rashly telling him it was his vocation to translate the whole of Greek Tragedy. But Carlyle did not much like the result—'Oh dear, he's a very foolish fellow. . . . He snips up sense and jingles it into rhyme. . . . I told him frankly I could not understand it.'

Browning, though often splendid in his lyrics, came to find in the

---

[1] Aeschylus, *Agamemnon*, 1326-33.

Ah, human life! Even its happiness
Fades as a shadow—its unhappiness
Grows a mere blur a wet sponge wipes away.
And *this*, to me, is still *more* pitiful.

Never the hearts of men are sated
With Fortune's favours; no voice warns *Her*
From gates of the mighty, where point all fingers;
To *Her* none cries: 'Thou hast come *enough*!'

grotesque the fascination that a moth finds in a tallow-candle. He grew obsessed with a desire to pull the nose of Beauty with one hand, and the noses of the British public with the other. Worse translations may exist than Browning's *Agamemnon*. But I have not found one.

Conclusion—fidelity itself, like most good things, can be badly overdone. Truth to the letter, but falsehood to the spirit, is one of the worst of all forms of falsehood. Better even the wildest licence, especially if the translator warns his readers beforehand in his *preface*, than the boorishly literal verse of Browning's *Agamemnon*, or the boorishly literal prose of Buckley's *Iliad*, as once quoted by Housman—'They cut off his ears with the sharp brass; but he, injured in his feelings, went about, enduring that calamity with frantic mind.'

This kind of crib-English was the curse of that curious nineteenth-century product, Bohn's Library of classical translations—the sort of stuff that, in Johnson's superb phrase, 'may continue its existence as long as it is the clandestine refuge of schoolboys'.[1] Labouchère, indeed, acclaimed Bohn as having done inestimable service—for he had finally shown up what a fraud the classics were. But it was Labouchère's way to be naughty.

*   *   *

Here is translation of a wholly different type—

> What else is Wisdom? What of man's endeavour
> Or God's high grace, so lovely and so great?
> To stand from fear set free, to breathe and wait;
> To hold a hand uplifted over Hate;
> And should not Loveliness be loved for ever?

This song of the Bacchants of Euripides, rendered by Gilbert Murray, has itself the loveliness it praises. It is beautiful, musical, noble. It could be sung at meetings of the United Nations, if the United Nations were given to song. But the Greek appears to me to say something extremely different, and far less idealistic. After all, the Bacchants are cruel and fanatical zealots. 'What is wisdom?' I take them to say (though the exact sense is disputed): 'What gift more glorious can the gods give man than to hold a stronger hand above the bowed heads of the hated? Dear is the glorious evermore.'

[1] Johnson said it of the translated Virgil (1718–31) of Joseph Trapp (1679–1747), first Professor of Poetry at Oxford (1708); who also inspired the epigram:

> Keep to thy preaching, Trapp; translate no further;
> Is it not written, 'Thou shalt do no murder'?

What is wisdom? What is fairer
Gift of God in human eyes
Than to bow, with stronger arm,
Hated heads that sought our harm?
Fair is fame and dear its prize.

Most unchristian; indeed inhuman; but, alas, very human too.

Gilbert Murray, unlike most verse-translators, was himself a poet. No man in our century did so much to transplant Greek poetry into the general English mind. Therefore, I criticize him only with hesitation and respect. But Murray was a romanticist and idealist. Now Euripides was likewise a romanticist and idealist; but he was also a realist. In him, romance and realism went strangely hand in hand; as indeed they not uncommonly do—in Homer, Chaucer, Shakespeare, in Balzac, Stendhal, Flaubert, or Dickens. But this realistic side of Euripides was apt, I think, to become muted in Murray; who remained a personality far gentler and more idealistic, tenderer-minded and less embittered, than the poet he honoured and rendered.

Even Murray's persistent use of the rhymed couplet for Greek dramatic dialogue, instead of blank verse, seems revealingly characteristic. For it creates a dreamier atmosphere—something more like the *Earthly Paradise* of William Morris than the theatre of Dionysus ever knew. Morris I love and admire, both as a poet and as a man; but his dreamy, wistful, though heroic, atmosphere is not the sharp air of 'sunlight-loving Athens'.

Conclusion—a translator must be true not only to the words, but also to the personality of his original. All great style, however impersonal, is alive with the writer's personality. 'The style is the man himself.' If the translator has a personality of his own, as Murray had, it risks distorting the personality of his original. This danger is hard to avoid; but it remains vital to avoid it. Or else the simple reader is deceived.

How difficult this avoidance of distortion can be, even in theory, is illustrated by Matthew Arnold, *On Translating Homer*. Homer's style, said Arnold, has four salient qualities—it is noble; it is rapid; it is plain in thought; it is plain in diction. The first three statements are true; but the fourth seems a most perilous half-truth. Homer's syntax, indeed, *is* generally plain enough; for he was not of the tribe of poets that prefer their water muddy. But 'plain in diction'? When we remember those magnificent polysyllables, those thunderous compound-adjectives—'ἐπὶ ῥηγμῖνι πολυφλοισβοίο θαλάσσης', 'κορυθαίολος

Ἕκτωρ', 'ῥοδοδάκτυλος Ἠώς', 'ἠεροφοῖτις Ἐρινύς', 'σκίδναται ἐξ ἀνέμοιο πολυπλάγκτοιο ἰωῆς'?[1]

Far from sharing Wordsworth's prejudice in favour of the speech of common men, Homer is so poetic in his vocabulary that even for the infinitive of that poor drudge, the verb 'to be', he employs no fewer than five variant forms. Greek epic elaborated a language never spoken by any race of men, but compiled from diverse dialects, and enriched with new coinages. As well call the style of Michael Angelo 'subdued'. When a customer said to William Morris, 'But I thought your colours were faint', he got the furious answer, 'If it's dirt you want, you can find it in the street.' Homer might have been less boisterous; but he might not have felt very differently about Arnold's 'plain in diction'.

Why did Arnold delude himself that Homer's diction is 'plain'? Simply because he *wanted* it to be. One side of Arnold (though not, luckily, the side which wrote *The Scholar Gipsy* or *Thyrsis*) felt strongly drawn towards asceticism. It is enough to recall his sonnet, *Austerity of Poetry*—that moral tale of the young Italian bride, crushed in a festival accident, who was found to be wearing, under her shining silks, sackcloth next the skin. Of such a story some would merely feel —'Poor child! Her brief life poisoned by those morbid and disgusting bigotries of the medieval mind!' But Arnold found it edifying. The poet's Muse, he says, should likewise wear sackcloth beneath her splendour.

Indeed Arnold at times made his own Muse wear the sackcloth outermost. And so, having this persistent sense of guilt about verbal splendour, he denied that splendour to Homer. But, for all that, the *Iliad* is *not* composed in the style of *Balder Dead*—a fine poem in its way; but not Homer.

In short, as the personality of Gilbert Murray to some degree distorts the personality of Euripides, so does Arnold's distort Homer's.

It follows that the translator must watch like a dragon to see that his own character does not mask the character of his original. Without personality a man is not likely to be a good translator, nor indeed a good anything, except a good nonentity; but, unless watched, a translator's own personality can perilously blur and disfigure the truth.

But I do not wish to take leave of Gilbert Murray on a note of criticism. Listen to another chorus from his *Bacchae*—

[1] 'Scatters before the bluster of the wide-wandering wind.' (Two words of three syllables, one of four, and one magnificent monster of five!)

Or where stern Olympus stands;
In the elm-woods and the oaken
      There where Orpheus harped of old,
And the trees awoke and knew him,
And the wild things gathered to him,
As he sang amid the broken
      Glens his music manifold.

Here the romantic side of Euripides is being truly rendered by the romantic Murray: the echo is faithful as well as lovely. There are, no doubt, some slight infidelities. In the Greek, Olympus is not 'stern'; and I do not think one should import this new idea. It does not greatly matter that 'the elm-woods and the oaken' in the Greek are merely 'many trees'; or that the last two lines—

As he sang amid the broken
      Glens his music manifold

—are really an expansion of a single Greek word meaning 'coverts', 'places where wild things lurk'. These expansions it might be rather pedantic and puritanic to condemn. The essential point is that this 'music manifold' remains true in spirit to its original, and yet, unlike most verse of the last thirty years, meets what is for me one test of true poetry—that its lilt should haunt one, ringing and singing in one's head, long after the book is closed.

*   *   *

So far we have dealt with translators who suffer either by being too free, like Pope and FitzGerald; or by being too literal, like Browning or Bohn's series; or by letting their own personality blur their vision of their original, like Murray or Matthew Arnold.

Now for a very different type of rendering, of which brief examples will be more than enough. Odysseus has just returned, after twenty years of war and wandering, to the wife of his youth.

'My dear,' answered Penelope, 'I have no wish to set myself up, nor to depreciate you; but I am not struck by your appearance.'

This is Samuel Butler. Actually the Greek says[1] something totally different, both in meaning and in tone—

Good sir, I do not speak so from arrogance, nor from contempt of you, nor because I am bewildered by surprise.

[1] *Odyssey*, XXIII, 174–5.

Homer is not Jane Austen. Samuel Butler translated the *Iliad* quite well, though he expurgated much of its poetry; but, having once decided that the *Odyssey* was written by a woman, he proceeded to give it at times the style of Mrs Bennett or Mr Collins. 'Bless my heart', cries Odysseus. 'Sweethearts', says Penelope to the suitors. The nymphs of Artemis become 'a bevy of beauties'; and in the palace of King Alcinoüs one 'meets all the best people among the Phaeacians'.

One can always delight the vulgar by vulgarizing great literature. Such successes can be cheaply bought: but cheap they remain. Butler was often a very clever man, sometimes a very wise one; but not, I think, here. Like his disciple, Shaw, he had a familiar imp; and here the imp ran away with him. I have the greatest admiration for Butler's *Notebooks*; but he should have left the *Odyssey* strictly alone.

Butler, like a number of more modern translators, wanted to bring Homer down to earth, to make him familiar, to adapt him to modern democracy. But Homer was *not* democratic in his sympathies; he sang for the aristocrats of Ionia; and to rob him of his dignity, of his grand style, of 'that large utterance of the early gods', is historic falsification.

Here are some further specimens of this jaunty type of translation:

Cyclops, here, have a drink after that jolly meal of mansmutton.

This is Odysseus addressing Polyphemus in the *Odyssey* of Rouse. The Greek, of course, has nothing whatever about 'jolly' or 'mutton'. It says simply—'Come, Cyclops, drink wine now, after feasting on flesh of men.' One must have a curious and odious conception of Odysseus to imagine him cracking callous jokes about 'jolly mutton' over the comrades he has just seen massacred and devoured before his eyes. Homer is not Jack the Giant-killer. This sort of thing makes me sympathize with the rage of William Morris striding down the aisle of some medieval church 'restored' out of recognition, and bellowing 'Beasts! Pigs! Damn their souls!'

Or again, here is Virgil in modern dress—

Aeneas, where are you off to? Don't welsh on your marriage contract.

So runs a recent version of Turnus' taunt to the fleeting phantom of Aeneas. Yet there is nothing colloquial to be found in the Latin original.

Quo fugis, Aenea? Thalamos ne desere pactos.

Where are you fleeing, Aeneas? Do not forsake the bridal pledged as yours.

Our twentieth century tends in this matter to run to the opposite extreme from the eighteenth. For them, the ancients were often too low; for us, they are often too lofty.

Thus, where Odysseus blinds the Cyclops, Pope wrote—

> Urg'd by some present god, they swift let fall
> The pointed torment on his visual ball.

We laugh. It reads like a parody; yet it is perfectly serious. To Pope's age it seemed too low of Homer to say simply—'They thrust the trunk of olive, pointed at its end, deep in the Cyclops' eye.' Accordingly the olive-trunk had to be elevated into the loftier abstraction of a 'pointed torment'; and the giant's eye to be polished into a 'visual ball'.

The result seems to us grotesque. But is our own opposite extreme any wiser? The reign of Whig aristocracy has been gradually replaced by the century of the common man. Probably England never enjoyed so much justice and happiness as under the Welfare State. That is all to the good. But perhaps not all to the good for literature. Quality tends to-day to be replaced by quantity. And because it is the age of the common man, our time tends persistently and incorrigibly to distort its versions of work written in ages less democratic. Our modern world has acquired a kind of demagogic resentment towards all poetic magnificence. We decry dignity. We despise grace. But the ancient writers wrote, often, for aristocrats rather than for common men. They talked, not only in a different language from ourselves, but also in a quite different *tone*. Milton recognized this—

> Som time let Gorgeous Tragedy
> In Scepter'd Pall come sweeping by.

But in modern versions Tragedy too often ceases to be gorgeous; loses her sceptre; and sweeps in a much meaner way.

And so, instead of exalting the ancients on stilts, like Pope, we now make them sprawl in the gutter. But both attitudes are equally false. If it is bad that a translator should let the character of his original be distorted by his own character, it is no better to let the character of his original be distorted by the character of his own age. And this seems to me one of our most inveterate faults to-day.

'Still,' it is objected, 'Homer wrote to please his contemporaries; a translation should be written to please ours.' 'The fiction of contemporaneousness', say the editors of *The Oxford Book of Greek Verse in Translation*, 'is the only reasonable fiction to adopt.' But is it?

So far from being 'the only reasonable fiction', it does not seem to me reasonable at all. We cannot possibly reproduce the effect produced by a writer like Homer on his contemporaries for two simple reasons. First, we are quite unlike Homer's contemporaries; secondly, we cannot even know what his effect on them was.[1]

I should have thought that the true object of translation was much simpler and more modest—that it should merely try to compensate the intelligent reader for his ignorance of the language concerned, and to give him, however imperfectly, the impression he would be likely to get, could he read the original fluently himself. Now when I read Homer, he does not, thank Heaven, seem in the least contemporary. He looms majestically out of the distances of a vast antiquity. To modernize him is like restoring Stonehenge, polishing its monoliths, and sticking them with advertisement posters. If I travel to Tahiti, it is not to see the parts of Tahiti that are just like Blackpool, with piers, cinemas, and motor-buses, but the parts, if there are any, that still keep their own unique and native character unspoiled. When I travel in time, instead of space, I want, as far as possible, the same. But some of us are like that type of British tourist between the Wars who wanted to drag everywhere with him the habits of Hampstead, and would yawp for his native bacon and eggs—not 'foreign kickshaws'—even in the Piazza della Signoria, or beside the Campanile of Saint Mark.

Homer, for example, belongs to a world long vanished and magically remote. He did not write yesterday, and he should not be made to read as if he did. When I read him in Greek, he seems like a forest of primeval oaks whose leaves are yet eternally young; I do not want him, in English, to recall the steel pylons of the latest electricity grid. Medieval painters, of course, could depict Roman soldiers as dressed in medieval armour. Yet that was because the medieval mind had an imperfect sense of history, and no sense of anachronism; but *our* sense

---

[1] Even odder, if that be possible, is the other suggestion that a translator should try to reproduce the impression made by Homer on a Greek of the age of Sophocles. Why the age of Sophocles? And how much can we conceivably know, anyway, of the impression Homer produced on Sophocles?

For *modern* translation one can often follow Belloc's principle—'What would an Englishman have said to express the same?' But Homer, or Omar, is essentially not a modern Englishman—in modern England they would have been unrecognizably different personalities.

of history is sharper and fuller—and I have no wish, even if I could, to lose it. It enriches life's variety.

> I doe love these auncient ruynes:
> We never tread upon them, but we set
> Our foote upon some reverend History.

The fact is that in all periods a great number of readers are too casual and vague-minded to care a pin for truth in general, or for historic truth in particular. They merely want what is familiar—the sort of thing they are used to. And so Chapman, in a 'conceited' age, sometimes tricked out Homer with the conceits of an Elizabethan wit; but this was travesty—for Homer was too wise to run after the merely clever. Pope, in a polite age, tried to make Homer a polished man of the world; but this too was travesty—for Homer's age was not polished like Queen Anne's; and 'men of the world' know far less of the real world than the real Homer knew. Samuel Butler, again, being a clever jester, was one of the first to begin the modern game of trying to rejuvenate the dead classics by making them all slightly vulgar; but if there was one character to whom Homer denied that wide sympathy which he could feel even for Polyphemus, it was the vulgar demagogue Thersites.

No doubt the modern world takes a different view. The modern reader often feels about tradition, strictness of form, dignity, grace, as Walt Whitman felt when urged to bind a work of his in vellum— 'Pshaw!' cried he, 'hangings, curtains, fingerbowls, china-ware, Matthew Arnold!' And no doubt this reaction against snobbery and Victorianism may be, in some ways, healthy. It may sometimes be better to be Philistine than precious. But let us remember that many other ages have held wholly different beliefs from ours; and to respect that difference is vital, if you care one tittle for historic truth.

Euripides was one of the first ancient writers to take a few tentative steps towards our kind of modernizing realism, with its impatience at traditional romance (though he was also, in other moods, himself a romantic). But at once this slight lowering of traditional dignity provoked the outraged fury of Aristophanes. Not without reason. Aristophanes could be crudely realistic himself; but only in comedy—which, to Aristophanes, seemed quite a different matter. And so in his *Frogs* he makes the ghost of Aeschylus fulminate passionately against Euripides for his meanly modernizing experiments.

> Poor wretch, can you not see
> That souls high-wrought, and mighty thought,
>   must speak with majesty?
> That heroes whose line is half divine, need words with a
>   nobler air,
> Just as their dress has a lordliness beyond our common wear.[1]

If, then, many modern poets prefer metres that hardly scan more than common talk, and the kind of matter-of-fact language heard in a railway-carriage, to the rigid metrical conventions and the fastidious diction of older poetry, they are completely within their rights. And so are the modern readers who agree with them. But in translating older literature there should be no deception, and no muddle. The authors should make clear at once in their prefaces that they are, in fact, 'adapting', or 'paraphrasing', not closely 'translating'; that, since to the marble style of Aeschylus they prefer something more like brick, to the ivory of Sophocles something more like bone, they have modified their originals accordingly. Then, at least, the public can cease being taken in; as at present they constantly are.

*   *   *

> Though he has watched a decent age pass by,
> A man will sometimes still desire the world.
> I swear I see no wisdom in that man . . .
> This is the truth, not for me only,
> For this blind and ruined man.
> Think of some shore in the north the
> Concussive waves make stream
> This way and that in the gales of winter:
> It is like that with him.

So runs a recent and typical translation of a chorus in Sophocles' *Oedipus at Colonus*.[2] It is the kind of version that is now turned out by the mile—studiously flat, and full of prosaisms like 'a decent age'. It is not flatly literal, like Browning or Bohn—on the contrary, it seems rather too free. It is flatness for flatness's sake. It is not vulgar, like Butler or Rouse—just deliberately drab. But it gives me quite a different feeling from the original. Take away the columns and pediments from a Greek temple, and you get something quite like the modern brick-box style of architecture. But you will have taken away a lot. And again the simple reader is deceived.

[1] *Frogs*, 1058–61.   [2] 1215–20, 1239–44.

Yet if one wishes to keep nearer to the spirit of the original, instead of adapting it to the utilitarian bleakness of much modern work, what then, is one to do? I think one must compromise. Dislike for aggressive modernisms need not mean that one should call 'cowherds' 'kine-wardens', or cultivate equally aggressive archaisms, like that Professor Newman justly mocked by Matthew Arnold for obsolete gibberish like 'bragly', or 'bulkin', or 'dapper-greav'd Achaeans'.

The problem is largely the same as for the historical novelist. 'Tushery' and 'what-ho without there!' have come to seem foolish and tiresome; but it becomes still more grotesque when the illiteracy of Hollywood makes an Elizabethan courtier reply to his sovereign 'O.K., Queen!'

Shakespeare in modern dress is one of those tricks that may amuse, the first few times they are played, just by showing that they *can* be played. After that, for me, they become tedious jackanapery. So with Homer or Sophocles in modern colloquialism.

The only solution I can see, then, is to avoid words or idioms that are either obtrusively ancient or obtrusively modern—there remain plenty that are neither. Such a comparatively neutral, timeless, dateless background will avoid jarring clashes either with modern habits of mind or with characters, events, and ideas that belong to a bygone age.

* * *

Here is yet another type of deformation—a complete indifference to the rhythm and sound of one's original.

> And all the gods pitied him;
> But Poseidon
> Steadfast to the last
> Hated
> God-like Odysseus.
> The sea-god visited
> A distant folk,
> Ethiopians,
> Who at the edge of the earth
> Are divided into two parts.[1]

[1] Θεοὶ δ' ἐλέαιρον ἅπαντες,
νόσφι Ποσειδάωνος· ὁ δ'ἀσπερχὲς μενέαινεν
ἀντιθέῳ 'Οδυσῆϊ, πάρος ἣν γαῖαν ἱκέσθαι.
ἀλλ' ὁ μὲν 'Αιθίοπας μετεκίαθε τηλόθ' ἐόντας —
'Αιθίοπας, τοὶ διχθὰ δεδαίεται, ἔσχατοι ἀνδρῶν.

(*Od.*, I, 19–23)

67

This imagist version by 'H.D.', of the opening of the *Odyssey*, which in its ladylike sippings suggests to me a hen drinking, is supposed to be a counterpart of the long gallop of Homer's hexameter. But to my ear the original makes a totally different noise—not like these truncated hiccups, but like the long roll of 'Ocean on a western beach'. The classical hexameter seems to me hopeless in modern European languages; but English can at least find metrical equivalents far less inappropriate than this.

Or, again, consider Housman's far finer version of a famous ode of Horace; which keeps admirably close, I think, not only to the literal meaning, but also to the melancholy nobility, the personality, behind the Latin.

> The snows are fled away, leaves on the shaws
>   And grasses in the mead renew their birth,
> The river to the river-bed withdraws,
>   And altered is the fashion of the earth.
>
> The Nymphs and Graces three put off their fear
>   And unapparelled in the woodland play.
> The swift hour and the brief prime of the year
>   Say to the soul, *Thou wast not born for aye.*
>
> Thaw follows frost; hard on the heel of spring
>   Treads summer sure to die, for hard on hers
> Comes autumn, with his apples scattering;
>   Then back to wintertide, when nothing stirs.
>
> But oh, whate'er the sky-led seasons mar,
>   Moon upon moon rebuilds it with her beams:
> Come *we* where Tullus and where Ancus are,
>   And good Aeneas, we are dust and dreams.
>
> Torquatus, if the gods in heaven shall add
>   The morrow to the day, what tongue has told?
> Feast then thy heart, for what thy heart has had
>   The fingers of no heir will ever hold.
>
> When thou descendest once the shades among,
>   The stern assize and equal judgment o'er,
> Not thy long lineage nor thy golden tongue,
>   No, nor thy righteousness, shall friend thee more.
>
> Night holds Hippolytus the pure of stain,
>   Diana steads him nothing, he must stay;
> And Theseus leaves Pirithöus in the chain
>   The love of comrades cannot take away.

That I find lovely.[1] But here again the sound, the rhythm, the music wake my misgivings. In themselves, they delight my ear; but they seem to me too different a tune from the original. Housman has used the ten-syllable quatrain of Gray's *Elegy*: but in Horace the long hexameters are strikingly alternated with lines of less than half their length. Surely that is something for a translator to aim at reproducing.

> Frigora mitescunt Zephyris, ver proterit aestas
> Interitura simul
> Pomifer autumnus fruges diffuderit, et mox
> Bruma recurrit iners.

I miss in Housman's English the sob of Horace's half-lines that bring home, by their own brevity, the poignant brevity of all human things.[2]

---

[1] I regret, however, that Housman has made summer a lady. The Latin *aestas* may be feminine; but in England, I feel, summer is a gentleman—though often an unmannerly one.

[2] Contrast two stanzas by J. B. Leishman, which are a good deal closer than Housman to the rhythm of the original, but seem to me far inferior in style.

> Chillness yields to the western wind, Spring's victim of Summer,
>   destined to perish as well
> soon as Autumn unloads her exhibited fruits; and, with sudden
>   numbingness, Winter returns. . . .
>
> Chaste Diana has failed from encompassing darkness to carry
>   chaster Hippolytus back,
> neither has strong-armed Theseus availed to unloose the Lethaean
>   chains from Pirithoüs bound.

Why 'unloads her exhibited fruits'? It suggests an agricultural show. The Latin has nothing about 'exhibiting'. Why is Hippolytus made 'chaster' than Diana? An insult to the goddess. The Latin merely calls Hippolytus 'chaste' and has no epithet for Diana at all. In strict 'translation' such licences seem to me unjustified.

The same translator has also tried to reproduce the Horatian alcaic:

> Eheu fugaces, Postume, Postume,
> labuntur anni nec pietas moram
>   rugis et instanti senectae
>   adferet indomitaeque morti.
>
> Ah, how they glide though, Postumus, Postumus,
> the years, the fleeting! Neither shall righteousness
>   cause wrinkles, cause onsetting Age or
>   unovercomeable Death to falter.

But how difficult is translation! For here attempted fidelity of metre seems to produce gross infidelity of style. The Latin flows; but the English jerks ('the years, the fleeting'). The Latin is natural; the English strained and contorted. One startles for a moment to read 'Neither shall righteousness cause wrinkles';

This difficulty of rendering the music of foreign verse is one of the translator's hardest problems. Clearly he can seldom keep as close to sound as to sense. In the phrase of Voltaire, you cannot 'translate music'. Sometimes, indeed, a foreign rhythm *can* be acclimatized; as Greek prosody by the Romans, or Italian blank verse by the English. But often this remains impossible. The English hexameter, for example, despite Arnold's curious infatuation for it, seems, as I have said, a broken-winded, galumphing thing.

But at least, where the original gallops, the translation should gallop; where the original was sung, to music now lost to us, the translation too should lilt and sing. Often, however, quite different means must be used to obtain something like the same end. Thus the nearest thing, for me, to the ancient dactylic hexameter is the anapaestic hexameter of Morris in *Sigurd the Volsung*; though I think that often he archaized his style a little too much, and polished and varied his rhythms rather too little.

> Then uprose Grimhild the wise-wife, and took the cup again;
> Night-long had she brewed that witch-drink, and laboured not in vain.
> For therein was the creeping venom, and hearts of things that prey
> On the hidden lives of ocean, and never look on day;
> And the heart of the ravening wood-wolf and the hunger-blinded beast
> And the spent slaked heart of the wild-fire the guileful cup increased:
> But huge words of ancient evil about its rim were scored,
> The curse and the eyeless craving of the first that fashioned sword.

There moves, across the fjells of Norway, a grimmer sister of Circe and Medea. But she too knows the magic that strikes swiftly, that hurries to their weird the lives of men—

> The curse and the eyeless craving of the first that fashioned sword.

Again, an exact equivalent to the Greek six-foot iambic may seem available in the English six-foot Alexandrine. But English Alexandrines, though magnificent in isolation, in bulk become odious. Though not seldom tried in translations from Greek drama, they break monotonously in half like bars of chocolate. On the other hand, for some mysterious reason, the French Alexandrine works perfectly. Metre

the simple 'instanti' and 'indomitae' give place to the exotic crudity of 'onsetting' and 'unovercomeable'; the strong *climax* 'morti' ('Death') is replaced as last word by the feeble 'to falter'. Nor is even the rhythm wholly true. 'Ah, how they glide though' suggests not $- - \cup - -$, but $- \cup \cup - -$.

remains a wayward, capricious, incalculable thing. And so, though you can render the six-foot iambics of Aeschylus or Sophocles into the six-foot Alexandrines of Racine, in englishing Greek tragic dialogue you had better stick to five-foot blank verse.

As for ancient lyrics, attempts to reproduce their metres, with each long syllable of the original replaced by a stressed syllable in English —or one that the translator tortures into a semblance of stress— almost always seem to me to move as awkwardly as an embarrassed town-lady picking her uncertain steps through a puddled farmyard. My own prejudice is that in translating lyrics one had better, as a rule, stick to rhyme—without rhyme it is hard to keep the lilt and swing that are the very life of the lyric form.

*   *   *

To resume, translation should be true to the meaning of the original, while remaining English (as Browning did not); it should be true (unlike Murray at times) to the personality of the original; it should be true (unlike Butler) to the historic tone of the original; and (unlike 'H.D.') it should be as true as possible to the rhythm and music of the original.

When all is said, I have to confess that perhaps the greatest monument in the whole history of translation remains, for me, the English Bible. Take, for example, the curse uttered by Job against the day of his birth.

> Let the stars of the twilight thereof be dark; let it look for light but have none; neither let it see the dawning of the day:
> Because it shut not up the doors of my mother's womb, nor hid sorrow from mine eyes.
> Why died I not from the womb? Why did I not give up the ghost when I came out of the belly?
> Why did the knees prevent me? Or why the breasts that I should suck?
> For now I should have lain still and been quiet, I should have slept: then had I been at rest,
> With kings and counsellors of the earth, which built desolate places for themselves;
> Or with princes that had gold, who filled their houses with silver;
> Or as an hidden untimely birth I had not been; as infants which never saw light.
> There the wicked cease from troubling; and there the weary be at rest.

There the prisoners rest together; they hear not the voice of the oppressor.

The small and great are there; and the servant is free from his master.[1]

The men who translated this were not concerned with petty cravings to be up to date, or in the movement of the moment. They did not care about being 'contemporary'. They did not ape the fashions of their own age—Sidney's style, or Lyly's, or Bacon's. They were not out to flatter the common man. They were concerned only to be true to an eloquence which for them was not only noble, but sacred. To add or omit a single image or idea would have been sacrilege. 'We presume not', wrote Gregory Martin in his preface to the Rheims Testament, 'in hard places to mollifie the speeches or phrases, but religiously kepe them word for word and point for point, for fear of missing or restraining the sense of the holy Ghost to our phantasie.' Indeed Martin may have carried such scruples too far, with less wisdom than Tyndale, or Coverdale, or the makers of our Authorized Version. And even in the Authorized Version there are passages that one feels can hardly have meant anything even to the translators. Here in Job, for example, why should kings build themselves 'desolate places'? One should more probably read 'pyramids'. But such things are minor details. The essential point is that this wholesome fear of twisting writers 'to our phantasie' seems to me to-day far too much forgotten. For all the great writings of the past are, in their way also, holy writ.

I do not know Hebrew. But comparing these verses from Job with the Greek Septuagint, and with the Latin Vulgate of Saint Jerome, I am impressed by the *closeness* of the rendering. The English is indeed, to me, more majestic than the Greek; but not more so (though very different) than the thunderous roll of the Vulgate.

And yet here too there are some to-day who want this venerable loveliness modernized. I do not know why. There seems to me nothing in the Authorized Version of the passage hard to comprehend except for idiots. But here is part of a modern version by the Rev. James Moffatt.

> Why died I not when born,
>   why perished I not at birth,
> Why was I not buried like an abortion,
>   like still-born babes that never see daylight?

[1] iii, 9–19.

Why were there knees to welcome me,
    why were there breasts to suck?
I would[1] have been lying still,
    I would[1] have slept in peace,
With kings and statesmen of the world
    who had built pyramids for themselves,
With princes, rich in gold,
    who had filled palaces with silver.
There villains cease to rage,
    and their victims are at peace,
Captives lying quiet together
    deaf to the slavedriver's shout;
High and low are there alike,
    the slave free from his master.

I do not say this is bad. But the whole magic, for me, is gone out of it. What devil tempted Mr Moffatt to change 'Why died I not from the womb?' into 'Why was I not buried like an abortion?' Why alter 'the wicked cease from troubling' into 'villains cease to rage'? Why, in the Gospel, does Mr Moffatt replace 'Solomon in all his glory' by 'Solomon in all his grandeur'? 'Glory' is far nearer to the Greek word, δόξα, than 'grandeur' is. And apart from the sound, the associations of 'glory' are, to me, finer and more magnificent. In short, I prefer King James's Bible to Mr James Moffatt's.[2]

---

[1] Better 'should'.

[2] The version of Ronald Knox seems much superior to this; but still inferior to the Authorized Version:

'Blacken its starlight, let it await the coming of dawn; the night that should have closed the doors of the womb against me, shut these eyes for ever to sights of woe!

'Had but the womb been the tomb of me, had I died at birth, had no lap ever cherished me, no breast suckled me, all would be rest now, all would be silence. Deeply I would take my repose, with the old kings and senators, that once restored cities for their whim, the chieftains that had such wealth of gold, houses full of silver; with babe still-born and babe unborn, hidden away in the sunless grave. There the unquietness of the wicked is stilled, and the weary are at rest; untroubled the thrall sleeps, his tyrant's bidding cannot reach him now; master and slave are there, and the slave masterless.'

Nor can I follow Knox when he says, 'A Biblical phrase like "O King, live for ever!" has got to be changed; nobody ever talked like that in English'; and suggests some pallid paraphrase like 'Long life to the King's majesty'. How anaemic and boring! Hyperbole is often part of the Oriental character. What would Knox have done with such phrases as this from ancient Egypt?—'Thou hast set him [Aknaton] there until the swan shall turn black and the crow turn white, till the hills rise up to travel and the deeps rush into the rivers'—or 'the

Here too the modern mind shows exactly the opposite aberration to that of the eighteenth century. For our neo-classics found the Authorized Version, like Homer, too simple, too inelegant. In 1761, for example, the Rev. Francis Fawkes produced some improved versions of Scripture. He polished the Song of Deborah. Even to-day, many will remember how the fleeing Sisera came to Jael—'He asked water, and she brought forth butter in a lordly dish.' But that was far too crude for Mr Fawkes. 'Butter' indeed!

> He ask'd refreshment from the limpid wave,
> The milky beverage to the chief she gave.

Again, when David mourns for Jonathan—'thy love to me was wonderful, passing the love of women', that too is embellished by the fastidious Fawkes—

> Thy love was wondrous, soothing all my care,
> Passing the fond affection of the fair.

Or there is Somerville's version—

> How wonderful his love! The kindest dame
> Lov'd not like him, nor felt so warm a flame.

Or again there was that Dr Edward Harwood who produced a 'Liberal Translation of the New Testament', where 'Jesus wept' became 'Jesus, the Saviour of the world, burst into a flood of tears'; at which Johnson 'contemptuously threw the book aside, exclaiming "Puppy!"'[1]

Where the eighteenth century was often too snobbish, the twentieth is often too crude. It distrusts romance. It regards beauty with suspicion. Sometimes its motto seems, 'Truth is crudity, crudity is truth.'

Modern scholarship has produced new light on the Bible; but, as style, it can hardly hope to produce a translation as good as the seventeenth century gave. We have more science but far less art. By all means correct the errors of the Authorized Version; but only where really necessary, only with fear and trembling. If others prefer that debasement called Basic English, let them.

Even after three and a half centuries, I think, the modern translator can keep in mind no better model, for general method, than the com-

obelisks which King Amenhotep had erected for a million millions of years'. 'No one ever talked like that in English.' So presumably Monsignor Knox would have translated simply 'for a very long time'?

[1] See Birkbeck Hill's note in Boswell's *Johnson*, III, 39.

bined truth and beauty of the best parts of the English Bible, polished by the labour of generations, as a boulder by the sea, during more than a century.

To-day most translation, despite more accurate scholarship, seems to me on a much lower level than the Authorized Version and, indeed, than many other translations of the sixteenth and seventeenth centuries.

The fundamental trouble is that those who lack a historic sense are apt to regard a historic sense as nonsense. Many moderns, partly owing to the multiplication of the half-educated, are far too preoccupied with this flickering point in space-time which we call the contemporary world. Men who would smile at the idea of proclaiming Little Piddlington the most important point in space, are often themselves just as grotesquely parochial about the ephemeral point which they chance to occupy in time. To-day translators, and readers of translations, seldom have enough respect for the past, and its differences. It is merely a sun which has set in order that *they* may hoot.

*   *   *

To sum up. The two main weaknesses of modern translation seem to me disregard for truth and disregard for beauty; which, indeed, if the original is beautiful, remains an essential part of the truth.

Truth in translation does not mean merely literal truth. It is multiple. It includes, above all, these four aspects, if the reader is not to be deceived.

(1) Translation should be true in meaning—no ideas added, none omitted—so that, ideally, it should be *conceivable* for the translation, if retranslated, to give back the original text.

(2) It should be true in rhythm, so far as the difference of languages admits. Often this does not admit much. English hexameters seem to me horrible. Greek lyrics seem to me better in English rhyme. But if the original lilts, the translation should lilt; if one gallops, so should the other; and so on. This is the objection to translating verse into prose.

(3) A translation should try to be true to the tone, the character, of the original author—not, for instance, turn deep feeling into cleverness, as Dryden when he adapted Chaucer.

(4) A translation should try to be true to the historic atmosphere, the spirit of a period; and not resemble an over-restored church, or Shakespeare in modern clothes.

75

In general, the chief dangers of translation are infidelity on the one hand, servility on the other. But, in addition, particular periods have particular dangers of their own. The translators of the eighteenth century tended towards snobbery and preciosity; those of the twentieth, to crudity and meanness.

I think, in short, that we are too ready to play pranks with the great work of the past—

> We do it wrong, being so majestical.

It may be that I have grown too fussy about truth of this kind. It seems to leave many people quite unconcerned. My college, for example, has portraits painted of its distinguished figures. In recent years we have had some of these distinguished portraits made by distinguished artists; and the results may (or may not) be distinguished pictures. My objection is that they are far less like the originals than even passport-photographs usually are. Posterity is going to receive a totally false impression of what these men were really like. We are, in fact, busy falsifying history. Yet this does not in the least worry the distinguished historians among my colleagues. I find it all very odd. But I continue to think that a portrait should be as like as possible, and a translation as true as it can be made.

Translators like Pope, FitzGerald, or Murray tend, I feel, to prefer what they think beauty to truth; translators like Browning, Butler, and many moderns tend to prefer what they think truth to beauty; but where the original seems beautiful, the translator, I believe, should try to serve truth and beauty equally; giving, when doubtful, the benefit of that doubt to truth.

At present, I have suggested, 'translation' is become a hopelessly confused term, covering a variety of different things; so that it would be less muddling to distinguish, first, 'close translation'; secondly, 'paraphrase'; and thirdly, 'adaptation'. But that is merely a suggestion for critics. Translators will never heed it. For one would be a simpleton to expect any writer to produce a work called 'Ronsard's sonnets, *paraphrased* by Mr Helicon'. Such a title would damage his reputation and his sales. For the simple reader still fondly loves to imagine he is getting something much more faithful than mere 'paraphrase'. To use such a word would seem an admission of inferiority. What I do suggest, however, is simply that every translator, to whatever school he belongs, should always prefix a preface, however brief, stating his own principles in the matter, so that his public can know how strictly, or how freely, he is at least trying to treat his original. It would, of course, be ideal if the original could always be printed on the opposite page; but that is too costly; and, in any case, it would help only those readers who knew the original language. But until translators are prepared to explain thus frankly what precisely they are endeavouring to do, there will continue to be this widespread and unscrupulous deception of the public by false interpreters, this continual fathering on original writers of meanings, ideas, and attitudes that they never dreamed of. Let 'translators' translate how they will. Liberty and variety have their value, as well as truth. But let them also say in their prefaces, far more candidly than most of them do, what they are at. We now expect editors of old texts to do this—to explain their guiding principles. Translators should do the same. As things are, the simple reader is constantly being duped, and the Italian adage keeps its contemptuous truth: '*traduttori—traditori*'—'translators are traitors'.

The Literature of Greek Travel

YRIAC OF ANCONA in the fifteenth century, asked by some bewildered contemporary what possessed him to wander in a wilderness of Turks and fleas, like Greece, replied 'I go to wake the dead.' That awakening was to be the Renaissance. Thanks to it the dead of Greece are still awake to watch with their calm marble eyes the frenzies of our fevered world. And yet even to-day every traveller in Greece still needs to waken those dead for himself anew. They are still there. That is why the call of Greece is so strong. Perfect travel, for me, demands two qualities in a country—that it shall be full of beauty; and that it shall be full of ghosts. Lands with too little past may thrill the eye, but not the memory. To make our lives fully living we need also the dead. Now no country is more beautiful in itself than Greece; none more haunted. And among its phantoms move not only the great figures of its own legend and history, but also that long succession of half-forgotten pilgrims, more varied even than Chaucer's, who have sailed Greek seas and toiled up Greek mountain-sides from Herodotus to Frazer.

Even a brief and inadequate survey like this may throw a little light from a fresh angle on three different things—on Greece itself, on the art of writing travel-books, and on some characteristic changes in human feeling through two thousand years, from the classical to the medieval and the modern.

It is not generally realized that the Rev. Thomas Cook, that Baptist temperance-missionary who started his famous travel agency, a century ago, by running special trains for meetings of teetotallers, was descended from Apollo. Religion, temperance, and travel were the interests of both. And not only did the God of Delphi know so much of European geography from Cadiz to the Caucasus that each band of early colonists consulted him, like a travel agency, before they sailed away; it was the fame of his oracle that brought the first foreigners to Greece—the envoys of King Croesus from Lydia, the two sons of King Tarquin (so legend told) from Rome. And from later Rome came the first foreign sightseers, men like Flamininus the Liberator and

Aemilius Paulus, who, after breaking the power of Macedon at Pydna, made a regular tour from Delphi to Olympia.

But Rome came not only to see, but to conquer. Already by this date Greece was becoming a land of historic ruins—Corinth, Delos, Mycenae, Sparta, Amphipolis—whose desolation inspires some of the loveliest laments of the 'Anthology'.

> Lost now are the homes of the heroes. Scarce here and there a city
>> From the dust lifts its head a little, where the sons of the gods were born.
> And such wert thou, Mycenae, as I passed, a thing of pity—
>> Even the goats of the mountain have pastures less forlorn.
> The goatherds pointed towards thee. And I heard an old man say—
> 'The Giant-builded City, the Golden, here it lay.'[1]

> Where are the towers that crowned thee, the wealth that filled thy portals,
>> Thy beauty, Dorian Corinth, whereon men stood to gaze?
> Thy proud dames sprung from Sisyphus, thy shrined Immortals,
>> Thy palaces, the myriads that swarmed along thy ways?
> Not a trace, not a trace, unhappy, hast thou left behind in falling—
>> All has been seized and ravened by the wild throat of War.
> We only, Ocean's children, are still left calling, calling,
>> The sea-mews of thy sorrows, along thy lonely shore.[2]

It is the same brooding over glory departed that inspires the first prose passage in the literature of Greek travel to become famous—that letter from Servius Sulpicius consoling Cicero for his daughter's death, which has now become linked for ever with the memory of Sterne's Uncle Toby. ' "Where is Troy and Mycenae, and Thebes and Delos, Persepolis and Agrigentum," continued my father, taking up his book of post-roads which he had laid down.—"What is become, brother Toby, of Nineveh and Babylon, of Cizycum and Mitylene? The fairest towns that ever the sun rose upon are no more; the names only are left; and those (for many of them are wrong spelt) are falling themselves by piece-meal to decay . . .

' "Returning out of Asia, when I sailed from Aegina towards Megara," (when can this have been, thought my uncle Toby), "I began to view the country round about.—Aegina was behind me, Megara before, Pyraeus on the right hand, Corinth on the left.—What flourishing towns now prostrate upon the earth! Alas! alas! said I to

---

[1] Alpheus of Mytilene (first century A.D.—perhaps time of Augustus); *Anth. Pal.*, IX, 97.
[2] Antipater of Sidon (second century B.C.); *Anth. Pal.*, IX, 151.

myself, that man should disturb his soul for the loss of a child, when so much as this lies awfully buried in his presence! Remember, said I to myself again,—remember thou art a man."

'Now my uncle Toby knew not that this last paragraph was an extract of Servius Sulpicius' consolatory letter to Tully:—he had as little skill, honest man, in the fragments as he had in the whole pieces of antiquity. . . . "And pray, brother," quoth my uncle Toby, laying the end of his pipe upon my father's hand, in a kindly way of interruption —but waiting till he finished the account,—"What year of our Lord was this?" "'Twas no year of our Lord," replied my father. . . . "That's impossible," cried my uncle Toby . . . "Simpleton!" said my father,—"'Twas forty years before Christ was born."'

In this Roman of Cicero's day, nearly two thousand years before Chateaubriand, it is strange to hear already the same music of mortality; so early, and so inevitably, even these most classic of ruins took the sunset colours of romance.

But if Greece was now captive, her conquerors thronged to her— students like Caesar, Cicero, and Horace; tourists like Catullus and Virgil, who caught his fatal malady one burning day among the ruins of Megara; exiles like Cicero and those victims of the Empire who found, like many a Greek Communist later, their St Helenas in the Cyclades; even Emperors like Augustus, Nero, and Hadrian.

Now that Greece had come to live on, and in, the past, guide-books were needed. We still have fragments of an early one, the so-called pseudo-Dicaearchus, round about 100 B.C.:[1]

'Oropus is a nest of cheats, a hive of swindlers, and nothing could surpass the extortions of its custom-house officers, whose unconscionable roguery has from time immemorial become bred in their very bones. They even charge duty on what is brought *into* their country. Most of the people are boors to meet, having long since knocked on the head the most intelligent among them. . . .

'Thebes, though ancient, is modernly planned, having been thrice in history destroyed on account of the surly arrogance of its inhabitants. It is an excellent country for horses. . . . As for the people, they are spirited and amazingly optimistic, but headstrong, supercilious, and insulting, quick to blows and reckless of common justice, alike with each other and with foreigners. . . . Accordingly their lawsuits never

[1] C. Müller, *Fragmenta Historicorum Graecorum*, II, 254 ff.; Frazer, *Pausanias and other Greek Sketches*, pp. 56 ff.

last less than thirty years. Anyone who dares utter a word in public about this state of affairs, unless he leaves Boeotia in a hurry, is likely to find himself murdered one dark night by those whose interest it is that lawsuits *should* go on. . . . The women are the prettiest in Greece. . . . The poet Lacon praises the Boeotians, but he is lying; the fact is he was caught making love to a Boeotian lady, and let off lightly by the injured husband. . . . Thence to Anthedon is 160 stadia. . . . At Thespiae is nothing but pretentiousness and fine statues.'

This puckish unknown is a great contrast to the serious Strabo, who under Augustus included Greece in his *Geography*. But Strabo's acquaintance with the country was slight; and an unhappy misdescription of Mycenae has convicted him, like some modern travel-writers, of describing what he had not seen. The one outstanding figure in the ancient literature of Greek travel is his successor Pausanias.

Pausanias was not a great writer. Like Strabo, he was not even a Greek, but from Asia Minor. And Greece, when he wrote her geography (as Plutarch her last great history) in the second century A.D., was only a poor shadow of herself. And yet, especially since Frazer's magnificent edition, Pausanias can be excellent reading. He is not read enough. He is no mere Baedeker. He has Plutarch's sense of the heroic past; so that when he tells of the repulse of the Gauls from Thermopylae, or the death-struggles of Messenia, that ancient Poland, a ghost of greatness rises in him. And Pausanias has also, what Plutarch lacked, a curious streak of romance, when he comes to tales like those of Coresus and Callirhoe, or of Argyra and Selemnus: 'For Selemnus was a young shepherd in the bloom of his years who was loved by Argyra, the Silver One, a nymph of the sea, who used to visit him and sleep by his side. But soon his flower faded, and the nymph came back no more. So in his loneliness he died of love, and was changed by Aphrodite into a river. But even when his limbs were turned to waves, he loved Argyra, as the tale tells that Alpheius loves Arethusa; and so Aphrodite granted him another grace, so that his water remembered Argyra no more. I have also heard tell that the stream of Selemnus cures love in man or woman; so that, if they bathe in it, they forget their love. If there is any truth in the tale, then great riches are less precious to men than the water of the Selemnus.' This last sentence sounds cynical; but Pausanias is no cynic: 'Pitiful indeed was the fate of the innocent youths and maidens who perished through Melanippus and Comaetho; pitiful too the lot of their kinsfolk. But the lovers, I hold, escaped calamity; for to man alone better it is than life itself to love and to be loved.' So with his romantic stories of the supernatural—the ghosts heard battling on the midnight plain of Marathon; the ghost of a sailor of Odysseus from whom the athlete Euthymus saved a maiden; or the sinister shrine of Zeus on Mount Lycaeus in Arcadia, where human sacrifice perhaps endured to Pausanias' own day, and where all creatures lost their shadows; so that the hunter might see his quarry standing there shadowless, yet dared not pursue it, for whoever entered the precinct died within the year. Pausanias makes such things moving still, because they moved him. He is a simple man. He faithfully records, like some medieval pilgrim, the sacred relics of the ancient world—at Panopeus, lumps of the clay from which Prometheus made the first man; a stuffed merman at Tanagra; the sceptre of Agamemnon; the hide of the Calydonian boar; even the egg of Leda, whence Helen sprang. At moments we are reminded of Herodotus; but only at moments. For the genius has departed; this is not the first, but the second, childhood of the race. Soon there were to be Greek travellers of a different kind; little more than a century after Pausanias, came Alaric the Goth, to be bathed and banqueted in a trembling Athens, and to leave sacred Eleusis in ruins.

Already the long silence of the Middle Ages is upon us. But a fine attempt to recapture what the tottering Greek Empire still seemed to the barbarian invader has been made by Kingsley in his 'Ballad of the Little Baltung' (unhistorical though it is) on the legendary poisoning of Athanaric by Theodosius, and the vengeance sworn then by the young Alaric.

The Greek Kaiser welcomes his Gothic guest with smiling perfidy:

> He showed him his engines of arsmetrick
>   And his wells of quenchless flame,
> And his flying rocks, that guarded his walls
>   From all that against him came.
>
> He showed him his temples and pillared halls
>   And his streets of houses high;
> And his watch-towers tall where his star-gazers
>   Sit reading the stars of the sky.
>
> He showed him ostrich and unicorn,
>   Ape, lion, and tiger keen;
> And elephants wise roared 'Hail, Kaiser!'
>   As they had Christians been.

But the Greek Emperor's poison is in the cup of Athanaric, and it is too late to regret the green forests by the Danube's side. This same contrast between the heroic simplicity of the North and the sinister sophistication of Byzantium recurs still unchanged half a dozen centuries later, when Viking Scandinavia comes south to 'Micklegarth' and the Greek Emperors rally round them that Varangian Guard described by Scott in *Count Robert of Paris*. Indeed, among our literature of Greek travel may be counted those romantic runes scored in the flank of the stone lion from Piraeus who now sits outside the Arsenal at Venice; and supposed to record a Greek exploit of that Harold Hardrada who was to fall one day at Stamford Bridge.[1]

A similar contrast between warlike West and cunning East recurs two centuries later, when the Fourth Crusade floods over Byzantium and fills Greece with that Frankish chivalry whose ruined castles still bring to the land of Achilles the ghost of Lancelot, and whose deeds are told in Lord Rennel of Rodd's *Princes of Achaia* and Miller's *Latins in the Levant*. Those who wonder what the Byzantine Empire looked like to a Crusader's eye will find tantalizing glimpses not only in Villehardouin's Chronicle, but also in the poetry of the Provençal troubadour, Raimbaut de Vaqueiras.[2]

But now reappear travellers in the ordinary sense. Between 1159 and 1173 the Jew Benjamin of Tudela travelled from Navarre to Bagdad and back. Unfortunately Benjamin was too race-conscious. He is mainly interested in how many other Jews he can find by the way. 'Thence in two days you cross to Corfu, which contains but one Jew, a dyer called Joseph.' Joseph may have been an excellent dyer, but he is not exactly the one thing we should choose to hear about in twelfth-century Corfu. But Benjamin plods on to find 50 Jews at Patras, 100 at Lepanto, 200 on Parnassus, 300 at Corinth, and no fewer than 5,000 in the fortunate city of Thebes. He is more interesting about the Vlachs, those nomad shepherds still familiar to the Greek traveller of to-day: 'They are nimble as deer, and from their mountains descend robbing and raiding into the plains of Greece. None dares make war on them, and no king can subdue them; and they are not Christians.' Anyone who has dealt with their dogs will agree.

The next visitor known to me after Benjamin of Tudela is the

[1] Cf. Snorri Sturluson's account in the *Heimskringla* of the deeds at Byzantium of both Harold and King Sigurd the Crusader; and the curious Byzantine episode which closes *Grettir's Saga*.

[2] Edited by Oscar Schultz (1893).

Englishman, John of Basingstoke, Archdeacon of Leicester, in the thirteenth century. He records that he had learnt less from all the doctors of Paris than from a certain young lady of Athens, Constantina, daughter of the Archbishop; who in her teens was already mistress of the Seven Arts, and could predict eclipses, earthquakes, storms, and plagues. Unfortunately the contemporary Archbishop of Athens, Akominatos, disclaims having any children. We are left to weigh the word of a Greek Archbishop against that of an English Archdeacon. But at least it appears that some relics of culture still survived in thirteenth-century Athens.

The fourteenth century brings us to a more entertaining traveller, Sir John Mandeville, whose work is even more of a traveller's tale than most. For, first, it is not by Sir John Mandeville; secondly, its compiler, a Belgian physician of Liège, seems to have travelled mainly from shelf to shelf of his library. Being about as veracious as Othello's tales to Desdemona of men with heads beneath their shoulders, his book enjoyed a wild success. His Greek section is brief; but he tells vividly of Justinian's statue in Byzantium, whose hand now refused to hold the magic apple long since fallen from it, and betokening his empire's lost provinces; and of Mount Athos (he should have said Olympus, but miscopied what he stole), who casts his shadow 76 miles, and has a summit so dry that certain wise philosophers, climbing it with sponges to their noses, found still unchanged the letters they had traced there in the snow a year before. He tells too of the Isle of Cos, where 'is yit the doughter of Ypocras, in forme and lykness of a gret dragoun that is an hundred fadme in lengthe as men seyn, for' (a characteristically perfidious touch) 'I haue not seen hire.' The unhappy lady had been thus afflicted by Diana; and a dragon she was doomed to remain, until kissed by a knight. Attempts had been made by various bold gentlemen; but their hearts always failed at the supreme moment —much to the fury of the slighted damsel. 'And whan the knyght saugh hire in that forme so hidous and so horrible he fleygh away and the dragoun bare the knyght vpon a rocke mawgree his hede. And from that rocke sche caste him in to the see.' This typical medieval jumble seems ultimately derived from the story of the nymph Callisto, changed by Artemis or Hera into a bear; from the sacred snake of Asclepios; and from the fact that Hippocrates had a son, or grandson, called Draco. But how much imaginative charm the world would have lost if the Middle Ages had been scientific!

Niccolò de Martini, a notary of Capua, who really did visit Athens at the end of the fourteenth century, found there not a single inn and only a thousand houses. But he eagerly records how there used to be an idol in an iron-bound cave above the Theatre, which sank hostile ships as soon as they came above the horizon—a far-off memory, doubtless, of the Gorgon's head which Pausanias describes on the Acropolis.

With our next traveller, the Florentine Buondelmonti, we can see the medieval idea of Greece, as a land of sinister magic, beginning to yield to the Renaissance sense of its departed glory. Early in the fifteenth century, while Henry V was conquering France, Buondelmonti visited Rhodes and the islands. He is still a credulous soul; he too tells of the daughter of Hippocrates in Cos. Yet there is a change. He comes to study Greek; and at Delos he and his companions, finding the great Apollo of the Naxians prostrate on the shore, have the novel idea of trying to set it on its legs again. 'But with all the machines and tackling of our galleys we could not, though we were more than a thousand.' The isle of Thera proved more perilous. 'Being in these parts on board a Genoese vessel, we saw an octopus, sixty cubits in compass, stretching forth his tentacles and advancing upon us. In panic we left our ship and hurried on shore, where from higher ground we could contemplate the monster. Soon however a fair wind swelled our canvas, and joyfully we sailed away.'

Cyriac of Ancona is still more of a Renaissance figure. Like Schliemann, he was a self-taught merchant with a passion for antiquity; and wandered all over Italy and the Levant, now hunting with the Greek Emperor, now employed as Greek reader by Mahomet II at the siege of Constantinople. Returning from Greece, we are told, when eighty miles on his way, Cyriac heard of an inscription he had missed—and back he went. He was inaccurate and uncritical; he imagined he had found Homer's grave in Chios 'by the roots of an old fig-tree'; there are faults in his Latin verses; he sometimes miscopied his inscriptions; he was even accused of forging them. But let him be forgiven—*quia multum amavit*. We see him like a great bumble-bee, drunk with the honey of antiquity, humming in wide, tireless circles about the Levant. A typical passage tells how a giant Spartan carried him across the Eurotas, then snapped in his hands a bar of iron: in celebration, the delighted Cyriac composed a sonnet.

Constantinople fell. Five years later, in 1458, Athens was visited by Mahomet II in person, anxious to see 'the mother of the philosophers'

—'dearest of the cities of his empire'. (We must remember that Plato himself left his mark on the Ottoman constitution, with its system of Janissaries.) There still exists a Greek guide of the period, perhaps composed for the Sultan's use. Accuracy is not its greatest charm. It describes the tiny temple of Nike on the Acropolis as 'a small school of musicians, founded by Pythagoras'. They must have been very small musicians.

Then, after Sigismondo Malatesta in 1463 had carried back from Sparta to Rimini the bones of Gemistos Plethon, that last star of Byzantine learning, with the later Renaissance there comes a gap. The Turkish conquest must have proved a serious barrier: in conflict with it at Lepanto, near where Byron was to lose his life, Cervantes lost his hand. But in the early seventeenth century the Greek hills saw one of the queerest of all their travellers, Thomas Coryate.

Coryate of Odcombe in Somerset, once a buffoon of Prince Henry's, won a grotesque fame by his *Coryate's Crudities*, describing how he walked 2,000 miles in five months; half of the way in one pair of shoes, which hung gloriously for a century after in Odcombe Church.

He had a head like a sugar-loaf, says Anthony à Wood, and 'a very coveting eye, that could never be satisfied with seeing'. In 1612, after a farewell oration to the citizens of Odcombe, Coryate set out on a new ten-years' walk, by way of Greece and Egypt, into India; five years later he died at Surat, from the over-generous hospitality of the English merchants there. He has not much to say of Greece proper; but his description of Troy makes extraordinary reading.[1] He arrived with fourteen other English and 'a Jew or Druggerman'. After they had wandered round the ruins, identifying Priam's tomb and the like to Coryate's satisfaction, his companion Robert Rugge, whipping out his sword and reciting some extempore doggerel, dubbed Coryate 'the first English knight of Troy'—much to the alarm of their two Turkish guides, who thought a murder was in progress. Coryate replied in more doggerel, their musketeers fired two volleys in rejoicing, and our hero then delivered an equally ridiculous oration on previous visitors to Troy, from Achilles to the Emperor Caracalla, and on the solemn warning that its fate afforded against adultery.

At this same period Scotland produced a rival eccentric in William Lithgow of Lanark, whose *Totall Discourse of the Rare Adventures and*

---

[1] *Master T. Coryate's Travels to and Observations in Constantinople and Other Places* (printed in the 1776 edition of the *Crudities*).

painefull Peregrinations of long nineteene Yeares Travaylles (1632) claims that he covered on his 'paynefull feet' over 36,000 miles. Greece he *says* he traversed in 1609. But his ideas of Greek topography and English prose are equally peculiar. 'Athens', he says, 'is still inhabited, standing in the East part of Peloponnesus, neere to the frontiers of Macedon, or Thessaly by the Seaside.' 'Thessaly . . . lieth betweene Peloponnesus and Achaia: Wherein standeth the hill Olympus, on which Hercules did institute the Olympian games.' Sailing east from Salonika, he had the good fortune to find Parnassus several hundred miles out of its usual place. It had 'two toppes, the one whereof is dry, and sandy, signifying that Poets are always poore and needy: the other top is barren, and rocky, resembling the ingratitude of wretched and niggardly Patrons'.

He grows eloquent over his hardships: 'But this I remember, amongst these rockes my belly was perished, and wearied was my body, with the climbing of fastidious mountains.' On ship it was as bad: 'Between Serigo and Carebusa we had sevenscore and twelve miles of dangerous and combustious seas.' Even a fastidious mountain must have been better than a combustious sea.

And yet there is a sort of Tom o' Bedlam lilt about Lithgow's prose, with its blending of the Old Testament and Ancient Pistol: 'Here in Argos I had the ground to be a pillow, and the world-wide fields to be a chamber, the whirling windy skies to be a roof to my Winter-blasted lodging, and the humide vapours of cold Nocturna to accompany the unwished-for bed of my repose.' However he consoled himself on this painful occasion by composing a satire on women, inspired by the memory of Helen.

Lithgow repays his reader; though a man who tells us he saw at Rome in 'the Library of the auncient Romans', 'the Saphicke verses of that Lesbian Sappho', with many other ancient authors 'all wrote with their owne hands, and sealed with their names, and manuall subscriptions', must rank high in the calendar of unblushing liars.

But two more serious travellers await us—that *entente cordiale*, Monsieur Jacob Spon and Mr George Wheler. Spon (1647–85), a Protestant of Lyons and a doctor by profession, had all the antiquarian passion of Cyriac: 'C'est mon feu, c'est ma passion que les inscriptions antiques.' In 1675 he found himself alone in Rome, his companion Vaillant having been carried off on his way from Marseilles by an Algerian corsair; he met Wheler, botanist and antiquarian, and together they set out for Greece. Spon returned loaded with manuscripts and copies of inscriptions; and his *Voyage* (1678) is our first serious account of Greek monuments since Antiquity. But poor Spon lost his patients, who thought so good an archaeologist must be a very bad doctor, and too likely to provide them with funeral monuments of their own. When he dedicated his book to Père La Chaise, Louis XIV's confessor, the father merely recommended him to turn Catholic. To this, Spon wrote, and published, a too boldly Protestant reply, which ended in his flight to Switzerland and untimely death at Vevey.

But Spon, though a deeper scholar, is less readable than his English companion, Wheler, who in 1682 dedicated to Charles II his *Journey into Greece*, courteously adding Spon's name on his title-page, just as Spon had added *his*. More fortunate, too, than Spon, he was knighted, took orders, and died only in 1723, after producing eighteen children and another work, clearly inspired by them—*The Protestant Monastery: or Christian Oeconomicks, containing Directions for the Religious Conduct of a Family*.

But Wheler's account of Greece is delightful. For him, fortunate man, the Parthenon was still intact; the Turks proved not too Turkish; and there were no tourists. Admirable is his description, with a mixture of sly humour and simplicity, of his adventure marooned on Delos; or of the wicked 'Haga' of Athens, who planned to blow up the church of St Demetrios, and was hoist by that saint with his own petard (though, alas, the Propylaea flew skyward with him); or of the Mainote village where the old woman of the house, asked by some travellers why she was weeping and tearing her hair, replied, 'Because my son is not at home to rob you'; or of the 'extream civil' pirates of Myconos; or of the old hermit whom Wheler met and envied at St Luke's in Stiris, under the quiet shadow of Helicon.

A storm at sea even inspires him to versify a psalm, with results less happy:

> The Waves lift up their voice, the Billows rage:
> No Mortal Pow'r their Fury can asswage.
> They foam and roar; they toss the Ships so high,
> That many times they seem to touch the Skie:
>
> Few there have any appetite to Meat;
> And those that have, can nowhere sit to eat.
> Like Drunken Men they stagger to and fro:
> On dancing Decks what mortal Man can go?

But Wheler's prose is very endearing: witness this picture of Achaea under the Turks. In the mountains he comes on thirty or forty shepherds 'sitting in a round heap together. This made me presently call to mind the pleasant stories I had heard of the *Arcadian* Shepherds, from whose Country we were now not far distant: I thought of nothing, but being diverted by some Festival, some Sport or other among them; or, at least, that there had been the Nuptials of some fair Shepherdess then celebrated. . . . But approaching nearer, I was soon undeceived; finding an old Grey-bearded Turk, sitting in the middle of the Circle, like a Conjurer, with his Lap full of Pebles, Pen, Ink, and Paper by him, and giving each of them their Task; which was to turn five of those stones into so many Dollers by the next day at that time, upon pain of being made Slaves, and sent to the Gallies, if they failed. . . . The number of Pebles that were then to be made Dollers, was Four hundred and thirteen; by a People, that I dare engage, knew nothing of the *Philosopher's Stone.*'

From now on, the stream of Greek travellers thickens fast. There is no time to dwell even on curious figures like Guillet de St Georges, who produced a book on Athens in 1675 without ever going there; and, being exposed by Spon, brazenly accused his accuser of not having been there himself. But St Georges is an amusing rogue; as when he describes a Turkish dinner where he and his companions, busy staring at the lattice concealing their host's harem, found the servants had slyly replaced the plates they were eating from, by others containing 'Coleworts and Turneps and little Kitlings newly born', which they put without noticing in their mouths. Nor is there space here for the admirable botanist Tournefort, or that queer maniac the Abbé Fourmont, sent by Louis XV to the Levant in 1729, who after copying his inscriptions smashed them. 'Depuis plus de trente jours,' he writes triumphant home, 'trente et quelquefois quarante ou soixante ouvriers abattent, détruisent, exterminent la ville de Sparte. . . . Imaginez-vous, si vous pouvez, dans quelle joie je suis. . . . Sparte est la cinquième ville de Morée que j'ai renversée.' Fortunately the Abbé seems to have been as mendacious as mad, and to have wrought little of the havoc that he claims.

Nor can we more than name here the worthy Chandler, who so delightfully describes the Dervishes dancing in the Tower of the Winds at Athens; or the careful and sober Leake; or the admirable Pouqueville, who had served under Napoleon and negotiated with

Nelson in Egypt, before he found himself a Turkish prisoner in the Morea. It is time to turn to those two supreme Greek travellers—Chateaubriand and Byron.

Chateaubriand's *Itinéraire de Paris à Jérusalem*, despite its lapses from sublime to ridiculous, is still unsurpassed. A great, though exasperating personality; a great subject; a great style—these three do not often meet in one.

He travelled in 1806, and published in 1811. The motives of his journey were three, as he admitted at different times. First, he sought colour and imagery for his prose epic of Christianity, *Les Martyrs*. Secondly he saw himself as 'The last of the Pilgrims'—'I shall perhaps be the last Frenchman to visit the Holy Land in the pilgrim spirit of old.' He was, that is, a follower of Joinville, in the cynical age of Talleyrand. Thirdly and incongruously enough, this romantic pilgrimage was to conclude with a romantic assignation at the Alhambra in Spain with Natalie de Noailles, Mme de Mouchy. Few champions of Christianity have ever been as pagan as Chateaubriand; the main tenet in his creed was really 'I will have no other God but me.'

In the end the Pilgrim duly arrived in the Alhambra, but, alas, two months late: and Mme de Mouchy was no Penelope. 'I am an unfortunate woman,' she once said; 'no sooner do I fall in love with one man, than I meet another I like better.' And so at the Alhambra Mme de Mouchy was in black and in tears; she had met a most charming colonel—and then he had died. However, Chateaubriand succeeded in consoling her. Yet tragedy crept into the comedy, when Mme de Mouchy grew jealous of the Duchesse de Duras, and during the Hundred Days at last went mad. It is well to feel all this in the ironic background, as one reads Chateaubriand's book.

Yet it remains one of his best. There is more than usual of that charming smile of his, which he denied to his sombre René; and less stilted solemnity, less brooding on his bored ego. Travel shook up Chateaubriand; and he needed shaking.

The work is not very learned, though not always above pretending to be. But he loathed libraries—those 'nids à rats'. And he scandalized Dr Avramiotti at Argos by just galloping up a hill for an eagle's-eye view, instead of conscientiously poring over the sites. But after all there are a thousand scholars for one poet like Chateaubriand. He has that strange Circe's wand which can transform even foolish creatures back into God's image—style.

Hence he must be read in full: he cannot be conveyed in summary. The reader must be lulled—except when some crowning absurdity breaks the spell, not unpleasantly, with a sudden gust of laughter—by the long roll of those melancholy sentences with which Chateaubriand first taught French to equal the surge of the English Bible, or the organ-march of Sir Thomas Browne.

Sailing from Venice, by Corfu and Ithaca, he landed at Modon in Messenia. 'Pas un bateau dans le port, pas un homme sur la rive; partout le silence, l'abandon et l'oubli.' Then enter bands of Janissaries and Turks. The roads proved for the moment unusually clear of brigands: for the Pasha of the Morea had just cleaned up the district of Mount Ithome by the simple method of drawing a cordon all round, and killing everyone within it. It is true that this cost also the lives of three hundred innocent peasants. One recalls the massacres of the Albigensian Crusade—'Slay on, and God will know His own!'

The cavalcade sets out: first, the guide with a spare horse; then an armed Janissary; then Chateaubriand, also armed; and at the rear his Milanese valet, Joseph, a little fair, fat man, sweltering in blue velvet through a Greek August. Each evening they reach an empty 'khan' or inn; the Janissary goes out to hunt a fowl, which Chateaubriand insists on paying for; they eat with their fingers, wash them in the brook, then sleep on the floor 'parmi toutes sortes d'insectes et de reptiles'. 'Voilà comme on voyage aujourd'hui dans le pays d'Alcibiade et d'Aspasie.'

Sometimes things are even worse, as at the approach to Sparta, where the khan is occupied by an old Turk squatted among goats and goat-droppings: 'J'avais mangé l'ours et le chien sacré avec les Sauvages; je partageai depuis le repas des Bédouins; mais je n'ai jamais rien rencontré de comparable à ce premier kan de la Laconie.' Sometimes things are better: 'Il y même à Misitra une maison grecque qu'on appelle *l'Auberge anglaise*: on y mange du roast-beef, et l'on y boit du vin de Porto. Le voyageur a sous ce rapport de grandes obligations aux Anglais: ce sont eux qui ont établi de bonnes auberges dans toute l'Europe . . . jusqu'aux portes de Sparte, en dépit de Lycurgue.'

True, the little Spartans of Mistra amused themselves by pushing pieces of the ruins on top of him; but there was the consolation of finding there his own *Atala* translated into modern Greek. What more could author desire? Then comes one of Chateaubriand's sublimely absurd moments. With difficulty he finds his way to the site of Sparta. The sun is just rising over the range of Menelaïon, amid the silence of the ruins: 'Je criai de toute ma force: Léonidas! Aucune ruine ne répéta ce grand nom, et Sparte même sembla l'avoir oublié.'

And yet a moment later the magic returns; as on the surface of a woodland-pool the ripples of some fallen pebble disappear, and the mirrored forest stands dreaming there again. Chateaubriand sees some blue lilies on an islet in the Eurotas—'j'en cueillis plusieurs, en mémoire d'Hélène; la fragile couronne de la beauté existe encore sur les bords de l'Eurotas, et la beauté même a disparu'.

He crosses Mount Parthenius; loses himself and catches a fever in the legendary marshes of Lerna; is led by a naked shepherd-boy to the tomb of Agamemnon and the ruins of Mycenae. Corinth produces a typical and comical flourish of grandiloquence: 'Je ne parle point de Denys et de Timoléon. . . . Si jamais je montais sur un trône, je n'en descendrais que mort; et je ne serai jamais assez vertueux pour tuer mon frère; je ne me soucie donc point de ces deux hommes.'

Beyond the Isthmus a Turkish commandant demonstrated to the Frankish stranger the excellence of his carbine by casually sniping a peaceful peasant on the neighbouring hill; the wretch crawled in, wounded and weeping, and was given fifty stripes by way of compensation.

So at last Chateaubriand arrived in an Athens whose Piraeus showed not a single sail, and only a single wooden shed for its Turk douanier: nothing now but the cry of wave and sea-bird by the grave of Themistocles. With a last description of dawn on the Acropolis we will leave Chateaubriand to sail on under Sunium for his Holy Land: 'J'ai vu, du haut de l'Acropolis, le soleil se lever entre les deux cimes du mont Hymette' (it has not two summits; but no matter): 'les corneilles qui nichent autour de la citadelle, mais qui ne franchissent jamais son sommet, planaient au-dessous de nous; leurs ailes noires et lustrées étaient glacées de rose par les premiers reflets du jour. . . . Athènes, l'Acropolis, et les débris du Parthénon se coloraient de la plus belle teinte de la fleur du pêcher; les sculptures de Phidias, frappées horizontalement d'un rayon d'or, s'animaient, et semblaient se mouvoir sur le marbre par la mobilité des ombres du relief; au loin, la mer et le Pirée étaient tout blancs de lumière; et la citadelle de Corinthe, renvoyant l'éclat du jour nouveau, brillait sur l'horizon du couchant, comme un rocher de pourpre et de feu.'

Three years later, in 1809, Childe Harold left England on *his* pilgrimage. By way of Lisbon and Malta he arrived in Albania, and at

Janina visited Ali Pasha, now a little plump man of seventy, who in his time had roasted enemies alive, and drowned a dozen women to humour a daughter-in-law. Ali liked Byron, and praised the high breeding of Byron's small ears and little white hands; while Byron was ravished by all this and by 'the glittering minarets of Tepalen', with their feudal pageantry that reminded him of Scott's Branksome Castle. At Janina he began *Childe Harold*. But Byron's poem lacks the perfection—and the poetry—of Chateaubriand's prose. Most moderns will prefer Byron's letters, with their Sancho Panzan picture of *his* valet, Fletcher; who, poor man, after the terrors of a fearful storm in the Albanian hills found himself facing still worse terrors at sea. 'Fletcher yelled after his wife, the Greeks called on all the saints, the Mussulmans on Allah; the captain burst into tears.' After trying to console Fletcher, who could only moan about 'a watery grave', Byron calmly lay down in his cloak on deck; and was delighted to be driven ashore at 1 a.m. among the picturesque cut-throats of Suli.

Like Chateaubriand, Byron was scornful of archaeological fervour. His companion Hobhouse, he says, 'would potter with map and compass at the foot of Pindus, Parnes and Parnassus, to ascertain the site of some ancient temple or city. I rode my mule up them. They haunted my dreams from boyhood; the pines, eagles, vultures and owls were descended from those that Themistocles and Alexander had seen, and were not degenerated like the humans.'

The trio arrives at Athens. 'Ah, my Lord,' cried Fletcher on the Acropolis, 'what chimney-pieces one could make with all this marble!' 'Magnificent!' exclaimed Hobhouse surveying the Parthenon. 'Very like the Mansion House,' said Byron. But that did not prevent him from trouncing in both prose and verse the vandalism of Lord Elgin, then busily at work.

They took rooms in Athens; Byron in the house of a widow with three fair daughters, all under fifteen, Theresa, Mariana, Katinka. It was for Theresa that he wrote:

> Maid of Athens, ere we part,
> Give, oh give me back my heart . . .
> Hear my vow, before I go,
> Ζωή μου σὰς ἀγαπῶ.[1]

Perhaps too it was for her that he wounded his own breast with a dagger, in the fashion of Eastern lovers, while the lady looked coldly

[1] 'My life, I love you.'

on. But (alas for romance) in the end poor Theresa married a Mr Black, and died at eighty, penniless.

After being nearly waylaid by some Mainotes at Sunium, Byron and Hobhouse sailed for the Hellespont, where Byron performed that feat he valued beyond all he had ever done, by swimming from Sestos to Abydos: and so to the Bosphorus where, perched on the Symplegades, he scribbled his parody of Euripides' prologue to *Medea*:

> Oh, how I wish that an embargo
> Had kept in port the good ship Argo!

Returned for a second stay to Athens, he lodged for a time in the Choragic Monument of Lysicrates, then part of a Capuchin monastery, busy teaching the Abbot's pupils to box, or rescuing young ladies on their way to be thrown into the sea in a sack; while even Fletcher, after all his complaints of the lack of beer, beef and tea, of resin in the wines and bugs in the beds, now consoled himself for the young bride he had left in England with an Athenian Circe.

There followed a second trip to the Morea, which enabled Fletcher to put his foot in a boiling kettle at Megara. At Patras Byron nearly died of fever, while Fletcher and the doctor both lost their heads. But Byron's Albanian servants swore to kill the doctor if their master died; the doctor wisely fled; and Byron recovered for fourteen years more.

I have recalled enough to send readers back to the strong and astringent letters in which Byron records these things. With his tragic return to Greece I need not deal. It belongs not so much to Greek travel as to the history of Europe. But one moment in it is worth reviving here. They were approaching Cephalonia; the plaintive but faithful Fletcher was still there: 'My master,' he confided, Sancho-like, to Trelawny, 'can't be right in his mind. Why, sir, there is nothing to eat in Greece, or to drink; there is nothing but rocks, robbers, and vermin. I defy my Lord to deny it.'

Byron overheard: 'I don't deny it. What he says is quite true to those who take a hog's-eye view of things. But this I know, I was never so happy as when I was there.'

It was true, I believe, for him as for many another Greek traveller. And to Byron life and death were kinder in Greece than in England. The tragedy of Missolonghi was his finest poem. And next to it may stand that part of his *Don Juan*, which tells of the love of Juan and Haidee among the Cyclades, and embodies those lines which, even though England has sometimes forgotten the spirit of Navarino, have already outlived those Dictators of a day who, of their grace and wisdom, told us we were tired of liberty:

> The mountains look on Marathon
> And Marathon looks on the sea,
> And musing there an hour alone
> I dreamed that Greece might yet be free.
> For standing on the Persian's grave
> I could not deem myself a slave.

This is far from exhausting the lively pageant of Greek travellers. We must leave Byron's own friends, Hobhouse and Galt, and that old pirate Trelawny, who came with Byron to fight for Greece, and outraged his friend's corpse, and married a whole seraglio, including the daughter of the Greek bandit Odysseus, and sat six weeks motionless in the cave on Parnassus where a traitor had shot him in the back, yet was eighty-nine before he was laid at last beside Shelley in the Protestant Cemetery at Rome; and Christopher Wordsworth, the poet's nephew, who came to Athens in 1832, when it was unsafe to stir beyond the walls, and there were no newspapers, while letters were cried in the streets and burnt if unclaimed; and Dodwell, whose *camera obscura* spread consternation among the Turks on the Acropolis, lest he should put them bodily in his 'magic box' and carry them away; and Edward Lear, who also painted Greece and had a poem written on his travels by Tennyson; and Lamartine, who is watery and disappointing; and Edmond About, whose impish *Roi des Montagnes* gave many of us at school our first picture of Greek brigands; and Flaubert, returning from Egypt; and Heinrich Schliemann, whose simple faith raised to life again the dead of Troy, Tiryns, and Mycenae; and the sensitive pen of Sir James Frazer in our own day.

But I have said enough to suggest how happily one can travel through Greece in one's head, as well as on one's feet. True, Greek travel has produced no work quite so famous as Johnson's *Hebrides* or Doughty's *Arabia*. It hardly will now: for to-day even Greece is fast being vulgarized. Athens itself in the last forty years has become defiled with vast, crawling suburbs. But in the pages of Pausanias, of Wheler, of Chateaubriand, of Byron, we can revisit an older Greece, dead now, yet safe for ever from the grinding march of the machine, in that Universe of Ideas where—

> A new Peneus rolls his fountains
> Against the morning star,

with no railroad through Tempe at his side. Published to-day, Chateaubriand would be giggled at, Byron silenced with jeers of 'Rhetoric!' It may even be that, neglected in a world of science and technology, those Greek dead whom Cyriac of Ancona went long ago to waken, may die for a while a second death. But, for the present, the Greek past is still ours: and this sketch may help a few readers, above all those who have had the good fortune to tread Greek soil themselves, to breathe again, for a moment, that clearer and cleaner air.

Testtuberculosis: the Menace of Science to the Humanities

I N a recent Essay Paper at Cambridge I set this quotation: 'We are menaced by a new Dark Age, with theologians and monks replaced by scientists and technicians. *Vicisti, Galileo!*'[1]
The quotation was, I need hardly say, invented. It is often much simpler to invent one's quotations. It was also deliberately exaggerated. But it involved, I thought, certain real and serious problems, on which it would be interesting to see what was thought by the young.

The result was catastrophic. If one sets six alternative essay-subjects, one hopes that each of them will attract a reasonable share of the candidates. Then the anguished boredom of reading them may at least be lessened by variety.

But this particular topic proved disastrously successful. I had evidently trodden on a very sore spot. Two-thirds of the victims—something like a hundred of them—flew straight for this one subject—as straight as crows. And did they croak! I was well caught.

Whether such alarm and despondency are widely common among the non-scientific young, I cannot tell. Nor can I say that such fears are wholly unfounded; but they do seem to me rather exaggerated. It may then be worth considering how one should face this problem of the triumph of science; and whether one need take views quite so disconsolate.

Obviously our scientific advance has also serious drawbacks. If all the monkeys in the Zoo were trained to fire machine-guns, liberally equipped with ammunition, and let loose in Regent's Park, it would hardly tranquillize the neighbourhood. And this, of course, is just what science has done. It has distributed dynamite in the human nursery; it has piled infernal machines into the paws of Caliban. The road to Hell is rapidly being paved with good inventions.

A Congo tribe used, I have heard, to call the white man 'the bat

---

[1] 'Thou hast conquered, O Galileo!' With reference, of course, to the traditional dying words of Julian the Apostate, mortally wounded on his Persian campaign—'*Vicisti, Galilaee!*' ('Thou hast conquered, O Galilaean!').

that flies hard it knows not whither'. At moments one may well wonder if these simple natives were not right. At moments one may be
reminded of the American inventor who spent two years contriving a
machine which should first chloroform, then decapitate him—and
succeeded. At moments one may begin to see the earth itself as just a
vast *mis*guided missile. Eighty-odd years ago Jules Verne's hero went
round the world in eighty days: now a dog does it in eighty minutes.
No wonder men grow giddy.

About all this the individual can do nothing. Epictetus, indeed,
wisely taught that we should never worry about things we cannot control. But that, for most of us, is a counsel of impossible perfection—
like Wellington's calm remark that he made a point of not lying awake
at night, since no good ever comes of it. Few are so strong-minded.
All the same, one can do worse than try to remember these wise men.
The hair is seldom improved by tearing; and few grow wiser by
becoming bald.

And even if these world-events are beyond our control, we have
still—for the present—our own lives to lead. Many students of the
humanities seem to me unduly worried, both by doubt about their own
careers, and by a needless sense of inferiority to these dominating
scientists who make us feel, at times, futile as fossils, or frivolous as
butterflies.

Well, what is the worst that a scientist might say to us? I will imagine one—a personage far more rude and ruthless than the amiable
and admirable scientists I have really known. For one can sometimes
exorcise what one fears, not by bolting from it, but by visualizing it at
its grimmest. So Caesar, when his men in Africa grew dismayed by
rumours of the vast hosts of King Juba, assured them with grim
humour that the King was indeed approaching at the head of hosts still
vaster—ten legions, 130,000 cavalry and light infantry, and no fewer
than three hundred elephants. 'So now', said he, 'let some of you stop
asking questions.'

*   *   *

Therefore this spectral scientist that I conjure up shall be something
of an ogre. And this is what he says.

'How frightened you look, you people of the past!—like a lot of
respectable bourgeois listening with pale faces to the strains of *The
Red Flag*. Well, no dog likes his day being done. Console yourselves

that you have had a very long day, you humanists and students of the arts. And we shall not liquidate you all. A certain quota of you may survive. But you must descend now from that lofty perch where for so long you have looked disparagingly down your noses at us scientists.

'Even in the later nineteenth century, remember, a man as gifted as Rossetti could preen himself on not knowing whether the sun went round the earth, or the earth round the sun. That Mr Herbert, who in Mallock's *New Republic* impersonates Ruskin, could indulge in arrogant Jeremiads because our modern world "would", as he puts it, "sooner look at a foetus in a bottle, than at a statue of the god Apollo, from the hand of Phidias, and in the air of Athens". And a writer as world-famous as Tolstoy could mock at scientists for classifying seven thousand kinds of flies; or propose that mankind should turn back from science to tilling the earth with sticks.

'Even in our own time, Gandhi could fool about with goats and spinning-wheels. But all that is over. Since then, India and China have developed five-year plans. Mystic meditations under bo-trees are at a discount. In fine, the boot is on the other foot. Or, as a fellow-scientist of mine once forcibly put it—"We are living in the age of the engineer, and the spark-gap is mightier than the pen."

'What you people feel', my scientist continues, 'is doubtless expressed by this sort of melodious wail uttered not long ago in the *Times Literary Supplement*: "What will almost certainly first strike anyone studying the plan *of* the buildings *of* the University *of* Melbourne" (three "of's" in a line!—how badly you arts people write!) is the pathetically small number and size of the buildings devoted to the arts—some four in all—compared with the profusion of scientific departments, ranging from biochemistry to tribophysics." (But of course you will not even know what tribophysics is.)

'This mandarin in the *Literary Supplement* admitted that what he calls "the liberal arts" (science, no doubt, being "servile") need far less space than laboratories; none the less he finds the situation "pathetic". Pathetic himself!

'Surely even this anonymous Jeremiah must know that this country and the Commonwealth are producing only a fraction of the scientists we need—that we had in 1956–7 only 10,000 researchers to Russia's 80,000; that Russia now turns out 100,000 engineers a year, against a third of that number in the U.S.A. Such a person might as well have complained in 1940 that the munitions-programme was interfering with the output of fiddles.

'Make what you can', smiles my scientist, 'of these hard facts. For the facts are as inevitable as hard. Why? Glance back for a moment at human history and resign yourselves to the irresistible. For you are caught up in a world-historic movement. You are impotent as pebbles in the resistless glide of a glacier.

'Man began with magic. The magician multiplied bison by painting them on cavern-walls; he made rain; he kept the stars in their courses. From such delusions sprang religion, art, science. Sorcerers grew into priests; seers into poets; astrologers into astronomers.

'Now the priests have had a long reign, and the poets a reign still longer, as the supposed teachers of mankind. Just as Homer three thousand years ago could be taken for a master of war and wisdom, so even in the last century your Matthew Arnold could still pontificate about poetry as "the criticism of life". To this day there persist literary pundits who presume that they can teach the world about "values". But what value have these "values" of amateurs, increasingly ignorant of what science has discovered about the world, including the human mind itself?

'This simple fact was pointed out, ages ago, by the earliest philosophers. For the great contribution of the Greeks lay, not, as is commonly pretended, in creating beauty—other races had already done that—but in recognizing that beautiful nonsense can often be very far from truth. And so Heraclitus said bluntly that Homer should be whipped; Pythagoras saw him hung in Hell on a snake-encircled tree; and Plato purged his Republic of all poets—inspired drunkards impudently posing as experts about life. The long war of philosophers and scientists against poets and artists is not a novelty; it is over two thousand years old.

'One of the most vital moments in history was when Thales of Ionia one day in the sixth century B.C. asked "Of what is the world made?"—and answered "Of water". He had answered wrong: but he had *asked*. For the first time the human mind had emerged from fairy-tales about world-eggs, or elephants that stood on tortoises that stood on nothing, to rational hypothesis.

'But because you literary people have enjoyed through centuries a corner in education, for a thousand persons who know something about Greek tragedy, there is perhaps one who knows a thing about

Greek science—that Eratosthenes got within fifty miles of the earth's true diameter; that Heraclides realized the earth's daily rotation; that Aristarchus anticipated Copernicus in centring the planets round the sun.

'And then, of course, there was the great Archimedes; of whom the literary merely know that he once had a bath, and that he was killed by an irritated soldier (with whom they perhaps sympathize) because he would not stop doing geometry.

'But unfortunately Greek science was bedevilled by slavery. Because slaves laboured, while gentlemen could chatter philosophy in porticoes, like you, mechanical science was thought servile; and because slaves did the labour, labour-saving seemed futile. Even so, there may have been more inventions between 330 and 130 B.C. than there were between then and A.D. 1600.

'If the Romans had bothered more about science, it might have saved the Empire from the Barbarians; just as Greek fire long saved Byzantium from Islam. But, instead, the West let itself be besotted by Oriental superstitions and fanaticisms. And so now began a period of over a thousand years in which the human brain was devoted to such pretty problems as whether the Holy Ghost were a female ninety-six miles high; whether the first two Persons of the Trinity were composed of the same substance, or only of similar substance; or how the resurrection of the body would work for cannibals whose bodies were constructed from other people's bodies which they had eaten.

'One is told, of course, with bated breath by medievalists that some of these medieval minds were incredibly subtle; I can only infer—as is indeed obvious from daily observation—that, without some scientific sense, minds incredibly subtle can become also incredibly silly.

'Medieval science, no doubt, is delightful—for the literary. There is in the hearts of horses a bone which drives away sorrow; if you walk with a staff of myrtle, you will never grow tired; if you put the tongue of a frog on the heart of a sleeping woman, she will babble all her secrets. How wonderful to know remedies so simple for weariness, or sorrow, or women's secrecy—you would think there must have been a wild stampede to put these easy panaceas to the test of practice. Not a bit of it! For minds like theirs the test of truth was, not experience, but the mouldiness of the authority. Topsell, for instance, has doubts about the pretty ways of unicorns, because he can find no authority for them *more* than five hundred years old; could he only have found an authority a thousand years old, doubt would have vanished. What wonder if medieval writers on nature remain about as rational as modern literary critics?

'And so it is with a gasp of relief that one comes in this foolish epoch on an eccentric like Roger Bacon who can make the astounding statement—"He therefore that wishes to rejoice without doubt in the truths underlying phenomena must know how to devote himself to *experiment*." Naturally such a man was hastily shut up; and is said to have paid for his originality with years of confinement.

'However, this unscientific Eden, this twilight sleep, was too good to last. The Awakening came. Leonardo da Vinci, wonderful as artist, was yet more wonderful as scientist. On the very day, it is said, that Michael Angelo died, Galileo was born. "It moves."

'Three centuries after Roger Bacon there appeared Francis Bacon, with those schemes for *experimental* research that flowered in the Royal Society, just three centuries ago. Naturally the Royal Society was at once jeered and sneered at by the literary, such as Samuel Butler, the author of *Hudibras*. But one of the Royal Society's first experiments (1661) seems marvellously symbolic.

'Everyone knew that nothing venomous could face either Irish earth (thanks to Saint Patrick), or unicorn's horn. The Royal Society did a simple thing that no one had dreamed of doing before.[1] They got some Irish earth; they got what purported to be some unicorn's horn; they got—how difficult!—a spider. They circumvallated the spider with these sacred substances. The creature could not have cared less— it just scampered over them.

'That trotting spider symbolizes the march of science. Tremble, little flies. Your romantic unicorn's horns are broken reeds.

'From 1700 to 1750, it has been estimated that there were 170 new inventions; from 1750 to 1800, 344; from 1800 to 1850, 861; from 1850 to 1900, 1,100. Think only of the nineties, within the memory of many of us—"the naughty nineties", when your decadents were crooning their sad little songs.

1890   First electric power-station in England.
1894   Maxim's steam aircraft flies 100 yards.
        First motor-race, attaining 15 miles an hour.
        First wireless signals.

[1] With the curious exception, apparently, of William Davenant.

1895   First X-rays.
1896   Steam aircraft flies 1,300 yards.
      Abolition of English speed-limit, for automobiles, of 4 miles an hour.
1898   Radium.
1899   Wireless between England and France.
1900   Freud's *Interpretation of Dreams*.

'The avalanche was gaining speed. What are political or artistic revolutions compared with this scientific revolution, which no counter-revolution ever puts back again? And now the world is so dependent on scientists that without them a large part of its grossly inflated population would starve. Particularly here in England, where we sit crowded like sea-birds on a narrow rock, our survival depends on leading, and continuing to lead, in the race of science.

'You do not want to see this harsh fact. A lot of you are still medieval-minded. In 1949 the Pope decided that the Blessed Virgin rose bodily to Heaven—is that sort of thing your answer to the sputnik?

'Some of you are students of languages. Well, we must have interpreters, till English, Russian, or Chinese becomes the world-language. But, anywhere you travel, you will find plenty of Cook's agents or the like, who can patter half a dozen languages for very modest salaries. Languages are no great accomplishment. Soon we shall leave quite a lot of translating to machines.

'Some of you are historians. I suppose we must have historians. But the man-hours devoted to history seem excessive. What matters to-day is not the past, but the future. We are in a life-or-death struggle for scientific supremacy. Let the dead bury their dead—or a good many of the living may need burial sooner than they like. This is no time for trained bores discussing the price of eggs under Edward I, or how much it might cost an eighteenth-century M.P. to corrupt the electors of Eatanswill.

'Some of you study philosophy. Philosophers are people who mystify themselves methodically about what is not yet scientifically known. For example, philosophers once argued that the planets must move in circles, because circles are perfect; then Kepler found that they do not move in circles at all, but in ellipses. The great Hegel demonstrated that there *must* of necessity be seven planets; within a week of his book's publication a disobliging astronomer discovered an eighth since then new planets have been found in shoals—thirty-one, for example, by a single astronomer in three months of 1928. Much philosophy, I suspect, is like the dying words of Gertrude Stein—so much more intelligent than the multitudes of them she published in her lifetime. "What is the answer?" she murmured; and then—"But then what is the question?"

'Again, a vast activity goes on the study of art and literature, ancient and modern. I should have thought that art and literature were produced, not to be studied, but to be enjoyed; and produced by men who were anything but students—men who would have had no hope of Ph.D.s, and not the remotest wish for them. Your elaborate output of criticism is largely a pseudo-scientific bubble-blowing. Professor Pismire quarrels with his colleagues for, say, pronouncing Pope a better poet than Dryden: Dryden, screams Pismire, is better than Pope. Better for whom? For Pismire. Then let him go and enjoy Dryden quietly in a corner. Why does he waste the world's time? Because the world is so foolish as to listen, and pay him for it. Has Pismire ever written a poem? No. Then he is like a man lecturing on cookery without ever having even boiled an egg. Universities are bad for art; and art for Universities. Art and literature merely get chewed up there by pontificating pedants; and nothing comes of it but dyspepsia and wind.

'And what has your literary and artistic world produced in this present century? A lot of synthetic insanities—of decadent, anti-rational maunderings. In fact, a general stampede from reason. Not unnaturally. For, more and more, the best intellects are now drawn into science; and its dazzling triumphs have set off wild flappings and screamings in the anti-intellectuals—like flabbergasted bats squirming and shrieking back into the shadows of a suddenly floodlit cave—minds nostalgic for medieval bigotry, or nostalgic for noble savagery. Savages reverence madness; now your madness reverences savages.

'After all, literature and the arts may by now have had their day. Renan, himself no mean writer, has written: "A time will come when the great artist will be an outworn, almost useless thing; the savant, on the contrary, will become ever more important." And Clifford Bax, describing how Leonardo da Vinci shifted his interest from art to science, once predicted: "Three or four hundred years hence poetry, like rattles and tooth-corals, will be found only in state-homes for incubated infants." In fact, art is perhaps only the opium of aesthetes.

'The dogs of the humanities may bark: but the caravan of science moves on. The time approaches when scientific knowledge will have so increased that nothing can be sensibly talked about—not even the weather—except by qualified experts.'

*　　　*　　　*

So speaks my spectral scientist. I have, of course, caricatured him into a mixture of truth and monstrosity. But how should we answer this terrible man? It is too easy—I have heard it done—to indulge in futile recriminations; too easy to mock at scientific Philistinism like Newton's, with his talk of sculpture as stone dolls, of poetry as 'ingenious nonsense'; or like Bentham's, with his queries whether pushpin were not better than poetry, and the game of solitaire than the bloodthirsty pages of Homer. One can cite—but it has been done too often—Blake growling at the loom of Locke and the waterwheels of Newton; or Lamb and Keats drinking confusion to Newton and the science which robs the rainbow of its divinity, angels of their wings. One can lament it as only too typical that science should now reveal fairy-rings to be the work, not of fairies, but of fungi! I have myself gazed up at the floodlit Parthenon, high on the Acropolis of Athens, with morose reflections that we can now floodlight what we can no longer build. I have seen Wordsworth's Tintern Abbey besieged by char-à-bancs fifty deep, and their dutifully bored occupants; or looked from the Pillar, above Ennerdale, to where on the Cumbrian coast squat the sinister towers of Calder Hall—with a heart that leapt up as little as Wordsworth's would have. I have vivid memories, too, of the air-display at Farnborough—dazzling machines, magnificent skill, and yet, among all that vast concourse of spectators, hardly one face one wished to look at twice. And behind it all there looms, always, the chance of being cremated alive, free of cost, on the most masterly scale.

But such complaints and laments hardly help. They may raise a laugh or a groan—but not the level of the discussion. And I have seen such talk tease scientists to anger; but nothing is gained by making honest men angry. Actually we can no more reverse the march of science than Eve could uneat the Apple. Science may bring world-catastrophe; but only a world-catastrophe could now stop science. Some may feel that the human Faust has sold himself to Mephistopheles. It seems too soon to say. But there is nothing to be done but to make the best of the bargain—to try to defend and preserve as much as possible of what we value. Having to sup with the Devil, we must look about for long spoons.

*   *   *

How, then, shall we give our accusing scientist an answer that makes sense?

First, I think, he is being rather unscientific. That is to say, an inadequate psychologist. He has asked too little what is our aim in living. Science offers us power, wealth, comfort. But these are not sufficient ends in themselves; they are merely means—sometimes very dubious means—to a satisfactory life. It seems to me true that nothing matters ultimately to us but mental processes that we can value.[1] Indeed we do not even know that anything exists but mental processes. What mental processes we value, depends on taste; but to find mental processes that we can go on valuing, depends also on wisdom and foresight. For any fool knows that there are plenty of tempting experiences that have nasty stings in their tails; plenty of jolly revels that leave vile headaches and foul tongues; plenty of alluring mirages that lead only to the dusty heart of deserts.

Honesty will, indeed, at once own that science too involves, not merely material gains, but also mental qualities that seem valuable— the thirst for knowledge, the love for truth, the curiosity that cannot rest in the face of unsolved problems. But there remain other mental qualities and activities no less important. And too exclusively scientific persons, or too exclusively scientific communities, are in some danger of forgetting that.

For one thing, science has perforce become crushingly specialized. Darwin himself, with his clear-sighted honesty, once called such specialization as his own 'an accursed evil for man'. Eight years on barnacles! He had lost his feeling for music, painting, poetry. Once he had passionately enjoyed Milton: he ended by finding even Shakespeare nauseously dull. Could he have lived again, said Darwin, he would have guarded against this. For, in his own frank words, 'the loss of these tastes is a loss of happiness, and may possibly be injurious to the intellect, and more probably to the moral character'. And again (to Hooker, June 17, 1868)—'it is a horrid bore to feel, as I constantly

[1] Sometimes put in the form, 'Nothing matters but *states of mind.*' But '*states of mind*' seems to me too static a phrase for our thoughts, which can no more stand still than time itself.

do, a withered leaf for every subject except science. It sometimes makes me hate science.'

When Sir Robert Walpole had fallen from power, one day in his library at Houghton he took a book from the shelf, then another, then another—then burst into tears. 'Good God!' he cried, 'I can't read.' It was not his sight he had lost, but his taste—decades of struggle for power in the Commons had destroyed for him the quiet pleasure of a book in a corner. Now his political power was gone; and nothing remained in its place. I have known scientists no less frustrated than Sir Robert, when illness kept them from their beloved laboratories. And I am not happy about the new system which now turns a large part of English youth into scientific specialists at fifteen.

But here my spectral scientist ejaculates 'Pshaw! Many scientists are just as well-read and cultivated as anybody else.'

Maybe. I am not out to attack scientists, but to defend non-scientists and the importance of the imaginative side of human personality; not only in literature, but also in life. For poetry and imagination deserve better than merely to exist squashed like moths in books; the hard, but vital thing is to keep them, also, in living. Think, for example, of John Stuart Mill, bred up in an educational hothouse by his father, to become what Carlyle unkindly called 'the patron-saint of rationalism, sawdust to the masthead'. What saved Mill from actual nervous breakdown was—the poetry of Wordsworth. Or there is the old Japanese painter in a novel by Malraux, who explains that if he ceased to paint, he would feel blind; and worse than blind—*alone*. For without his imaginative vision he would have ceased to see the world; without the power to communicate that vision, he would have felt isolated from his fellow-men. The out-and-out realist sees, in fact, only a part even of reality. I do not believe in ghosts; but I believe in the importance of ghosts— the ghosts one conjures up for oneself from what one has learned of the world's memories. Always there besets us danger of becoming like Frances Cornford's woman seen from the train—

> O fat white woman whom nobody loves,
> Why do you walk through the fields in gloves,
>   Missing so much and so much?

Since the book of life is so vast, as illustration of this need for imagination take a single one of its chapters—love. 'En amour', said that great scientist, Buffon, 'il n'y a de bon que le physique' (which did not prevent his becoming absurdly sentimental over Mme Necker). 'L'amour', echoes Chamfort, 'est l'échange de deux fantaisies et le contact de deux épidermes.' But how prosaic it would be *without* the fantasies! For Romeo, if he grows too scientific, Juliet may become merely a specious midge-dance of particles—a light-brigade of electric charges. But if that is all his vision of Juliet, how dull! Again, from a scientific point of view, poor Juliet is made up mainly of empty space; remove that, and the really solid part of her would be reduced to an almost invisible speck. And yet again, if Romeo reads philosophy as well as science, he will realize that even these particles composing Juliet are of questionable reality. He can be certain only of his own visions—whether fantasies or no.

> Nature has lost her soul; the World, its shaper;
>   The Singing Spheres have stilled their silver notes;
> The Hosts of Heaven melt to wisps of vapour,
>   The whole Creation to a dance of motes.
>
> And yet all is not taken. Still one Dryad
>   Flits through the wood, one Oread skims the hill;
> White in the whispering stream still gleams a Naiad;
>   The beauty of the earth is haunted still.
>
> Where lonely lakes, of all their Gods forsaken,
>   Mirror grey Heavens that Time has left as bare,
> Where sleeps the glade no fays nor fauns awaken,
>   O unforgotten face, still *you* are there.

No doubt imagination and intuition, sometimes of a very high order, are needed by the scientist also, to conceive his hypotheses. But they are imagination and intuition of a very different type from the poet's, or the novelist's. One great drawback, I feel, to excessive specialization in science is that most of it deals, not with people, but with things. There is medicine of course; but that deals mainly with men's bodies. And there is psychology—to me, the most fascinating of all the sciences; but that remains as yet an infant science—some think, a bastard one.

The humanities, on the other hand, seem to me to have a vast advantage in that their subject-matter is so largely human—however inhuman the pedants may sometimes make it. And in real life, as in books or plays, the most vital element remains, for me, not facts, nor events, nor even ideas, but people—character—human nature.

This preference, no doubt, is partly a matter of taste. But not, I think, wholly. I suspect that it is hard for an individual or a society to remain balanced, healthy, and sane, unless the interest in things is balanced by interest in people—I do not mean in sherry-parties, but in the human heart. Science is knowledge; and knowledge is excellent; but less excellent than wisdom. Now it is very far from clear that science is apt to add appreciably to human wisdom.

Obviously, Socrates or Montaigne knew far less of science than a modern schoolchild. Indeed Socrates turned away from the physical science he had pursued in younger years, because it seemed to him so unimportant compared with the problems of the human soul. And yet, though we know so much more than Socrates or Montaigne, are men with wisdom like theirs one jot commoner to-day than two thousand years ago?

Science, one may feel, is like its ancient god, Hephaestus, or Vulcan —a potent deity, a worker of marvels, yet tending at times to lameness; because it is thus limited to things rather than men; and, in men, to the rational side of a creature who, both for better and for worse, is so much more, and less, than rational.

One would expect, again, that minds trained in scientific method would at least think with more scientific precision than others, outside as well as inside the laboratory. Yet in practice it does not always seem so. Just as Newton could busy his leisure with such theological extravagances as demonstrating the Church of Rome to be the eleventh horn of the fourth beast in the Book of Daniel, so a number of modern scientists have shown, for instance, a curious tendency to become the naïvest dupes of Marxism, or at least fellow-travelling agencies. Emerged from their laboratories, they proved 'innocents abroad'.

In September 1938 I made the forlorn effort of collecting at Cambridge certain distinguished signatures to a protest against the folly and ignominy of appeasing Hitler at Munich. I penetrated the mysterious recesses of the Cavendish Laboratory: one of the chief names in nuclear science refused to sign. I went to John's, and climbed the long stair of Coulton. There at the top sat the old medievalist, in a picturesquely medieval chaos, his empty lunch-plate perched precariously on a medley of old cardboard chocolate-boxes that overflowed with dusty papers. But Coulton had no hesitation about signing. His mind might dwell in the twelfth century; but it saw far more shrewdly than some of his scientific colleagues into the twentieth century also. For to-day those who cheered loudest for Munich have taken good care to forget it.

I do not quote this as an argument. For then I should have to prove that a larger proportion of historians in general, than of scientists, saw Munich for the ignoble sham it was.[1] But I do quote this as an *illustration* of my point—that science does not always give sense.

In 1938–9 Otto Hahn found a way to split the uranium atom. But when it was pointed out to him that this might lead to an atomic bomb, the good man is said to have exclaimed—'That, surely, would be against the will of God.' Such ignorance of history, such innocence about life, supposing the story to be true, seems almost to baffle comment. Science does not always give sense. Could scientists, indeed, but discover how to increase the sum of wisdom in the world—ah then, how one's misgivings about them would vanish!

But so far there is little sign of *that*. And if one asks the psychological reasons why science should sometimes seem to breed such stupefying naïvety, the answer, I suspect, may be partly that most scientists are little concerned with emotions, apart from curiosity and ambition; and may therefore be often less aware than others of the terrible power of passion and desire—in politics, for example—unconsciously to blur and distort the reason. One has at times the impression that such men, emerging from their emotionally sterilized laboratories into the dusty tumults of the market-place, can be as strangely swept away by foolish feelings as unimmunized Polynesians by so mild a virus as measles.

* * *

Secondly, the scientific specialist, adept at dealing with the complex problems of his own narrow field, perhaps tends to underestimate the still greater complexities of life at large. Experts can be excellent servants, but perilous masters. In the *Affaire Dreyfus*, not for the only time, the handwriting experts were terribly sure, and terribly wrong. One should, I believe, always try to consult experts; but one should always distrust them.

When Shane Leslie was at Eton, he was visited by his cousin,

[1] Whether we gained by the year's respite that Munich gave us, can be endlessly debated. What remains unpardonable in the behaviour of the British Government and people at the time is their stupid optimism, their canting excuses, their ignominious nagging at the Czechs who had trusted us in vain.

Winston Churchill; and received from him a piece of advice I have never forgotten. 'Don't', said Winston, 'turn your mind into a damned ammunition-wagon: turn it into a first-rate rifle, for shooting off other people's ammunition.' Admirable! Who does not know people who are hogsheads of knowledge—and mere hogsheads they remain.

I am not attacking science, but only excess of science. For I doubt if it is healthy, either for an individual or for a society, to grow too exclusively scientific. The earth's crust is larded with the fossils of species that overspecialized. And think how much man owes to the unspecialized versatility of the human hand. For most of his life H. G. Wells dreamed of the coming reign of science; yet he ended his days in tragic horror that the world, which had so strangely fulfilled so many of his prophecies, should now, for sheer lack of common sense, seem plunging irreparably to doom.

Further, though science has revolutionized our lives, it remains very curious how little, so far, scientists have succeeded in actually dominating mankind. On the contrary, our age has repeatedly seen scientists become like captive djinns, either imprisoned in bottles, or forced to scour heaven and earth on the errands of some tetchy and whimsical despot. Hitler was no scientist—he naïvely believed in astrology. By temperament he was a tenth-rate artist. But because he was an intuitive master of one thing—the psychology of mobs—and devoid of any prudence or any scruple, he soon had the scientists of Germany slaving as his docile drudges, and feeding from his bloodstained hand. Stalin was no scientist—he was an ex-theological student, reared in a Tiflis seminary where they discussed such scientific topics as the precise language talked by Balaam's ass when it launched into human speech. Yet, because Stalin too was pitiless, unprincipled, and a past master of intrigue, he called the tune for the scientists of Russia; so that the great biologist Vavilov was sent to his death, while Trofim Lysenko, knowing less perhaps about cultivating ears of wheat, but more about cultivating the ear of Stalin, rose to power and honour. (Unfortunately Marxist orthodoxy seems to meddle less with Russian physics than with Russian biology.)

Science, in short, is now amazingly important; but still, in some ways, amazingly impotent. It has given men miraculous powers; but not the power to use rather than abuse them. If we want a civilized humanity, not a super-antheap, science alone seems, as yet, very far from being enough. It has rearmed Goliath the Philistine, in place of a spear like a weaver's beam, with strength to lift mountains on his little finger; but Goliath remains Goliath still. Caliban in a space-ship is still Caliban. What a welcome colonist for other worlds!

And so, to return to our practical problem, I do not see why those who still study the humanities should feel so anxious or inferior, so frightened or futile. Consider a few particular subjects.

*   *   *

First, modern languages. Year by year the free world is being squeezed into closer unity by the pressure of totalitarianism. This makes only greater, not less, the need to know each other's languages. Translations are not enough.

Again, the greater the power of Russia and Asia, the more urgent the need of Russian and of Asiatic tongues.

The Russians see this. Russian education may give first priority to science and engineering; but next to this, it seems, come languages. In Russian secondary schools, recently, 40 per cent were learning German, 40 per cent English.

And this is not only a question of dull utility. The old Roman poet Ennius boasted that, knowing three tongues—Latin, Greek, and Oscan —he had three hearts, where men less fortunate had only one. The boast was not idle. 'What should they know of England, who only England know?'

Secondly, literature, ancient, medieval, and modern. Science is, it has been said, a race; art, a dance. Science progresses: art changes. The scientist rises on the shoulders of his predecessors: the artist often feels crushed beneath their feet, or obscured by their giant shadows. There is no evidence that the human brain has improved in quality for tens of millennia. Homer has never been surpassed; for me, never equalled. Through art and literature, then, it is open to the living to meet the best dead minds of the last three thousand years. What an opportunity to throw away! It may sound cynical, or misanthropic, to say that the dead are often better company than the living; but surely it is true. They are not less important than electrons and neutrons. True, these damned particles may in the end take our lives, and are already fast changing them. But though they may take one's life, why let them obsess it? A platitude: yet apparently needed.

Thirdly, history. It is an ancient gibe that men learn from history only that men never learn from history. But that seems over-clever. Wiser, I think, was he who said that the best reading for youth was the life of a good man; and next best, the life of a bad one.

General philosophies of history may contain much pseudo-science. Minds like Hegel and Marx, Spengler and Toynbee may often have busied themselves in building mares' nests. But if men can learn from their own experience, surely they can learn also from the experience of others. Many of us to-day are perhaps in danger of too much forgetting the past. For the present hustles and changes us, faster and faster; the future preoccupies us with dreams of scientific progress, or menaces of scientific annihilation; the past itself grows ever longer, and the knowledge of it more formidably overwhelming, so that the mere mass of it can dismay. No doubt, by looking back too much one may turn, like Lot's wife, to a sterile pillar in a barren land. Too much 'recherche du temps perdu' can become merely 'du temps perdu'. On the other hand, by looking back too little one may degenerate into a fretful midge, a rootless will-o'-the-wisp, dancing fitfully across the morasses of modern life.

Civilization, as Burke never forgot, has been built on tradition. Tradition can become an incubus. But tradition is like steel. From steel you can forge chains; but from it you can forge also armour and sword and ploughshare.

If English history, for example, despite its blots and blemishes seems to me less unhappy, less stained with enormities, than that of any other land I know, this is no doubt partly because of our blessed insularity; partly because of English commonsense, and good humour, and willingness to play fair and to compromise. But this good sense and good humour and fair play owe much of their strength to the enduring tradition that these qualities are English—that it is un-English to lack them. A verb without a past is 'defective'; so is a nation. 'Look unto the rock whence ye are hewn.'

The Locrians of ancient Greece kept always in their line of battle a vacant place of honour for the shade of their national hero, the Locrian Ajax, who had fought at Troy; just as Spanish convents kept at their tables a place vacant for Saint Theresa. A fine conception, and a wise one.

> Well for the race whose past abides—which rises bolder
>   To meet the days of menace with its pride of memory;
> Whose great dead loom from the darkness as Oeta's mountain-shoulder
>   Above Thermopylae.

When the British navy was suffering disastrous losses in evacuating the army from Crete, it was questioned whether the operation should be abandoned. Admiral Cunningham answered: 'It takes the Navy three years to build a new ship. It will take three hundred years to build a new tradition. The evacuation will continue.' It continued.

The other great value of history seems to me its poetry—the epic, the tragedy, the comedy of man. The imagination of the living grows fatally impoverished if they forget the dead. Because their landscapes were full of ghosts I care about, I went to Iceland and, five times, to Greece. But I have never greatly wished to see the Rocky Mountains, or the Victoria Falls; for they are haunted by no spirits that I care about; they remain but stone and water. Narrow perhaps; but one feels as one feels.

'I', said Taliesin the Bard, 'have borne a banner before Alexander . . .
I was in Canaan when Absalom was slain; . . .
I was at the crucifying of the merciful Son of God; . . .
I was an overseer of the work of Nimrod's tower; . . .
I was in Asia with Noah in the Ark,
I saw the destruction of Sodom and Gomorrah.'

That gramary of Taliesin's lies within the grasp of all of us. On the magic carpet of history we can escape the tyranny of Time. It is impossible, they say, for bodies to travel faster than light. But minds can. They can travel to the furthest galaxy in the twinkling of an eye.

Then there is philosophy. Here I can hardly presume to speak. I feel like a butterfly fluttering to the defence of that bird of wisdom, the owl. I see it look at me with great, round, wondering, meditative eyes.

I will say merely this. The best philosophers, for me, are the cannibal philosophers who have eaten up their too credulous and dogmatic colleagues; the sceptical philosophers who have exposed human bigotries and superstitions. I prefer the doubting Socrates to Plato; Hume to Hegel; Russell to Bergson. Sceptical thinkers such as these seem to me invaluable and indispensable. Perpetually the human mind sprouts nettles and thistles. And against false philosophies the remedy must be—philosophy. Even scientists as eminent as Jeans or Eddington have been apt, when they wandered into philosophic speculations, to stagger horribly. It is hard to imagine a world in which men would not philosophize; harder still to imagine such a world very intelligent.

Further, the all-important field of values is a part of philosophy—of ethics. To that, science—even psychology—has so far contributed little.

*   *   *

There remains the practical problem of careers. In education and research it seems inevitable that science will encroach still further on the humanities. But in the wider fields of government, administration, and business I am doubtful if science (though here too it will encroach) gives the best training. For here it is often a question of dealing with people rather than with things. And though on this territory the psychologists begin to infiltrate, it will be long, I think, before they master it.

Further, the complexity of practical life seems to need minds of general and flexible intelligence, as well as minds closely and rigidly specialized. Thus it used to be said that men who had taken Classics at the University often did better in the Law, despite their later start, than men who had taken law degrees. Again, I can recall a period in the last war when there was urgent need for men who could learn Japanese within a year, instead of the four years pronounced by experts to be the minimum. The department concerned wisely defied the experts, combed the universities for brilliant young classics, and found, I gather, that they could master their Japanese in the period pronounced impossible.

Thucydides puts into the mouth of his Pericles the claim that free Athens, in contrast to sternly disciplined Sparta, could produce individuals 'able to meet every variety of circumstance with the greatest versatility—and with grace'. The same may still be true, in a measure, of the Athens of the humanities in contrast to the Sparta of science. *Both* types are needed. Without both Sparta and Athens, Greece would have fallen to the Persian; and the whole story of Europe and the world till now would have been changed.

If I stress so much the value of the broader, more flexible type of mind, it is because so often the specialist seems to become like that grotesque kind of Olympic athlete who spends years of his life trying to jump half an inch higher or longer—a sort of human flea.

After all, it has long been the British system of government to mingle general with expert intelligence; so that, for example, over the sea-dogs at the Admiralty we set, as First Lord, a landlubber who might be seasick in crossing the Solent. It has worked.

117

I once asked the Cambridge Appointments Board what happened to men who took English without doing brilliantly, or becoming teachers of it. For I was worried lest it might be proving, for many, a blind alley and a dead end. Their reply was quite unruffled. Business firms in general, they said, cared little what subject a man had taken honours in, provided the honours were decent. In that harshly practical world of business to have done reasonably well at Oxford or Cambridge, no matter in what, had acquired, apparently, prestige enough. Long may it remain so! But this seems one more reason for thinking that some non-scientific students may be over-anxious and needlessly dismayed.

What, in fact, are the essentials of a career? Happiness and useful-ness both depend largely on having work one likes, and (whatever may be the common view to-day) plenty of it. To live only for that fraction of life which is leisure, is to be only fractionally alive, and pre-ponderantly a slave. Therefore in choosing a career temperament and taste, not rewards, should count first. For science many have no taste, or no aptitude, or neither. Then they should not dream of it as a career. To become a third-rate scientific technologist—a sort of glori-fied plumber—for the sake of cash or security seems a lamentable sur-render—as stupid and squalid as marrying merely for money. Those who choose the humanities may now risk being paid less; but their scale of values must be cheap if they are not prepared for that. 'Better is a dinner of herbs where love is, than a stalled ox and hatred there-with.' I respect those who take holy orders, though I do not share their convictions, because they have the courage of those convictions, and are not afraid to chance a less comfortable life. If one prefers studying Homer to flatworms, one should be prepared to pay. The real artist scorns pot-boiling; so should those who care for the arts. I admit that the scientific often seem happier than the artistic. Julian Huxley, for example, seems to me a saner and more balanced mind than Aldous Huxley. On the other hand the artistic may often be in less danger of growing narrowed and dulled; though, of course, one need not look far, inside or outside universities, to see scientists who do not grow dulled or narrowed, and literary persons who do.

*   *   *

As for the universities themselves, even if the proportion of arts students should sink, as seems inevitable, regrets may be needless as well as useless. For some arts faculties might well gain in quality what they lose in quantity. History and English, for example, seem to-day over-popular, and would not suffer by becoming more confined to those with a real gift for them, and a real zest. When Hannibal was about to march from Spain on Italy, he told the fainthearts who had misgivings about facing the Gauls, the Alps, and the legions, to go home. He was probably wise.

Again, we could do with a good deal less of that demented research which writes theses on Merovingian hairpins, or the indefinite article in Bernard Shaw.

As for the future of the world at large, here too there seems to me no reason why followers of the humanities should feel futile or inferior, if they know their business. For they may be able to do something to prevent the New Jerusalems of Welfare States being built wholly within the borders of Philistia.

It is not my object, I repeat, to attack science, but to defend the humanities. The greatest dangers of the future seem to me to come, not from rational science, but from minds irrational and anti-rational, from the vulgarians and the barbarians. In face of these, science and the humanities should see each other, not as enemies or rivals, but as allies. That they should squabble is as if the right eye should quarrel with the left. Both are needed for true vision.

What, for example, have been in my own lifetime the worst and deepest roots of evil? Not human wickedness (though there has been plenty), but human blindness and hysteria, folly and fanaticism. I have seen our country fight three serious wars—the South African, which was simply to make South Africa safe for the Afrikaners; the First World War, after which the politicians flung away what millions had died to win; the Second World War, by which the devil Hitler was cast out to make more room for the devil Stalin. Ten years—nearly a quarter of my adult life—have gone on war-service; yet I was one of the luckiest of my generation—most of my fellow-undergraduates of 1914 are dust, these forty years, from the Somme to the Euphrates. These world-conflicts were largely fought and won by science; yet science itself was powerless against the folly and fanaticism that both caused these wars and threw away their victories.

And now our civilization is still threatened, perhaps more than ever, by vulgarity, barbarism, fanaticism. Science enables us to hear round the world—but largely things it would not be worth crossing the street to hear. Science enables us to see across continents—but largely things it is not worth turning one's head to look at. We are B.B.C.-sick. As if we had already reached the Termite State, our very houses sprout foolish antennae. The other day, typically enough, when a bevy of modern damsels were questioned on television, a few of them, it turned out, *had* heard of Eisenhower, but thought him Prime Minister of the United States; a few *had* heard of Nehru, but thought him a Russian; *all* had heard of a jigging gentleman called Elvis Presley; but not one had even heard of Mr Khrushchev. And by now these ladies enjoy votes. In such fumbling hands lie the choice of British Governments, and the policy of the British Commonwealth.

Here, again, are two specimens of what modern barbarism can make of science in education. One from *Eugenics Pamphlets*, Sacramento, California:

> Has your kiddie ever had the fun of raising butterflies from caterpillars? Since it takes skill as to food plants, it is *highly educational*.[1] Has he had the *fun*[1] of watching a watertiger eat all other water animals in his aquarium? ... Has he watched a wasp accurately sting the nerve ganglion of a spider, then tuck his 'refrigerated' food away in a clay jug along with the egg that is the promise of next year's wasps? ... The child whose parents utilized his natural instinct for acquisition to give him nature-study education ... may have thus started the germ of his becoming a world-renowned scientist.

The other is from the *McGehee (Ark.) Times*:

> R. T. Webb, assistant farm-agent, and Mrs Lois Perkins, assistant home-demonstration agent, visited the Coon Bayou school Monday, and gave some wonderful demonstrations to the boys and girls. Mrs Perkins gave a demonstration on candy making. Mr Webb demonstrated how to get rid of hog lice. The attendance was good.

Not long ago our Greek Professor at Cambridge was sniffed at for busying himself with such dead mutton as the war for Troy. Yet, for civilizing the young, one may still wonder if Homer is so inferior to hog lice.

And let us not look down our noses at such utterances as mere Americanisms: we in England can be as crude. 'Every schoolboy', we were recently told in the *Daily Telegraph*, 'should know what is going on, not only in Zeta, but also in Bepo, Dimble, Pluto, Gleep, and the rest.' And a wise man from Epsom wrote hastily to agree: 'Surely

---

[1] My italics.

what happened at Troy and its environs, while all very well for medi-
tation in a peaceful, stable world, will never affect the course of a
neutron inside a reactor.' How true! Yet will Zeta and Pluto, Bepo and
Gleep, these strange deities of our new Heaven, save men from the
danger of becoming themselves mere reactors, neutrons, and robots—
as soulless as hens in a battery?

Science thus worshipped as a fetish can become not only barbarizing
to the mind, but demoralizing to the character. The American authorities, alarmed by the behaviour of American prisoners captured in
Korea, conducted a scientific investigation which revealed that numbers of them had died from their comrades' neglect, and numbers more
had collaborated with their Chinese captors. The conduct of their
Turkish fellow-captives made a curious contrast. *Their* record showed
neither the casualties (for the poor simple Turks helped one another),
nor the collaboration with the enemy (for the poor simple Turks kept
their discipline and loyalty). Why? These tough primitives, the
researchers concluded, had not been softened by the comforts and
corruptions of a too sophisticated society. Science does not always give
sense: it does not always give character. One is tempted to adapt
Goldsmith's warning—

> Ill fares the land, to hastening ills a prey,
> Where *Science* accumulates, and men decay.

Modern civilization, like that of Rome, is faced by the double
menace of barbarism and fanaticism. Science and humanism, both children of the Renaissance, should not bicker, but combine to meet these
common enemies. The scientist remains half-lame without some knowledge of the arts; the arts-student is half-blind without some interest
in science. Men like Leonardo, Goethe, Chekhov have shown how
possible, and profitable, it can be to pursue both. Einstein himself was
capable of taking the trouble to play records of Bach for an obscure
youth to whom Bach's music was unknown. 'That', said the kindly
Einstein, 'is the greatest activity of which man is capable—opening
up yet another fragment of the frontier of beauty'. England in 1940
might well have been lost without radar and the Spitfire; but it might
also have been lost without Churchill. Science *and* the man.

To all this it may be answered: 'These are fine-sounding phrases.
"Écrasez l'infâme!" "À bas les barbares!" A common crusade of
science and the humanities against the barbarism and fanaticism that

threaten to engulf the world. But, even if you could persuade us, how much chance of success?' I have no notion. The immediate future is generally unpredictable. The ultimate future, beyond the brief moment of geological and astronomical time that our present civilization has existed, is utterly unknowable. There are no guarantees of success. But even if we fail, we shall not know it. The monks whose tired fingers copied out pagan poets while round them, often, their harried lands were red by day with blood, by night with flame, could not dream that their work would one day help to revive the ancient world, and build a new. Yet, in the end, it did. And even if this battle against modern barbarism were doomed to fail, one may at least, perhaps, save one's own soul. The early Christians believed the millennium at hand. Gradually realizing it was not, they too turned towards saving their own souls. Their methods were sometimes peculiar—such as not washing for fifty years. But I am not recommending their methods.

*   *   *

Perhaps I may sum up these slight conclusions.

(1) Some of us who study the humanities seem over-anxious about the dominance of science. This is a mistake. One should remain true to one's own tastes and aptitudes. Good men in other lines will still be needed. If some scientists earn more cash or laurels, let them. Money is a bad guide to a wife or a profession.

(2) If the proportion of scientists in universities rises, never mind. The value of faculties is not measured by numbers. Growing fewer, they may sometimes grow fitter. Quality matters, not quantity.

But (3) if the scientists increase at Oxford and Cambridge, those universities themselves should not. They are both too big already. Better build new ones. Remember the dinosaur. Elephantiasis is a horrid and degrading disease.

(4) The danger of testtuberculosis—of the scientific over-specialization which sends the human mind into a decline—is perhaps greatest in our schools. For scientists—I have seen it with my own children—real education is now tending to stop by sixteen. This seems mad. Even in Russia, I gather, they give two years more. We are risking the production of bright young scientists knowing neither history, nor English, nor French, nor German, nor Russian. The universities could counter this if they would only use the stranglehold they possess through their scholarship and entrance examinations. But I suspect that

science examiners find it too hard to resist any brilliant young physicist or biologist, however ill-educated in other ways. They are being short-sighted.

(5) The artistic and the scientific should not squabble and recriminate. That is as futile as the seventeenth-century War of Ancients and Moderns. To-day the humanist is probably wise to know some science, if only by spare-time reading; and the scientist to know something of the arts. Not enough time? There might be, if we wasted less. But this is an age, not only of unprecedented time-saving, but also, perhaps, of unprecedented time-wasting. Even one's Sunday paper is now as big as a book. And next day what remains?[1]

We have seen the Battle of France, the Battle of Britain, the Battle of the Atlantic: now we may have upon us the Battle of Civilization. Possibly I am alarmist. I am unlikely to live long enough to know. If there is a risk of 'a new Dark Age', it is not simply the fault of the scientists. It may not be the fault of anybody. But it may also be partly the fault of both scientists and humanists in failing to combine more effectively against the brutal and infatuated savagery of a century that has so largely lost its sense of life's values in hysterical surrenders to unreason.

[1] The Sunday issues *alone* of one American daily consume yearly the annual growth of a forest the size of Staffordshire (1,250 square miles). So swiftly can our civilization transform beauty to waste paper.

Of Books

SOCRATES in Plato's *Phaedrus* playfully tells how the Egyptian god Thoth (whose ibis-head still peers from many an ancient Egyptian wall), having invented writing, along with other arts such as arithmetic, geometry, and astronomy, submitted these brilliant finds to the judgement of his fellow-deity, Thamus of Thebes. But over the hieroglyphs Thamus shook a gravely disapproving head. Writing and reading, said Thamus, might indeed speciously pretend to aid memory; but in reality they would ruin it. This seeming staff would prove a crippling crutch. By writing and reading, men would degenerate into encyclopedic smatterers and superficial polymaths.[1]

However, the god Thoth was not only ibis-headed, but also pig-headed. To the warnings of Thamus he paid no attention at all. Might human history have been happier if he had—or, rather, that humanity without any history which would have taken our place? Some may think so. 'What a good riddance', they might sigh, 'of all those depressing necropolises called libraries, pathetically haunted by myriad ghostly dreams of immortality! Why, our public libraries, given time enough, would end by pushing us all, like Gadarene swine, into the sea. Without writing, we should be spared this spate of twenty thousand new books a year in England alone; instead, we might possess memories like those individuals in ancient Athens of whom we hear that they knew all Homer by heart.'

But, unfortunately, we should have lost Homer. So simplified a world might have pleased Lao-tse or Rousseau. Yet even Rousseau wrote and published. Plato himself, having imagined this playful *boutade* against writing, proceeded to write it. Perhaps, indeed, he wrote too much. For among his many excellences I can hardly count brevity.

Goethe too once called writing an abuse of speech. But he was here

---

[1] Socrates had a further objection to books—he could not ask them questions. But perhaps he was a trifle too fond of captious questioning—like a Cambridge philosopher I recall, who, if one ventured that it was a fine day, would reply in a high-pitched croak, 'And what exactly do you mean by "a fine day"?'—until some of his guests began to regret the disuse of hemlock.

thinking of writing, not (like Thamus) as corrosive of memory, but as perversive of style. No doubt writers *are* apt to grow artificial or obscure; and their writing *would* often be better, were it nearer to good talk. Still Goethe, like Plato, continued to write.

It remains, however, true—and curious—that ancient literature did begin to decline as libraries began to grow. Euripides (*c*. 485–406 B.C.) and Aristotle (384–322) were among the first recorded collectors of books; the Hellenistic age saw the first great public libraries of Alexandria and Pergamum, in the third and second centuries B.C.; and it is Seneca, in the decadent Rome of Claudius and Nero, who first talks of private libraries being thought as essential to houses as baths. (There were to be medieval monasteries—and indeed, as late as this century, Cambridge colleges—that thought libraries much *more* essential than baths.)

Possibly it was no mere coincidence that ancient books thus declined as men grew bookish. Literatures may tend to swamp themselves; till at last they lose all freshness and spontaneity. It could be argued that Shakespeare or Burns would have written worse, had they read more; that Propertius or Ben Jonson or Gray would have written better, had they read less. Certainly, with the infinite volumes of our book-ridden world on our backs, some of us feel as the earthworms may have felt (if there were any) when above them was piled the pyramid of Cheops.

But though a hydrogen-bomb, by reducing to carbon the whole literature of the past, might stimulate to fresh youth and originality the literature of the future, at *that* price most of us would sooner make do with the literature of the past. And though Johnson saw libraries as sad embodiments of the vanity of human wishes, and Chateaubriand abominated them, even in private houses, as 'nids à rats', none the less I have long counted myself more fortunate than millionaires, in having a million and a half books a hundred yards from my door. No temptations to move elsewhere have ever weighed with me against *that*. My luck was all the more incredible in that this mountain came to me, not I to it. Ten years after I had settled in my home, the University Library obligingly waddled across the Cam, to sit down beside me on what had been a cricket-field. (Which some will consider a lamentable exchange.)

True, the thought that this vast mausoleum annually engulfs 2,000 feet of new books—two miles of them every five years—is a nightmare that might give anyone writer's cramp. But sometimes it is better not to think.

*　　　*　　　*

In August 1918 I was interrogating German prisoners in the Third Army Cage at Candas, in Picardy. Among the grey figures pacing gloomily under the summer sun behind that black barbed-wire was a pleasant young Fähnrich or Ensign, whom I liked the better because he refused to give me any information. I did not press him. Luckily there was no need. The German rank-and-file, already war-sick and dis-heartened ('Deutschland', they grunted, 'ist kaput'), felt also such veneration for officers—even enemy officers—as a higher order of beings, that they usually talked readily enough; especially with the aid of a cigarette or two. Besides, there were the Alsatians. The German High Command, distrusting them, had broken up their regiments and distributed them through the rest of the German army. An admirable help. For it meant that most German units now contained a sprinkling of Alsatians, eager to tell us all they knew.

With my Fähnrich, therefore, I soon wandered off into a friendly general conversation. What were we both going to do after the war? I have never forgotten his cry of unfeigned horror, when I said I should go back to the University, left at the end of my first year—'Was! Ein Bücherwurm werden!'

A bookworm, the next year, I again became. Forty years have passed since then. But (though luck has perhaps more hand in such things than wisdom) I doubt if I should have been happier—or as happy—as any other kind of creature. Though it was probably also lucky to be dragged away from books for ten years by wars; for it may well be better for one not to do the same things in life too long. A bookworm, indeed, I had already been since childhood—too much, perhaps, and too soon.

*　　　*　　　*

Should one ever let oneself grow autobiographical? It is something of a problem. On the one hand, how much more interesting most people become in conversation, if only they can be drawn to talk of their *own* lives, and how it went with them! There, after all, they know what they are talking about. We should be vastly the poorer without the frank irreticence of writers like Montaigne, or Rousseau, or Boswell, or Trollope. And my wife, whose judgement I value, has long complained 'But you always write so *impersonally*.' That, indeed, is not my own impression. But there . . . Who sees himself?

On the other hand, especially to the English, there is apt to seem something odious and ridiculous in prosing about oneself. We have an inhibition about such exhibitions. We think of Andersen's absurd Emperor striding naked down the street. 'Le moi est haïssable.' And then it is so hard to be honest. Even Montaigne did not always succeed. No form of candour is so liable to turn into its opposite—insincerity. For the writer is constantly tempted away from his job of interesting, or serving, the reader, into trying to impose a certain picture of himself. We enjoy Rousseau or Boswell; but we tend to think less of them. Even Pepys seems a little ridiculous; even Chateaubriand, an inveterate poseur.

Conclusion? Full autobiographies are perhaps better left to others to write. For the fullest autobiography is never complete; the most truthful, never the whole truth. Anyway, nothing could induce me to attempt one. Besides, even if honest, they cannot avoid taking liberties with the privacy of others, usually without the victims' leave. Indeed there have been authors quite ogreish in using other people's skins as writing-material—like Alfred de Musset and George Sand romancing in print about their unhappy romance in Venice.

On the other hand, it may be a little over-reticent to withhold even scraps of one's own experience that might offer some use or amusement. The drawbacks of full autobiography need not apply to autobiographical glimpses and fragments of the kind given us by Montaigne. As Mme du Deffand put it, defending him against Walpole's charge of egotism: 'Le *je* et le *moi* sont à chaque ligne, mais quelles sont les connaissances qu'on peut avoir, si ce n'est pas le *je* et le *moi*?'

Finally, the memories that I have here in mind are already so remote, that I seem speaking really of another person, vanished years ago.[1] After all, perhaps not a molecule of him survives in my present body. And perhaps a few recollections of that strangely different world of Victoria and Edward may now acquire a certain interest, not because they are striking in themselves, but because they already seem so oddly distant from the world of to-day. 'Where,' said his friends to a Parisian actor, 'do you get such strange hats?' 'I do not *get* them. I *keep* them.'

---

[1] Like my son of ten who, watching a film of his own infancy, spontaneously cried out (with much more justice), 'Isn't he sweet!'

So with other things than hats. Time can add a certain interest even to the trivial; anyone who lives long enough begins to become something of an ancient monument. And I have, alas, lived long enough to have seen the great Queen herself. 'Vergilium vidi.' True, she was one of my first-remembered disillusionments. I expected a majestic lady in a golden crown; but, held aloft in my nurse's arms upon Blackheath, I saw only a little, old, black-bonneted granny in a black barouche. Still, I am glad to have seen her. Not only for her own sake. It seems also a link with remoter history to have seen in the flesh someone who, I suppose, had seen her grandfather, George III; who may well, in his turn, have seen Sir Robert Walpole; who may have seen Charles II strolling in Whitehall, almost three hundred years ago.

*   *   *

One of my earliest memories is of groaning to my mother, at the age of three, 'Oh, I wish I could read!' For I was then an only child, and a lonely one, in London. And in those days—luckily, I still think—neither wireless nor television existed to console me with their mental lollipops; so that salutary boredom did in effect goad my indolence into learning to read by four. My children have had a gayer time (though I have kept television out of the house). All the same I do not wholly envy them. There is, I believe, no substitute for the love of books. And when not long ago, for example, I overheard the B.B.C. Children's Hour vulgarizing the story of Moses, with the usual falsetto over-acting, and a vile dialogue that wobbled between seventeenth-century and twentieth-century English, as if the Authorized Version were not good enough, I gnashed my teeth and fled from the tea-table. Even my small daughter, I noted with satisfaction, turned the thing off. When a recent report on 'Television and the Child',[1] edited by Dr Himmelweit, consoles us that most children are *not* 'heavily addicted' (the average amount of viewing is, for groups aged 10–11 and 13–14, merely 11–13 hours a week), then one may perhaps wonder what *would* be 'heavy', and what proportion of a school-going child's whole leisure these dozen hours represent. We are told that television has not diminished but increased the number of books read in general. Yet the day has still only twenty-four hours. And it may be suspected that though some may read now, who before would have read nothing,

[1] Oxford University Press, 1958.

many others who would have read more, must now read less. This
levelling-out may be 'progress'. But I wonder.

*   *   *

Childhood memories are fickle things to trust. But the other day I
came on documentary evidence—a dusty notebook of crayon draw-
ings from my sixth or seventh year, mainly devoted to horrific pictures
of seas and mountains (largely volcanoes in frenzies of eruption), or
equally volcanic naval battles between French and English ironclads
(for the Entente Cordiale of 1904 was still some three years away).
Among these mountain-ranges, however, there is one *not* in eruption
—white summits, green slopes, a straggly firwood like a moulting
hedgehog, and a river in bluest chalk, of most improbable straightness;
with the inscription—'Lonely is the place were the wild time grows'.
That garbled version of Shakespeare's Oberon, whom I had sometimes heard my mother quote, was perhaps my first glimpse of poetry.
And, in a way, I have been looking for that place ever since. Oberon's
'thyme' might be pleasant enough; but a place where *time* grew wild
for the gathering, with armfuls to spare—*that* would be a place to
discover! For of time I have never found enough—that curious herb
which, the longer it grows for us, grows only shorter. Even a forty-
eight-hour day would seem too brief. What a hapless figure is that
pessimist who wanders through Thomson's *Castle of Indolence*,

> Ne ever uttered word, save when first shone
> The glittering star of eve—'Thank Heaven! the day is done!'

But it is strange how easily children can be caught by poetry without
understanding it—a habit that (despite present fashions) I admire less
in adults.

Almost the next page of the same notebook shows a ship with the
legend, 'Alone on a wide wide sea'—another phrase that must have
caught my childish ear. But though this seascape shows a setting sun
like the Ancient Mariner's—a sun very red in the face, with spiky
beams—the ship is, most incongruously, a four-funnelled cruiser of
the *Terrible* class, long since forgotten on the scrap-heap. (I must have
been very aggressive and bellicose then—life was to prove more than
generous enough in the way of wars.) But it was the seas of *The*

Ancient Mariner that captured me. Reading the poem at seven, I seem to remember, I did not think much of the dicing of Death and Life-in-Death (nor do I now); and still less of the seraphs.

But before this, at six I suppose, I had made heavier weather with *The Pilgrim's Progress*. Christian's combat with Apollyon was well enough; but I was shocked at poor Ignorance being dumped through a sort of coal-shoot into Hell, just when he had used his initiative to reach the Heavenly City by an unauthorized short-cut; and the picture, in my edition, of Giant Despair was so terrifying that I used to evade him by turning over several pages together when I knew I was approaching his abominable presence. Nor could such precautions save me from sweating awake at night in my small bed with horrors of the Day of Judgement. Johnson, I suppose, though he suffered the same horrors, thought them salutary, since he would not give a farthing for Bishop Percy's little daughter when he found she had never read *The Pilgrim's Progress*; but I am more inclined to keep my disapproval for parents who let small children read it. However, there can be small danger of that to-day. *The Fairchild Family* and all their grisly kindred are well buried. And good riddance—provided their place is not taken by sadist films and comics. For our age, so microbe-conscious that I have heard (whether truly or no) of children kept so spotless that their health suffered for lack of some necessary mineral, like copper, remains curiously careless about mental bacilli. As for Bunyan, he will live on by his style; but style is for adults.

The same seems to me true of the Bible. One may think it deplorable that the average modern now knows little or nothing of the sombre, barbaric splendour of the Books of Kings, the melancholy wisdom of Ecclesiastes and Proverbs, the unsurpassed cursings of the Prophets (often most unpleasant, but most eloquent persons), or the tragic magnificence of Job. But little of all these is meat for babes; though many of the simpler (and less odious) Bible narratives may be. At all events in my dame-school the Bible became a burden, as we learnt, like little parrots, things we no more understood than that French innocent who, confused between La Fontaine's crow and Jehovah's dove, began the Lord's Prayer—'Notre Père, sur un arbre perché.' What I did understand, I revolted at. 'The Lord is my shepherd', we piped. But I lacked the least wish to be a sheep. No one explained to our young minds that, if the Bible shows an excessive passion for sheep, that was natural enough in the imagery of a pastoral people.[1] But to a small Londoner sheep were silly, cowardly creatures, familiar only as mutton; and so, when cold, and white with congealed fat, quite loathsome. I did not want to be a sheep in the Lord's flock one bit.

And so the Bible, whose style and imagination have long since won my astonished admiration, found me then a reprobate little heathen and rebel—*anima naturaliter pagana*—who intuitively disliked the New Testament Jews as 'pi' and mawkish, the Old Testament Jews as nastily ferocious, yet feeble beside such bonny fighters as Achilles, or Diomede, or Dietrich of Berne. Jehovah I found (and still find) a most disagreeable deity; Pallas Athene was much more to my liking. I envied her beloved Odysseus.

This early aversion for Hebrew literature was strengthened by a bored detestation of being taken to church. How I prayed—though not literally—for rain! Quite unmusical, I could find no consolation in that gracious side of Anglican worship. During the service my father used to indulge in an eccentric habit of reading pagan Latin authors. (Just as Marie Antoinette—though few human beings could have been less like Marie Antoinette than my father—had, one is told, Gresset's *Vert-vert*[2] bound as a prayer-book.) Such solaces however were not as yet for me (though some years later I *was* allowed a Greek Testament to read). Nor was there much relief in the sermons; though there still sticks in my memory a fleeting glimpse of our little rotund and rubicund vicar, as he polished his pince-nez on his surplice, fulminating against the faithless sheep who strayed away to listen, instead, in Greenwich Park to 'the braying of a brass band'. That sonorous alliteration must have pleased him; but his modesty would have been astounded to know that those six words of his, over which we laughed afterwards, would still echo in one pair of human ears after half a century. So strange is the power of phrase.

[1] So Homer calls his kings 'shepherds of the people'. All the same, this image, though shared by Hebrew and Hellene, is edged with unconscious irony. For shepherds do not rear their sheep as pets; they rear them for shears and slaughter-house. Long ago the bitter Palladas of Alexandria (*c.* A.D. 400) made *that* grim point:

> For Death we all are nurtured, the greatest and the least,
> Like fatted swine for the slaughter—to die as dies the beast.

[2] The story of a convent parrot, borrowed for its eloquence by another convent; the too observant bird, however, arrived with a vocabulary lamentably enhanced by listening, as it travelled, to the language of the bargemen; and so fell into dire disgrace.

The truth was, my childhood had already found its sacred books elsewhere—two of them, oddly enough, from the pen of an Anglican Dean. For, at nearly seven, I was given Dean Church's honest, straightforward retellings of *Iliad* and *Odyssey* in prose, with illustrations from Flaxman. They, and an excellent book on mythology called *Gods and Heroes*, and Kingsley's *Heroes*, were my first glimpses of those Greek shores that were to fill so much of my life's horizons.

There was, too, another book of those years that I remember with gratitude, though perhaps it is now forgotten—Dr Wagner's *Epics and Romances of the Middle Ages*. With its legends of King Rotha of Bari, Dietrich of Berne, and the like, it gave a certain sense of Europe's second heroic age, as Homer of the first. The modern child, in an age which has specialized in meeting children's tastes, might find it stuffy. But I can still re-feel my anguished distress over the end of King Ornit, who rashly bought dragon's eggs from a wandering merchant, and hatched them with only too great success.

> I had an aunt in Yucatan
> Who bought a python from a man,
>   And kept it for a pet.

But the fate of Ornit was not at all comic. I can still see in memory what was to me the nightmare illustration of his end—the sleeping king, gone out to defend his people; the faithful dog that vainly leaps and barks to wake him; and the loathly 'lindworm' as it stalks nearer and nearer, on its four legs, breathing fire. That scene has become linked in my mind with the helpless horror of the years 1933–8, when it looked as if the lindworm of the Third Reich might engulf a sleeping England, which nothing seemed able to wake from the deathly torpor of appeasement. Indeed King Ornit is a fitting type of human tragedy —the shining egg we covet, and obtain, and cherish till a monster comes out of it; the drowsy blindness that wakes only when waking is vain. In those early days I could not bear unhappy endings. Can any children? Things like 'Cock-robin' or 'The Babes in the Wood' may be thought fare for babes; but I suspect that they were first contrived by, and for, more adult tastes, and only later got pushed down into the nursery. For the nursery, I suspect, all's well that ends well. Horrors and agonies can be endured, and enjoyed, by the way; but they *must* end well. About the age of three or four I disconcerted my parents by frenzies of lamentation for a certain 'Hen-len' who perished, if I remember, by pecking up a nut which choked her. Years later I found the end of Kingsley's *Hereward* painful and that of Hugo's *Notre Dame* quite unendurable. And yet—so strangely do our tastes and feelings sometimes reverse themselves—in adult life I was to spend years on Tragedy, and tragedies; and have long felt comedy an inferior form.

Yea. Tragedy is true guise.
Comedy lies.

* * *

What seems to me lucky now is that I was left to run loose in my father's library; with little guidance, during childhood, but with very little interference. For any child with an itch to read, that may be, quite often, the best way. No doubt I frequently floundered out of my depth; but on the whole—like Johnson's Warburton, though in quite a different sense—I 'floundered well'. I had a feeling of adventure and exploration and independence, which no conducted tours can ever give. There I was, running and roaming at large, like a little pig after truffles.

To-day, when writers and publishers have discovered that the un-grown, like the uneducated, are numerous enough to make a most profitable public, we have avalanches of books designed for the im-mature of all ages. Of the children's books, many are admirably con-trived. Yet, even so, there may be certain drawbacks. The diet of the Victorian child may have included a good many dry bones (I can recall a disgusted birthday when I received a life of Livingstone, and Samuel Smiles's *Self-help*); yet the bones contained sometimes a good deal of marrow—even of lion's marrow—not wholly replaced by the modern child's fare of shortbread and meringues. No doubt, William Morris was an extraordinary person; and there may be exaggeration in the story that he had read his way right through Scott's novels by the age of seven. But to-day the reading even of a boy so exceptional would probably be less in quantity, and a good deal less in quality. For now that publishers cater so abundantly for all ages and tastes, the ungrown and the untaught are no longer driven to explore higher levels, *faute de pis*.

All this may be part of a general tendency of life in Welfare States to grow more comfortable, yet in some ways smaller. Everything becomes middle-class; and everything may become merely middling. However, this is only a guess; I shall not waste time lamenting, where lamentation is either needless or useless. English children to-day may well be healthier and happier than ever before. Gone are the barefooted street-arabs that to my own childhood were familiar sights. All the same I cannot regret that from six to eleven I was allowed to run loose in a library. It was a tiny example of free enterprise; and the wastefulness of free enterprise may be a small price to pay for independence. Ever since, I have felt a passionate contempt—perhaps excessive—for people who want to be taught, instead of teaching themselves; for the packs of little jackals that run yelping together in literary movements[1] or critical cliques; for all who cannot walk alone in the isolation of totally unpopular opinions, with the disdainful aloofness of cats. Loyalty to one's battalion or one's war-department is quite another matter; it is mere conformity and 'togetherness' that make me quiver with nausea. No one but the magnificent old Ibsen has put that feeling with intensity enough for my content. I see that this emotional nonconformity may be extreme; that early Christianity and modern Communism both show how formidable, how irresistible sometimes, is the force of organization. But my abomination of gangs remains.

So my feeling is that modern parents should read aloud things worth reading, but not read aloud too much—enough to implant a taste for reading, but not enough to produce laziness about reading alone; and that they should be careful of wireless. We worry, reasonably, about radioactivity; but not, most unreasonably, about that dangerous form of it which comes out of boxes in our own homes. And I think children's books can be overdone. Only a fanatic would be ungrateful for the best of them—for Lewis Carroll, or Edward Lear, or Beatrix Potter. But, mentally as well as physically, weaning can be delayed too long. With intelligent children it may be best to have a wide range of good books on the shelves, and to leave some lying about as bait.

Some modern parents may find a problem in comics—always vulgar, often worse. I own that, perhaps needlessly, I have. Indeed, comically enough, they link up with one of the eternal and fundamental problems of ethics. Prohibition of a desire may either suppress or intensify it; indulgence may bring either satiety or drug-like addiction. One never knows which. Long ago, the puritanical Plato came down on the side

---

[1] No doubt the French Pléiade and the English Pre-Raphaelites had a certain effectiveness; no doubt the drowsy attention of the public is more easily awakened by groups than by individuals; but even in these two instances the banding together proved brief. And 'log-rolling' is a poor business, best left to those who deal in mere lumber.

of prohibition; the more reasonable Aristotle on the side of reasonable indulgence. So, in this matter, did my wife; loving liberty even more than I loathed comics, I acquiesced; and time has proved her right. Quite spontaneously in the end (though it certainly took time) my dining-room has ceased to be coloured with the garish exploits of 'Dennis the Menace' and his kin. 'But', whispers Plato's ghost, 'the harm was done.' I shall not, however, believe him. At some comics I should draw a firm line; but not at *all* comics. Illogical? So is life.

To list the reading of my later childhood, even if I could, would quickly become a bore. But I remember being fervidly absorbed in the *Lays* of Macaulay—so that to please myself I learnt a lot of *Horatius* by heart, and found with pained astonishment that my mother was completely cold to it. (It takes one long to accept the painful truth that those one loves best are often far from sharing one's other loves in literature and art.) On the other hand I was bitterly recalcitrant at being made by my father (it still seems to me odd of him) to learn by heart Longfellow's *Psalm of Life*—

> Tell me not, in mournful numbers,
>   Life is but an empty dream!
> For the soul is dead that slumbers,
>   And things are not what they seem.
>
> Life is real! Life is earnest! etc.

Little wonder I loathed it. For, in the first place, the 'mournful numbers' that regard life as 'an empty dream' include very few small boys;[1] and, secondly, it is not abnormal for small boys to detest such moralizings.[2] Still, in fairness to poor Longfellow for whom few have a good word now, I must add that I liked his *King Olaf* (not knowing its far finer source in old Snorri's *Heimskringla*). And I can still recall the sinister fascination of Christina Rossetti's *Goblin Market*; though even then my rebelliousness found its ending too mawkishly improving. (Poor Christina was over-scared of goblins; true, they ate her brother, Dante Gabriel; but she and her sister Maria were no less eaten by angels—the angels being, as so often, only goblins in white sheets.)

[1] Obviously, by 'mournful *numbers*' Longfellow meant 'mournful strains', 'mournful poetry'; but how could a child know that?

[2] Poor verse it still seems to me. What a lame trochaic is line 4!—'And things áre not whát they séem.' For one's natural impulse is to say—'And thíngs are nót what they séem'; to the total annihilation of the metre. Not the first time that poor thought and poor technique have gone together.

All the same, though as a thinker Christina Rossetti remained always a child, as a poetess she *was* the real thing.

However, *the* poet, for me, in those years was Tennyson. This was not merely because we went every spring, with monotonous iteration, to Freshwater in the Isle of Wight—a Freshwater not yet 'developed' and ruined. (Indeed, my earliest memory is of sitting, aged two, in Tennyson's Lane, by Farringford, wreathed with ivy by the small village-girl who looked after me.) I loved his stories, such as *The Lady of Shalott* or *The Voyage of Maeldune*; the smooth perfection of his music; the lovely loneliness of landscapes like *Mariana* or *The Dying Swan*. There still comes back to my nostrils the honey-and-almond scent of the yellow, sun-warmed gorse-bushes, where I sat reading him on High Down, below the granite cross that recalls his memory, and above the then still unspoilt fields and copses that hid the shy poet's home.

In prose one of my happiest finds at this time was a complete translation of Herodotus—one of the few books that can delight any age, from ten to a hundred. For here is a great artist who yet seems artlessly natural; a wise, tragic ironist who yet talks as simply as a child. And a little later I discovered that much more artful and artificial genius of history, the great Gibbon. He seems to me, now, absurdly precocious reading for ten (my children at that age would as soon have thought of reading through a dictionary); and I can still remember lifting my innocent little head from those sombre pages to ask my mother the meaning of some frightful word, which led her to murmur anxiously, 'I don't think that's quite fit for you to read.' At once I shrank back my small snail's-horns, and lay low; while she, being both indulgent and embarrassed, said no more. From that moment I continued my tête-à-têtes with Gibbon in discreeter silence. I suppose it was largely my queer passion for Romans that drew me on. I had enjoyed the history of the Roman Republic better. For I liked the Romans to win. And though the campaigns of Hannibal caused me anguish, till he was smashed by Scipio, in the end the Republic always did win. But in Gibbon the Romans were always losing and declining. Still, they were Romans.

Gibbon himself loved them less—'I am convinced there never, never existed such a nation, and I hope, for the happiness of mankind, there never will again.' I love them a good deal less myself, now, as a nation; though, had Gibbon seen the twentieth century, he might have had a kinder word for Rome. For one does not easily imagine Hitler or Stalin or Mao-tse-tung inaugurating another Age of the Antonines.

Further I regretted, like Julian the Apostate, the twilight of the Olympian gods; and after that eccentric reactionary had fallen on his Persian campaign, I do not think I had the heart, then, to struggle much further. Incapable, as yet, I suppose, of savouring Gibbon's wicked ironies, I did not doubt the truth of Christianity. I should merely have preferred paganism to be true; but there—it just was not. Indeed, when about that time I was taken up to my mother's room and the bed-clothes were drawn back to reveal a small brother, overwhelmed by this totally unexpected shock I rushed to my own bedroom, burst into tears, and knelt down to pray I might be nice to the creature. (My daughter, at two and a half, was more modern and less inhibited, when confronted with a like situation—'Jenifer get roses for Mummy. But NOT for Oliver!')

All the same my pagan sympathies remained. When I wrote, about this time, my first remembered poem, it bore the title, sufficiently ludicrous for ten years old, of 'The Rape of Proserpine'.

Already, I suppose, my essential tastes had been moulded—for Greece and Rome; for lonely scenery; and for poetry or prose about action, rather than fussy chatter about feelings and passions.

*　　　*　　　*

When I was about eleven, my father turned closer attention to my schooling; and with a good deal of daring and originality, being dictator in his own school, he set me to work a large part of my time alone in his private study instead of in class. I will not pretend that in this privacy the mouse did not sometimes play. But I am grateful for his curious experiment. Alone I learnt my first Greek, which he went through with me in the evenings. Wisely, he did not waste much time on rudiments—we plunged almost at once into Homer; and I can still recall the excitement of meeting old friends like Achilles and Odysseus in their native tongue. Most teachers of languages and prescribers of set books seem to me unconscious saboteurs—so unerringly do they choose authors who are either incorrigible bores, or far above the heads of children. The 'dead' languages were doubtless doomed to a second death anyway; but their doom has been hastened by pedants' insistence on dead grammar and inappropriate writers.

For most of the next eight years I became a little exam-passing animal (too much so); no longer tumbling about an English library, but soaked in the classics of two thousand years before. In a sense, it seems fantastic—the upbringing of a mandarin. But though I grudge now some of the time spent at Rugby on grammatical subtleties, or on Greek and Latin proses and verses, on the whole I have no great regrets. (Which illustrates perhaps the absurd human tendency, while readily grumbling over what one has suffered, to remain tolerably, or intolerably, content with what one has become.)

Still that ancient Mediterranean world is not only a world of many perfections. It keeps also, in the first place, a compact, rounded unity of its own, free from the chaotic multitudinousness, the crushing multifariousness, of modern life. It offers high quality, in manageable quantity. Secondly the values of the Greek mind seem to me often saner and healthier than those of later times. More and more I come to honour and admire the efforts of this race, which could so easily rage with passion, and plunge into folly, none the less to keep its balance, its honesty of mind, its clarity of thought. To have lived through the first half of our own raving century has only deepened my distrust and hatred for the moonstruck and the hysterical. Thirdly, that dead world, which is still so living, keeps a stability, a sense of enduring permanence which modern man is fast losing. For now it is as if we were all crowded on an endless, endlessly moving staircase, that moves faster and faster, beyond control; or as if the earth whirled faster and faster beneath our feet, till it nears the speed where bodies (and minds) fly to pieces and disintegrate. But that small ancient world stands clear and calm and changeless, above the turbid racing of the tides of time.

Yet it is not an easy world to enter. Its 'Open, Sesame' must be spoken in its own tongue. You may try translations; but the infection of our modern Babylon is on them, and they grow vulgarer year by year. You may try Greek tours in white-painted liners, packed with bishops and lecturers and evening-frocks; but Athens has grown huge and horrible in the forty years since I first saw the Acropolis rise up against the sunset from the Saronic Sea; and even in the Greek countryside mountain-paths that in 1920 seemed hardly changed since Byron or Chateaubriand, Oedipus or Odysseus passed there, are desecrated now with the tarmac and char-à-bancs of barbarians from the West. Once more 'Great Pan is dead'. To know the real Greece one must read Greek, alone.

Then, as in the changeless world of Plato's ideas, can at least be glimpsed what the earth will never see again.

> Long since your bones have mouldered; long, Dōricha, the binding
>   Of your curls, long all the fragrance from your robe has passed away,
> That you flung round fair Charaxus, and caught him in its winding,
>   And breast to breast lay drinking, at the dawning of the day.
> But the loved song of Sappho lives on and lives for ever—
>   White pages still proclaiming your name thrice-blest the while,
> That Naucrātis shall remember as long as towards her river
>   The ships stand in from seaward, up the lagoons of Nile.[1]

> One told me, Heraclitus, you were dead; and left me weeping,
>   As once more I remembered how often down the west
> We talked the sun to setting. And now—dust in earth's keeping—
>   Old friend from Halicarnassus, long since, it seems, you rest.
> Yet still the songs you sang us, your Nightingales, abide:
> Not Death himself shall seize them, that clutches all beside.[2]

*　　*　　*

Possibly this course of education, which many will now find fantastic, though it was the ordinary thing in a public school then, should have contained more science. But unless one is going to be a scientist, I am not sure that, for the layman, science is not better read about at leisure, especially in one's later years. At twelve I was given a quite expensive chemical laboratory of my own, in a room under the roof; and great fun I had, generating gases or analysing complicated mixtures of inorganic salts, though at times it made the house hardly habitable. But though it may conceivably have taught me something of scientific method, that little, I suspect, could have been done much more quickly (though far less amusingly).

The *results* of science seem to me often fascinatingly and fantastically poetic; to go through life in ignorance of them would be like walking blindfold through the Sistine Chapel. But the *details* of scientific investigation seem often as arid as the Arizona Desert; demanding the narrow patience of pismires and, more and more, a mathematical skill far beyond most of us. Take astronomy, for example. One can well

---

[1] Poseidippus (third century B.C.?). Sappho's brother Charaxus, trading to Naucratis in Egypt, was fascinated by the courtesan Doricha or Rhodōpis.
[2] Callimachus (*c.* 310–*c.* 240 B.C.).

understand that ecstasy which inspired in Ptolemy (if it is genuine)
one of the few good poems ever written by scientists[1]—

> I know well I am mortal, a feeble thing and fleeting,
>   Yet when I watch the wheelings of myriad star on star,
> My feet touch earth no longer. It is as I were eating,
>   At the high God's own table, of Heaven's ambrosia.[2]

But though many can share that emotion, the mathematics of epi-
cycles, or of Einstein, remains a field for very few. We are now putting
much science into education: but I doubt if we can get much real
education out of science. Of that, however, more elsewhere.

No doubt it would have been wiser to give more time, too, to
modern tongues (one should take advantage of the tenacity of a young
memory); wiser, perhaps, to do more mathematics (though most of us
use our mathematics only for the rudimentary purposes of wrestling
with income-tax returns, and of helping our children with their
homework, so that they in their turn may help theirs; and so *ad in-
finitum*). But, when all is said, I count myself happy to have made
friends early in life, and *for* life, with minds like Homer and Herodotus, Plutarch and the poets of the Palatine Anthology, Lucretius
and Virgil, Horace and Tacitus. They have, I suppose, certain qualities
in common—style, vitality, intelligence, compassion, courage, and,
sometimes, gaiety; no maundering credulities; and they never scream
—as even Greek Tragedy, even Shakespeare, sometimes scream.

I can see that a critic might object: 'But it was a narrow world, and
has narrowed you. Literature since Greece and Rome has become infinitely more various, and less rule-ridden. You are haunted by these
antique ghosts, with their limited perfections. Consequently many
later writers only half-please you, or do not please you at all. Either,
like Blake, Shelley, or Browning, they seem to you too intoxicated;
or, like the Metaphysical Poets, too often silly-clever, strained, and
"frigid"; or like many modern novels, trivial and squalid; or like
Henry James, fussy and effeminate; or like D. H. Lawrence or Joyce,
barbarous. You belong in a tomb by the Cerameicos or the Appian
Way. Go back there!'

There may be some truth in this. However I doubt if my faults are

---

[1] Lucretius was a great man. But the really poetic parts of his *De Rerum Natura*
do not seem to me very scientific; and the strictly scientific parts are hardly
poetry.
[2] *Anth. Pal.,* IX, 577.

really the fault of the classics. More and more I suspect essential character to be inborn. We are influenced, of course, by what we read; but we go on reading it largely because, for congenital reasons, we find it congenial. One can, of course, warp children's character with neuroses; or, contrarily, give them full freedom to become themselves; but the same environment can still produce personalities as opposite as Charles II and James II. Our good or evil genius lies largely in our genes.

*　　　*　　　*

Compared with the ancients, English Literature took a very small place in the Rugby of those years; though, by modern standards, we seem to have been often overworked. (I must frequently have done ten hours a day—more than I ever did again, continuously, till the Second World War.) But in the Twenty we had one of the most remarkable of masters. Robert Whitelaw was then, I suppose, about seventy—a little frail figure, surmounted by a vast spectacled head like that of Wells's Grand Selenite in *The First Men in the Moon*. This great boulder of a cranium looked still odder from being traversed by a marked lateral valley or depression, that ran across its top from ear to ear. But that huge headpiece was also well filled; and the small body that supported it was still so tough that, at an age when, under the modern system, he would long since have been superannuated, Robert Whitelaw never even sat down in class—he stood by the hour at a heavy lectern, which in moments of Dionysiac fervour he would perambulate about the floor, leaning it towards him and rotating it alternately to left and right. He was a passionate martinet—'Wait', said my master in the form below, 'till Mr Whitelaw gets his claws in you!' But he was an excellent martinet. Though his heart was above all in the classics—he would cross swords with the great Sir Richard Jebb, and his complete verse-translation of Sophocles is still the best I know—no one could forget his *Hamlet*. When his high-pitched old treble began to *sing* Ophelia's songs, they seemed, indeed, doubly crazy; but Shakespearian tragedy can seldom have been so well taught. And as I look back, across that room falls the shadow of a tragedy deeper even than Shakespeare's—not many of those who laughed there were to see another seven summers.

In the Sixth there was even less of English literature, except as something to translate into Greek or Latin. Yet there are worse approaches. I never felt more vividly the splendour of that ending of *Sohrab and Rustum* where the human tragedy loses itself in the majestic flow of

Oxus from Pamir to the Aral Sea, than when turning it into Latin hexameters. Translation can bring home the essentials of a poem better, sometimes, than the critical pontifications of schoolmasters. Too often I have heard undergraduates say of a book, in tones of nausea, 'Oh, I would rather not write on *that*—we did it at school.'

But to a master who ran a literary society for the Sixth I did owe my first encounter with two writers who have mattered to me lastingly. For he read us a paper on the *Playboy* of Synge, then only three years dead; and another on William Morris's *Sigurd the Volsung*. Since then, Synge has long taken his established place, for those who love Ireland, irony, and style; but to-day no one reads *Sigurd*. Though Shaw called it the greatest epic since Homer, I have met only two people in my life who shared my admiration for it—McTaggart, the philosopher of Trinity, and Lawrence of Arabia. But numbers are not everything. For me, at sixteen or seventeen, it was a thrilling discovery of that spirit of the North which I was to meet again in Ibsen, and the Icelandic sagas, and Iceland itself; which was to bring me, thirty years later, a Swedish wife, and a Sigurd and a Signy as son and daughter. Here was an individualism even intenser than the Greek—indeed, carried to a point that a Greek would have found impious; an individualism whose iron creed it was—

To beseech no man for his helping and to vex no god with prayer.

To-day I see well enough the poem's faults—its unbalanced construction; a certain roughness and lack of revision in its verse; an excess of iron in some of its characters. All the same, if there have been greater heroic poems, I still know no poem more heroic. It gave me just what I wanted—a world of men who did without brainsick enthusiasms or amiable illusions; who cooked up no false consolations; who relied on nothing in heaven or on earth but themselves. Morris himself, like Hardy, still seems to me a real and splendid person, much superior as a human being to most men of letters that have ever lived. And if his poem became for me then a sort of breviary, I was soon to need it. I still have somewhere a notebook with passages copied from *Sigurd*—some of its pages smudged and grimed with drifting TNT from German shells of 1917, that burst while I read it by Grandcourt at the sources of the Ancre. A critical test of an unusual kind; but not, perhaps, without a certain stringency.

* * *

But meanwhile Cambridge from October 1913 to June 1914 was—so it seems in retrospect—the calm sunset of a lost Golden Age. Sinister clouds might hang on our eastern horizon; but though we *saw*, at moments, a certain menace of danger, we did not really *feel* it. Generations of peace and civilization, long-standing belief in progress—in liberalism—in fundamental human decency, lulled most of us still to security. No doubt, individuals suffered and would always suffer. And there is often a strain of pessimism in the young. But the world at large seemed good to us, with good prospects of growing better. Even suppose there were a war—well, Europe had seen plenty of wars. Like 1870, even if unpleasant, it would all be quickly over. Little we dreamed what modern war would be like, what modern human beings could become. So we thought and talked of quite other things. It was, indeed, the talk of those months that mattered to me, even more than books. 'What!' cried Bielinsky to the young Turgenev, after a six-hours' argument, 'we do not know yet if God exists—and you want to dine!' We were rather like that. 'Sancta simplicitas!' The modern young might have thought us almost infantile. We did not walk about everywhere hand in hand with girls, like lost Babes in the Wood. Healthier if we had? Possibly. I do not know. Young women can take up an infernal lot of time. And I have misgivings about the child-marriages so popular at the moment.

> If hours be years, the twain are blest,
> For now they solace swift desire
> By bonds of every bond the best,
> If hours be years. The twain are blest,
> Do eastern stars slope never west,
> Nor pallid ashes follow fire:
> If hours be years, the twain are blest,
> For now they solace swift desire.[1]

But suddenly to meet, at nineteen, people like Lowes Dickinson, Keynes, Sheppard, G. E. Moore, Roger Fry, Desmond MacCarthy, was an intoxication I had never known before. And among undergraduates there was the brilliant F. K. Bliss (younger brother of the composer), soon to be killed in France; and the charming Hungarian, Ferenc Bekassy, soon to be killed by the Russians in the Carpathians. Had one only guessed, how much more one would have used that brief time to know them! And yet, of course, it was better not to guess.

[1] Hardy, 'At a Hasty Wedding.'

Perhaps such talk still exists somewhere. But nearly all those I have named are dead; and I have never come on it again. For that age of confidence is dead also. We have found out what men can become—not merely the men of five centuries ago, but contemporary, 'civilized' men. After Cressida, Troilus (had he lived) could easily have loved anew; could perhaps have loved better and more wisely; but never again with the same buoyant trustfulness in life. Perhaps something analogous has happened to us who have lived through this last half-century.

Besides, youth is the time for ardent argument. Then one may still believe that arguments lead somewhere. Now I have come to suspect that the arguer seldom clears anyone's mind but, sometimes, his own. And many of us, having read our Freud, have grown more sceptical than ever; seeing reason no longer as a searchlight, but usually as a gust-swept candle guttering amid the winds of emotion and the night of the Unconscious. And so, though good talk remains the pleasantest of pastimes, it now seems no more than that. It is also rare. Would one learn more of life and reality, it may be better to talk with the dead—in books.

*　　*　　*

Of writers, apart from my eternal ancients, only three names recur to me now as specially associated with that golden year, 1913–14—Shaw, Swinburne, Housman. An incongruous trinity perhaps. But they have in common two qualities easily congenial to a mind of eighteen or nineteen—youthfulness and rebelliousness. The young often tend to be angry. One can only ask that they should escape becoming merely peevish. Anger can at least breed energy, if nothing else; but what atom of good ever came of peevishness, it would be hard to say.

If, since then, parts of these writers have long worn out for me, that too is natural. Many books do wear out; and not a few immortals are, unfortunately, too mortal to last even a human lifetime. The Swinburne of *Atalanta* and *Poems and Ballads* still seems to me a metrical magician, a musical prodigy. But he seemed a good deal more than that in 1913, when many of the walls of Victorianism were still standing; though they had long begun to crack and totter. Then one could still hear him as an inspiring thunder on the left.

Shaw, again, has long appeared to me what even then Tolstoy had said he was—a person with 'more brains than is good for him', whose 'triviality is astounding'. But in those days he had just done, I think, his best work, with no sign as yet of the long decline to follow, or of those *trahisons de clerc* which were to leave him at last the pettifogging defender of Mussolini and Stalin. If he was already overfond of standing on his head and grinning through a horse-collar at the British public, he was still a very effective advocate of socialism. And at sixteen or seventeen I had become a socialist (which did not make much for popularity in a public school of 1912). Time has duly brought us socialism in plenty; and, as the way of time is, plenty of new problems —among them, that of averting the excesses of socialism itself. Shaw still seems to me a wonder of wit and style; but one who might have done better with less wit and more wits, less cleverness and more honesty of mind. His master, Samuel Butler, with all his whimsies, was the better man.

*   *   *

But the time had come for flinging books away. I was bicycling with my father by Loch Etive and Loch Awe, when the War came and, even on lonely Highland roadsides, there began to appear posters of a stern Lord Kitchener calling with outstretched finger for his hundred thousand volunteers. I recall what follows merely for the strange glimpse it gives of a world now vanished beyond belief. When I shyly suggested that I ought to join up, my father, to whom my career was more precious than his own, knit his brows above his gold spectacles and snapped angrily—'Only wasters go into the army.' It was not lack of patriotism. He was soon to accept the harsh necessity. But it was a kind of last desperate cry from that vanishing Victorian world where the soldier, though he might be idolized at intoxicated moments, as after Balaclava or Mafeking, was normally viewed by many an honest citizen as a caste apart, and an outcast, with some of the disdain of the Chinese mandarin or scholar for the mere brutish man-at-arms.

So in that autumn of 1914 I stowed away my books and lecture-notes in my cupboard at Trinity, wondering if I should ever take them out again; with much the same feeling as when, twenty-five years later, in September 1939, I stored my manuscripts in King's Chapel, and on the line where the luggage-label on my tin trunk said 'Per . . .', wrote with a sudden impulse that sombre verse of Virgil—

Fortuna omnipotens et ineluctabile Fatum.

Both times, 'omnipotent Fortune' and 'ineluctable Fate' proved kinder to me than to most.

For twelve years I had lived largely in books; now, suddenly, I was to learn to live—and live happily—without them. Easily one grows to think books indispensable in life. It is wrong—they are not; or, if they become so, something is wrong with oneself. However, I admit that there are very few things that I would not sooner dispense with.

Those years 1914–18, though an unspeakable disaster to mankind—worse perhaps than we realize even yet—brought me individually, I suppose, more good than harm; despite a year and a half in hospitals, a deaf ear, and damaged lung. Hard though it was at first to make the adaptation from academic Cambridge to an officers' mess in the winter mud of Purfleet on the flats of the lower Thames, still one was in the open air, bursting with health, constantly interested, with a platoon one became deeply fond of. And we were all so young. And the war, whether or no it could have been avoided, was now unescapable, and vital not to lose. That Christmas we all jumped in our mess-chairs as the ineffectual anti-aircraft gun on the water-tower by our camp suddenly split the air; we ran out, to see flying up the Thames the first hostile aircraft, I suppose, ever to blacken British skies. Turning back later, it fell into the sea. Little we guessed of what it was to prove the harbinger in the thirty years to come—or we might have felt like Charlemagne in the story, weeping prophetically at sight of the first sinister galley of the Northmen, sighted off Narbonne.

*   *   *

Through 1915–16, though poor Homer bumped about Picardy in my valise, it was things like the *Bystander* that I read, in the rare moments that left time and energy enough to read at all. True, even then, bits of remembered poetry ran sometimes through one's head; at rare intervals one might scribble verse; but even when my parents posted me literary broadsheets provided by a paternal *Times*, I only wish my dug-out had seemed as dry as they. Yet I was soon to re-discover, as never before, the use of books.

My first wounds had only disabled me three months; during which I came on Kipling in my convalescent home, and Boswell's *Johnson* by the Dorset sea. But in March 1917 gas brought pleuro-pneumonia, and for a fortnight I sweltered, too ill to be moved, in a hutted casualty-clearing station at Dernancourt, with a temperature of 103–4 degrees reinforced by an infernal stove blazing night and day at the bed's foot. At night I was chased by nightmares which drove me for the only time in my life to sleep-walk, till rushed at by a startled orderly; but —blessed be books!—all day I read. Afterwards I could not even recall the titles of what I read, except the first of them—*Guy Mannering*. And when, years later, I reread it, the whole novel seemed quite new, except Meg Merrilies. But those books passed me through the interminable days while my parents in England puzzled vainly to reconcile War Office telegrams that I was dangerously ill, with nonchalant notes of grumpy boredom from me. I do not remember being even conscious of danger—the printed page screened off any shadowy death's heads at the bed's foot—until one day when the Medical Officer on his evening rounds asked how I felt, and I answered wearily that nothing seemed to make any difference. I did not mean it despairingly—I was just mortally tired of being parboiled day and night, while the snow-squalls of that late spring of 1917 pattered drearily against the hut-windows, and convoys of wounded passed in or out at all hours of light or darkness; tired of never being able to lie flat, lest I suffocate, and of having hollow needles pushed into my back to pump my pleural cavity, under local anaesthetics much too local, while I crushed a long-suffering nurse's hand. But to my surprise, that evening, the doctor answered sharply, 'You mustn't talk like that!' He thought I was letting myself go. I had no more notion of doing that than Shakespeare's Barnardine of letting himself be executed. But had I just lain and thought, instead of being drugged with books . . . ? As it was, I had been most effectually distracted; and was much more disturbed a little later when an eminent R.A.M.C. general, Sir Ralph Hemingway, appeared and observed to my M.O., in a low voice that did not escape my damaged hearing—'You'll have to resect.' 'Resect' sounded horrid. It was. But an eight-inch rubber tube through a hole in a sawn rib proved magical. And again I had cause to bless the inventor of printing. It was the worst crisis of the U-boat blockade; and so when we embarked at Le Havre, it was not in order to reach England in twelve hours, but to spend fourteen solid days on our hospital ship, the S.S. *Asturias*, moored in the harbour, while disaster followed disaster in the Channel outside. This delay on the very threshold of home would have been maddening, had not some kind soul opened the liner's peacetime library. For that fortnight I could gorge alternately meals and books.

The year in hospital that followed was in its way a return to the book-rambles of my childhood. Once again I read omnivorously and at random, as the whim took me; first in the splendours of Dorchester House in Park Lane, then in a Dorset convalescent-home. It was one of the queerest, yet not least happy periods of my life; divided between bicycling about Hardy's Wessex and pillaging the excellent Public Library of Bournemouth. Week after week, month after month, as summer changed to autumn, winter, spring, I rode and read. Beaulieu, Lyndhurst, Brockenhurst, Ringwood, Wimborne Minster, Cranborne Chase, Shaftesbury, Blandford, the Winterbournes, Milton Abbas, High Stoy Hill, Egdon Heath and Dorchester—they lay only the more peaceful in the quiet sunshine that was lighting the dust and smoke of battles oversea.

Hardy, d'Annunzio, Nietzsche, Schopenhauer, Samuel Butler, *The Golden Bough*, Pater, Heine, Rossetti, Meredith, Hafiz, Montaigne, Anatole France[1]—on them too lay a timeless peacefulness; even though one did not know if one would see another year's return; even though whole days were sometimes poisoned by the disclosure of sordid secret treaties, by the leading articles of too pugnacious journalists, or by the bellowings of politicians far less inspiring than Churchill and Roosevelt in the Second War. But, above all, 1917 remains for me Wessex and Thomas Hardy. Sometimes I rode past Max Gate. Years after, Mrs Hardy blamed me for not daring to knock at its door. I deeply regret it. Yet it still seems inevitable. How should an unknown subaltern have the impertinence to intrude on precious time like his?

All this was a most haphazard and rambling way to read. I can hardly imagine doing it now. I have come to distrust higgledy-piggledy reading. But at twenty-two it may have been right. One has to find one's tastes, like a dog casting about for a scent, before one can follow them.

*   *   *

[1] My introduction to Anatole France I owed to Desmond MacCarthy, who sought me out in Dorchester House, led me into a bookshop, and charmingly gave me *L'Etui de Nacre*. A couple of months later *Thaïs* was given me by, of all people, a Roman Catholic aunt; who must, I suppose, have imagined the book (surely on the Index) to be an edifying story, because it was about an early Christian hermit and a converted Magdalen.

It was during my third term in France, on the Intelligence Staff of Third Army, in the summer of 1918, that I met my Fähnrich who had such a horror of becoming 'ein Bücherwurm'. But actually his own army seemed to contain far more bookworms than we. For I remember finding an abandoned German field library at Solesmes, east of Cambrai, full of standard authors in buff paper-backs such as it would have been astonishing to find in British soldiers' hands at any time, let alone the middle of a campaign. It was even broad-minded enough to include translations of enemy writers—such as Pierre Loti's *Pêcheur d'Islande*.

Now I saw a lot of German soldiers that autumn—only too many; till I began to dread the sight of each new column of shambling figures snaking down the dusty white roads to the Army Cage at Bapaume or Le Quesnoy, while exultant Alsatians, already segregated into a cage of their own, shouted mockingly at them through the barbed wire— 'Ist Hindenburg da?' Yet the average German did not seem a better soldier than ours (though they taught us a lot of expensive lessons first), nor fundamentally so decent. Which suggests once more that 'Kultur' is by no means the same as civilization; and that one should not expect too much from books. A suspicion which is not weakened by the contrast in the last war between Japanese brutalities in the field or in prison-camps, and the exquisite sensitiveness of their tea-ceremonials or flower-arrangements or calligraphy. Human character remains oddly incalculable.

On the other hand there *were* Germans—not only in their Air Force —who still thought in terms of 'chivalry'; which depends on tradition; which, in its turn, depends not a little on books. On November 11, 1918, there were brought to the Army Cage the Commander, Adjutant, and Machine-gun Officer of a Würtemberg battalion; and, the War being at last over, we invited them to tea. Not unnaturally, they were deep in gloom over the prospect of captivity in England at this fifty-ninth minute of the eleventh hour. Then, as I talked to them, it emerged that they had been captured only *after* the Armistice began— they had ridden forward with a white flag to complain that we were advancing faster than had been agreed. And the Battalion Commander ended: 'Wir verlassen uns auf die bekannte ritterliche Ehre der Engländer' ('We put our trust in the known chivalry of the English'). I think he meant it, and was not merely indulging in Machiavellian flattery. In any case, they were very pleasant words to hear, so that they have stuck forty years in my memory; and I am glad to remember too that, after I had sent a report by dispatch-rider to Third Army H.Q., in the small hours of that night an English car arrived to take them safely back to their own retreating column.

And now yet again I found the boon of books. In the deadly flu-epidemic of that autumn my lung-wound had suddenly reopened; for six weeks it was daily dressed by the little black Jamaican doctor of the Army Cage, who did not even wash his hands for the purpose (his time was largely taken up with buying Iron Crosses for cigarettes from the prisoners); but now that the War was over I could come back to Cambrai to be cut up again. The day after the operation I had lost too much blood to digest anything; but in consolation I was able to devour Wells's *Joan and Peter* from cover to cover. Years after, when Wells seemed pathetically to have survived his old reputation, I seem to remember that I was at least able to write and tell him of that debt.

Two months later I was an undergraduate again. Twenty years of books; then on 3–9–39 a naval uniform knocked at my gate and asked how long I needed to pack; and so began another almost bookless interval—six years this time. And yet—though it seems almost disgusting—never was I happier. For, firstly, there was work to be done both fascinating and vital. Secondly, I have never had better colleagues to work with. Thirdly, the Home Office (with a generosity that always stops my mouth when I am moved to rail at bureaucrats) allowed my Swedish fiancée to enter an England where, as they had warned me, every extra mouth might count. However long I live, I shall always remember with nostalgia the quiet of Buckinghamshire villages, there at the very heart of England, and of English nature, and of English good nature; the sunlight in hours off duty among the fir-woods above Woburn Sands; the blaze of bluebells in Duncombe Wood by Great Brickhill, that no terrors oversea or overhead turned pale in their spring glory; the brave thunder, as we worked through the small hours, of the night-expresses for Holyhead and Carlisle which not all Hitler's bombardments could keep from their indomitable course. Books with a purpose may often suffer; but life rammed with purpose is surely the best. I should shudder at the thought of such a time's return; but I would not have missed it. And now I suppose that books will remain my chosen field again till the end of the chapter; since the hydrogen-bomb, despite the somewhat undignified scream-ing that it now produces, may none the less prove a beneficent invention that puts an end to major wars, by making them too unprofitable for any side, too dangerous for all.

*   *   *

But why, in general, should one read? And what? And how? And how much? Not for me to lay down laws about it—I am merely asking myself what, rather to my own surprise, I seem never to have asked myself systematically before. And even if my tastes and ideas seem to the reader mere quirks and eccentricities, they may yet be of some slight service. For it is by comparison with the views of others, however wrong-headed, that one can often clarify and fortify one's own.

Why read? Precisely that question was recently discussed by a leader in the *Times Literary Supplement*. For a nice young man at an Adult Education College, after dutifully reading the good books prescribed him, had politely asked 'What use?'—it took, he complained, such time and trouble, with no return that he could see. One suspects, indeed, that he was the wrong sort of young man for books; or else that it was the wrong sort of college, and prescribed the wrong sort of books. The heart-breaking thing about much of the academic teaching of literature which now rages all over the world is that it so often consists in trying to teach the unteachable to the unteachable. For the love and knowledge of literature are things far more self-taught than taught.

Told that imaginative literature would give him more insight into human feelings, this young man replied by asking if all that would not be better done by psychology. Such a reply seems typical of that unscientific superstition about science which plagues our scientific age. For one would have thought it obvious that science, whose main concern must be facts and ideas, could hardly be a substitute for art, whose main concern is with feelings; that, though psychology can throw light on Shakespeare, it cannot conceivably replace Shakespeare. On the contrary, one of the wisest psychologists I ever knew used to stress the vital importance, to any psychologist, of a wide knowledge of literature.

At this point the writer of the leading article offered a new defence of reading—'that we do not fully live in our age unless, in some degree at least, we possess the higher culture of that age'. But suppose the young man answered—'I do not want to "live fully" in our age.

I loathe our age, precisely because it makes it so hard to live fully. I can live fully only out of it, and in opposition to it. Its "higher culture" seems to me far from high. In this at least I am like your Flaubert who took for his patron-saint Saint Polycarp with his cry—"Dans quel siècle, mon Dieu, m'avez-vous fait naître!"'

To which, of course, the answer would be: 'But if—as well you may—you find the present often so emetic, then literature offers you the best flying-carpet in the world for escaping all these tyrannies of place and time.'

The leader-writer, however, ended on a note of some despair; as if disheartened by such a recalcitrant young man. 'It would', he concluded, 'be almost impossible to-day for somebody, asked what the value of literary culture to life is, to give such a sturdily honest answer as Dr Johnson's:

> The greater part of readers, instead of blaming us for passing trifles, will wonder that on trifles so much labour is expended, with such importance of debate, and such solemnity of diction. To these I answer with confidence, that they are judging of an art they do not understand; yet cannot much reproach them with their ignorance, nor promise that they would become in general by learning criticism, more useful, happier or wiser.

'Dr Johnson was talking of the discipline of textual criticism, but his answer applies to literary culture in a broader sense.'

But at this, surely, Johnson would have bounded with fury. 'Sir,' he might have roared, 'to literary culture my words do *not*, and *cannot*, "apply". I spoke of *textual* criticism; which directly concerns only the editors of books. Does one man in ten thousand edit a book? Are you so blind as not to see the difference between editing books and reading them? Or so irreligious as to forget that God Himself has bestowed on men two *books*, the Old Testament and the New, with the direct and sole purpose of making them "more useful, happier, *and* wiser"? Did I not tell Percy's little daughter that I would not give a farthing for her because she had not read *Pilgrim's Progress*? Instead of talking about what I might have said, let me remind you of things I did say—"I am always for getting a boy forward in his learning . . . because you have done a great deal when you have brought him to have entertainment from a book."—"It was the maxim, I think, of Alphonsus of Aragon that *dead counsellors are safest*. The grave puts an end to flattery and artifice, and the information we receive from books is pure from interest, fear, or ambition. Dead counsellors are likewise most instructive, because they are heard with patience and with reverence." Much as I loved talking, I denounced the idle, superficial notion that knowledge enough can be got from conversation. "The foundation", I said, "must be laid by reading. . . . In conversation you never get a system." I told Bozzy to have as many books about him as he could. And do you suppose I could have talked so well myself, if in younger years I had not read like a Turk?'

*   *   *

It does not seem really so hard to find answers to the type of modern youth who jauntily observes 'Reading's had it.' For, firstly, how many pleasures are there so accessible, so inexpensive, so permanent, so harmless, in a world which few but crabbed ascetics can think over-provided with enjoyments—particularly with enjoyments that do not carry stings in their tails? Of course one can, if one is fool enough, ruin one's health and vitality over books, like the young Leopardi. But if one is to reject all pleasures that are not also fool-proof, one's life is likely to remain exceedingly austere. And reading is a pleasure that can also be an anodyne, for all pains and griefs that are not too acute; even though few of us may be as resilient as Montesquieu, who never had a sorrow—so he said—that an hour's reading could not cure.

*   *   *

Secondly, there is the knowledge which reading can convey more swiftly and surely than whole armies of sages in the past, or all our multitudinous babblings out of boxes in the present. For one can read faster than anybody can talk. One can skip. One can reread what a first reading left obscure. Some may think mankind has amassed more knowledge than it can digest, and would be better with far less of it. But such a view seems too like nostalgic regrets for the noble savage, the noble peasant, or the infant trailing glories from on high. These ideal figures are suspect; in any case regret for them is vain. For the world will incorrigibly continue to accumulate knowledge; and ignorance must tend more and more to get left behind and enslaved. Besides, in a world where so many pleasures become so quickly a weariness or a vanity, one of the last impulses to grow surfeited and fail, even in the old, is the curiosity that craves insatiably to know and understand. Whatever else age takes away, while a man keeps his curiosity, all is not lost. The old Socrates in prison, says the story, asked a musician to teach him an air. 'What use, when you are going to die?' 'So as to know it *before* I die.'

No doubt, as Thamus objected, books have weakened our memories. But they have given us wider memories in exchange. Not Thamus himself could have memorized the contents of a single modern encyclopedia. If I can have extensions of my grey cells sitting in black and white on my study-shelves, surely the gain is mine. Besides, old Thamus was no psychologist. He did not realize how memory can become a fallacious cheat and traitor under the influence of our fears or desires. And anyway the brains that remember most are very seldom among those that think the best.

*   *   *

Thirdly, it seems intelligent to wish to be intelligent. That too has been questioned. Sophocles and Meredith, in splenetic moments, have both suggested that sanity is unhappier than the blissfulness of insanity or insentience.[1] But happy idiocy is rare; and those who romanticize it can hardly have glimpsed the blood-freezing interior of a mental home, or thought of those who have to tend imbecility. There is more force in the argument that doubt whether life be worth living is far more common in intellectuals than in gardeners. But this may well be because gardeners are usually healthier, rather than because they are stupider. And if the intelligent let themselves get unhealthy, it often shows only that they are insufficiently intelligent. *Of course* intelligence is dangerous; but so is the lack of it. Anyway one seldom meets anyone who honestly wishes he were weaker in the head.

But, supposing it to have value, intelligence is surely a good deal dependent on contact with other minds; the sharper, the better. However Arcadian the ancient Arcadia may have been, its mountains with

---

[1] ἐν τῷ φρονεῖν γὰρ μηδὲν ἥδιστος βίος (Sophocles, *Ajax*, 553—Ajax to his infant son).

'For life is happiest in senselessness.'

The Meredith passage is in *Modern Love*, XIX:

If any state be enviable on earth,
'Tis yon born idiot's, who, as days go by,
Still rubs his hands before him, like a fly,
In a queer sort of meditative mirth.

all their beauty never bred intellects such as grew up on the coasts of sea-going Athens or Ionia. The wisest of Homeric heroes, Odysseus, was also the greatest wanderer of them all. This contact with other minds can sometimes be found in talk—as Greek philosophers found it, or eighteenth-century *salons*. 'En effet,' says Taine, 'nous nous sommes civilisés par la conversation; les Anglais, point.' Unfortunately what Johnson called 'solid talk', where real things are 'discussed', was always rare, and now seems rarer still. It is not produced by putting a dozen persons round a room, to conduct half a dozen perfunctory duologues; it demands the maintenance of one general conversation among all—an art which most moderns (and most modern hostesses) not only lack, but do not even know to exist. Even in the eighteenth century it cannot have been common. But with a good book one can always enjoy, tête-à-tête, the mind of a man that one likes and respects. And indeed few authors are, in my experience, as good in the flesh as in print.

The ideal, no doubt, would be to combine both good talk and good books; so gaining from the first that readiness, from the second that fulness, which Bacon so wisely says they give. But since good talk is hard to come by, all the greater the need for good books. Even if successful writers are themselves often not very intelligent, having gained their success rather by being imaginative or sensitive, the reader can still grow more intelligent in their company, if only by asking where they go wrong. The man who reads can become older in experience by three thousand years; if he does not become thereby a little wiser also, the fault must be his. An active mind can develop as constant a hunger for ideas as the body has for its daily bread. It is not the unhappiest type of mind. And its happiest hunting-ground must be found in books.

No doubt, book-wisdom is suspect. Careers like those of Lamartine or Woodrow Wilson can show how justified, sometimes, is the common man's distrust of the bookish, and of their power to cope with crude reality. But after all the Clemenceau who baffled Wilson was also a man of books, though a sharper and tougher-minded one. And so was Winston Churchill.

* * *

Fourthly, one can read to make friends—friends who are never not at home; never out of temper; never false. Perhaps all my critical judgements are eccentrically personal. A book, to me, means a person, rather than a thing. There are authors that I love better than all but a handful of people I have known in the flesh; authors that I loathe and despise with an intensity that, fortunately, no living acquaintance has ever aroused. Reasonable? A foolish question. Feelings are not matters of reason; reason can decide only what one does about them. And I am quite content to do nothing about these violent feelings. They only make my contact with books more alive.

There comes to my mind an old lady of ninety, with failing health and sight, a lonely exile since many years from Austria, prisoned in one room of a suburban lodging. Once in far-off days in far-off Vienna a famous author loved her; but all that world has long since vanished into utter oblivion, leaving only a few dusty or rusty fragments of fact in the glass-cases of history. And yet she still reads on indomitably, indomitably taking notes. Those little know what they lose who have never made friends with dead writers, who will not die.

*   *   *

Lastly, as Flaubert put it, 'ne lisez pas comme les enfants lisent, pour vous amuser, ni comme les ambitieux lisent pour vous instruire. Mais lisez pour vivre.' No doubt Flaubert himself read too much. But there remains more life in some books dead a thousand years than in much that passes for living, but remains really as futile as froth-blowing.

All the same one should not claim too much. The literary are in danger of thinking literature even more important than it is; as the artistic do with art. The best is not got from books by bookworms. One of the great qualities of Professor Raleigh, as of the Johnson he admired, was a steady refusal to exaggerate the place of letters in life. Asked in 1914 to sign a literary album to be presented to the King of the Belgians, Raleigh replied with terse irritation: 'The best present to give the King of the Belgians is Belgium. Two of the men of this household are at the front, and the third is drilling. Yours truly. . . .' Carried too far, this attitude could grow tiresome. Some thought it so in him. But perhaps it was a healthy corrective. In 1940, while civilization tottered, there were still industrious researchers busy with such fruitful themes as 'The anti-Catholic use of Catholic material in the imagery of eighteenth-century literature', or 'Personal pronouns in Henry James'. Even if sane beings could study such topics at the best of times, one may wonder if in 1940 they might not have been better employed in at least filling shells.

*   *   *

And what should one read? Infinitely as the answer must vary with the individual, there may still be some fairly general principles. One may read either to pass the moment, or for lasting gain, or both; either to enjoy, or to remember, or both. I must own that, whenever possible, I have always wanted, in defiance of the proverb, both to eat my cake and to have it. It is part of the great art of having things both ways; and, whatever people pretend, one often can. Now it is irksome to find, a month later, that one remembers nothing of a book but its title; and a year later, perhaps, not even that. No doubt life is a kind of mist we all have to walk through—as the fog of the future clears before us, the fog of the past closes in behind. But it becomes a disconsolate, suffocating sensation when the past grows too quickly and thickly blurred. Therefore I strongly dislike not remembering what I read, and reading what I shall not want to remember; frequently though one must do both. This miserly obsession with time is perhaps more than ever an eccentricity in a Welfare Age so largely content with mere pastimes. We kill ourselves to save time—on the roads and in the air; then, having saved the time, we do not know what to do with it, and kill that too. To kill people to save time, and then kill the time as well, seems a rather curious procedure. Able-bodied people who kill time, when it perishes so fast anyway, seem to me only half-alive themselves. So perhaps it would be intelligent if we considered more closely what is worth reading.

Besides, even the unremembered reading of the moment may have effects more than momentary—may train the mind or muddle it, strengthen the character or weaken it. No one knows how much the unconscious remembers. The great Chatham would refuse even to look at certain prints. 'You *must not*', said Schumann, 'play bad music. You *must not* even hear it, unless compelled.' Over-squeamish? Perhaps. But perhaps, too, we are not squeamish enough.

With reading that one *hopes* to remember, naturally it becomes still more important what one reads. For one of the most important things to know is what not to know.

This, I find, is not the general view. The half-educated have often a superstitious faith in the value of the most futile scraps of information;

like the Emperor Tiberius baiting the erudite with inane questionings on such matters as the name of Hecuba's mother. Hence the success of the young Northcliffe's *Answers*; and the popularity of 'quizzes'. The general-knowledge questions set by newspapers and schoolmasters deal often with such imbecile trivialities that the prize should really go to the person knowing, not most, but fewest of them.

Yet this fetish is not confined to the half-educated. Johnson once denied that there was such a thing as useless knowledge; though in a wiser mood, as so often, he contradicted himself—'Life is surely given us for higher purposes than to gather what our ancestors have wisely thrown away, and to learn what is of no value but because it has been forgotten.' Housman, again, valued every grain added to the heap of established fact. Lord Keynes, recalling the generation of his youth at Cambridge, records that they passionately denied any distinction between knowledge useful and useless. And when I have set the same problem in examinations to the youth of modern Cambridge, it has become clear from their answers that to most of them the idea of knowledge being sometimes futile had never even occurred.

This attitude, I must say, leaves me stupefied to the limit of stupe-faction. 'Useful' and 'useless' are here, of course, idle terms unless one asks 'for whom?'—'for what?'; and unless one takes them to mean '*relatively* useful'—'*relatively* useless'. The essential question is not what knowledge is likely to serve for a particular job, but what is likely to serve an intelligent person for getting the most from life; given that lives are brief, and memories briefer. If nothing in life matters ulti-mately but states and processes of mind that one can value, this ques-tion does not seem by any means empty. To say that *nothing* would be useless for a man about to travel six months with only one suitcase, would be mad. Well, we have perhaps sixty adult years to travel through life; with little time to learn, and little leisure to recall or refresh what we have learnt. Yet the world of knowledge seems full of White Knights painfully clattering and staggering on their way under monstrous loads of egg-whisks and mousetraps.

And so, for some, the dominant mood induced by dutifully scan-ning the weekly reviews is that of Diogenes at the fair—'Immortal Gods, what a lot of things Diogenes does *not* need!' There has been, one reads, a book of 732 pages on Edward Marsh; and one of 933 on Lord Northcliffe. (Surely even Caesar or Napoleon need not take up such a wasteful wilderness of words. Tacitus did Agricola in 30 pages

—and will last thirty times as long.) There is a volume of 475 pages on death. (A fine way of using up one's life.) So-and-so has written a novel telling how attempts to improve fig-culture in South Italy led to a whole village being doped with aphrodisiac. (How hopeful! How hilarious!) Then there is *The Story of Cheese-making in Britain*—347 pages; *The Fine Art of Mixing Drinks*—362 pages; *Guide to Lovebirds and Parrotlets*. . . . And the whole periodical may be rounded off by some disinterment of half a dozen-odd letters from a famous writer, hitherto unprinted, and so bumblingly dull that they would far better have remained so.

And yet perhaps such criticisms are peevish and intolerant. Perhaps one ought to be grateful that, amid our growing mass-uniformity, such a strange diversity of human types and tastes can still survive. And even 'parrotlets' are more intelligent than football-pools. Still I shall not read these great works.

What *should* one read? No man can here be another man's judge. This is merely a personal record of some things that it seems to me worth while to have read.

Perhaps the most important and fascinating subject for the human mind is—the human mind. If one feels so, one turns to books about people rather than about things—to poetry, drama, history, biography, fiction, psychology (though some would include the last under fiction).

Verse, once supreme, seems to me still to have certain advantages over the prose that has largely dethroned it. First, it *can* be briefer (though, as Tennyson said, most poems are too long). It can jump transitions more boldly. Poetry can be a grasshopper—a cicada— where prose is often an ant. A good instance of this is provided by the best ballads; few prose short stories have ever attained such artistic economy.

Secondly, poetry, when perfect, can seem more perfect than prose. A good line of verse can seem the one right, inevitable expression of its idea; whereas even with fine prose one feels less convinced that the writer could not have been every whit as effective had he worded what he says in half a dozen different ways.

Thirdly, verse takes far firmer hold on the memory. This is not merely a convenience. It has meant that poetry has had far more influence on men's lives. Think if Homer or Shakespeare had been all in prose! Prose can be as poetic, as imaginative, as any verse; but it is less able to become a part of oneself, like the inward voices that guided Socrates or Joan of Arc.

Lastly, the poetic imagination, though it can exist in prose-writers and in men that do not write at all, has had its nativity, and its most constant home, in verse. When Lytton Strachey said of Bacon, 'It is probably always disastrous not to be a poet', he was, I think, tempted by epigram into exaggeration. 'Always' is a big word; 'disastrous', a strong one. And the Bacon of the *Essays* was not seldom, in his own way, a poet. But in Strachey's dictum there remains a good deal of valuable truth; and those who have gnawed and worried his memory might sometimes have been wiser and fairer had they possessed more sense of poetry themselves.

* * *

In 1946 a selected thousand persons, of all ages, classes, and incomes, were catechized by painstaking inquirers about what they were reading. Of those who pleaded guilty to reading anything whatever (about half), no fewer than 70 per cent were reading fiction. Political or social science, the next most popular subject, occupied a mere 8 per cent; poetry—2 per cent! This hardly makes the heart leap up. Though perhaps the poets themselves are most to blame. The public can scarcely be expected to maintain its interest in men who stick their heads in rabbit-holes, and gabble. Yet this dominance of fiction may surprise by its crushing completeness. For in addition to this 70 per cent of book-readers one must take into account also those other temples of fictitious living, the theatre, the cinema, broadcasting, television, and the magazine.

But this extraordinary passion for unreality—for happenings that never happened, and for the lives of people who never lived—is not perhaps, after all, so unnatural. This is the age of the common man; and the common man has always loved stories. And no harm in that— if only the stories were not, often, so muddy. Most of us, if we worked in the shops, offices, or factories of some glum and overgrown city would not acquire much taste for poetry or Nature, for dignity or grace (except, for a few brief years, in feminine form). Immured in that greyly prosaic world, we should need to piece out our prisoned life with imaginary lives, spiced with a mixture of realism and romance, above all with the great twin themes of crime and sex.

It surprises me much more to find even among the happy few,

elaborately educated and fortunately circumstancely, a similar passion for fiction, which seems to me oddly disproportionate (though of course I may merely be odd myself). Thus I can recall an eminent Cambridge philosopher who was said to refresh his grey cells, after the labour of settling the Universe, by devouring a novel a day from the Union or elsewhere. Over three thousand five hundred novels every decade! What stuff, at that rate, he must have passed through him. A stomach like iron. But why should fantasies seem so preferable to the fascinating strangeness of reality? I am as puzzled as a naturalist might be, who saw his fellows crowding along museum galleries filled only with faked chimeras, centaurs, basilisks, mermen, mandrakes, phoenixes, sirens, sea-serpents, harpies, and hippogriffs.

At this point I hear some exasperated novel-lover protest—'Are you so blind to the powers that the novelist wields?—how he can create worlds of his own, more or less like the world we know, yet more complete, more unified—charming us as a model or a map can charm, by a compactness that we can grasp, as we cannot grasp the full-scale original—worlds illumined by the poetry of a vivid imagination, by the beauty and energy of a living style?—how he can people these visioned worlds with characters that seem rounded off and transparent to our gaze, as real people can hardly ever be? For even if we met Uncle Toby or Mr Micawber in the flesh, they could not be as constantly characteristic, as consistently amusing, as they are when we summon their obliging phantoms from the shelf. And even if real men like Pepys or Boswell have sometimes made themselves as vivid and intimate as the best characters of fiction, surely you must admit that great stretches of their writing remain not very individual or very interesting. Biography cannot possibly replace the novel. Even the most startling characters of history, like Peter the Great or Byron, grow dimmed with some of that confused unreality which settles like dust, deeper and deeper, on all past reality. Across such faces Time and Death have let fall their veil of mystery: these men too have become wraiths, like the comrades of Odysseus when he met them again by the blood-filled trench on the Ocean-shore. James Boswell was as much born for Samuel Johnson as Sancho Panza for Don Quixote; yet even in that most famous of *Lives* Johnson is not wholly there—we feel that he keeps an unseen side like the moon; whereas of Don Quixote, or Falstaff, we seem to know all—or almost all—that there is to know. And again has even *The Life of Johnson* an artistic unity comparable, say, with that of *Madame Bovary*? Has his career, however tragic its end, the artistic compactness of her briefer and swifter ruin?'

As regards the greatest novels I must grant much of this defence to be true. My objections are to the droves of minor novelists whose off-spring have a death-rate of 99 per cent per annum, while hardly one in ten thousand survives ten years.

First of all, they are so terribly wordy. Renan, if I remember, said he would have liked to read novels if only they were provided with *manchettes*—marginal summaries or newspaper headlines. That, in-deed, might help. But such summaries could only give the story; which may, even in a good novel, be the weakest point.

Secondly, the philosophies of novels seem frequently foolish; their values, valueless; their plots and characters, equally improbable and un-important. As outlined, week after week, in reviews, they leave my simple mind staggered at the hordes of rats and rabbits, decadents, neurotics, perverts, and psychopaths that my fellow-creatures appar-ently think it worth giving years of their lives to write or read about. 'We just don't know', moans the hero of a recent New York novel, *The Notion of Sin*, 'why we're here, or where we came from, or where we're going. The others *know*—God how they know, and how tire-somely they know. We can only shrug. To those of us who are agnostics, my question is: What morality do we live by?' What a generation of jellyfish! The modern decadentsia seems to live with one ear cocked for the whimper of the egghead, the other for the whoop of the caveman. But it is also very interesting. That same cry once rang out, like a ghostly wail, from the declining centuries of Rome. And, recalling it, one begins to listen anew for the tramp of the barbarians.

'If you can get', wrote Lawrence of Arabia in a letter, 'walking and talking people, you have got one-third of what the novelist wants. The other third is something keener seen than the earth of our eyes to set them in; and the last third is something for them to say better and richer and riper than the stuff we can say ourselves.' 'If all we did', he added, 'was to invent people who were passably real, it would be easier and more realistic yet to procreate real children on any woman.' 'Easier' seems a trifle wild (Lawrence was something of a misogynist). But with the rest I could not agree more. Yet how very, very few are the novelists by whom those exacting requirements are fulfilled!

Thirdly, if fiction is made as extraordinary as real life can be, it tends to fail—we cry 'How improbable!' If it is made less extraordinary than real life—well, that is precisely my point—it *is* less extraordinary. The novelist competes with life at a disadvantage. Fiction, if it grows fantastic, often ceases to fascinate: but with a true story, the more fantastic it grows, the greater, very often, its fascination. And in fact Time has produced tragedies, comedies, and romances more dramatic than Shakespeare's. The supreme story-teller is Life. Ivan the Terrible and Peter the Great outdo the most bizarre characters of Dostoievsky; indeed Dostoievsky and Tolstoy themselves had lives and characters stranger than anything imagined in their novels. Gulliver is a figure far less enthralling than Swift; Rasselas than Johnson. The autobiographies of Alfieri, Rousseau, and Chateaubriand still grip readers who could never drag themselves through *Mirra*, or *La Nouvelle Héloïse*, and who find even *Atala* rather faded and '*fade*'. Goethe is more interesting than the young Werther. Byron and Shelley never conceived destinies as poignant as their own. The true story of Alfred de Musset and George Sand still moves us, though his *Confessions d'un Enfant du Siècle* and her over-lyrical romances have come to seem falsetto. Balzac never conceived a scene of dramatic irony so bitter as his own homecoming with his *comtesse lointaine* from Poland to the Rue Fortunée. And in all the *panache* of *Hernani* or *Notre Dame* there is no rhetoric so fine as the old Hugo's own manifesto at Brussels to the fugitives of the Paris Commune, in defiance alike of Belgian mobs and Belgian bureaucrats—'I offer to the vanquished the asylum refused them by the Belgian Government. Where? In Belgium. I offer it at Brussels. I offer it at 4 Place des Barricades.'

No doubt, strangeness is not everything; no doubt, the great novelists have other qualities in compensation. But it is worth noting that Tolstoy, who certainly knew something about fiction, came in the end to a position still more extreme. He had once dramatized an episode from real life; then two of the characters concerned came and begged him not to publish; and, with that honesty which was one of his finest traits, Tolstoy records: 'Once more, as so many times previously, I was convinced how much feebler and less real are the psychological motives that one invents to explain actions. . . . After talking with these people I cooled to my work.' And he asks himself whether the novel will not finally disappear altogether, as the long poem has already disappeared. 'It seems to me that in time works of art will cease to be invented. It will become a shame to invent a story about some fictitious Ivan Ivanovitch or Marie Petrovna.' That I doubt. It will at least be a very long time. And I should be sorry. But this view is very interesting in the mouth of Tolstoy.

Lastly, one may suspect not only the philosophy, but also the psychology, of many novelists. Their task is to present people one can care about and believe in. One may believe in characters without caring sixpence about them; but one cannot care, unless one believes. Yet when one is asked to believe that character C in situation S would have adopted behaviour B, too often one cannot oblige. One remains unconvinced. Too often the behaviour of C throws more light on the curious character of the author who conceived this poor puppet, than on human character in general.

Genius, of course, can create worlds of its own. I cannot deny that persons like some of the characters of Dostoievsky or Henry James *could* exist—even may exist (though to live with them might drive one to murder or suicide). All the same I am much more interested in creatures of this world; and much prefer those writers of fiction (or drama) whose psychology really convinces me—such as Ibsen, Chekhov, or Maupassant.

But not only must the characters of fiction, and their feelings, seem true; they must also seem to matter. I grudge a single minute to the emotions of flatworms, or the trivial agonies incurred by over-delicate and under-employed personages from sitting on crumpled rose-leaves. Even a master like Proust tends at times, I feel, to fuss excessively with splitting psychological straws, picking up pins, and incatenating fleas. Still more Henry James. Exquisite sensitiveness may be well enough; but it can become morbid, like the gouty toes of eighteenth-century gentry—the penalty of being too well-to-do, with too little to do.

It may be that the modern novel has come to live dangerously near the frontiers of science—an uncomfortable neighbour. Once philosophy was a province of poetry. But poets tend to be poor philosophers, and philosophers poor poets; consequently, with the growth of specialization, the philosophers soon hunted the poets, as frivolous amateurs, off their territory. Something not wholly unlike might happen between psychologists and novelists; the novelists in their turn might likewise find themselves mocked as frivolous amateurs. Even now I believe that, if it is human nature one really wants to know about, one can learn far more from the case-histories of a good psychoanalyst than from legions of novels. Psychologists' theories are still often fantasies; but their recorded facts are reasonably reliable—and at times both staggeringly strange and amazingly revealing.

For all these reasons I hardly read six novels a year. Were I a person of leisure, the total might rise to four times as many; but I doubt it; even at the risk of being torn in pieces by wild novelists.

*   *   *

As compared with fiction, there seem certain advantages in drama. Like the short story, it is a form less wordy, and more concentrated, than the novel (which is terribly subject to elephantiasis). For few audiences will endure more than a couple of hours. Again, drama is rather less liable than fiction to fool about with obscurities and eccentricities; partly because drama, like architecture, is a costly art and imposes *some* caution; partly because drama fails unless it succeeds, at once, in pleasing simultaneously a quantity of persons highly diverse in quality. Further, the dramatist cannot, like the novelist, indulge in prolix analyses of his ideas and characters—they must speak for themselves.

True, good acting is rare, and the theatre less convenient than a chair. But good plays are no worse for being read. Often they are better. Comedy, no doubt (for instance *The Merry Wives* or *The Alchemist*), can gain a lot from actors who know their stage-business. Similarly with more serious plays not of the first rank. But with the best drama it may be hard to find producers and actors good enough. Here the ideal would be both to see and to read. But I seem to have got more from the best of Aeschylus, Shakespeare, or Ibsen in the study than on the stage. Though this may be largely a matter of personal preference. (And now perhaps I shall be rent also by angry actors.)

*   *   *

Then there is biography—one of the most precious of all forms of literature, if it is human nature that one most cares to know. But a difficult art. It requires not only a good biographer but a good biographee—that is to say, a personage who has character; who is not too remote, nor too unimportant, nor too inactive; who is known about in sufficient detail, including things he has himself said or written. For people's actions (even if it is certain that they did them) are often less revealing (for they may have had a dozen motives) than their own words and style. Thus Queen Victoria was, for all these reasons, a most excellent subject; and it was from her that Lytton Strachey made perhaps his finest book. Whereas Queen Elizabeth remains a little too remote and enigmatic for a really satisfying biography; her portrait tends to become either too romantic or too dull.

It is, indeed, sometimes curious how much more alive a man may become when dead, in a book, than he ever seemed to one, when living, in the flesh—unless one was as intimate with him as Boswell with Johnson. And yet this is natural enough. Even persons of some note may not be brilliant, or even tolerable talkers. In a few casual meetings such a character has probably neither the time, nor the wish, nor the power to strip bare his past experiences, or his present feelings. One has seen only his mask—or one of his masks—through a mask of one's own. Yet most people seem to take far more trouble to meet live lions, or even monkeys, than to study a dead lion through a Life of him—though the dead lion may offer a far more extensive and intensive view. When two gentlemen called full of ardour to see the great Professor Porson, he ironically ordered candles so that they could see him better. It may be doubted if they saw much. Whereas the life of Porson makes astonishing reading. Biography seems to me a greatly undervalued form, considering how much knowledge it can bring of a kind supremely worth knowing.

*   *   *

History, as de Tocqueville pointed out long ago, has tended to be seen by aristocratic societies and individuals as a process dominated by great personalities; whereas more democratic communities, familiar with the comparative impotence of the common man, have regarded history rather as an inevitable working out of general movements and impersonal forces (as in Marxism). A similar tendency perhaps exists in fiction and drama. And perhaps in all these fields the tendency has to-day become a little overdone. Mass-men may dislike and decry the individual; but one wonders if the 'inevitable' forces of the twentieth century might have not found some markedly different 'inevitability' without (for example) Lenin, Hitler, or Churchill.

The history, then, that seems worth while to me generally deals with persons rather than things—unless the things are ideas as living as those of Montesquieu or de Tocqueville. One of the most abominable books, for instance, that I ever failed to read was *The Shorter*

Cambridge Medieval History. Page after page, it piled up dead facts, of a quantity that no brain could hold, and of a quality that no decent brain would wish to—all rammed on one another like Tamburlain's pyramid of skulls, with not one living face to be seen. Everything was so abbreviated that the whole thing could well have been abbreviated still further, into eight words—'They were born; they were wretches; they died.' It might serve for reference, like a dictionary; but for nothing else. The true life is in details. The substance of a man may be boiled down to the compass of a bottle; but by then the real substance of the man is gone. The ideal historian, I believe, should also be a philosopher, a poet, and a psychologist. But few historians seem good enough psychologists—not even Macaulay or Michelet. In the past century history has had to be rewritten in the light of new economic knowledge; in the century to come it may have to be rewritten again in the light of new psychological understanding.

*   *   *

With psychology we come to the stern frontier of science; though perhaps only, as yet, to the frontier. For psychology is still a young science, with a good deal of chaotic babble and confusion. But though the theories of Freud may prove in some ways as primitively inadequate as those of Copernicus, Galileo, and Newton, they may prove no less historic. For no science seems likely to become more important— or more perilous. Man has an equal genius for discovering knowledge and for abusing it; and if the tyrannies of the twentieth century have become in some ways more terrifying than any before, it is partly because they have learnt to make use, even if only a fumbling use, of psychology. Anyone who is a bad practical psychologist may succeed well enough in most sciences; but he is likely to do little good in fiction, drama, biography, history, oratory, or politics. He cannot be trusted in philosophy; particularly in ethics, which has long been bedevilled by crass ignorance of human nature. And he is likely to flounder badly in economics, or sociology. Bad psychology is the quicksand which undermines Plato and Marx.

No doubt this field of psychology is dangerous and confusing for the layman. Yet I seem seldom to have spent time better (though I take in general no great pleasure in reading German) than in ploughing through the voluminous case-histories of Wilhelm Stekel; who stands out, for me, partly because he gives a far greater proportion than most writers on his subject to concrete individual instances in practice, as contrasted with general theories. It is the instances that the sceptic seeks and values. The thousands of pages left by Freud and Stekel bring home, above all, both the pitiable irrationality of the human mind and the vital need to view and treat that irrationality with the coolest rationalism.

*   *   *

Then there is science in general. It has become the Colossus of our modern world between whose bulging legs we creep. Constantly we are adjured to read more of it. Certainly let us read it. But some of these counsels do not seem wholly reasonable.

We are told, for example (to quote Sir Charles Snow, one of the most rational of scientists), that it is as uncultured not to be able to describe the Second Law of Thermodynamics as not to have read any Shakespeare.

At this I draw a deep breath. Let us leave aside the word 'culture' which has been defiled by literary prigs and aesthetic snobs; the question is whether the thoughts and feelings involved in understanding the Second Law are really as valuable—add as much to life—go to make as admirable a type of person—as the thoughts and feelings involved in understanding Shakespeare.

Both the Second Law and Shakespeare make one think. Which is valuable. Knowledge of the Second Law also satisfies the emotion of curiosity; but are not the emotions roused and satisfied by Shakespeare rather wider, deeper, more varied, and more valuable? There is also, we are told, aesthetic beauty in some mathematical and scientific reasonings; but to appreciate this may well require more specialized expertise than most of us can hope to attain.

'Your values', it may be replied, 'are merely subjective preferences.' In the short run, yes. But preferences have also consequences. One may enjoy pleasure P; but not perhaps the effects of P. After the bottle, sometimes, the headache. To put it as concretely as possible—which would one sooner choose as friend or companion for life, other things equal, a man or woman who knew all about entropy, or one who could fully feel *Hamlet* or *Antony and Cleopatra*? Might not the entropist, however admirable, risk turning out a little cruder and rawer, more insensitive and ununderstanding in personal relations—in a word, prosaic? Could such a one—

> Minister to a minde diseas'd,
> Plucke from the Memory a rooted Sorrow,
> Raze out the written troubles of the Braine,
> And with some sweet Oblivious Antidote
> Cleanse the stufft bosome of that perilous stuffe
> Which weighs upon the heart?

Let us by all means try to make the best of both worlds, science and art. But the cause of science is hardly helped by the present tendency to exaggerate the spiritual blessings of being able to define 'mass' or 'acceleration', or to describe the beauties of the Yang-Lee experiment. One might urge a scientist to read Homer; but why on earth should he be expected to master the details of the digamma or the Aeolic dialect?

What matters for the ordinary reader is the broad results of science —often beautiful, often astonishing, sometimes gruesome; not the detailed processes by which they are attained. The idea, for example, of the expanding universe is extraordinary; but it is the conception that matters, to most of us, not the mathematics.

The world is in some ways like an incredible factory full of inconceivably elaborate machines. But men remain more than machines. One is wise to know *something* of motor-car engines; but one would be a fool to spend three months in a garage learning intricate repairs which, under the division of labour, it is far better to have done by a mechanic. For with the time and energy thus fribbled away one might have done something less philistine, like making an acquaintance with Chinese literature, or walking round Greece.

So let us by all means read science. But let the scientists not badger us to read them overmuch. They are doing too much harm as it is, in England at least, by over-specializing the young. There are too many other fascinating chapters in the Book of Life into which it is a pity never to have dipped. And there are too few mortals able to realize that they are not immortal, or willing to do that simple arithmetic which tells us how little we have time on earth to do. Nature remains, I feel, not only less interesting (that is a personal taste), but also less important to know, than human nature.

For the Nature revealed by natural science seems not so much majestic, or beautiful, or wonderful, even, as infinitely odd. She gives the impression, if for clarity one momentarily personifies her, of a wild Romantic, loving infinite extravagance, in both senses of the word;

here fantastically lavish, there grudgingly niggard; here incredibly vast, there incredibly minute; here inconceivably hot, there inconceivably cold. True, she sometimes punishes excess—if a species grows too bulky, or too specialized, or too heavily armoured, she ruthlessly treads it out; and only a few fossils survive to tell that it ever walked the earth, or saw the light. But for such human qualities as measure, moderation, mercy, Nature seems to have little use. 'But you too', she might reply, 'are my children, your qualities too come from me.' All the same, we are unnatural and rebellious children; all our civilizations are a defiance of her, which she tolerates until one of them goes a step too far—and then she sometimes wipes it from the world.

So the Nature-worship of minds like Wordsworth or Meredith remains, for me, hard to understand. Nature seems far less worshipful than bizarre; like the many-breasted Diana of the Ephesians. And odiously callous. The Magnificat of Job is magnificent; but the poet of Job very carefully selected the marvels he invites men to admire. The bands of Orion, the sweet influence of the Pleiades are imposing enough; but mixed with such sublimities there are all the mean little tricks and cruelties that Nature stoops to. Consider, for instance, the wiggly snail. The snail picks up from birds' droppings on the grass a certain parasite; once safe inside the snail, the guest ingeniously swells out its host's horns, so that they can no longer be withdrawn inside the protecting shell; turns them to gaudy colours; and makes them wiggle. Some foolish bird, attracted by this flamboyant advertisement, makes a meal off the snail, and starts the parasite's eggs off again on another round of their eternal cycle.

If one applied to this little masterpiece of diabolical ingenuity Paley's argument about the Watch and the Watchmaker, and his inference from creation to Creator, the conclusion might not be very edifying. One might begin to wonder if the wisely shaping goddess of Wordsworth and Meredith were not perhaps more like an inventive genius declined into sadistic second-childhood. But this is the sort of grotesque impasse in which science frequently leaves us landed; hence, in part, my preference for humanity and the humanities.

Like Wordsworth, Hardy could turn for lessons to a vernal wood.

> Heart-halt and spirit-lame,
> City-opprest,
> Into this wood I came
> As to a nest;

> Dreaming that sylvan peace
> Offered the harrowed ease—
> Nature a soft release
> From men's unrest.

But Hardy's conclusion was very different from Wordsworth's (which seems to me also true in its degree; but much less profoundly true, being too Panglossy).

> But having entered in,
> Great growths and small
> Show them to men akin—
> Combatants all!
> Sycamore shoulders oak,
> Bines the slim sapling yoke,
> Ivy-spun halters choke
> Elms stout and tall. . . .

> Since, then, no grace I find
> Taught me of trees,
> Turn I back to my kind
> Worthy as these.
> There at least smiles abound,
> There discourse trills around,
> There, now and then, are found
> Life-loyalties.

Science can be fascinating, like a visit to some desert with its hidden life of toad and centipede, spider and scorpion; but too often the fascination is chilled by a sense of futility, disgust, even revolt. Too often the ingenuity is blended with brutality; the beauty with horror. Not there would I fix my home.

*   *   *

And *how* should one read? In youth there may be much in favour of roving widely at random. Young years can be *Wanderjahre*, spent exploring in search of one's real self and one's real tastes. But later, when one has found oneself, there may come a time for more system— for reading groups of books on a given subject rather than rushing after whatever has just fallen piping hot from the press. New books, like new bread, are of course more appetizing; but there may be better diets. To have read the latest literary wonders may enable one to prattle at tea-parties; but, had one only waited a year, they might all have blown over, like last year's leaves. And is it kind to one's mind to cram it higgledy-piggledy with whatever is just out; much as if a monthly van came and shot pell-mell into one's cellar sardines and skipping-ropes, sugar and seed-potatoes, coal and looking-glasses? There is surely the same drawback here as with those periodicals, learned and unlearned, which cram the reader with a hotch-potch of information, and leave in the most orderly mind an impression only of chaos.

If one reads with a definite purpose—say, to lecture or write—that of itself introduces a certain logical pattern. The drawback here, I find, is that I have been driven to read hundreds of books not really worth reading, while there remain hundreds of far better ones I have left unread—and now I shall never live to read them.

Still, there are some compensations. If one writes as well as reads, there results a balance of imports by exports which makes, I think, as much for the healthy comfort and well-being of a mind as of a community. For if one only reads, one may soon come to feel like a stuffed animal. Again, I have now a more coherent knowledge of a few topics; indeed, I begin to feel as if one only began to know something of a subject when one has been to the pains of writing a book about it. But in that case, life being so short, one can know terribly little. Besides, the more one learns of a subject, the more one sees how much one has left unlearnt. As the building grows, so does its shadow.

However, it will be all the same in a few years' time. And, looking back, I realize that I never enjoyed reading more than when writing *From Many Times and Lands*. To be able to read up connectedly, with an abundant library at hand, things like Egyptian or pre-Islamic Arab literature, or Chinese or Persian poetry, or the history of Genghiz or Tsar Ivan, made me realize what unsuspected treasure lies off the beaten track. I had the pleasures of a truant vagabond, for my real field was English; and yet it was not really truancy, since all literature is, in the end, one.

I would add that it seems to me as natural and necessary to keep notes, however brief, of one's reading, as logs of voyages or photographs of one's travels. For memory, in most of us, is a liar with galloping consumption.

*   *   *

And *how much* should one read? It is not so easy to hit the happy mean. One may have too little taste for reading, and fail to acquire more; as is happening, I suspect, with many of the modern young. Or one may lose the taste, from over-preoccupation with other activities; as Sir Robert Walpole in the tussle of politics, or Darwin wrestling with species. In later life H. G. Wells told Arnold Bennett that he was losing his capacity to read; and excused it by eyestrain. But, added Bennett, who recognized the same symptom in himself, 'It isn't his eyes.' It was age and over-writing. In such a plight I should feel like a witch robbed of her broomstick.

On the other hand most of us know people who read too much. 'Le livre', wrote Anatole France, 'est l'opium de l'Occident. Il nous dévore. Un jour viendra où nous serons tous bibliothécaires, et ce sera fini.' We may feel that those days of Anatole France were a happy time indeed, if men had nothing worse to fear than this exaggerated menace. Still the race of over-readers has a long, if not much honoured descent. Antiquity already produced such portents as Didymus (c. 80–10 B.C.), nicknamed 'the brazen-bowelled' because of all the works he had consumed, and 'the book-forgetter' because he forgot what his own works contained (not inexcusably, since he is credited with writing 3,500 or 4,000 of them; now all lost except for fragments). Then there was Hermogenes, so famous for his erudition at fifteen that he was presented to the Emperor Marcus Aurelius; but imbecile by twenty-five, so that he was a man in his youth and in his manhood a child; and was found, when he died in old age—a nicely horrid touch —to have his heart covered with hair! There was the Elder Pliny, who used to begin work at one or two on winter mornings; had books read to him even while being scraped and rubbed after his bath; was attended by a secretary even in his litter; and rebuked his nephew, the Younger Pliny, for wasting time by walking—to such effect that when Vesuvius erupted and the uncle lost his life in scientific curiosity, the nephew foolishly lost much of that historic spectacle by sitting on in his study, still scribbling.

The Renaissance in its turn produced book-devourers no less pro-digious, like the great Casaubon; Scaliger, with his thirteen languages; Huet, Bishop of Avranches, who had read everything, and ploughed through the Bible, in Hebrew, twenty-four times.

Yet one suspects that such monsters of erudition got far less from life, very often, than the truant and scandalous Wandering Scholars of the Middle Ages.

Souls, like poor moths, too often moulder
Crushed within tomes—as spring grows older,
    Take the road!
April's sweet smile grows never older;
Lighter our hearts, when again our shoulder
    Lifts its load.

Come, Juvenal! Come, Cicero!
Trudge! Where we part, no man may know,
    Comrades divine!
I diced Dan Ovid at Saint-Lô,
My subtle Senek—by Bordeaux
    He paid my wine.

Bacchus, Venus movent bella
Suaviora quam sunt mella.
    North and South,
From Canterbury to Compostella,
I have tasted many a cellar,
    Many a mouth.

Books and the road, they make man wise;
Folly he learns from woman's eyes;
    Be mine all three!
Wide still the world before us lies—
Keep each poor scholar till he dies,
    Fair Trinity!

Chaucer too knew how to hold the balance. The eagle might tax him with going straight from his books at the Custom-house to other books at home—

    Thou gost hom to thy hous anoon,
    And, also domb as any stoon,
    Thou sittest at another book
    Tyl fully daswed is thy look.

But Chaucer had sense enough to pursue half a dozen other occupations also; not forgetting the open road to Canterbury.

Hobbes, who observed that if he had read as much as other men, he would have known as little, has made, and keeps, more of a name in the world than the omnivorous Huet. And the warning of Boileau has not lost its point—

Que les vers ne soient pas votre éternel emploi.
Cultivez vos amis, soyez homme de foi:
C'est peu d'être agréable et charmant dans un livre;
Il faut savoir encore et converser et vivre.

Boileau would not have approved one of the most picturesque figures in my Cambridge memories, now vanished—a most worthy professor who, the better to concentrate on his beloved erudition, hid himself in a hermitage next a public-house, far out on the Newmarket side of the town. When an ex-pupil, now an antipodean Bishop, had searched out the house and rung in vain, he consulted (so rumour told) the adjoining publican. ''E don't want to see yer', replied that worthy. ''E's writin' 'is books. 'E's thrown 'is doorbell in the brook.' Eventually the Bishop, taking Heaven by storm, forced his way in through the boothole window; and was discovered by his old master floundering in a sea of boots.

But this seems carrying the love of learning over-far.

The secret, I suppose, of finding the best balance between life and books—a difficult one—is to hit the point where reading ceases to increase the aliveness of one's life, and begins to lessen it. For life is lessened when books start to encroach on real experience. The ageing d'Alembert, weary of mathematics and philosophy, murmured regretfully—'Je n'ai pas été assez galant.' Perhaps he was right (though he might have been only unhappier—Julie de Lespinasse cost him pain enough). Ibsen seems to have felt the same. And I have heard a similar regret attributed to Bernard Shaw. Again over-reading can seriously sap vitality, as Montaigne was acutely aware: 'Les livres ont beaucoup de qualitez agreables à ceulx qui les sçavent choisir: mais aulcun bien sans peine; c'est un plaisir qui n'est pas net et pur, non plus que les aultres; il a ses incommoditez, et bien poisantes: l'ame s'y exerce, mais le corps, duquel ie n'ay non plus oublié le soing, demeure cependant sans action, s'atterre, et s'attriste. Ie ne sçache excez plus dommageable pour moi, ny plus à eviter, en cette declinaison d'aage.'

On the other hand, though they cannot compete with the most vivid moments of active living, books can heighten these and to some extent replace them. The first moment when I saw, at sixteen, the white curve of the Matterhorn against the blue sky above an unseen Italy was more intense than anything in books; yet it would not have seemed so miraculous but for the nineteenth-century writers who first realized the magic of Alpine sun and snow. The first time I saw the cloud-topped mountain-ridges of Acroceraunia from the Adriatic, or the Leucadian Promontory white with sun and storm, or Hymettus, purpled with sunset, from the Saronic Sea, was something intenser even than poetry. But the same shapes and colours would not have seemed the same in New Zealand or the Rockies. Half their transfigured splendour came from the poetry of two thousand years before, or the memory of that other sunset on Hymettus when the hemlock was brought to Socrates.

Books can still wield the magic powers of Michael Scott, or Faustus, or Prospero. Eyes that never read, remain blind to the phantom dead and to the unseen presences that walk the earth—cannot call up the past world to redress the troubled balance of the present—cannot move, like Persephone, both amid the fleeting beauty of the living spring and among the ghostly meadows of eternal asphodel.

> Among my roses, under my apple-tree,
>   I sat with Milton. By us stole the hours.
> I glanced up—at the pomp of Poetry,
>   Her groaning greatness, her tormented powers,
> Mortal beside her immortality,
>   Smiled the flowers.

But though the rose may smile disdainfully at the poet, she would have been less beautiful without Propertius, Ausonius, and Omar, Ronsard, Shakespeare, and Herrick. And when the rose-petals have fallen and mouldered, even amid December frosts the books remain. They escape, a little, from the tyrannies of place and time. A book, runs the Persian saying, is like a garden in the pocket.

Living eyes can hold a light lovelier even than that Venus of Botticelli who floats in her pensive beauty over a flower-strewn sea. But their gaze can gain a still deeper loveliness by association with hers; and when they have been dimmed by the dust of Time, and one more golden head has turned silver, the Venus of Botticelli still endures. The beauty that we can possess is mortal; the beauty that is immortal we cannot possess. Yet each can make the other deeper and more intense. And as the years pass, we may come to feel that it is the seeming dead of art and literature who are really alive; and we, the seeming living, who remain only the flitting phantoms of a transient mortality.

'Fool's-errand to the Grave': the Personality and Poetry of Housman

AFTER a quarter of a century the ghost of Housman can hardly be said to be very lively in Cambridge. For Classical scholars, no doubt, he remains a formidable ancestor; but for years together the English Tripos has often shown no sign of being aware that a poet called Housman ever existed; and I suspect that he is little read by the academic young.

This might be attributed to a certain east-windy chill in the Cambridge climate, which even two centuries ago could make Gray write ironically to Walpole, of his Eton Ode: 'I promise you, few take to it here at all, which is a good sign (for I never knew anything liked here, that ever proved to be so anywhere else).' Cambridge may be geographically flat; but intellectually a lot of it lies at the glacial altitudes of the higher brow.

Indeed Housman himself could remark (though of course he was being humorously naughty): 'After having been at Cambridge for twenty years, I realize that it is an asylum in every sense of the word.' And again—'The kindest action the Dons have ever done me has been never to mention my poems.'

But one may suspect that the general attitude to Housman is much the same at Oxford also, and in England generally. Current fashions in poetry and criticism have pushed him far down the precipices of Parnassus. It may quite well be that he still sells pretty steadily—for the intelligent public and the critical pundits are often, I believe (especially after going into the sales of Tennyson), far further apart than the pundits usually realize.[1] But the views of the intelligent general reader, though it is these that really matter most, remain silent and subterranean; for years now I have not come across any critical enthusiasm for Housman, except in a scholar who writes to me from remote Japan.

[1] Cf. Proust: 'Il y a plus d'analogie entre la vie instinctive du public et le talent d'un grand écrivain qui n'est qu'un instinct réligieusement écouté, au milieu du silence imposé à tout le reste, un instinct perfectionné et compris, qu'avec *le verbiage superficiel et les critères changeants des juges attitrés*.'

Whether this disparagement is right or wrong, I shall not discuss; believing that 'right' and 'wrong' have a clear meaning with reference to statements of fact; a hazier meaning in matters of ethics; but in questions of aesthetics no meaning whatsoever. At the influence-value of a book one can, indeed, guess: of its pleasure-value every cultivated person must judge for himself. Much of the current chatter about 'evaluation' is pretentious cant, better left to auctioneers. I shall merely try to explain why, for me, some of Housman's poetry still keeps its magic; and, still more, to understand better this tragic, intriguing personality and his strange, embittered view of life.

*　　*　　*

Alfred Edward Housman, the eldest in a family of five sons and two daughters (among them two other writers, Laurence and Clemence), was born just a century ago, in 1859, near Bromsgrove in Worcestershire. He was thus no 'Shropshire lad'. But Shropshire lay on his western horizon, golden with the magic of setting suns. And as Housman himself pointed out, Tyrtaeus the poet of ancient Sparta was likewise, according to legend, no Spartan, but an alien from Athens.

The Housman stock is said to have originated from Flemish immigrants named 'Haussman', who had crossed to Yorkshire by the fourteenth century, and moved into Lancashire by 1500. On his mother's side the poet came from the Devonshire Drakes, whose arms bore a symbolic dragon (Drake—Draco). Certainly the great Sir Francis himself was hardly more dragonish to Spanish dons than his descendant to the dons of universities—especially in Germany.

The poet's father was a Bromsgrove solicitor, not very successful in business, nor strong in character, who seems in later years to have grown both impoverished and bibulous. Probably Housman owed more mentally (as happens commonly enough) to his mother, the daughter of a divine of some intellectual distinction, Dr John Williams.

But on his twelfth birthday his mother died.

Over all that long reticence which was Housman's life there hangs a mystery unlikely ever to be dispelled. Was this early blow in boyhood the real beginning of his lifelong gloom? It may well have contributed a good deal; even if inborn temperament contributed still more. For this wife of a not very satisfactory husband had taken her eldest son for confidant; and perhaps that maternal figure, so prematurely lost, never wholly relaxed its hold on him. We know better now the dangers of a mother's influence that is never fully outgrown—how enduring love for the woman who gave him life can lead a man, paradoxically enough, to care most for that other love which seems 'passing the love of women'.

Even at eight years old, by Housman's own account, Lemprière's Classical Dictionary had 'attached my affections to paganism'. Now, at thirteen, he became a deist; at twenty-one, the atheist that he remained.

Like the young Rossettis, the young Housmans had an intellectual vitality that made poetry-writing a family amusement. Alfred would set his younger brothers and sisters to compose. At thirteen, for example, he prescribed them the theme of 'Death'—one stanza each. The subject sounds sombre enough—especially in a home so recently made motherless. And the shadow of Death was to brood insistently over Housman's poetry to the end. Yet one must not exaggerate. For we are told that the poem which resulted on this occasion moved Alfred and the elders of the family to roars of laughter. It is largely this changeful mixture of gaiety and gloom, of ironic wit and melancholia, that helps to make Housman, all his life, so elusively hard to grasp. But perhaps he who created Hamlet and the Gravediggers would have understood.

Housman's own boyish verses seem equally precocious in their sadness and in their technical skill. Here, for example, is part of a song from a drama on *The Execution of Lady Jane Gray*, set for the Family Magazine which he edited—a song for the eve of the scaffold:

> Breathe, my lute, beneath my fingers
>   One regretful breath,
> One lament for life that lingers
>   Round the doors of death.

And here is part of a poem called 'Summer':

> Summer! and after Summer what?
> Ah! happy trees that know it not,
> Would that with us it might be so.
> And yet the broad-flung beechtree heaves
> Through all its slanting layers of leaves
> With something like a sigh. Ah no!
> 'Tis but the wind that with its breath
> To them so softly murmureth;

For them hath still new sweets in store
And sings new music evermore;
Only to us its tones seem sighs,
Only to us it prophesies
Of coming autumn, coming death.

Each time the closing word is 'death'. Soon after, at Oxford, the pictures on Housman's walls were to be Dürer's 'Melancholia' and 'The Knight, Death, and the Devil'. Of course it is common enough for juvenile poets—like the young Tennyson—to write as if they were already ninety, and encamped, with both feet in the grave, in a Vale of Bones. All the same the boyish melancholy of the young Housman seems to me beyond the common. So does his promise.

Along with his lifelong sadness, there already appears in this early work his lifelong love for biting irony and mocking anticlimax—

An acorn tumbled from the oak,
Who knows how many years ago,
How many years of nights and days?
Perhaps when over woodland ways
The hoary Druid came and broke
The consecrated mistletoe.

And now the oak-tree throws a shadow
And bears an acorn of its own,
That ripens in its fairy cup,
Looking at heaven; and being grown
Falls rustling to the autumn meadow;
And pigs arise and eat it up.

But there was too, side by side with these poems of youthful gloom, plenty of high-spirited nonsense-verse, as gay as that rather later, and most admirable, parody of Greek Tragedy printed when Housman was twenty-four. If a thunder-cloud hung even over his youth, its edges were still brightly sunlit.

In 1874 there reveals itself another characteristic trait. Of a visit to London the boy of fifteen writes to his stepmother (for his father had now taken, as second wife, a cousin of fifty): 'But I think, of all I have seen, what has impressed me most is the Guards. This may be barbarian, but it is true.' To the end, soldiers were to enjoy a somewhat bizarre prominence in Housman's verse.

In 1877 he went to St John's, Oxford, and there met M. J. Jackson, scientist and athlete, who was to become for him rather what Hallam had been for Tennyson at Cambridge, nearly fifty years before. In 1879 Housman duly got his first in Mods. But in 1881 occurred that other mystery, his failure in Greats. The simple explanation seems that he cared little for ancient history, and even less for ancient philosophy. Already his real interests were textual, and he was busy emending Propertius. And so, just as in mathematical Cambridge the headstrong young Wordsworth had refused to grind at mathematics, so the headstrong young Housman seems to have defied the authorities of Oxford to make him read historians and philosophers. Possibly he relied too confidently on getting through by his general classical knowledge alone; possibly he had spent too many hours in the company of his friend Jackson, who was easily sure of his own first in science; possibly there were emotional tangles now undiscoverable.

At all events, in the exam he left a number of questions not even attempted; and so failed. As Raleigh put it, 'the nightingale got no prize at the poultry show'. But, after all, this image seems more amusing than true, or fair to Oxford. The analogy does not really work. Nightingales do not take part in poultry shows; nor is Oxford a mere poultry-yard. But Housman *was* a scholar as well as a poet; and at this particular show, had he chosen, he could have been cock of the walk. Whether the real reason was heedlessness, pride, or self-punishment, he wantonly ran his own head against a painful stone-wall. And one may note that, persistently and implacably though Housman denounced the injustice of the Universe, he never seems to have complained of any injustice from the University.

None the less, in a family now impoverished, the blow was bitter. It cost Housman himself ten years as a minor civil servant in the Patent Office, starting at only £100 a year; and none knows how much silent mortification it cost him as well.

However, with really strong characters defects, or defeats, are often over-compensated. Just as the stammering Demosthenes made himself at last the paragon of orators, so this rejected classical candidate proceeded to make himself in his spare hours a portent of Latin scholarship; so much so that in 1892 he found easy access to the Chair of Latin at University College, London. Indeed, after his Oxford failure, Housman's career became almost monotonously simple—ten years (1882–92) in the Patent Office; eighteen (1892–1911) as Professor in London; twenty-six (1911–36) as Professor at Cambridge.

But there were also other, bitterer dates that have left muted echoes in his verse. In 1887 his close friend Jackson, with whom he had lodged in London and worked in the Patent Office, left England to become head of a college in remote Karachi, and finally to die at Vancouver in 1923.[1]

> He would not stay for me; and who can wonder?
> He would not stay for me to stand and gaze.
> I shook his hand and tore my heart in sunder
> And went with half my life about my ways.

In 1892 Jackson's younger brother Adalbert, to whom Housman was also devoted, died of typhoid.[2] In 1901 his own youngest brother fell in the South African War.[3]

Meanwhile his work went on—in addition to learned articles, the five books of *Manilius* (1903–30); *Juvenal* (1905); *Lucan* (1926). The first edition of *A Shropshire Lad* (1896) took over two years to sell its 500 copies; and brought him £2 5s. 3d.[4] Though steadily reprinted by Grant Richards, it seems to have won wide popularity only in the changed atmosphere of the First World War. Things went very differently with *Last Poems* (1922), of which 21,000 copies were printed by the end of two and a half months.

Finally, on May Eve, 1936, the troubles of that proud and angry dust found their final peace. His ashes were laid, in earth from his Worcestershire home, under the north wall of Ludlow Church.

> Between the trees in flower
> New friends at fairtime tread
> The way where Ludlow tower
> Stands planted on the dead.

---

[1] Jackson's marriage in 1889 seems to have inspired Housman's 'Epithalamium' (*Last Poems*, xxiv); though this piece was apparently not finished till long after, in 1922.

[2] Remembered in *More Poems*, xli, xlii.

> Strange, strange to think his blood is cold
> And mine flows easy on;
> And that straight look, that heart of gold,
> That grace, that manhood gone.

[3] Cf. *L.P.*, xvii; *M.P.*, xl.

> [4] I hoed and trenched and weeded,
> And took the flowers to fair:
> I brought them home unheeded;
> The hue was not the wear.

> Our thoughts, a long while after,
> They think, our words they say;
> Theirs now's the laughter,
> The fair, the first of May.

* * *

As a personality Housman remains enigmatic, because he seemed to possess several personalities, not easy for an outsider to reconcile. For there was Housman the relentless scholar; Housman the social gorgon, who could freeze men to stone; Housman the epicure, as precisely fastidious about food and wine as about the purity of classical texts; Housman the gloomy, yet humorous ironist; Housman the generous helper and passionate friend; Housman the literary critic (though that title he disclaimed); and Housman the poet. One cannot understand the last of these figures without knowing something of the other six.

On Housman the scholar we have the sufficient witness of Professor Garrod (1929)—'He stands to-day the first scholar in Europe; if this country has had a greater scholar, it will be only Bentley.' Comparisons with Bentley goaded Housman himself to modest rage; though he *was* willing to be compared with Porson. Clear enough, at all events, that in his own field he ended by overtopping, not only the examiners who had once failed him, but almost every Latinist in Europe.

Yet even in his scholarship paradox remained. The main efforts of that superb brain and encyclopedic knowledge were spent on establishing the text of a poem hardly read, and largely unreadable—the astrological epic of Manilius, edited through half a lifetime (1903–30). True, this poetic Roman astrologer, who lived in the years of the Star of Bethlehem, but is mainly remarkable for his knack of being simultaneously metrical and arithmetical, does also rise at moments to real eloquence. But it was not for such literary qualities that Housman as scholar cared. Indeed, if my memory is correct, he once began a course on Lucretius VI by saying he had chosen this Sixth Book because it possessed no literary qualities to distract one from the pure problems of the text.

His Cambridge lectures I found impressive, but repellent. The lecturer himself, immaculate in his starched linen and icy in his impassive aloofness as the Pole Star, seemed the awesome embodiment of a steely, mathematical precision; but his faith that *all* knowledge was precious, whether or no it served the slightest human use, revolted me then, as it revolts me still. I imagine I might have felt the same rebellious repugnance in listening to the great Calvin preaching, with inflexible, yet absurd logic, on Predestination at Geneva. I sensed something morbid and unhealthy in this formidable ascetic pressing into his own skin the harsh folds of his intellectual hair-shirt. It seemed too like the brilliant perversity of Pascal. All things may in the end be vanity; but meanwhile some things seem much vainer than others. If anything matters, it is surely not knowledge in itself, but mental states and processes that we can value. For a healthy mind, life remains, I feel, too precious, and too brief, to be spent on futilities, even if they are facts; on trivialities, even if they are true. Poor Shenstone was himself an inferior poet; but he deserves to be remembered at least for his wise remark, too often disregarded still, that 'it is idle to be assiduous in the perusal of inferior poetry'. I have no use for remorse—itself one of the worst of futilities; but looking back on life, I think perhaps my greatest mistake has been to spend too much of it on the perusal of inferior books— largely of the learned kind. For there are a great many works of erudition of which one can only say that it is an outrage to ask any decent brain to swallow, let alone absorb them. We are far too careless of our mental diet.

Further, with this passion for collecting and establishing facts that seemed often worth no more than rotten apples, Housman combined a passion, no less puzzling, for scalping bad scholars with the ferocity of an Iroquois. At times he recalled that Renaissance type of inhuman humanist who would write to some rival, in boiling ink—'May God confound you for your theory of impersonal verbs!' Indeed, some of us who could not have cared less about textual cruces in Manilius or Lucan, would frivolously scan Housman's prefaces for the entertaining violence of their invective; just as medieval Scots would laugh over the flytings of Dunbar, or old Melancholy Burton at the endearments bandied by Oxford bargemen. For example—'I imagine that Mr Buecheler, when he first perused Mr Sudhaus' edition of the Aetna, must have felt something like Sin when she gave birth to Death.' 'Among their pupils are several who comprehend neither Latin nor any other language; and whom nature has prodigally endowed at birth with that hebetude of intellect which Messrs Vahlen and Buecheler, despite their assiduous and protracted efforts, have not yet succeeded in acquiring.' 'Buecheler died in 1908, and the troop of little dogs which trotted at his heels was scattered abroad in quest of other heels to trot at.

These were soon found.' 'Not only had Jacob no sense for grammar, no sense for coherency, no sense for sense, but being himself possessed by a passion for the clumsy and the hispid he imputed this disgusting taste to all the authors whom he edited.' The conservative critic 'believes that the text of ancient authors is generally sound, not because he has acquainted himself with the elements of the problem, but because he would feel uncomfortable if he did not believe it; just as he believes, on the same cogent evidence, that he is a fine fellow, and that he will rise again from the dead'. 'Critics who treat MS evidence as rational men treat all evidence, and test it by reason and by the knowledge they have acquired, these are blamed for rashness and capriciousness by gentlemen who use MSS as drunkards use lamp-posts,—not to light them on their way but to dissimulate their instability.' Or again, in oral circulation, there was that couplet on the mares' nests of the perversely ingenious Verrall (who does not lack counterparts among the Shakespearian critics of to-day)—

> When Verrall's roaming footsteps fieldward fare,
> Quakes for her callow young the brooding mare.

Verrall sometimes deserved that. Yet, even as vitriol, the vitriol was not always worthy of its author's intellect. To observe, for instance, that Herr Elias Stoeber came from Strasbourg, 'a city famous for its geese', was something that Johnson too might have said in conversation, but that Johnson would probably have considered too puerile to print. And the wonder grows when one finds that Housman even stored up in his notebooks an arsenal of little barbed remarks, all ready for discharge at peccant pedants.

It would be foolish to dwell on this strange foible in a man fundamentally kind, and at times quixotically generous. It gave a good deal of pain at the time; but it becomes unimportant now—merely a pity, and a puzzle. It is a pity because, while Housman's butts are largely forgotten, this violence does not raise his own reputation. (So wise, for once, was old Bentley in holding that a man is damaged, in the end, not by what others write, but by what he writes himself.) And it is also a puzzle. One can understand well enough that shoddy thinking could exasperate that clear brain as excruciatingly as bad playing can exasperate a sensitive musician. (Did not Lulli sometimes break the fiddles of his players over their own heads?—though his fundamental kindliness would console them with new instruments afterwards.) Yet even so, such violent rage seems out of all proportion. It is galling enough punishment for the average scholar to be confuted, without being also insulted into the bargain. I suspect that a lot of pent-up pain within himself lay behind Housman's passion for inflicting it on erudite incompetents.[1]

Similarly with Housman the social gorgon. If he often made others suffer, it was that he himself suffered agonies of shy self-consciousness. The nervous dog bites. 'Can *you* make him talk?' growled Robert Bridges. 'I can't.' And George Calderon, after meeting this Cambridge Sphinx, observed to Rothenstein: 'Well, William, so far from believing that man wrote *The Shropshire Lad*, I shouldn't even have thought him capable of reading it.' I can myself recall sitting through an agonizing feast at Trinity next this grey eminence thirty-five years my senior, whom I had never spoken to before, and feeling as if I were trying to conduct a conversation from the ground with St Simeon Stylites atop of his pillar. It was not only the impression Housman gave of ruthless intellect; that fastidious mouth—the mouth of the gourmet —always seemed drooping, under its drooping white moustache, with an unutterable distaste—as if the wine of life itself were corked.

No thunders fell on me then—the mountain merely remained hidden in chill, impenetrable mist. But there *were* times when Housman could be not only mute as a Trappist, but crushing as a Duchess. Wellington once observed that he himself had no small talk, and his colleague Peel no manners; there were unfortunates who might have complained that Housman was Peel and Wellington in one.

Yet this prickliness, as I have said, may well have been only the unhappy defensiveness of a spirit intensely shy, intensely sensitive, and intensely repressed. Had I known more of life, and of him, I should have boldly rushed in where angels feared to tread; reckless whether he thought my conversation nonsense or not. For when some bore departed from Trinity, and other members of its High Table were heaving loud sighs of relief, Housman quietly remarked—so I was told—'Oh, *I* liked him—he used to *talk* to me.' The child could put its hand on the hole of the asp. In the same way guileless young

---

[1] I remember once, at a trial-lecture by some candidate for a classical Chair, sitting just behind Housman, who was one of the electors; from anywhere else nothing would have been visible but the usual immobile figure and impassive face; but I could see, all the while, how on his knees his hand continually twisted, round and round, the silk tassel of his mortar-board, as if it had been the neck of some unfortunate goose.

Frenchmen and Americans could ply Housman with audacious personal questions—and actually obtain answers from him—where strong men from the highest tables in Cambridge would have sweated ice at the bare idea of such temerity.

For behind this Iron Mask was a man unhappy and poignantly affectionate; and—almost stranger still—behind the intellectual ascetic was an epicurean lover of good cheer. Housman had no great use for philosophers; but to the Stoics he preferred Epicurus; and to Epicurus himself, Aristippus the hedonist. Some were astonished to find that a person whose mental diet seemed to consist largely in chewing stones and dust, was also a delicate connoisseur of food and wine. Yet so it was. In Paris he attained a distinction that very few Englishmen can ever have won, for Monsieur Frédéric of the Tour d'Argent contrived in his honour a dish called 'barbue Housman'. (*Barbue* is a kind of turbot.) And Grant Richards's admiring volume on the poet whom he published for so long, contains pages and pages of pure gastronomy, such as—'next day, September 2, we drove to Quingay and fed at the Truite de la Loue, drinking a Pouilly Fuissé 1921, and an undated Montrachet. We did better at Besançon with a Hermitage Rochefine 1920 at the Hôtel des Bains, and a Chambertin 1915 next night *chez* Gavillon in the rue des Granges. I think we came to the conclusion that Besançon was hardly worth two nights; but that, perhaps, was due to the rain.' Poor Besançon! For bread-and-butter, on the other hand, Housman entertained such horror that it distressed him even to see people eat the stuff.

All this is extremely odd to a barbarian like myself who would rather drink water from a mountain-stream on a hot day than all the alcohol that ever came out of bottles. But one is glad that Housman found at least some intense pleasures in his lonely life. And it should be stressed that, if a *gourmet*, he was never a *gourmand*.

More human still was Housman the humorist; though the humour, naturally, tended to be drily ironic. His letters are full of an engaging *pince-sans-rire* that usefully corrects the false impression of him as a man of impenetrable gloom. He might, like Heine, see life tragically; but, like Heine, he contrived to lighten its shadows with irony and comic relief. For example—

(To Grant Richards.) 'If you go, I shall be there about nine o'clock, just drunk enough to be pleasant, but not so incapable as a publisher would like an author to be.'

(To the same, on crossing the Channel after the torpedoing of the *Sussex* in 1916.) 'After all, a quick death is preferable to a slow journey; and as I am only an author and not a publisher, I am comparatively well prepared to meet my God.'

(To the same, in 1928, with a refusal to let A. J. A. Symons include something from *A Shropshire Lad* in an anthology.) 'He may be consoled, and also amused, if you tell him that to include me in an anthology of the Nineties would be just as technically correct, and just as essentially inappropriate, as to include Lot in a book on Sodomites.'

(To Laurence Housman, on a letter from their sister Kate about *A Shropshire Lad*.) 'Kate writes to say that she likes the verse better than the sentiments. The sentiments, she then goes on to say, appear to be taken from the Book of Ecclesiastes. To prefer my versification to the sentiments of the Holy Ghost is decidedly flattering, but strikes me as a trifle impious.'

Even the night before he died, when his doctor tried to amuse him with an improper story, he remarked: 'Yes, that's a good one, and tomorrow I shall be telling it again on the Golden Floor.'

Further, as well as humour, Housman possessed humanity. From early years repressed and neurotic, he had hidden this human side of him so deep that even a member of his own family, reading the first half-dozen poems in *A Shropshire Lad*, could cry out in astonishment, 'Alfred *has* a heart!' Four words that speak worlds. But those who really knew him, knew they were true. This terror of dons could yet visit his bedmaker in her last illness, or rush off to Venice, at sixty-seven, because the one-eyed gondolier[1] he had employed on his visits there since 1900 was attacked by consumption. Housman arranged to put the man out of want for life; returned after three days; and never set foot in Venice again. Then, remembering how the great twelfth-century Campanile of St Mark, fallen in 1902, had been painfully rebuilt in the ten years that followed, he wrote (with no sign, I think, of failing powers) what must be one of the last of all his poems, on the tower that would never be rebuilt for him, and the city he would never see again.

[1] He had, improbable though this may sound for a Venetian, lost one eye by *the kick of a horse.*

From dusty wreck dispersed
Its stature mounts amain;
On surer foot than first
The belfry stands again.
At to-fall of the day
Again its curfew tolls
And burdens far away
The green and sanguine shoals.

It looks to north and south,
It looks to east and west;
It guides to Lido mouth
The steersman of Triest.
Andrea, fare you well;
Venice, farewell to thee.
The tower that stood and fell
Is not rebuilt in me.

Again, in 1914 when the War came, Housman took what many would think the bizarre step of sending to the Chancellor of the Exchequer a free gift of several hundred pounds; similarly in the financial crisis of 1931. And the few individuals who did get behind the defences of his reserve could be astonished at his kindness. Enough to quote from the letter of a fellow-clerk in the Patent Office, when Housman got his Professorship—'I like you better than any man I have ever known. There is, as far as I could ever discover, absolutely no flaw in your character, and no one would ever hope for a better friend.' A curiously un-English letter; but there seems no motive for doubting its sincerity.

Even I, who only twice in my life exchanged a word with him, got a glimpse the second time, though the circumstances were quite trivial, behind the Iron Mask. Our first meeting had been at that unhappy feast in Trinity; the second was at a feast in John's. On this occasion, though no lover of feasts, I felt more secure, for there sat as buffer between us our host, Heitland the classical historian (whose shrewd old face used to make more picturesque the streets of Cambridge with a little pointed hat above his little white beard, so that his small figure suggested a Swiss dwarf, or gnome, just emerged from the interior of a mountain, and capable of vanishing into thin air again before one's eyes). But when we rose at the end, and Heitland disappeared from between us, I was astonished to find Housman turning towards me and saying—'I have been battening on your flatteries in the weekly press.'

At this point I can hear some reader exclaiming: 'Good God! How it pays to be grumpy! Here is Housman being celebrated for doing, exceptionally and after a mellowing dinner, what any ordinary person would have done any day out of common politeness.' But it was not quite so simple. To the difficult Housman the synthetic amiabilities of social intercourse did not come easily; and there was something curiously touching about his tone that night. Johnson justly found ludicrous the reciprocal civilities of authors; but this shy poet and irritable scholar could easily have thought me an impertinent youth. For in the *New Statesman* I had been rash enough to describe his lectures—'this quiet, immaculate figure, setting straight with even-voiced, passionless, unresting minuteness the jots and tittles of a fifth-rate ancient whose whole epic was not worth one stanza of his own'. 'One came away', I had added, 'feeling as if one had been watching a disguised Apollo picking the oakum of Admetus—divinely, but oakum!' Men had been shrivelled to ashes by him for less. 'Ah,' the cynic may answer, 'but even gods like incense.' Yet to talk to Housman of his poetry, no matter with what deference, could be perilous as touching the Ark. To an unfortunate stranger at Trinity High Table, who went up and said how much *A Shropshire Lad* had meant to him in the 1914 War, had not Housman replied (in words already quoted)—'The kindest action the Dons have ever done me has been never to mention my poems'—and then turned his back? He was not, and is not, easy to understand.

There rises before my memory another figure no less remarkable, and no less enigmatic, whom I knew a little better—Lawrence of Arabia. For both were brilliant minds, ruthlessly self-repressed and elusive, who yet at moments laid bare their hearts in striking verse or prose. Nor is this parallel merely fanciful. Of himself Lawrence wrote in *The Seven Pillars of Wisdom*—'There was a craving to be liked—so strong and nervous that never could I open myself friendly to another. The terror of failure in an effort so important made me shrink from trying. . . .' In the margin of that passage Housman wrote—'This is me.'

Both men could be charmingly gay, like Johnson; but, as with Johnson, their fundamental mood was tragic, not so much with the bitterness of circumstance, as with a deeper and more incurable unhappiness of temperament. When in 1933 Housman had heart-trouble, his comment in a letter is revealing: 'The real bother is what I have often had before in my life, depression and causeless anxiety.' And he had written thirty-eight years before (September–October 1895):

> Oh, on my breast in days hereafter
> Light the earth should lie,
> Such weight to bear is now the air,
> So heavy hangs the sky.

'Causeless depression' does not mean depression uncaused—one may doubt the existence of such a thing; it means depression whose causes are locked from the conscious mind. The strange paradox that was Housman—both ungenerous and wildly generous, both kind and harsh, both humorous and joyless—cannot really be explained. Even the most modern psychology can only guess at the true explanations. But this should at least help us to avoid false ones. The cause of Housman's tragedy was not in outward events. He lived most of his life under conditions that most would think fortunate; he enjoyed the still greater good fortune of keen faculties successfully used, and strenuous labours brilliantly accomplished. Nor was the cause of his unhappiness simply in the gloom of his philosophy of life; Hume, for example, though probably still more sceptical, was yet far happier. One may suspect that before Housman was thirteen, perhaps earlier, the real harm was done.

But though we know too little to explain why he became so, this view may least help us to understand a little better the kind of person he became. Housman's fine qualities, I think, were of his essence; his faults were unhappy accidents. Somehow the crystal was flawed; but it was no common stone. Somehow the tree grew warped; but it was no ordinary tree. Of Housman could have been written, as of a very different scholar—

> Cut is the branch that might have grown full straight . . .
> That sometime grew within this learned man.

*   *   *

There remains Housman the writer—the critic and poet. The title of 'critic' he always disclaimed for himself; believing those really worthy of the name to be extremely few—rarer even than good poets and, in fact, 'the rarest of the great works of God'.

I wonder if this disclaimer is not a little wayward. One *can*, if one wishes, use the word 'critic' to mean *only* 'a superlatively good critic'.

But that is not the best way to make oneself understood by one's fellow-countrymen; for most of whom 'critic' means simply 'one who passes judgements, especially on the arts', no matter whether the judgements passed are sagacious or insane. The phrase 'a detestably bad critic' remains perfectly good English. And Housman's own use of English seems to me a little peculiar when he asserts that 'the literary critic' appears only 'once in a century, or once in two centuries'; as if he were talking of a sort of Phoenix.

One can agree, however, that superlatively good critics, or even good critics, *are* strangely rare—even as compared with good poets. Why Sainte-Beuves should be so infrequent, I do not know; but seemingly they are. I do not think Housman himself was a superlatively good critic (it was, as he emphasized, no field of his); but his opinions—not least when light-heartedly thrown off in talk or letters—seem to me often highly interesting, even when one may differ. It is interesting, for example, that he shook hands with Bridges over their agreement that Chaucer's most perfect piece was *The Nun's Priest's Tale*; that he found no pleasure in reading *through* plays by Shakespeare because, though some parts were magnificent, others were 'so slovenly that the effect of the whole is disagreeable'; that, unlike Mr Robert Graves, he thought Milton unique in English for 'the dignity, the sanity . . . the just subordination of detail, the due adaptation of means to ends, the high respect of the craftsman for his craft and for himself, which ennoble Virgil and the great Greeks'; that Hardy was his favourite novelist, 'next to Jane Austen'; that he had, not surprisingly, a special cult for Matthew Arnold, whose poems he ranked far above his own;[1] that he thought posterity would value Christina Rossetti above Swinburne; that he admired Patmore, though not 'his nasty mixture of piety and concupiscence'; that he found Joyce's *Ulysses* unrewardingly barren, and only 'one or two half-pages amusing'; and that he felt for Galsworthy a dislike so passionate that he could scarcely be persuaded even to become Galsworthy's fellow-pall-bearer at Hardy's funeral, and refused the Order of Merit at least partly because Galsworthy had received it. One is not compelled to like Galsworthy's writings; but as Galsworthy the man appears to have been an unusually fine character, this vehement aversion seems puzzling, and hardly to be understood without more private knowledge.

[1] Typically, among Arnold's poems, he particularly liked 'Creep into thy narrow bed'.

But of course Housman's main venture into regular criticism—one might almost say, his only serious one—was the Leslie Stephen Lecture of 1933, when he was seventy-four—*The Name and Nature of Poetry*. He did not want to give it, and was exhausted by giving it; but, listening on that classic occasion in the Senate House, I failed to detect any sign of effort or strain. After it was all over, one member of the English Faculty observed, I was told, that it would take 'us experts' ten years to undo the harm it had done. This growl appears to have been reported by some officious person, as the way is, to Housman himself; for a letter of his drily attributes a remark on similar lines to 'the leader of our doctrinaire teachers of youth'.

Housman attached no great weight to his own lecture. He had been asked to do it; did it; and was glad to have done with it. Its first and most obvious distinction lies perhaps in a style whose strength and simplicity recall the better, simpler manner of that Johnson who was also one of the ancestors of Housman's poetry. It was pleasant to hear; it is pleasant to read; and that quality is something not to be belittled in a world where, for some curious reason, so much that is written about writers is written by men who simply cannot write.

Secondly, as often happens when creative authors turn to criticism, the lecture is perhaps most interesting for the light it throws on the author himself—particularly that closing passage about Housman's own methods of composing poetry; about his reliance on the spontaneous inspiration sometimes provided by a pint of beer and an afternoon walk; and about his extreme difficulty in filling by deliberate brain-work the gaps that capricious inspiration sometimes left.

Here Ronsard, Burns, or Shelley would have agreed with him; but Johnson, Crabbe or Scott, Morris or Trollope, Balzac or Flaubert, might have risen in vehement protest. Not, perhaps, without reason. Housman admits, indeed, that he cannot assume other poets to have composed in the same way as himself; but he inclines, I feel, to generalize a little too confidently about the passiveness of the early stages of composition, the spontaneous secretion of poetry by the poet, as of turpentine by the fir. Of some lyric poets all this may be true enough. But could poets of epic length rely on anything so wayward and capricious as such fits of 'inspiration'? Or those Attic dramatists who, decade by decade, turned out their regular four dramas a year? Surely simple arithmetic forbids. One hears indeed of Aeschylus, Cratinus, or Jonson turning for stimulus to the winepot, or Balzac to the coffee-pot; but often the simple inkpot has served—and served better. Inspiration has consisted merely in drawing up a chair to a table, and doggedly picking up a pen. No doubt there have been poets whose symbol might have been a spasmodically leaping grasshopper; but there have been many others who would have found a better emblem in the patient perseverance of spider, ant, or bee.

Indeed, on Housman's own admission, though inspiration may compose more easily, it does not appear that it composes any better. He instances a poem of his own, two of whose stanzas flowed into his head, while a third 'came with a little coaxing after tea'; a fourth, however, took twelve rewritings, and over twelve months. Now Housman refused to say which stanzas were thus 'inspired', or which was the one composed by sheer doggedness; and though, of course, some readers may think they can guess, I defy them to reach any agreement about it. Q.E.D.

Again, there was the hard, deliberate brainwork of Housman's constant revisions. His first thoughts for poems, jotted in his notebooks and printed by T. B. Haber, are often strangely banal; and were only perfected by much afterthought. In short, Housman himself may often have been a good deal less spontaneous and intuitive than he seems to suggest.

It is also curious that a writer whose own poetry would seem to many moderns contemptibly lucid in meaning, should yet in his lecture so emphatically belittle the importance of meaning in poetry. Housman's arguments for this strange attitude seem to me no less strange. 'Meaning is of the intellect, poetry is not. If it were, the eighteenth century would have been able to write it better.'

But what, precisely, does one mean by 'meaning'; by 'intellect'; by '*of* the intellect'? I suppose Housman to be asserting that true propositions, unlike poetry, are produced, and judged, by the reasoning, logical side of the mind. But even were poetry always so instinctive—which I doubt—could one really maintain that the mad Christopher Smart's *Song to David* needed no 'intellectual' qualities to write it, and has no 'meaning' as written? Could it have been composed by a Mongolian idiot? Is it mere sound and fury, signifying nothing?

One could similarly say, 'True statesmanship is of wisdom and goodness; successful oratory is not.' For the essence of oratory is simply to persuade. The successful orator is one who can intoxicate multitudes—for example, make very many people very angry at the same time. But it would surely be odd to argue that a man with oratorical genius is not far more valuable if he possesses *also* wisdom and goodness. For without these he can become a disastrous pest—like Cleon or Hitler.

So with poetry. There have been poets neither sane, wise, nor good; but can one suggest that they were not a penny the worse for lacking these qualities—that Homer's poetry is not far more valuable, and more moving, for possessing them? This is beyond my powers to swallow.

From his later remarks, and his examples, Housman seems really concerned to stress that a man as wise and sensible as Hume may yet be unable to produce a single line of true poetry—which is indeed obvious; and that, since the essence of poetry is to intoxicate and thrill, its clearest indications are things like a shudder down the spine, a stab in the stomach, or a gash in the face when one is shaving. For some people such symptoms may be true enough; though, of course, other causes might produce a like effect without being poetical at all—for instance, if a skull suddenly looked at one out of the shaving-mirror. But to prove that poetry may coexist with madness does not prove that poetry is none the better for being combined also with the good sense of Horace, the compassion of Virgil, or the nobility of Ronsard. In poetry, as in life, truth is not always beauty, and truthfulness does not always make beauty; but it *can* make beauty still more moving—as, for me, the loveliness of Hardy's best poems becomes far more poignant for seeming so profoundly true. One can build enchanting buildings in dream or cloud; but most men value them still more if built of solid stone on solid earth. Poetry can be merely an ivory opium-den; but it can surely be something better.[1]

Housman, however, having decided that poetry was just 'a way of saying things', and that the sense of what it said remained immaterial, was naturally tempted to deny that 'there are any such things as poetical ideas'. Take, for example, the saying—'Whoever will save his life shall lose it, and whoever will lose his life shall find it.' That, for Housman, is 'the most important truth which has ever been uttered'. (How one can establish such orders of merit wholly passes my comprehension.) But, for all its importance, he finds in it nothing poetical.

[1] Housman himself later commented: 'I did not say poetry was better for having no meaning, only that it can best be detected so.' But that is not quite my impression from the lecture itself.

I wonder. But in any case why should the poeticalness of ideas have anything to do with their *importance?*

'Longinus' (perhaps in the first century A.D.) thought exactly the opposite—that some ideas *are* sublime, however they may be worded —-for instance, that sombre silence of Ajax when Odysseus meets his spectre in Hades. And here, I think, 'Longinus' was right—that moment would be magnificent, even if described in Iroquois or Urdu. Similarly, the bare fact that a notebook scribbled by Napoleon as a young gunner-officer breaks off with the entry 'Sainte-Hélène, petite île . . .' seems to me touched with a tragic poetry, however you may word it. Life too can be a poet. And there can be poetry in its happenings, as Hardy knew so well, quite independent of any words.

Further, in arguing that poetry does not depend on its meaning, but may even be marred by it, Housman seems tempted into some very curious examples. Poe's *Haunted Palace*, we are told, is one of his best poems so long as we do not realize that its palace-door is really Roderick Usher's mouth, its yellow banners his hair. But here the poem seems harmed, not by having a meaning, but by having *two* meanings —one of them foolish. The real point under discussion is not the value of allegory (often, as in Spenser, a bore), but of simple straightforward meaning.

Again, as an instance of words poetical without meaning, Housman adduces the stanza of Blake—

> Tho' thou art worship'd by the names divine
> Of Jesus and Jehovah, thou art still
> The Son of Morn in weary Night's decline,
> The lost traveller's dream under the hill.

But this does not appear to me meaningless either. Blake's symbolic sense here may remain, except for Blake scholars, wrapped in mist; but at least the literal meaning stands out clearly enough, especially in the last and most striking line. Who does not see with vivid vision that forlorn wanderer, like a weary Jacob asleep under the climbing stars of Beth-el?

Still less can I understand why the lyric from *Measure for Measure*, 'Take, O take those lips away', should be described as 'nonsense'— 'saying nothing'. To the forsaken Mariana in her moated grange I should have thought its bitter significance only too poignantly plain. Indeed, had the lyric only been written in Greek or Latin, I suspect that the classical scholar in Housman would have known extremely well what it meant; would have infallibly emended any textual corruptions which blurred that meaning; and would have performed a war-dance on the bodies of other unfortunate critics who had failed to grasp the sense.

Why, asks Housman, is he moved to tears by 'six simple words of Milton'—

> Nymphs and shepherds, dance no more?

'What in the world is there to cry about?' Quite a lot, I should have thought. Is there not a picture by Poussin, an Arcadian scene of happy swains, where the painter has set also the tomb of a dead shepherd, with the legend—'Moi aussi, j'ai vécu dans la douce Arcadie'? Surely Milton's words are moving because they remind us, as pastoral so often does, from the *Lament for Bion* down to *Lycidas* and *Thyrsis*, that even from the happiest Arcadia man must in the end depart—that there too appears 'la Ravisseuse de toute jouissance, la Dislocatrice de toute intimité, la Mort'. Is there a sadder pair of words in the English language than the last two of these six—'no more'? Well Tennyson knew that.[1]

The poetic feelings that Housman finds mysterious are so, I think, mainly because they move on less conscious levels of the mind; just as the sense of the uncanny, the *unheimlich*, or the sense of the *déjà vu*, are traced by modern psychology to emotions repressed and forgotten. We can be strangely moved by chains of association that have become invisible; as the man who looked out of the inn-window and unaccountably lost his appetite for breakfast, realized afterwards that it was because he had unconsciously recognized in the courtyard a government-spy. But, though strange, such things are not perhaps after all so inexplicable.

What does need explaining is the paradox that this ultra-romantic and anti-rational view of poetry should have been adopted by a person like Housman, whose own scholarship was conducted by an intellect as keen and cold as the blade of a guillotine, and whose own poetry remained almost always passionately and unambiguously clear. Why, in critical theory, was the less conscious, less intellectual side of

---

[1] It need hardly be pointed out that in their original context in Milton's *Arcades* these six words have no such note of sorrow; but what moved Housman, I take it, was independent of any context.

poetry so stressed by one who was in practice the most conscious and self-conscious of intellectuals?

Possibly, as so often, this 'although' was really a 'because'. Housman's life was bleak and forbidding; his scholarship was the rigid discipline of a monk; and so the poet in him was shy and half-ashamed; this may have been partly why, when he came to think and talk of poetry, he thought of it, rather, as a shadowy dreamland away from the harsh light and austere repressions of real life; and talked of it as an irrational, intoxicated, spontaneous activity—a sort of golden automation in a silver twilight.

But it is all the more piquant to watch how this theoretical contemner of meaning in poetry abruptly changes tone as soon as he becomes a practical critic of poems by his brother Laurence. For here he shows no mercy at all to any meanings left woolly and obscure. '*Prisoner of Carisbrooke* ought certainly to be included, as it has more root in earth than most of its author's lays, and occupies the proud position of distinctly meaning something from beginning to end. . . . What makes many of your poems more obscure than they need be is that you do not put yourself in the reader's place and consider how, and at what stage, that man of sorrows is to find out what it is all about. . . . There are others where throughout the first half of a poem the hapless reader is clawing the air for a clue. . . . *The Two Debtors*. I do not understand this; and perhaps that is why I think it perfectly odious.'

Here, in this merciless insistence on meaning and clarity, there speaks out a quite opposite side of Housman—the side I respect and admire. Now it is true that this letter to Laurence Housman was written many years earlier, in 1894; and Alfred might have changed his views by the time he gave his Leslie Stephen Lecture in 1933. But I doubt it. His own verse-style, as late as 1926, had not changed. It seems to me a case, not of altered views, but of differing moods.

There are many kinds of poetic emotion, ranging from the drugged phantasmagorias of opium to the stimulated elevation of good wine not drunk to excess. All may have their values. Which of them one prefers, is mainly a matter of temperament. The present fashion is largely for opium; and, detesting all intoxications, I detest it. But it too will blow over. Anyone who does not regard mere literary fashions with contempt, is himself contemptible. One can always say, like the young Abbé de Bernis when warned by a crabbed and aged bishop to expect no promotion from *him*, 'J'attendrai'.

The rest of *The Name and Nature of Poetry* seems less important. One may regret that it should add yet another to that tedious series of discussions since Aristotle about the 'right' meaning of 'poetry'. Surely there is no one 'right' meaning—there are half a dozen, listed in any decent dictionary, and all established by good usage. One meaning of 'poetry' connotes metre, another does not; one meaning implies artistic excellence, another does not; and so forth. To argue which is *the* true meaning is like arguing whether 'box' really means a receptacle, or a kind of tree; whether 'chest' rightly means a receptacle, or a part of the human anatomy. It may be regrettable that human tongues should make the same noise to indicate totally different objects, leaving it to the context to settle which. But so it is. One should try not to sully the stream of language by one's own use of it; but it is idle to try making that stream flow backwards.

More interesting are the indications, written partly between the lines, of Housman's own preferences—a taste, now sufficiently uncommon, for eighteenth-century hymn-writers like Watts;[1] a distaste (like Johnson's) for Metaphysical Poets; a dislike for the character of Dryden; a distrust for modern poetry. Here, while agreeing that our age, with its infatuation for the silly-clever, has often become far too Donne-ish, one may question if it is quite fair to Metaphysical Poetry to dismiss all its conceits as 'purely intellectual' and 'intellectually frivolous'. Safer perhaps, remembering things like Marvell's superb *Coy Mistress*, to say that they *often* are. And again, without much liking Dryden personally, one may wonder if it is not a little extreme to assert that, where Pope had a soul (not always a very pleasant one), Dryden had 'nothing but a lump of clay'.[2]

---

[1] Housman quotes from Watts:

> Soft and easy is thy cradle;
>   Coarse and hard thy Saviour lay,
> When his birthplace was a stable
>   And his softest bed was hay.

The simplicity of vocabulary, syntax, and word-order, the bell-like clarity of rhythm, are both curiously like Housman's own verse.

[2] The lecture contains also what seems to me a curiously false analogy. Why, it asks, do men resent the imputation of being deaf to poetry, but not of being deaf to a bat-squeak? But the parallel seems faulty. For there is nothing discreditable in being unable to hear an abnormally high note—dogs can hear still higher ones; but there *is* humiliation in admitting an inability to appreciate the most honoured part of literature.

And so, I repeat, this lecture seems to me, though enjoyable and stimulating, to throw light not so much on poetry as on Housman the poet. This last is the Housman who, for me at least, matters most. And perhaps the most extraordinary thing about Housman the poet is that he could ever coexist with Housman the scholar.

Familiarity soon blurs the strangeness of life; as the silvery bright-ness of new-cut lead quickly dulls back to the familiar leaden grey. And yet that this drily scientific dissector of the corruptions of a dead language, prim and precise with all the stiff conventionality of academic life, should have produced the passionate self-revelations that cry aloud through the pages of *A Shropshire Lad* and *Last Poems* is really almost as bewildering as if Browning's Grammarian turned out to have writ-ten Browning's lyrics; almost as fantastic as if Great St Mary's changed overnight into a haystack, while the Proctors progressed down King's Parade with scythe on shoulder and straw in mouth, and flocks of sheep scampered to vote in the Senate House.

* * *

About the value of these unlooked-for poems there has been some savage debate—often more savage than impressive. Now there may be a good deal in the view that it is wise to read some literary history and biography before approaching an author's works, but *not* to read liter-ary criticism of their value till one has read the works themselves. Otherwise one's feelings may get warped beforehand. Neglect of this principle vitiates, I suspect, much teaching of literature, especially in universities (so far as literature can be taught at all). One is unlikely to get a good picture by photographing on a film already exposed by someone else. So if any of my readers should happen not yet to have read Housman's poems, I would suggest that it *might* be better to put this book aside and read them now.

About aesthetic works all argument seems to me idle, except where it is a question of suggesting a writer's ideas to be irrational and so intellectually undesirable, or unhealthy and so socially undesirable —as, for example, where Housman himself objects to Patmore's 'nasty mixture of piety and concupiscence'. But though we smile at the good eighteenth-century Abbé Raynal objecting to *George Barnwell* that it is '*naturally*' ridiculous for a play to have as heroine a prostitute, we are still not always much wiser ourselves. Of his aesthetic feelings every man who is not a sheep, must, I believe, be his own and only judge;

but he may be able to judge his own feelings more clearly if he has also listened to those who admire a work explaining why, and to those who do not admire it likewise explaining why. I shall therefore try here to put the case for both sides; and employ a Devil's Advocate to put the case against.

'To begin with,' the Devil's Advocate may protest, 'the very nature of Housman's poetry is *unnatural*. It is pastoral—disguised pastoral— a particularly false form of a form essentially false. It embodies a collection of poems about Shropshire lads of the village, by a man who was not in the least a village-lad, nor even from Shropshire. Housman learnt much from Johnson: a pity that he did not also learn Johnson's scorn for artificial rusticities. 'Is my team ploughing?' What did Housman know of ploughs? Except in Greats!

'Mere arithmetic', the enemy may continue, 'is enough to give the thing away. *A Shropshire Lad* reiterates the word "lad" no less than sixty-seven times. This unfortunate monosyllable, happy enough in Shakespeare's "Golden lads and girls", has thus been made unusable for whole generations to come.

'Why, even his Shropshire topography is bogus. Hughley Steeple, for example, is *not* "a far-known sign"—it stands in a hollow; the church had no steeple at all; and its north side is embellished with no buried suicides.[1] "Now that Hughley is burnt down," Housman wrote in 1925, "it is curious to think that I never saw it; though it cannot have been much to see." He merely liked its name.

'In fine, Housman posing as a young yokel is as frivolously artificial as Marie Antoinette milking cows at le Petit Trianon. Meredith in his Box Hill seclusion has been laughed at as a Marie Antoinette with whiskers. But even Meredith deserved the gibe less than Housman.'

In answer, one may admit that there does indeed seem an excess of 'lads'. But it seems excessive, also, thus to condemn all the flocks and herds of pastoral indiscriminately to the slaughter-house. Why did Housman develop this strange passion for Shropshire rustics? As well ask why Wordsworth developed a passion for Westmorland shepherds,

[1] North, for a soon-told number,
    Chill graves the sexton delves,
And steeple-shadowed slumber
    The slayers of themselves.

Bicycling round Housman's Shropshire as an enthusiastic undergraduate in 1919, I discovered with some disillusion that this was a myth. Much it really matters!

goodies, and idiot-boys; why Hardy wrote of Gabriel Oak, Jude the Obscure, and Tess of the D'Urbervilles; why Lawrence of Arabia, when there lay open to him the most select society of London, yet preferred the society of recruits in the R.A.F.

Man seems an animal partly tamed, yet still partly wild. Often in the artificial cages of cities he sickens. For there he has lost his own liberty, and taken liberties with Nature; which, in the long run, Nature has nasty ways of punishing. Attic salt may be excellent in moderation; but too much of it can make a Dead Sea.

Hence the historic revolt of Rousseau, whom one sees stifling in the polished eighteenth-century salon, smashing its windows with frantic fists, and rushing, lacerated but irreconcilable, out into the night. Or there is that passionate protest of Gordon: 'I dwell on the joy of never seeing Great Britain again with its horrid wearisome dinner-parties and miseries. How we can put up with those things passes my imagination. It is a perfect bondage. At those dinner parties we are all in masks, saying what we do not believe, eating and drinking things we do not want, and then abusing one another. I would sooner live like a Dervish with the Madhi than go out to dinner every night in London.' Or, again, there is Hardy's summary of London as 'that hot-plate of humanity, on which we first sing, then simmer, then boil, then dry away to dust'.

Even four thousand years or more ago the Mesopotamian epic of Gilgamesh already drew, in contrast to the corruption of cities, that noble child of nature, Engidu, who plays Jonathan to the David of Gilgamesh himself. European pastoral goes back to the first giant-city founded by European hands—Alexandria. Men begin to value Nature as they begin to lose her. No doubt pastoral, which started as a flight from artificiality, has often become itself the height of artificiality; because it fell into the hands of chair-bound writers capable of believing that partridges suck, and rabbits lay eggs. Yet it seems rash to condemn so sweepingly a form that has inspired authors as diverse as Theocritus, Virgil, Ronsard, Spenser, Shakespeare, Milton, Herrick, Burns, Crabbe, Wordsworth, Clare, George Sand, George Eliot, Tennyson, Hugo, Arnold, and Hardy. A theme so persistent must surely meet some persistent human need. The Forest of Arden can claim its rightful place on the map of literature.

There has grown up among modern intellectuals a naïve belief that complexity is in itself a virtue. Why? Simplicity too can be a virtue. Simplicity can even be subtle; like the lines of the Parthenon which are subtly curved in order that they may not look curved. Donne or Hopkins is far more complex than Homer; but they are far from being Homer. An atomic bomb dropped on London would produce a mess of considerable 'complexity': but hardly pleasing. On the other hand a mere drop of water on a cabbage-leaf can be strangely beautiful. So I do not see why we should condemn pastoral wholesale—why we should assume that leech-gatherers are necessarily inferior to aesthetes, or Tess of the D'Urbervilles to some cat's-cradle of a woman out of Henry James.[1]

'Very well,' rejoins the Devil's Advocate, 'let the pastoral for the moment be reprieved. But these particular rustics of Housman's remain so morbid, and so monotonous. Their lives, like his own, are stupidly obsessed with death. In what inordinate numbers do these lads either turn soldiers and stop bullets; or shoot themselves; or slit their own throats; or take short cuts to prison and the gallows! One is driven to suspect in the poet some neurotic complex, such as makes masochistic undergraduates truss their limbs in cords, then hang themselves from ceilings. Richly he deserved the parody of Hugh Kingsmill:

> What, still alive at twenty-two,
> A clean, upstanding chap like you!
> Sure, if your throat is hard to slit,
> Slit your girl's and swing for it.
>
> Like enough you won't be glad
> When they come to hang you, lad.
> But bacon's not the only thing
> That's cured by hanging from a string.
>
> When the blotting-pad of night
> Sucks the latest drop of light,
> Lads whose job is still to do
> Shall whet their knives and think of you.'

Here I think one must concede a good deal to the accuser. Housman himself had the humour to remark of Kingsmill's parody that it was 'the best I have seen, and indeed the only good one'. Personally, then, I should be prepared to sacrifice most of Housman's poems on suicides; on gallows-birds; and on soldiers (though *not* his *Army of Mercenaries*).

[1] It could also be urged that Housman's Shropshire lads are a morbid, though unconscious, product of middle-class homosexuality, viewing romantically the young men of a poorer social class. But that would be guessing. In any case it seems unfair to judge writing by its supposed causes, rather than by its results.

But the part of Housman's poetry that really matters seems to me largely uttered, not through the lips of 'lads' at all, but through the poet's own; and its themes, though simple, are often universal and eternal—Nature and love, the bitterness of life's frustrations, and the chill *Nunc Dimittis* of death.

*   *   *

First, Nature. That beauty of the English countryside which we are now rapidly destroying, has been praised so often and so long, that it was no small feat to make themes so ancient new again; to have quickened Shropshire and the Welsh Marches, Wenlock Edge and the Wrekin, Buildwas and the vanes of Shrewsbury, with associations of his own, just as Hardy has done for Wessex—for Egdon Heath, and the Vale of Blackmoor, and Shaftesbury on its hill. Like his own Hermes, for some of us, Housman still leads over English hill and valley his band of ghostly memories—

> Across the glittering pastures
> And empty upland still
> And solitude of shepherds
> High in the folded hill. . . .
>
> By blowing realms of woodland
> With sunstruck vanes afield
> And cloud-led shadows chasing
> About the windy weald. . . .
>
> Buoyed on the heaven-heard whisper
> Of dancing leaflets whirled
> From all the woods that autumn
> Bereaves in all the world.

But though the rush of this is splendid as the sweep of a south-west wind under a blue-and-golden sky, Housman, unlike his Hermes, is seldom a 'Merry Guide'. For him, the beauty even of Nature is typically blended with a recurrent bitterness. His hills may grow white with spring-blossom, yellow with the swaying dance of daffodils; but the nettle too is there.

> The charlock on the fallow
> Will take the traveller's eyes,
> And gild the ploughland sallow
> With flowers before it dies,
> But twice 'twill not arise.

The stinging nettle only
   Will still be found to stand:
The numberless, the lonely,
   The thronger of the land,
   The leaf that hurts the hand.

It thrives, come sun, come showers,
   Blow east, blow west, it springs;
It peoples towns, and towers
   About the courts of Kings,
   And touch it and it stings.

There was plenty of nettle in Housman. Never mind. Grasp it. It even gives one a certain confidence. For here is a mind that will not merely prettify the world, leaving out less pleasant things. Housman was tough-minded; and to the tender-minded I much prefer the tough. By 'tough' I do not mean 'hard'—Hardy too was tough, yet the gentlest of men; I mean 'stoical and undeceived'.

*   *   *

So too with love. There too Housman finds less honeysuckle than nettle. Even in *Epithalamium* (said to have been inspired by the marriage of his friend Jackson in 1889, but not begun till 1900, nor finished till 1922, the year before Jackson died), though Epithalamia like Funeral Orations are licensed to lie sweetly, one senses only a half-hearted gaiety, with a sad undertone of loss.

Friend and comrade, yield you o'er
To her that hardly loves you more.

Far more frequent with Housman is the theme of love left lonely, as in that adaptation of Sappho which seems to me even more poignant than its Greek original.

The weeping Pleiads wester,
   And the moon is under seas;
From bourn to bourn of midnight
   Far sighs the rainy breeze:

It sighs from a lost country
   To a land I have not known;
The weeping Pleiads wester,
   And I lie down alone.

Yet no Greek island is so lonely as the giant-cities of to-day can be.

> And I lie down in London
> And turn to rest alone.

Those are fortunate who have never repeated to themselves that sentence of utter desolation.

Or, again, Housman expresses the bitter sense of waste that darkens a devotion kindled in vain, because it falls on some heart of stone which cannot kindle in return.

> From far, from eve and morning
> And yon twelve-winded sky,
> The stuff of life to knit me
> Blew hither: here am I. . . .
>
> Speak now, and I will answer;
> How shall I help you, say;
> Ere to the wind's twelve quarters
> I take my endless way.

Or, even if the love is returned, it is chilled by the shadow of fate that dooms it, as in *Bredon Hill*; or by the shadow of human forgetfulness, that consoles itself elsewhere.

> 'Is my girl happy,
> That I thought hard to leave,
> And has she tired of weeping
> As she lies down at eve?'
>
> Ay, she lies down lightly,
> She lies not down to weep:
> Your girl is well contented.
> Be still, my lad, and sleep.

True, there is another mood when the poet sees that without this healing gift of forgetfulness life would grow intolerable.

> Blue the sky from east to west
> Arches, and the world is wide,
> Though the girl he loves the best
> Rouses from another's side.

Those lines, too, so unusual for Housman in their comparative optimism, must have run in many memories when love proved fickle or unkind. And rightly. For there are times when they need remembering. Yet one seems to catch a note of desperation in the cry of the poet grown lawless—

> Come to the stolen waters,
>   And leap the guarded pale,
> And pull the flower in season
>   Before desire shall fail.
>
> It shall not last for ever,
>   No more than earth and skies;
> But he that drinks in season
>   Shall live before he dies.

For Housman himself was by nature too fastidious to follow Aphrodite Pandemos. Like the Shakespeare of the Sonnets, he saw too clearly the reaction to follow such indulgences.

> The fairies break their dances
>   And leave the printed lawn,
> And up from India glances
>   The silver sail of dawn.
>
> The candles burn their sockets,
>   The blinds let through the day,
> The young man feels his pockets
>   And wonders what's to pay.

Or there is that other dawn of disillusion, with the same ruthless juxtaposition of romance and realism, of life's splendour and its squalor, of Nature's heedless, stainless beauty and the human sense of guilt—

> In the blue and silver morning
>   On the haycock as they lay,
> Oh they looked at one another
>   And they looked away.

Evidently Housman's view of love, the passion which has moved more poets to ecstasy than any other, remains very far from gay. His nearest approach to a warm faith in it is perhaps that poem, *Hell Gate*, which celebrates the redeeming love of friends. But even that has its scene set in Hell. Nor does this somewhat naïve fantasy seem to me on a level with its author's best work.

And so it is no surprise to come on love-lyrics of Housman's whose conclusion is a final renouncement and despair of love itself.

> When I was one-and-twenty
>   I heard a wise man say,
> 'Give crowns and pounds and guineas
>   But not your heart away;

> Give pearls away and rubies
>> But keep your fancy free.'
> But I was one-and-twenty,
>> No use to talk to me.

And again—

> His folly has not fellow
>> Beneath the blue of day
> That gives to man or woman
>> His heart and soul away.
>
> There flowers no balm to sain him
>> From east of earth to west
> That's lost for everlasting
>> The heart out of his breast.[1]

That, to some ears, is lilting as a Siren's song; and in certain moods it can chant itself in their heads as the bitterest of truths. That is part of its justification. For bitter moods that have found perfect utterance can lose, in part, their sting.

Hardy too, a mind of more gentleness but no less fortitude, felt a like hesitation between the impulse to cry 'Yes' to love and the impulse to cry 'No'.

> By briefest meeting something sure is won,
>> It will have been:
> Nor God nor Demon can undo the done,
>> Unsight the seen,
> Make muted music be as unbegun,
>> Though things terrene
> Groan in their bondage till oblivion supervene.

And yet—

> Out of the night there looms a sense 'twere better
> To fail obtaining whom one fails to miss.

And again—

> But go your courses, sweet Aurore,
>> Kisses are caresome things.
>
> The paths of love are rougher
>> Than thorofares of stones.

[1] It is interesting that this cry of supreme disillusion seems one of the earliest of the poems—before 1890.

But, though ascetics would disagree, such moods that renounce and refrain do not seem to me the wisest or finest. Is life worth living? Many at least think so—or act as if they so thought. And *if* life is worth living, then there seems to me much less doubt that love is worth loving. Love may be perilous—not only a passion-flower, but often an edelweiss above an abyss. Yet without it what a sterile desert! One who cannot lose his heart, will never really find it; though it may be a pity, when losing one's heart, completely to lose one's head as well—as Romantic writers have often thought it admirable to do. But better, surely, to take the plunge anyway, than to shiver all one's years upon the barren brink.

I remember, when hardly more than an undergraduate, writing to one of the most brilliant minds of our century with a frustrated regret that there was no soul in the world I could call my own. He replied that, in his own case, he thanked Heaven for precisely that. Soon afterwards, to our astonishment, he married—very happily. He never returned to that topic; for though wise, as well as brilliant, he was also proud, and not one of those, still wiser, who smile when time mocks their wisdom. But his friends smiled. Now he is dead, and to smile would seem rather heartless. But the memory remains.

True, there have been minds more unbending, like Lucretius who counselled men to escape the tyrannic illusions of Eros in the physical promiscuity of 'Venus volgivaga'; like Flaubert, exasperated by 'l'Hâmour'; like Rivarol, proclaiming how much better it was to be the master of facile beauty than passion's dupe and fool—'Félicitez-moi: ma maîtresse a toujours quinze ans, et je ne reçois pas des billets du matin.' Yet observation suggests that this dusty side-track, though it may suit some temperaments, is apt to lead to a weary land, where grow apples, not of Wisdom, but of Sodom, with ashes at the core.

Alfred de Musset came likewise to disaster. He was too Romantically in love with love itself. Yet there remains, I think, sense as well as eloquence in that confession of faith uttered by Musset's Perdican in *On ne badine pas avec l'amour*: 'On est souvent trompé en amour, souvent blessé et souvent malheureux; mais on aime, et quand on est sur le bord de sa tombe, on se retourne pour regarder en arrière, et on se dit: J'ai souffert souvent, je me suis trompé quelquefois, mais j'ai aimé. C'est moi qui ai vécu, et non pas un être factice créé par mon orgueil et mon ennui.'

That seems to me braver, and more widely true, than some of Housman's love-poetry in its more desperate and morbid moods. For though one may regret certain passions in one's life, few can wish that they had never loved at all. Yet I seldom fail to find his love-poems moving. Even when they have a certain Siren-deceptiveness, it is still a Siren that sings.

* * *

But if Housman looked on the beauty of Nature and the intoxication of love with eyes so sombre ('I thought', said my Uncle Toby, 'that love had been a joyous thing'), little wonder that about life and death in general he grew more sombre still.

Max Beerbohm has put it with his usual sprightliness—

> T.H. and A.E.H.
> How compare either of these grim two?
> Each has an equal knack.
> Hardy supplies the pill that's blue,
> Housman the draught that's black.

Yet even Hardy is less uniformly sad. Across Hardy's blasted heaths can soar, at least sometimes, a lyric carolling like a lark, as when he waits for 'Lalage's coming'; and at times he could allow himself a romance as rosy as *Under the Greenwood Tree*. But Housman, though sometimes humorous, never seems really gay. Did he not say himself to one expressing a hope of more poems from him that, as he seemed able to write only of death and the grave, he thought he had better stop?

> Be still, my soul, be still; the arms you bear are brittle,
> Earth and high heaven are fixt of old and founded strong.
> Think rather,—call to thought, if now you grieve a little,
> The days when we had rest, O soul, for they were long. . . .
>
> Ay, look: high heaven and earth ail from the prime foundation;
> All thoughts to rive the heart are here, and all are vain:
> Horror and scorn and hate and fear and indignation—
> Oh why did I awake? When shall I sleep again?

The embittered despair of this 'proud and angry dust', retorting in the face of God a *Dies Irae* of its own, recalls those tersely grim epitaphs found sometimes on Roman tombs such as lined Appian or Flaminian Way—

> Manus levo contra deum qui me innocentem sustulit.
>
> I lift my hands against the God
> Who gave to death my innocence.

> Dii irati aeterno somno dederunt.
> The gods in their anger gave me to eternal sleep.

> Non fui, fui; non sum, non desidero.
> I was not, I was; I am not, I would not be.

Yet here the Devil's Advocate breaks in with redoubled irritation—
'But how monstrously monotonous is all this cheap pessimism! If one really finds life so awful and so longs to "sleep again", then it would be more logical to hop off a cliff than edit Manilius. And how irrational was this atheist scolding an Almighty whom he did not believe to exist, and cursing

> Whatever brute and blackguard made the world!

It is less intelligent even than the infant who belabours the "naughty table" on which the little idiot has banged his own head. It is sillier even than Swinburne's "the supreme evil, God", over which Christina Rossetti piously pasted a scrap of paper in her copy of *Atalanta*. And why all this outcry? Because May has been wet, and by next May one will be twenty-four! How appalling!'

Well, the wisdom of this last poem[1] I certainly cannot defend; however lovely the landscape-painting, even here, and however telling its intensity of phrase. One *could* argue that it is put in the mouth of a Shropshire lad; but that, I feel, would be dishonest. For no village-boy even if he thought thus, ever talked in such a style. The hands may pretend to be a ploughman's; but the voice is Housman's own.

To the more general charge of morbid melancholia Housman has given his own humorous defence in the well-known verses that begin:

> Terence, this is stupid stuff:
> You eat your victuals fast enough.[2]

His argument is simple. Alcohol gives more gaiety than any philosophy; but its effect, alas, is singularly transient.

> Therefore, since the world has still
> Much good, but much less good than ill,
> And while the sun and moon endure
> Luck's a chance, but trouble's sure,
> I'd face it as a wise man would
> And train for ill and not for good.

---

[1] *L.P.*, ix.

[2] This suggestion of gross and hearty appetite seems comically incongruous for Housman the delicate epicure. True, it is again a Shropshire lad who speaks. But would Shropshire lads tell erudite tales about Mithridates? Still it would be pedantic to let such discrepancies worry one.

(Perhaps a wiser man might train for both.) Accordingly, just as Mithridates died old because he had immunized himself to poisons by gradually increasing doses of them, so by facing life's sorrow in poetry one may grow stronger to bear it in reality.

But here the objector cries out: 'How stupid! First, on Housman's black view of life, Mithridates only suffered still more by dying old—he would have done far better to die young. Secondly, and more important, this fixed idea about meeting trouble halfway is as idiotic as the religious mania that preached, for centuries, that one should live constantly thinking of one's death. People who take to sleeping in their coffins may be justly suspected of more necrophily than good sense. Any husband knows that he may be left a widower; any wife, that she may be left a widow. On Housman's principle they should "train" themselves in readiness by constantly meditating on this pleasant prospect. How crazy!—unless, of course, they are secretly looking forward to it. To torment oneself about things one cannot alter is futile folly. And anyway half the things we torment ourselves about beforehand, never happen. On the very next page to the gloomy "Be still, my soul, be still!" Housman put (I suppose deliberately) a quite opposite, and much more sensible, view—

> Think no more, lad; laugh, be jolly:
>   Why should men make haste to die?
> Empty heads and tongues a-talking
> Make the rough road easy walking,
> And the feather pate of folly
>   Bears the falling sky.

A pity he did not remember that, and practise it, more often.

'In short, Housman's defence of his poetic gloom is sophistry. His reasons are not reason, but mere pretext. He wrote gloomy poetry, not as a public service, but just because he was a gloomy individual. Take his own confession—

> I to my perils
>   Of cheat and charmer
>   Came clad in armour
>   By stars benign.
> Hope lies to mortals
>   And most believe her,
>   But man's deceiver
>   Was never mine.

214

The thoughts of others
Were light and fleeting,
Of lovers' meeting
Or luck or fame.
Mine were of trouble,
And mine were steady,
So I was ready
When trouble came.

'Exquisite movement, no doubt—a dirge that dances like a fairy-wedding. A grace, I dare say, beyond any living poet—most of them do not know that such a quality exists. But what an extraordinary theme for self-congratulation!—that one spent one part of one's life in looking for trouble, the other part in finding it! Existence may be often horrible—the Universe indifferent—Nature a beautiful bitch. But why brood so? What does one hatch?

'And then, to crown all, this despairer disliked being called a pessimist. "As for pessimism," he wrote to a young American shortly before his death, "I think it almost as silly, though not as wicked, as optimism." (Why is optimism "wicked"?) "George Eliot", he went on, "said she was a meliorist; I am a pejorist." What a quibble! A pessimist is not one who thinks this the worst of all *possible* worlds. Who does? "Pessimist" is perfectly plain English for anyone who thinks that life contains "much less good than ill"; and that "high heaven and earth ail from the prime foundation". This pessimistic view may be true; but why on earth pretend it is not pessimistic?'

In these objections there seems to me much force; though they have little relevance to purely poetic values. Why Housman, like Hardy, so resented being called a pessimist, I do not know. Both apparently felt that, as Lawrence of Arabia once said to me, 'the whole thing had better stop'. That I call 'pessimism'. But does it much matter? It is only a rather trivial wrangle about words.

That Housman's poetry, again, is not always consistent, or balanced, or perfectly wise, seems to me also true. But, poetically, is this so very important? How many poets in all history have always been all these things? Certainly not Shakespeare himself.

*   *   *

Strange that even to-day such truisms should need repeating. But seemingly they do. Poets are not often sages—frequently they have lived the lives of fools; creative writers are not often thinkers of deep and balanced wisdom—frequently they have been over-emotional, frequently neurotic, sometimes mad. Yet recurrently, incorrigibly, pathetically, men have craved, not only to listen and enjoy them, but also to sit at their feet and call them 'Rabbi'.

There were some grounds for this in early periods, like those of Homer and Hesiod and Empedocles, when life was still unspecialized and even philosophers could write in verse. But that is a long-vanished world. The Middle Ages thought Virgil a magician; he is; but not in the way they thought. Yet even to-day there still recurs a tendency to talk about literature as if it were necessarily wisdom-literature (when in fact a lot of it can seldom have been more foolish than now), with all the hyperbolic claims of critics like Sidney or Shelley. In part, this tendency may be helped by the decay of religion—men rush about looking for oracles elsewhere.

At this moment I happen to be deep in examination-papers. One set of the young has learnt that the study of literature should be a sort of pseudo-science. They approach a poet with the glassy stare and cold concentration of a biologist disentangling the intestines of a cockroach. They have not acquired one spark of poetic feeling. They are prosaic as plumbers. Yet they cannot even write tolerable prose. One might as well think to study architecture by gnawing holes in floors with one's teeth. Another set has learnt to treat the study of literature as a sort of pseudo-religion. The poor dears have been taught to believe that they can learn all about life from the novel, as if fiction were a larger and better Bible. John the Baptist and St Paul are replaced, say, by D. H. Lawrence and James Joyce. Jane Austen becomes a major prophetess (which would have greatly astonished that sensible woman); and Henry James's works are exalted into new epistles of St James. After a pontifical laying-on of donnish hands, these neophytes rush with the fervour of young curates to preach that life's most complicated problems are now settled, its most debatable values established, by a few imaginative artists. 'Mais qu'ils sont drôles, les universitaires,' cried Flaubert, 'du moment qu'ils se mêlent de l'art!' No doubt Flaubert exaggerated; but not, alas, very much. Realists like Walter Raleigh, humanists like 'Q', grow lamentably rare.

What, really, are the main qualities of a creative writer? I should have thought, imagination, style, intensity of feeling, and force of personality. Artists, literary and other, have often been, like Lulli, all genius and no sense. A good instance of this is Strindberg. To expect such sensitive and passionate types to be *also* great thinkers, seems asking a lot. And in fact Leonardos and Goethes have been few. Within a quarter of a mile you may well find a dozen schoolgirls less naïve, and more rational, than Christina Rossetti; but you might search all England for a dozen adults with her imagination and her style. The contempt of Bernard Shaw or T. E. Lawrence for Shakespeare as thinker may be excessive; but I am not impressed by attempts to torture him into a profound philosopher; I believe his magic lay in style, power of sympathy, and personality.

Even if a writer's ideas do seem sound, it is often hard to know if they are new. Ibsen appears to me a far saner and more forceful thinker than most; but it would need vast research to discover which ideas of Ibsen's were really Ibsen's own. Nor does it much matter; what matters is his power to express and embody them in a new and vivid life.

What does one really want of a creative writer? If one shares his view of life, excellent—that is an added pleasure; but, inevitably, not a very common one. What *is* essential is that I should share, or that he should make me share, a sufficient number of his moods and emotions. In a word, sympathy. Lastly, even if his ideas seem stupid, and his emotions unattractive, he may still interest my curiosity, as a human being with a world of his own. Space-travel leaves me more than cold; the mere idea of infecting heavenly bodies with such mischievous little vermin as men in the mass often are, seems perfectly nauseous. But every person one passes in the street is a universe walking on two feet, which it may be harmless and fascinating to explore. The world of Balzac, for example, despite his realism seems often wildly, sometimes romantically, unreal. I do not much like him as a person. I should not dream of taking him for guide and philosopher. He might pique himself on being 'docteur en médecine sociale'—one merely asks, 'How many cures?' There may, even, be more truth in Sainte-Beuve's bitter epigram on him —'le romancier qui savait le mieux la corruption de son temps, et il était même homme à y ajouter'. And yet, even if Balzac had no artistic merits, it would be worth exploring Balzac's world and its fantastic creator. So, again, with Baudelaire.

Therefore it does not seem to me so important that one can pick all these holes in Housman's view of life. I enjoy him as a poet because I share a good deal of his pessimism; share a good many of his moods and emotions (including, of course, his feelings about what makes beauty of style and rhythm); and find him, even when my sympathy lessens, a deeply interesting personality to explore.

*　　*　　*

As regards his actual pessimism (I do not say this with any dogmatic assurance; but the reader may care to compare, or contrast, his own impressions), I should feel fuller agreement if it were rather less dogmatic; less indignant; more enlivened by a gaiety like Voltaire's; more softened by a compassion like Hardy's.

First, the dogmatism. When one considers the atrociousness of human suffering through history, the atrociousness of that carnage in the animal world which makes it often as ghastly in its horror as it can be dazzling in its beauty and ingenuity, then those who feel at all must feel, again and again, how tragic existence is. Yet one cannot know. One cannot judge the universe after an infinitely brief contemplation, with one's infinitely small capacities, of an infinitely small fragment of space-time. 'Am I', says the forcible Chinese phrase for ignorance of another's thoughts, 'a tapeworm in his belly?' Evidently one cannot be a tapeworm in the bellies of all creation. One cannot know. But a deep suspicion of infinite blindness and indifference may remain.

Secondly, indignation. What use? What grounds? May not the answer to the universe be, after all—'Forgive It, for It knows not what It does'? 'Whatever brute and blackguard . . .'—I find this angry defiance (like that of the legendary Nimrod shooting against God in Heaven arrows which fell bloodstained back to earth) as curiously irrational as that gentler, though seemingly ironic, farewell to the Creator which Housman wrote to be sung—and which *was* sung—at his funeral. (The Church of England is at times amazingly tolerant.)

> We now to peace and darkness
> And earth and thee restore
> Thy creature that thou madest
> And wilt cast forth no more.

All the same, one may prefer the silences of Alfred de Vigny—

> Le juste opposera le dédain à l'absence,
> Et ne répondra plus que par un froid silence
> Au silence éternel de la Divinité.

> Gémir, pleurer, prier, est également lâche.

Thirdly, gaiety. This may seem an odd quality to demand of pessimists; but I mean it. It is Voltaire's gift of laughter that makes *Candide* a more genial work than *Gulliver*, a livelier and more living tale than *Rasselas*. So too in poetry the wry irony of Heine illustrates how wise Nietzsche was in advising pessimists to laugh. It is, indeed, their best safeguard against being laughed at. Because of this lack of laughter the idea of living Housman's life would freeze me to the bone. But I am very grateful that he lived.

Fourthly, compassion. In real life Housman's kindnesses could sometimes be overwhelming; but in his poetry there is a certain strain of somewhat egocentric hardness that contrasts with the pity for the world which speaks in Virgil, or Po Chu-i, or Hardy. In Housman one hears often Hardy's Spirits Sinister and Ironic; but less often the Chorus of the Pities.

On the other hand I have always found Housman's pessimism stimulating and fortifying rather than depressing. His gloom remains, for me, far less a burden to the spirit than the unhappiness of writers like Clare, or Christina Rossetti, who suffer so helplessly that it is like listening to some anguished child crying in the dark.

> Fall'n Cherube, to be weak is miserable.

Such weakness is far more painful to watch than

> the unconquerable Will,
> And study of revenge, immortal hate,
> And courage never to submit or yield.

In Housman's Valley of Darkness that stoic fortitude burns like a gloomy flame. He does not whine or whimper like some now admired poets. The final consolation is to have learnt to live without consolations.

> What evil luck soever
>   For me remains in store,
> 'Tis sure much finer fellows
>   Have fared much worse before.
>
> So here are things to think on
>   That ought to make me brave,
> As I strap on for fighting
>   My sword that will not save.

A very ancient piece of philosophy—this thought of the better men who have fared even worse. Homer's Achilles used it to the cowering son of Priam; from Homer Lucretius took it, to rebuke the craven soul that dreads the grave to which the great kings of early Rome, and even the glorious wisdom of Epicurus, must bow themselves long ago; and in its turn it was caught up by Matthew Arnold when he put the words of the son of Thetis in the mouth of Senancour. A very ancient reflection; but there are many worse.

In fine, there are moods when I feel Housman's view of life to be in essence only too true; and then its truth deepens the sombre beauty of his verse. There are more frequent moods when I feel his view too uncompromisingly nihilist; but even then the beauty of his verse goes far to atone for its deficiency in truth. For him the world *was* so. And if we can traverse even Dante's fantastic hell, though glad to return and see the stars, we can visit Housman's world likewise, dark though it may be as some desolate mountain-corrie, with lowering clouds that creep like winding-sheets about the crags above its ink-black tarns.

Indeed, Housman's poetry has become linked in my memory with a scene from years ago. It was at Kotor—Cattaro—far up the Adriatic gulf that bears its name. At midnight on the terrace below my window a Jugoslav girl was singing to a party of her young countrymen, apparently about to leave for their national service, while overhead an intermittent thunderstorm rolled its echoes among the black mountain peaks that guard the gates of Montenegro. Now there seems in Jugo-slav singing something alien to the West—some touch perhaps of that Orient which brought to Serbia so many tragic centuries. For I have something similar from Indian lips. But what startles the Westerner in such singing is its unspeakable intensity—a self-abandonment to desolation and despair that may make even Gluck's 'Che farò senza Euridice?' seem by comparison restrained and self-controlled. I felt then, as never before, what Aristotle meant by the passionate 'pur-gation' of passion; what Homer meant when he made his characters 'take their fill of lamentation', or spoke of '*immeasurable* lament'. And I would give much to hear again that girl under the midnight crags of Cattaro, who made one realize with what anguish beyond our guessing the choruses of Athens may once have chanted for the dooms of Thebes and Troy; or the women of Synge upon the cliffs of Aran. Some echo of that despair, terrible but enchanting, I find again in the best of Housman; who, sending a poem to his sister when her son had fallen in Flanders, added that he saw it as a purpose of poetry 'to har-monize the sadness of the world'.

*   *   *

However, Housman's poetry, like most (especially lyric poetry), depends for its effect less on content than on form, less on its meaning than on its music. The two are not wholly separable. But by 'meaning' and 'content' I mean what would survive in a good prose translation into another tongue.

Here, of course, the Adversary again grows loud; accusing Housman's style of cliché, falsetto, and repetition; his metre, of a tom-tom monotony of thump like Macaulay's. And here we drift out into the unfathomable ocean of taste, and the incalculable currents of fashion. It would be interesting if some clever psychologist would analyse more clearly the psychology of aesthetic taste. For often human tastes seem like—much *too* like—the conditioned reflexes of Pavlov's dogs. Certain things become accepted as pleasurable. Men grow conditioned to like them, because they are familiar and recognizable. But in time, for the more rebellious and restless minds, the familiar pleasure begins to pall with satiety and saturation. They revolt and innovate. The majority at first howls disapproval. But more and more of them become familiarized and reconditioned. So a new taste, a new fashion establishes itself, till the whole rather silly cycle starts again. Not a very dignified process for a supposedly rational animal. Indeed it seems even less intelligent than ladies' fashions, which husbands and fathers are apt to find a little foolish. For ladies at least do not shrilly proclaim that this spring's hats represent a final discovery of absolute beauty, which will henceforth reign supreme—they know it will reign only till next spring. Nor do they pour pitying contempt on last spring's hats (unless belatedly worn by other ladies). But in aesthetic fashions men constantly commit the equivalent of both these follies. They are tied to the spluttering Catherine-wheel of 'contemporaneity'—to use a word as ugly as the thing. And how is one to tear free from this wearisome Wheel? Only, so far as I can see, by admitting, firstly, the complete relativity of taste. Secondly, by an obstinate individualism, a laughing contempt for all modes, movements, and majorities, pundits, prophets, and popularity. Thirdly, by travelling as widely as possible in the art and literature of many times and lands. Fourthly, by seeing that, while fashion is merely frivolous, things like bad thinking or fanaticism, mental unhealth or decadence are not merely subjective whimsies, but vital realities, with vital consequences, often though these are neglected by frivolous criticism. No one dies of a spring-fashion (unless dangerously denuded); but a rotting influence, like a spring influenza, can have costs of a very different kind.

* * *

Of Housman's style and metre, then, I can only say what I enjoy; in the hope of perhaps increasing a little the enjoyment of others. Apart from certain blemishes like the sixty-seven unhappy 'lads' of his first volume, a perhaps too frequent use of 'oh', and a tendency to repeat certain words or phrases like 'yon', 'forlorn', 'earth's foundations', or 'for aye', his style at its best keeps a clarity and purity that still delights me after close on fifty years.

There are famous writers who go proud in gold and purple, seeking elaborate words from the archaic past, or from their own invention, or from the dictionary. Such are Aeschylus or Pindar, Spenser or Shakespeare or Milton. There are famous writers who give a twist of their own to diction, grammar, and syntax, like a strong man bending horseshoes in his hands. Such are Shakespeare, often, or Meredith or Hardy. There are famous writers who, while keeping often a plain enough vocabulary, twist and torment their thoughts. Such are the Metaphysical Poets.

All these aim at strong effects. They would rather seem strained than weak, exaggerated than flat. At their best, they are magnificently effectual; but in their weaker moments, or in their weaker imitators, the effect can fail; and then the rider pitches from his high horse into the dust.

In reaction against such pomp and circumstance, with all their perils, others have protested like Montesquieu, or Wordsworth (in theory), or Samuel Butler, or Verlaine, that to strain for the sublime is 'unnatural'. It leads to the inflated, the affected, the false. Far better walk plainly afoot, with steps firmly planted on the honest earth.

But here too there is danger. Those who go too much afoot can become pedestrian—muddy or dusty, flat-footed or down-at-heel; like the worser Wordsworth, or the Patmore of *The Angel in the House*. The democrat who is too vain of having no dress-clothes may grow both boor and bore. The pride of Antisthenes, peeping through the holes in his rags, was an ostentatious arrogance not even redeemed by any magnificence. Our age knows too well the depressing bareness of that brick-box style produced by cubist architects in reaction against past flamboyance. It takes a very strong and original personality, like Swift's, or Cobbett's, or Bentham's, or Samuel Butler's, to prevent the plain style from sinking into the dull and ugly, or the vulgar and commonplace.

But, between the extremes of the purple and the plain, there exists a middle way of writing, which looks easy, but is far from it—a style whose power lies in its simple purity. It is to be found, I think, in Sappho, in Sophocles, and in Terence; in the best of Ronsard and Racine; in the letters of Dorothy Osborne and some other women of the seventeenth and eighteenth centuries, especially in France; in the prose of Montesquieu or Voltaire, the plays of Alfred de Musset, the verse of Walter Savage Landor and Christina Rossetti. 'Ayez des idées nettes et des expressions simples.'[1]

Such a style may seem the language of every day: but it is not the language of every-day people. Its thoughts are not twisted: but they can have plenty of point. Its words are not jewelled or precious: but they are not colloquial or mean. Their charm is to seem exactly and unerringly right. The constructions are never tortured: but the syntax remains clear, natural, and flawless—even if written by women who cannot spell. Indeed women sometimes excel at this kind of writing; just as they sometimes know, while dressing in the simplest grey or black and white, how to attain a perfect distinction of style. It was a woman who wrote—

> Only the light from common water,
> Only the grace from simple stone.[2]

This kind of writing is a highly civilized gift, never common in prose, still less in verse; and certainly not common now. But, for me, it still exists in the best prose of Bertrand Russell, and in the best verse of Housman.

> Life, to be sure, is nothing much to lose;
> But young men think it is, and we were young.

> But men at whiles are sober
> And think by fits and starts,
> And if they think, they fasten
> Their hands upon their hearts.

> But when the snows at Christmas
> On Bredon top were strown,
> My love rose up so early
> And stole out unbeknown
> And went to church alone.

[1] Mme de Charrière to Mlle L'Hardy.   [2] Edna St Vincent Millay.

> Then, 'twas before my time, the Roman
>   At yonder heaving hill would stare:
> The blood that warms an English yeoman,
>   The thoughts that hurt him, they were there.

> In midnights of November,
>   When Dead Man's Fair is nigh,
> And danger in the valley,
>   And anger in the sky.

> And silent hills indenting
>   The orange band of eve.

Like the words, the word-order is simple and unstrained. And only sparingly is some startling or exotic, poetic or archaic word inserted, like a solitary red poppy in the greenness of a field—

> And burdens far away
>   The green and *sanguine* shoals.

> Or beeches strip in storms for winter
>   And *stain* the wind with leaves.

> There flowers no balm to *sain* him
>   From east of earth to west.

> Star and *coronal* and bell
>   April underfoot renews.

> The nations of the *nadir*.

> The Spartans on the *sea-wet* rock.

> I see the air benighted
>   And all the *dusking* dales,
> And lamps in England lighted
>   And evening wrecked in Wales.

> And up from India glances
>   The *silver sail* of dawn.

That this easy-flowing style was the result (despite Housman's stress on spontaneous inspiration) of much difficult revision; that his 'coloured counties', for example, were previously 'sunny', 'pleasant', 'checkered', 'patterned', and then (in a dream) 'painted'—all this is now familiar. But there is a stanza in 'The Merry Guide' whose variants seem worth a moment's comparison. At first it ran—

> By windy shires of woodland
> With steeples dim-revealed
> And cloudy shadows racing
> On all the endless weald.

Then it became—

> By blowing realms of woodland
> With sunstruck vanes afield
> And cloud-led shadows racing
> About the windy weald.

The gain seems to me striking. Whole 'shires' of woodland are surely exaggerated. 'Blowing' is windier than 'windy'—one sees the branches shake. With 'sunstruck' vanes the sun suddenly comes out; whereas 'steeples dim-revealed' had suggested a grey August haze, recalling the 'dim-discover'd spires' of Collins in his *Ode to Evening*. Similarly with 'cloud-led' shadows, in place of 'cloudy' shadows; the clouds too come alive and take an *active* part. And with 'windy weald' the ancient device of alliteration once more shows that it has not lost its power. Like blank verse, alliteration looks easy, but is not; and Housman loved it as well (but more wisely) as that far earlier poet of the western shires—William Langland.

*   *   *

As for Housman's prosody, though here too tastes remain irreconcilable, it is worth noting what an appeal Housman's verse has had for musical composers; though he cared little about their labours, and seems to have been goaded even to fury by Vaughan Williams. This metrical charm, for those who feel it, is easier to feel than to analyse. But I suspect that one element in its haunting power is this.

As is well known, in Greek or Latin, where metre is based mainly on quantity, most syllables *must* be long or short according to rigid rules; and though a few syllables can be made long or short at the poet's convenience, such 'common' syllables are relatively very uncommon. In English or German, on the other hand, where metre is based mainly on stress-accent, the great majority of syllables—even syllables as unimportant as 'of' or 'by'—can be stressed, or not, at the poet's will.[1]

---

[1] Cf. Swinburne: 'The thunder *of* the trumpets *of* the night.' This does not of course mean that 'of' is *heavily* stressed—merely that it is in either case *more* stressed than the syllable *immediately* before or after. The stresses of metre are *relative*; its undulations (in iambics or trochaics) like the undulations of a telegraph wire, which *sinks* between each pair of telegraph poles, whether these climb up a hill or sink to a valley.

Consequently, it is far easier in English or German than in the classical languages to write metre *of a sort*. Our poets are carving alabaster, where the Greeks and Romans had to work in marble, or even granite. Carved alabaster can be lovely; but a soft medium may become dangerous for the facile and the lazy.

Because, in English, the metrical pattern can do so much of the work, for both writer and reader, there is a temptation to make it do too much of the work. Take, for example, two lines of Flecker:

> I have seen old ships sail like swans asleep
> Beyond the village which men still call Tyre.

The first line depends to a dangerous degree on the metrical pattern running in the reader's head. It must scan—

> Í have seen óld ships sáil like swáns asléep.

For one cannot say: 'I háve seen óld ships' (as if someone had challenged the statement). Still less can one say (without metrical chaos): 'I have seen old shíps sáil.'

I have chanced on an example still more extreme in Masefield—

> The snow whirled, the ship bowed to it, the gear lashed,
> The sea-tops were cut off and flung down smashed.

Metrically this seems to me as degenerate as the blank verse of plays by Davenant or Suckling. (All the more strangely because at other times Masefield's metre can be masterly.)

Now Housman's verse is the very antithesis of such laxity. His prosody is boldly incisive. It resembles young mountain-ranges like the Alps, where peak and valley are sharply and precipitously cut; in contrast to our British mountains that aeons untold have slowly rounded and ground down, like aged teeth. Indeed, it often brings back to my memory that line of the *Chanson de Roland* on the Pyrenees:

> Halt sont li pui e li val tenebrus.

> High are the peaks, and darksome are the vales.

This is a type of landscape—or earscape—that I like. Housman's stressed syllables tend to be intensely stressed, both by normal English pronunciation and by the sense of the sentence; his unstressed syllables to be as markedly unstressed; so that his verse sings itself, and even fools could hardly mis-scan it. Instead of having to impose the metrical pattern on a huddle of syllables, the reader finds the metre passionately imposing itself on *him*.[1]

> The rainy Pleiads wester,
>   Orion plunges prone,
> The stroke of midnight ceases
>   And I lie down alone.

> On Wenlock Edge the wood's in trouble;
>   His forest fleece the Wrekin heaves;
> The gale, it plies the saplings double,
>   And thick on Severn snow the leaves.

> Fall, winter, fall; for he,
>   Prompt hand and headpiece clever,
>   Has woven a winter robe,
> And made of earth and sea
>   His overcoat for ever,
>   And wears the turning globe.[2]

This clear-cut impression in Housman's metre, as of some unusually deep-hewn relief, seems at times reinforced by a kind of quantitative effect. That is to say, the stressed syllables, very often, are not only stressed—forcefully pronounced—but also long—lengthily pronounced—as in Greek or Latin; and the unstressed syllables are not only unemphatically uttered, but also briefly uttered.

> The ōld decēīved divīner
>   Awākes in Hell to fīnd
> The web of dōōm spun fīner
>   Than any mōrtal mīnd.

> By Sēstos town, in Hēro's tower,
>   On Hēro's hēart Leānder līes;
> The signal tōrch has būrned its hour
>   And sputters as it dīes.

---

[1] Heine too has often the same masterful clarity of rhythm—

> Aus alten Märchen winkt es
> Hervor mit weisser Hand,
> Da singt es und da klingt es
> Von einem Zauberland.

[2] Curiously 'Metaphysical', at first sight, for Housman; but perhaps really influenced, I think, by the Greek of Theognis (ll. 425–8):

> Not to be born at all is the happiest lot for mortal,
>   Never to open eyelids on the bright shafts of the sun:
> Or, born, as soon as may be to pass beyond Death's portal,
>   To pull *earth's heavy mantle* above him and have done.

> They sāy my vērse is sad: no wōnder;
>   Its narrow measure spans
> Tēars of etērnity, and sōrrow,
>   Not mīne, but man's.

This effect of quantity may still further increase the effect of stress in augmenting, as the verse surges forward, the distance, and difference, between the wave-crests and the troughs that intervene. The subtilizers may object that its results grow too crudely clear. I let them.

Another device of Housman's is the monosyllabic foot.

> Is my | team | ploughing
>   That I was used to drive
> And hear the harness jingle
>   When I was man alive?

Replace the initial trochee and the monosyllabic second foot by normal iambics like those of the other lines—'Are now my horses ploughing?'—and the verse is spoiled.

The monosyllabic foot is a difficult creature; but it can sometimes do wonders, as in some lines of Meredith's *Love in the Valley*:

> Often she thinks, were this wild thing wedded,
>   More love should I have, and múch | léss | cáre.

Another device of Housman's is a sudden check in a stanza's metrical flow; as water may seem to pause on the brink of a waterfall.

> Wenlock Edge was umbered
>   And bright was Abdon Burf,
> And warm between them slumbered
>   The smooth green miles of turf;
> Until from grass and clover
>   The upshot beam would fade
> *And England over*
>   Advanced the lofty shade.

To which the nearest parallel I can recall is a delightfully dancing measure of Campion's, three centuries before.

> Kind are her answers,
> But her performance keeps no day;
> *Breaks time as dancers*,
> From their own music when they stray.

Perhaps Housman's verse-rhythms are not so unsubtle after all; nor the composers whom he attracted, so eccentric. In an age when most poets, whatever may be their other merits, have become as songless as Australia's birds were once supposed to be, I find a special pleasure in this verse that sings itself. Metrical analysis can easily grow a bore. 'Do *you* understand all this about prosody?'de la Mare once said to me. '*I* don't.' But then de la Mare had by nature a marvellous ear. Housman, on the other hand, as is betrayed by a tantalizingly reticent passage at the beginning of his Leslie Stephen Lecture, was full of metrical theory. However, the main value of such theories is merely to amuse the curiosity of those who like to find reasons for their own feelings and sensations.

*   *   *

What then, it may be asked, is the exact rank of Housman among English poets? Such questions seem to me rather foolish, and arrogant. I do not understand the passion that some have for classing authors (as if one were a celestial examiner conducting a Day of Judgement) in rigid orders of merit. Just as Housman rejected the Order of Merit for himself, so literature rejects orders of merit in general. If you ranged all the English poets in a precise hierarchy, the next person asked would widely disagree; indeed, in another month, or another mood, one might disagree with oneself.

For real poetry Housman's own tests were curiously physical—it must make him bristle like a terrier at a rat, or make him cut himself shaving, or shiver down his spine, or feel a stab like a spear in his stomach. But some of us would put more trust in experiences less bodily, and longer-term. If a poet runs in my head, year after year; if he rises up in my memory at moments of emotion, whether pleasant or poignant, glad or gloomy—then, for me, his poetry is real. And real for me, by that test, Housman remains.

Ever since, half a century ago, I bought as an undergraduate that small, red, sixpenny volume which lay in the Cambridge bookshops of 1913, phrases and lines and stanzas from it have rooted themselves in my mind as phrases of the Old Testament in the minds of Covenanter or Puritan. Which? That would grow too intimately self-revealing; and I have none of the ardour of Rousseau for stripping in public. One instance, impersonal enough, will suffice. How often in the Second World War, as I came home at one or two in the morning from my war-job to the peace of my Buckinghamshire village, while the sky flickered and droned, or was left to the sinister silence of the stars, I found myself murmuring those lines printed after Housman's death!—

> I wake from dreams and turning
>   My vision on the height
> I scan the beacons burning
>   About the fields of night.
>
> Each in its steadfast station
>   In flaming heaven they flare;
> They sign with conflagration
>   The empty moors of air.
>
> The signal-fires of warning
>   They blaze, but none regard;
> And on through night to morning
>   The world runs ruinward.

Naturally, with his small output and narrow range, Housman remains 'a minor poet'. But there are two kinds of minor poets. There are those that resemble greater poets, and are merely less good—as many Elizabethan dramatists or sonneteers seem like small Shakespeares, who can write at moments very like Shakespeare, but are very far from being Shakespeare; or as many eighteenth-century poets are miniature Popes. But there is also another type of minor poet, much more valuable—men who, though not giants, yet give something of their own that no one else, not even the giants, has given. Miss *them*, and you will find nowhere else the particular thrill of pleasure, the particular personal relationship, that they can offer, and they alone. Their cup may be small; but it is their own—even if no bigger than an acorn-cup. They are unique. Such, for me, are Herrick, or the Marvell of the *Coy Mistress*, or Crabbe, or Beddoes, or Landor. And such, too, is Housman.

No doubt the keen-nosed hounds of criticism have scented in his poetry a surprising number of influences—Homer, Sappho, the Greek Anthology, Lucretius, Catullus, Horace, Propertius, the Border Ballads, Shakespeare (especially his songs), the Bible (especially Ecclesiastes and Job), Milton, eighteenth-century hymns, Johnson, Scott, Heine (who *is* important), Matthew Arnold, Tennyson, Swinburne, Christina Rossetti, Kipling, Bridges. The hostile may snort 'Professorenpoesie!' And yet, just as in de la Mare's poem, by some strange miracle, 'Whatever Miss T. eats Turns into Miss T.', so, whatever his sources, Housman, like those other greater plagiarists—Webster, Sterne, Goldsmith, André Chénier—remains unmistakably his strange self; whom others in their turn have tried to imitate, but with very small success.

It is not to be expected that lovers of Housman should agree which poem of his they love best. The favourite of Hardy and Wilfrid Blunt was 'Is my team ploughing?' Despite its metrical grace, it is not my own preference. Though cynical irony can be enjoyed, there are other things in life more valuable. And though this poem's bitterness has only too much truth, still its truth remains largely bitterness.

My own choice would be, rather, one of the last pieces Housman ever wrote—his valediction to Nature and to that beauty of the English countryside he had loved so long. It always recalls to me one of the most tragic scenes in ancient tragedy, where Hippolytus—another stoic figure on whom the laughter-loving Aphrodite never smiled—bids farewell to the virginal Artemis, Our Lady of Wild Things, whom he had followed so faithfully on the hills; recognizing with a touch of dying bitterness that, though the Goddess has revealed herself for an instant to comfort his last agony, yet the Immortals can sorrow only a moment for the dooms of the sons of men.

> Lightly Thou leavest our long comradeship.

So Housman too bids his mistress, Nature, an eternal, passionate, not unembittered farewell.

> Tell me not here, it needs not saying
>   What tune the enchantress plays
> In aftermaths of soft September
>   Or under blanching mays,
> For she and I were well acquainted
>   And I knew all her ways.
>
> On russet floors, by waters idle,
>   The pine lets fall its cone;
> The cuckoo shouts all day at nothing
>   In leafy dells alone;
> And traveller's joy beguiles in autumn
>   Hearts that have lost their own.
>
> On acres of the seeded grasses
>   The changing burnish heaves;
> Or marshalled under moons of midnight
>   Stand still all night the sheaves;
> Or beeches strip in storms for winter
>   And stain the wind with leaves.

> Possess, as I possessed a season,
>   The countries I resign,
> Where over elmy plains the highway
>   Would mount the hills and shine,
> And full of shade the pillared forest
>   Would murmur and be mine.
>
> For nature, heartless, witless nature,
>   Will neither care nor know
> What stranger's feet may find the meadow
>   And trespass there and go,
> Nor ask amid the dews of morning
>   If they are mine or no.

All this I have felt so exactly, and repeated to myself so often, that I half feel at moments as if the poem were my own. Of its kind there is, for me, nothing more perfect in the whole range of English poetry.

*   *   *

Housman was not, indeed, one of those poets, like Crabbe, who seem to have a botanist's or ornithologist's love for nature's tiniest details; he had not the short-sighted Tennyson's microscopic eye. His iron will made him walk his five or six miles daily in the dull, flat outskirts of Cambridge; but he is described as walking with eyes on the ground, or—as I have seen him—fixed straight and impassively ahead. Of trees, however, he does seem to have had a special love and knowledge.

> Give me a land of boughs in leaf,
>   A land of trees that stand;
> Where trees are fallen, there is grief;
>   I love no leafless land.

For centuries there had stood on the Backs of Trinity that noble avenue of limes whose phantom shades still rise in Tennyson's *In Memoriam*—

> Up that long walk of limes I past
> To see the rooms in which he dwelt.

But in our own day these seventeenth-century limes of Trinity, grown gaunt and decrepit, had regretfully to be felled, and replaced by a new generation of saplings; and then, to hide the horrible nakedness of the land where they had stood, two rows of flowering cherries were planted parallel, on the outside, to the rows of young limes. That happy idea I gather to have been Housman's.

> Loveliest of trees, the cherry now
> Is hung with bloom along the bough,
> And stands about the woodland ride
> Wearing white for Eastertide.

Housman never lived to see his cherry-trees at Trinity in their full glory; yet they remain a fitting memorial of the poet who had praised so often the blossoming whiteness of the English spring—cherry and chestnut, pear and plum and sloe; just as Proust, asthmatic prisoner in his closed carriage, would drive in springtime among the orchards of France, to glimpse once more 'l'ombre des jeunes filles en fleur'.

The Nymphs, like the Gods, heed little the passage of man's mortality. But every spring when I see the cherry-trees of Trinity tossing their white arms like a Greek Chorus of Dryads, their carefree forgetfulness takes back my memory to the lonely, gifted, unhappy man through whom they were planted there.

Happiness

I T was an observation of Johnson's that 'he had never passed that week in his life which he would wish to repeat, were an angel to make the proposal to him'. 'I have always been considered', said Goethe, 'one of Fortune's chief favourites. Yet there has been nothing but toil and care: I may say that in all my seventy-five years I have never had four weeks of genuine well-being.' 'The Caliph Abdurahman', observed Tolstoy to Gorky, 'had during his life fourteen happy days; but I am sure that I have not had so many.' And Anatole France, if we can believe his secretary, was more disconsolate still—'On me croit heureux. Je ne l'ai jamais été une heure, un jour.'

These seem to me astounding confessions. No doubt artistic temperaments are often tempestuously moody, or histrionically exaggerated. But even if we suppose that these four men enjoyed ten times —a hundred times—more happiness than they owned to, the result remains sufficiently dismal. Had Tolstoy's Caliph Abdurahman been happy for fourteen *hundred* days, instead of fourteen, that would still make less than four years; now most people would consider only four years' happiness in a whole lifetime to be a tragically poor allowance.

If brains so exceptionally keen as Johnson and Goethe, Tolstoy and Anatole France, could capture only such beggarly fragments of felicity, the ordinary man might surely be excused for despairing of life.

Yet he does not. Indeed, it would be extraordinary to hear any ordinary man giving so doleful a summary of his own existence. How many of us have ever met anyone who said, or whom we could even imagine saying, that he had never enjoyed a single month's content? On the contrary, most men and women seem to look back to periods of happiness measured in no such niggardly doses of 'days' and 'weeks'.

No doubt it remains extremely hard to be certain about this. For people do not commonly or readily discuss a matter so intimate. But such at least is my own experience. I cannot, indeed, claim to have been as happy as Montesquieu, who never had a grief, he says, that could not be cured by an hour's reading. He knew nothing, apparently, of griefs that make it impossible even to read. A strangely placid temperament. And since it is silly to pose as wiser than one is, I must admit, too, occasional moods of general depression when all human effort seems a beating-up of desert dust, and all human relations hollow, and 'vanity of vanities' the final word. One may ask oneself which of these moods, the gayer or the gloomier, sees life more truly; just as the Chinese sage who had one night dreamed himself a butterfly, wondered whether he were really a butterfly dreaming itself a man, or a man dreaming himself a butterfly. But since the moods of gloom have so far been far the fewer, and seemed linked with a less balanced state of mind, I am inclined to discount them. Often such megrims can be explained by being out of condition and overworked; one may find common sense again out of doors, where open air restores an open mind. On the other hand, I have never been convinced by optimists. 'Il y a horriblement de mal sur la terre'; and if I have fared better, it has been largely by unusual good luck. Indeed both extreme optimists and extreme pessimists seem to me to suffer both from too much imagination and from too little. All the same, whatever the future may bring (and I cannot, at my time of life, expect it to go on being as happy as the past), I shall have had, in the aggregate, periods of happiness totalling, not days or weeks, but many years. Why is it, then, that the world's cleverest minds have often reported so blackly of it? Why have they proved often so much less clever than their inferiors at getting from life a good deal of what they want?

A queer paradox; and a fascinating problem. One might have supposed it also an important one, since most men make happiness—or imagine they make it—their prime object and their main pursuit. No doubt there are some prudent persons who cleave to the paradoxical conviction that to pursue happiness is only to lose it, since it can be captured only by *not* pursuing it. Yet this, after all, is only a subtler method of pursuit—an attack in flank, instead of in front.

None the less my encyclopedia, which discusses topics by the ten thousand from 'Aabenraa' to 'Zwyndrecht', and deals with subjects as vaguely general as, for example, 'Intelligence', finds no room for any article on 'Happiness'. Even the index ignores it. *There* you will find that less elusive, but more treacherous thing—'Pleasure'; but not 'Happiness'. Did the editor think the problem too difficult?—or not think of it at all?

Surely it is a little odd, too, that even this scientific age, which leaves not the humblest natural phenomenon unstudied, and pries into the private lives of amoeba or flatworm, and probes the remotest abysses of both time and space, and devotes some of its subtlest brains to the problem of roasting alive the greatest possible number of human beings in the shortest possible time, should yet apparently search so little, even unscientifically, into this question of happiness; which remains, for most of us, the most vital of all?

In the days when happiness was looked for only, or mainly, in a future life, bookshelves groaned, as one would expect, beneath rival itineraries to the New Jerusalem. But to-day, when most men look much more, if not wholly, for felicity in this world, the guides seem curiously few.

Of course, there have been, and are, austere philosophers and moralists, such as Carlyle, who would reply, 'So much the better. Men should seek, not happiness, but something higher.' 'The will to happiness', to quote a Nazi writer, 'is lacking in us, and the idea that it is possible to work and struggle for individual happiness is not only foreign to us, it is positively revolting.' Such pundits can point in triumph to all the historic figures who seem to have pursued, not pleasure, but pain; not happiness, but sacrifice and martyrdom. But perhaps these altruists are overquick to cry 'Victory!' It may, indeed, be true (and a bleak sidelight on life) that men really occupy much, sometimes most, of their time, not in pursuing either happiness or pleasure, but in fleeing from unhappiness or pain—the pain, it may be, of gnawing conscience, however irrational; the unhappiness of thwarted impulses, however blind. To escape these they may be glad enough to choose other pains or unhappinesses that are at least less. Better stake and faggot than eternal Hell; better death at the front than contempt, and self-contempt, at home. But, even so, the pleasure-pain principle still holds.

'Cher Paphnuce,' says Nicias in the *Thaïs* of Anatole France,

ne crois pas que je te trouve extrêmement ridicule, ni même tout à fait déraisonnable. Et si je compare ma vie à la tienne, je ne saurais dire laquelle est préférable en soi. Je vais tout à l'heure prendre le bain que Crobyle et Myrtale m'auront préparé, je mangerai l'aile d'un faisan de Phase, puis je lirai, pour la centième fois, quelque fable d'Apulée ou quelque traité de Porphyre. Toi, tu regagneras ta cellule où, t'agenouillant comme un chameau docile, tu rumineras je ne sais quelles formules d'incantation depuis longtemps mâchées et remâchées, et le soir, tu avaleras des raves sans huile. Eh bien! très cher, en accomplissant ces actes dissemblables quant aux apparences, nous obéirons tous deux au même sentiment, seul mobile de toutes les actions humaines; nous rechercherons tous deux notre volupté et nous nous proposerons une fin commune: le bonheur, l'impossible bonheur!

This seems to me both true and untrue. It seems untrue in suggesting that all men always *consciously and directly* aim at happiness. That is quite inaccurate. Paphnuce *may* indeed have eaten his oilless radishes with a clear calculation of gaining the bliss of Heaven; but he may, on the other hand, have condemned himself to lifelong austerity from the curious notion that God ordained that he should, or that it would add to the pleasure, or the glory, of God, or from other crotchets equally bizarre; or merely from a blind sense of compulsion that he could not explain even to himself. Therefore to say that Paphnuce *must* be only pursuing happiness seems to me false—unless, of course (as is not uncommon with ascetics), he was a masochist, in whom the painful expiation of guilt had become perverted into pleasure; like, for example, Ignatius of Antioch, who wrote, on his way to martyrdom at Rome, 'Oh that I may *enjoy* the wild beasts!'

On the other hand, supposing it is asked what compelled Paphnuce to obey his conscience, and resist the temptation to exchange virtuous radishes for wicked pheasants, the probable answer still seems to me that the pain of his sense of guilt, the torment of disobeying his sense of obligation, outweighed, for him, the pleasures of the pheasant. To seek the agreeable and avoid the painful may not always be men's conscious motives; but pleasure and pain remain, I think, the ultimate sanctions that, consciously or not, make those motives prevail. Much human behaviour seems as little reasoned as the conditioned reflexes of Pavlov's dogs; but it was by pleasure and pain that Pavlov established those reflexes—by tasty morsels or electric shocks.

Dr Johnson, we are told, had a compulsion to touch posts in the street. Touching posts can hardly have given him much of either pleasure or happiness. But, if he missed a post, the result was a disquiet and anguish so acute that he was constrained to go back and touch it.

Perhaps I may be forgiven for recalling, though trivial, the clearest case I can myself recall of an acute moral conflict, needing instant decision, which I seem able to analyse. Near Grandcourt-sur-Ancre in 1917 a party from my company was carrying up, in single file, bombs and water, for a night attack. There were no communication-trenches; and the Germans, having seen us, I suppose, silhouetted against the last red of the winter sunset, very promptly and accurately put a series of salvoes into the rear half of our long column in Indian file. One voice said to me: 'Your job is to bring up these supplies. Go forward.' Another voice answered: 'But if you are afraid to go back and do what can be done for the wounded, the memory will be a torment.' To go back was perhaps a curious form of hedonism. But such it seems to me still. Others may work differently. But, in essentials, I doubt it.

In short, pleasure and pain, happiness or unhappiness are often not the goals visible before men's eyes; but I suspect they are always, whether consciously or no, the driving-force at their backs. The bullet may be aimed at all sorts of different targets; but the propellent is always one, or both, of these impulsive powers.

The hedonists then may indeed oversimplify, if they say that men above all seek happiness; it may be truer to say that men seek, above all, to live out their impulses—often irrational, often disastrous though these are—because they often find the frustration or restraint of those impulses intolerably painful. But this is rather a shift of emphasis from pleasure to pain, than a confutation of hedonism. In essence, I believe that Anatole France's Nicias spoke the truth.

If this is so, then the superiority of altruists lies, not in their being sublimely exalted above considerations of pleasure and pain, but simply in their chosen satisfactions and dissatisfactions being often socially more valuable.

In any case, if to wish for happiness is debased, debased I remain. And so it seems worth inquiring a little why happiness should be thought, and found, so difficult; and how, perhaps, it might be made a little less so. By 'happiness' I mean a state of satisfaction of some appreciable duration and stability. For though we can speak of 'moments of happiness', the idea of 'happiness' suggests to most of us more than mere transient gleams. 'Happy' meant originally no more than 'lucky'. Perhaps that etymology suggests a certain pessimism in popular experience, as if happiness were a pure gift of fortune; just as the Greek for it, εὐδαιμονία, means that one has a good genius watching over one. But though Bernard Shaw thought the direct pursuit of happiness a folly,[1] I do not see why intelligent beings need leave the problem so fatalistically to luck or demons.

*   *   *

[1] Cf. Flaubert: 'Le bonheur est une monstruosité; punis sont ceux qui le cherchent.' But that admirable man could be morbidly extreme.

A natural beginning for these unscientific musings is to consider first some of the views of our fathers before us. Here the difficulty arises that so much of our evidence comes from literature; and literary minds are so often abnormal or untypical. Still literature must remain an important witness, if only for lack of others. It turns out, however, to be often a far from cheerful witness. No one, so far as I know, has ever formed the dismal project of compiling an Anthology of Pessimism. But it would certainly make a far fatter volume than an Anthology of Optimism. And not only a far fatter volume, but, as literature, a far finer one.

I have no intention of here assembling anything so doleful, to depress my fellow-creatures. Yet it may be worth casting a cursory glance over some of the material such an anthology could use. For, first, I am astonished by its abundance; secondly, it seems to me to illustrate how unbalanced, very often, creative writers are in forming judgements, unsurpassed though they may be at expressing feelings. It sounds very fine to talk, like Shelley, of poets as 'the unacknowledged legislators' of the world; and no doubt, the best writers have often been voices of the better conscience of humanity; but creative literature as a whole seems more often an intoxicating stimulant— sometimes precious, sometimes pernicious—than an oracle of wisdom. More of it has been inspired by Dionysus than by Pallas Athene.

At the very beginning of history the Sumerian epic of Gilgamesh already lifts up a cry of pain. Man's life on earth, it laments, is only bitterness; already the civilization of cities has corrupted the native goodness of the heart; and beyond the grave, in the dust-covered House of Ereshkigal, the souls must flit like flocks of dishevelled birds, with only clay to eat for all eternity.

Ancient Egypt, under the funereal shadows of its pyramids, seems often no gayer.

> Those who built their tomb-temples,
> Their place is no more.
> Behold what is done therein,
> Behold the places thereof;
> Their walls are dismantled,
> Their places are no more,
> As if they had never been.
>
> None cometh from thence
> To tell us how they fare;

To tell us of their fortunes,
To satisfy our heart,
Until we too get us gone
To the place whither they have departed.

From Israel, travailing century after century beneath the Egyptian lash, or amid the parched stones of the wilderness, or under kings that do evil in the sight of the Lord, or in foreign captivities, there comes the answering cry that all is vanity, and increase of wisdom only increase of sorrow.

For what hath man of all his labour, and of the vexation of his heart, wherein he hath laboured under the sun? For all his days are sorrows, and his travail grief; yea, his heart taketh not rest in the night. . . . Wherefore I praised the dead which are already dead more than the living which are yet alive. Yea, better is he than both they, which hath not yet been, who hath not seen the evil work that is done under the sun.

True, Ecclesiastes is exceptionally doleful, as well as entrancingly beautiful. But there are also those eloquently sombre pages of the Books of Kings, the tragic protests of Job, the wailings and gnashings of many of the prophets.

*　　　*　　　*

Turn north-west across the Cretan Sea, from Hebrew to Hellene. Through the clearer and more critical vision of the Greek race, despite their radiant vitality, there fall often the shadows of a melancholy yet deeper, and more persistent still; from Homer nine centuries, perhaps, before Christ, to Palladas, four centuries after.

For never a thing more wretched, than man, e'er comes to birth,
Of all that breathe and creep upon the ways of earth.[1]

Not to be born at all is the happiest lot for mortal,
　　Never to open eyelids on the bright shafts of the sun:
Or, born, as soon as may be to pass beyond Death's portal,
　　To pull earth's heavy mantle above him and have done.[2]

He that craves in life a span
Past the common lot of man,
Sets his heart, past questioning,
On a vain and empty thing. . . .

[1] *Iliad*, XVII, 446–7.　　　　[2] Theognis, ll. 425–8.

Never to be born is best;
Next to that, far happiest
He that hastens from his birth,
Fast as may be, back to earth.[1]

If there is life in Hades!—
But I pray there may be none! For if the dead
Must find, there too, more sorrows to endure,
Ah whither should we turn?[2]

Dionysius, of Tarsus, here doth rot,
Sixty, ne'er wed. Would God my sire had not![3]

But perhaps no passage is more characteristic of Greek pessimism than that meeting between Solon and Croesus which, whether true or no, remains, by its simplicity and its grace, its civilized dignity and its melancholy wisdom, one of the most wonderful things even in Herodotus. It will well bear repetition.

The aged Solon, so runs the famous story, after reforming his native Athens, travelled through Egypt and Asia, till he came to the court, at Sardis, of the rich Croesus, lord of Lydia. The king had his guest conducted round his bulging treasuries; and then, like a complacent millionaire, asked the Greek who was the happiest man he had ever known. To his disgust, Solon answered: 'Tellus the Athenian.' Who, then, was this Tellus? And why so happy? Solon replied that Tellus had the happiness of living in a city nobly governed; of seeing his sons grow up good men, and his grandsons growing up in their turn; and of dying splendidly in the supreme moment of a victory he had won for his countrymen against neighbouring Eleusis.

Then Croesus asked irritably whom Solon placed next after Tellus; hoping at least for second place. And Solon answered:

Cleŏbis and Biton. They were men of Argive race, endowed with sufficiency of goods, and with such strength of body as you shall hear. For both alike were victors in the games, and this tale also is told of them. At a festival of Hēra among the Argives the rites required that their mother should be drawn by an ox-team to the temple. But the oxen were not brought from the fields at the hour appointed. Then, since time pressed, the youths yoked themselves to the waggon, and drew their mother on it to the temple, a distance of five and forty stadia.[4] And when they had done

---

[1] Sophocles, *Oedipus at Colonus*, 1211–14, 1224–7.
[2] Macaria in Euripides, *Heracleidae*, 591–5.
[3] *Anth. Pal.*, VII, 309.   [4] Some five miles.

this in the sight of the assembled multitude, they found the best end life can have; and by it God showed that it is better for man to die than to live. For the men of Argos, pressing round them, blessed the youths for their strength; and the women of Argos blessed their mother for bearing sons like these. And their mother, overjoyed at the feat her sons had accomplished, and at their glory, standing before the holy image, prayed for her children Cleŏbis and Biton, who had brought her such honour, that the Goddess might give them the best blessing man can find. And after her prayer, when they had sacrificed and feasted, the young men lay down to sleep in the temple, and never rose again. Such was their end. But the Argives made statues of them, and set these up at Delphi,[1] in honour of their noble worth.[2]

Now it is not hard to find flaws in this poetic tale of Solon's wisdom. If Tellus was happier than Cleŏbis and Biton, then the benign goddess should have granted them, not death, but lives like his. If, on the other hand, death is always better than life, then Cleŏbis and Biton were happier than Tellus, and should have been placed first.

Again, the logical conclusion from Solon's view would be suicide. But perhaps one should never press sages to logical conclusions.

Thirdly, the historical Solon, at all events, appears to have been far from desiring to die young. Mimmermus the Ionian had written a poem praying for death at sixty (since life, for him, was worthless, once the days of love-making were past)—

I would that, free from sickness, untouched by cares or tears,
The doom of death might take me at the end of sixty years.

But to this Solon replied with a counter-couplet suggesting that 'sixty' would be better emended to 'eighty'.

But however that may be, the striking thing is the persistence with which this despair of human happiness runs through Greek literature and legend. Of Trophonius and Agamēdes, builders of the first temple at Delphi, it was likewise told that they were rewarded by the gods for their pious labours by a slumber from which they never woke; and again, when King Midas captured the wild woodland deity, Silēnus, and asked him what was best for man, he received the same grim answer as Theognis and Sophocles gave—that the best for man is not to be born; the next best, to die.

It seems to me perpetually amazing that a race fired with such tire-

[1] By a strange coincidence, these statues have been excavated. They are far less beautiful, however, than the story.

[2] Herodotus, I, 32.

less energy should yet have been so subject to moods as world-weary as Hamlet's; and, again, that these moods of world-weariness should yet have left them so unlike Hamlet, still burning with tireless energy. Perhaps the answer is, that just because they were so intelligent, optimism became, for most of them, impossible. Buoyant optimists tend to be obtuse. And, again, just because life is always brief and often bitter, they may, in part, have flung themselves into the intoxication of activity, as baser souls take to the bottle.

> Dear heart, if once escaping this battle's shock we might
> Live deathless still, and ageless, henceforward evermore,
> Ah *then* I would not thrust me to the forefront of the war,
> Nor urge thee too to the battle that brings man's name renown:
> But—since so many shapes of doom about us frown,
> Numberless, that no mortal may shun or escape at all—
> Forward!—whether the glory to us or the foe shall fall.[1]

It is also interesting that these men who conceived or repeated such tales of disillusion as those of Solon or Silēnus clearly assumed that there was no life beyond the grave, but only the peace of not-being. They dream neither of Pindar's blessed Elysium, nor of Homer's desolate Hades, so much worse than any life on earth that the wraith of Achilles would rather, he cries, be even the bondman of a landless labourer than lord of all the dead. For Herodotus and Sophocles and Thucydides, as perhaps for most thinking Greeks after 500 B.C., death has become only a dreamless sleep; and such rest, they think, is perhaps the best that man can find.

All the same these extreme denials of the possibility of human happiness on earth seem to me to transgress that golden rule of the Hellene, 'Nothing too much'. It is, of course, possible enough that it might be better had life on earth never begun. We have not the vaguest means of knowing: but it seems, at least, not very plausible to deny that *any* human lives are ever, on balance, happy. For this presupposes that honest men who have affirmed with the sincerity of their dying breath the happiness of their own lives, like Hazlitt or William Morris, were either lying or deluded. Which appears improbable (strange though it may remain that the tormented and irritable Hazlitt should have felt so well content).

* * *

[1] *Iliad*, XII, 322–8. Quoted in Greek, as he worked on his deathbed in 1763, by John Carteret, Earl Granville.

Rome was tougher than Greece. But among Roman writers too our anthologist of pessimism would find no shortage of material. There is Lucretius, for example, with his vision of the newborn babe crying out ('as well it may') like a little shipwrecked sailor on the stony shores of life; his bitter protest that always the waters of joy are tainted at the source with bitterness, and wormwood hidden among all life's flowers;[1] his single, all-sufficing consolation that there is at least no danger of our living beyond the grave. There are, too, Virgil's 'lacrimae rerum' and the 'anni fugaces' of Horace; the noble gloom of Tacitus, to whom it seems as if the gods cared only to punish the guilty, not to save the innocent; and the terse summary of the Elder Pliny, that there lives nothing more wretched, though nothing haughtier, than man—'nec quicquam miserius homine aut superbius'. There is Lucan's bitter epigram—

> And from the living, that they may endure
> Still to live on, the high Gods keep it hid
> That death is happiness.[2]

And there is that sombre Tenth Satire of Juvenal which the melancholy of Johnson was to rewrite as *The Vanity of Human Wishes*.

* * *

Christianity brought a new hope into the world—but it was hope of another world, which often left this one only darker, by contrast, in the shadow of God's reprobation. The pagans too had sometimes believed in legends of ancestral guilt. Yet, for them, such hereditary curses as haunted the houses of Pĕlops or of Labdăcus were only rare, local, and short-lived. But now the shadow of ancient sin fell across the whole human race, from its first ancestor to its last survivor.

It was a curious relapse, after classical civilization, to the more primitive idea of collective responsibility, where the individual has not yet emerged distinctly from his group, and every member of a clan is fully answerable for the guilt of his fellow-clansman. True, there was now a hope of redemption. But human perversity soon rekindled also the flames of Hell—and for how many? For all unbelievers; for all the unbaptized; and perhaps for the vast majority even of Christians. So

---

[1] Medio de fonte leporum
Surgit amari aliquid quod in ipsis floribus angat.
(IV, 1133-4)

[2] *Pharsalia*, IV, 519-20.

some theologians held; calling in grim texts to support them—'strait is the gate'—'many are called, but few are chosen'—'*justus vix salvabitur*'.[1]

How could human beings enjoy an hour's happiness in the face of this possibility of torment unending? Why did not every man and woman rush headlong to the nearest monastery or nunnery, to take the tonsure or the veil? How could they so cruelly drag the innocent unborn into an existence loaded with that appalling risk? How could they fail to feel such callousness criminal enough in itself to merit Hell, if anything could? How was it that they did not refuse parenthood, like the Essenes, and leave Christendom to die out; so that one day Mongol and Turk might have galloped through a lifeless Europe to the shores of the Atlantic, beyond which the New World might have lain undiscovered to this day?

Yet this did not happen. On the contrary, wives of Bath gaily led husband after husband to the altar; worthy citizens guffawed over the ribaldries of the *fabliaux* or *The Decameron*. Men do not seem to have enjoyed life, or loved it, noticeably less, because it might be followed by everlasting torture. They did not risk life, nor take it, less readily than we—on the contrary. So vastly more powerful, it appears, are human instincts and passions than human reason, or even than human credulity. The unconscious mind is often far more potent than the conscious. For some, no doubt, through those centuries the hereafter remained a waking nightmare, as later for Cowper or Johnson. Yet even Cowper could play with hares, and Johnson make his laughter resound through midnight London.

And so, though medieval writers are often sombre, they are not perhaps more often so than those of other ages. To a modern mind the universe of Dante with its Inferno, or that of Villon with its 'corps pourris et ames en flamme', appears far ghastlier even than the gloomy world of Theognis or Leopardi; yet it did not appear intolerably gloomy to Dante or Villon. If, among medieval literature, that of the Anglo-Saxons seems peculiarly lacking in gaiety, this may well be a matter, not of beliefs, but of national temperament and tradition. The stoic fortitude of the Scandinavian sagas has a tone far more buoyant. Even comedy soon breaks into them, as it breaks into the heroic *chansons de geste*, into the romantic *Aucassin and Nicolette*, or into the lyrics of the troubadours. While Langland lies dankly lamenting

[1] 'The righteous shall scarcely be saved.'

among the mists of Malvern Hills, there rises in answer the healthy
laughter of Chaucer's pilgrims gaily clattering through

> a litel town
> Which that ycleped is Bobbe-up-and-down,
> Under the Blee, in Caunterbury weye.

Dunbar might tremble as he lamented fellow-poets dead and gone—

> Our plesance here is all vain glory,
> This fals world is but transitory,
> The flesh is bruckle, the Feynd is slee.
> *Timor Mortis conturbat me.*

He might shudder at the darkness,

> Ubi ardentes anime
> Semper dicentes sunt Ve! Ve![1]

And yet not Rabelais himself could shake with heartier mirth than
Dunbar at the infernal saraband of the Seven Deadly Sins, or the unfortunate aeronautics of the Friar of Tungland, or the blasphemous
testament of Andro Kennedy.

> A barell bung ay at my bosum,
>   Of worldis gud I bad na mair;
> *Corpus meum ebriosum*
>   I leif on to the toune of Air.

Such is human hopefulness that no doubt the ordinary man trusted,
even then, that he himself would somehow slip through into Paradise,
like the good thief; and such is human beastliness that some pious souls,
like Thomas of Cantimpranus, looked forward with added relish to a
Heaven made only the more heavenly by a splendid view from its
precincts of the roasting of the damned.

*   *   *

With the rediscovery of the ancient world, and the discovery of the
new, there dawned for a moment a new, and often arrogant, optimism.
But it did not last; the laughter of Ariosto and Rabelais died away; new
religious frenzies brought new wars and new horrors; and if men had
dreamed their new universe more spacious, they still found it led, for
each of them, only to a six-foot grave. The banners of Tamburlaine,
the books of Faustus found the same inevitable end. And so among the

---

[1] Where in the flames, for evermo,
The souls that burn, cry 'Woe! woe! woe!'

later Elizabethans and the Jacobeans an anthologist of pessimism could gather poisoned disillusion to his heart's content.

> Beauty is but a painting: and long life
> Is a long journey in December gone,
> Tedious and full of tribulation.
>> (Dekker)

> Man is a tree that hath no top in cares,
> No root in comforts: all his power to live
> Is given to no end, but to have power to grieve.
>> (Chapman)

> Oh wearisome condition of Humanity!—
> Born under one law, to another bound,
> Vainly begot, and yet forbidden vanity,
> Created sick, commanded to be sound!
>> (Fulke Greville)

The earth with men upon it (the divineness of souls excepted) will not seem much other than an ant-hill whereon some ants carry corn, and some carry their young, and some go empty, and all to and fro a little heap of dust. (Bacon)

> Pleasure of life, what is't? Only the good hours
> Of an ague. (Webster)

If God had made life happier, He had also made it longer. Stranger and new halcyon, why wouldst thou longer nestle amidst these unconstant and stormy waves? (Drummond)

But though the first hopes of the Renaissance had thus faded, the patient rediscovery of science, the seeming triumph of reason, the new faith in progress slowly built up again, for a while, a more sober and more solid confidence. It is impossible to measure such things; but one is sometimes tempted to believe that the general mood of educated society in France and England was never more comfortably optimistic, or at least cheerful, than between the closing years of the seventeenth century and the closing years of the eighteenth.

No doubt there appeared in England, in place of plague, that new and dread disease—the spleen, hypochondria, or, as foreigners called it, 'the English malady'. 'A celebrated French novelist', writes Addison, 'enters on his story thus: "In the gloomy month of November, when the people of England hang and drown themselves".' Then there is that delightful letter of Voltaire's in 1727 describing how, on the sunlit shores of the Thames near Greenwich, he was met by revels of Arcadian gaiety; and yet on the morrow in a café he found the affable merchants of the day before transfigured into monsters of surly gloom. Had he committed some frightful offence, such as preferring Paris to London, or French cookery to English?

> Ne me sentant coupable de rien, je pris la liberté de demander à l'un d'eux, avec un air de vivacité qui leur parut fort étrange, pourquoi ils étaient tous si tristes: mon homme me répondit d'un air refrogné, qu'il faisait un vent d'est. Dans le moment arrive un de leurs amis qui leur dit avec un visage indifférent: 'Molly s'est coupé la gorge ce matin; son amant l'a trouvée morte dans sa chambre, avec un rasoir sanglant à côté d'elle.' Cette Molly était une fille jeune, belle et très riche, qui était prête à se marier avec le même homme qui l'avait trouvée morte. Ces messieurs, qui tous étaient amis de Molly, reçurent la nouvelle sans sourciller. L'un d'eux seulement demanda ce qu'était devenu l'amant: *Il a acheté le rasoir,* dit froidement quelqu'un de la compagnie.

Some forty years later Diderot describes the Baron d'Holbach's impressions of England—vast and costly pleasure-domes,[1] where one could hear a mouse creep; tall, silent women strolling about to delicious music as gloomily as Egyptians defiling round the tomb of Osiris; and a retired spot in St James's Park with a pond reserved for ladies only—to drown themselves.

It would make an interesting subject for research to discover statistically how far this idea of suicide as our national sport was anything more than an international joke. For it seems doubtful whether the eighteenth-century belief that the English spent their lives killing themselves can have had any more foundation than the medieval persuasion that the English were cursed with tails. But the 'English malady', of spleen or 'hyp', cannot have been mere fable; probably it came, like the gout, from over-generous eating and drinking, rather than from metaphysical conviction.

None the less, for the happy few, the age which produced Montesquieu and Diderot, Hume and Fielding, Goldsmith and Jane Austen, the music of Handel and Mozart, the canvases of Reynolds, the architecture of Georgian Bath, seems to me markedly happier, or at least calmer and more balanced, than most; even if here too it is notable that the writers remain often melancholy voices—like Gray, for instance,

---

[1] Presumably an allusion to Ranelagh with its great rotunda.

or Swift or Johnson with their conviction that man is only happy when 'well deceived' or 'when drunk'.

Perhaps hopefulness reached its climax with the coming of American, French, and Romantic Revolutions. Indeed it grew, at times, almost imbecile.[1] But that Heavenly dawn was quickly overcast. Soon Romanticism turned, instead, to Stanzas in Dejection or Odes to Melancholy.

*　　　*　　　*

No doubt it is hard, often impossible, to settle the proportions of contentment or misery between one age and another. Such generalizations can be safely pursued only with extreme scepticism. But it remains, I think, significant that while many eighteenth-century minds complained of life, and some dallied with the noble savage, very few of them before Rousseau had complained specifically of the eighteenth century. They left it to nineteenth-century Romantics to talk of 'le mal du siècle'. With these revived an older form of pessimism, based on the nostalgic idea that other periods had been at least better to live in. When Leopardi cries 'fango è il mondo', or Chateaubriand that 'la vie est une peste permanente', they are only repeating the laments of Ecclesiastes or of Sophocles; but many Romantics find a fresh source of sorrow in the thought that their own era is specially accursed. Tossing aside the neo-classic idea of progress, the optimism of *les philosophes*, they revert to the older idea of other ages more golden, in a past beyond recall. (It may indeed be that some Romantics, being infantile and loth to grow up, in regretting past ages of mankind were really regretting the clouds of glory wreathed about their own lost childhood.)

---

[1] For example, in Joseph Priestley (1733–1804): 'Knowledge will be subdivided and extended . . . nature, including both its materials and its laws, will be more at our command; men will make their situation in the world abundantly more easy and comfortable; they will probably prolong their existence in it, and will daily grow more happy each in himself, and more able (and, I believe, more disposed) to communicate happiness to others. Thus, whatever the beginning of the world, the end will be glorious and paradisiacal, beyond what our imaginations can now conceive. Extravagant as some suppose these views to be, I think I could show them to be fairly suggested by the true theory of human nature, and to arise from the natural course of human affairs.'

Priestley has proved partly right; and *might* one day prove wholly so. But that day seems to me at least very remote; and I suspect that his 'true theory of human nature' contained some grave gaps.

Et ils parlèrent tant et si longtemps, que toutes les illusions humaines, comme des arbres en automne, tombaient feuille à feuille autour d'eux, et que ceux qui les écoutaient passaient leur main sur leur front, comme des fiévreux qui s'éveillent. . . . Il leur restait donc le présent, l'esprit du siècle, ange du crépuscule qui n'est ni la nuit ni le jour; ils le trouvèrent assis sur un sac de chaux plein d'ossements, serré dans le manteau des égoïstes, et grelottant d'un froid terrible.

L'éternité est une grande aire, d'où tous les siècles, comme de jeunes aiglons, se sont envolés tour à tour pour traverser le ciel et disparaître; le nôtre est arrivé à son tour au bord du nid; mais on lui a coupé les ailes, et il attend la mort en regardant l'espace dans lequel il ne peut s'élancer.

(Musset)

How beautiful this is; yet how imperfectly true! Despite these dismal prognostications the nineteenth century still contrived to roll on its way, as we now see it in retrospect, with Philistine energy and often, except for its poor, with a robustly *bourgeois* satisfaction. None the less the verdict of its creative writers still remained largely sombre and dissatisfied.

There are, no doubt, vigorous exceptions like Scott, or Macaulay, or Trollope. And there is Wordsworth, who said Coleridge was not happy enough to understand his poetry (though some of Wordsworth's poetry is sad enough). The buoyancy of Browning goes without saying; unfortunately it too often went without thinking, either; so that to some his optimism is more depressing than any pessimism. And again there is the sometimes rather crude heartiness of Meredith; but then I find it hard to understand the worship of 'Nature', who, were she really a person, would be a vampire as repulsively callous and perverse as she is beautiful.

Yet throughout the nineteenth century too, the voices praising life seem far outnumbered by the voices that accuse or lament it—the sardonic disillusion of Byron, the 'immeasurable sadness' of Tennyson ('*In Memoriam* is more optimistic than I am'), the stoic resignation of Vigny and Arnold, the epicurean melancholy of FitzGerald, the dreamy sadness of the Rossettis, the boyish rebelliousness of Swinburne, the 'dreadful night' of James Thomson, the disillusion of Flaubert and Maupassant, the scornful indignation of Housman, the bitter old age of Yeats, or the ironic pity of Hardy, whose Creator repents that he ever made the world.

As when, in Noë's day,
  I whelmed the plains with sea,
So at this last, when flesh
  And herb but fossils be,
And, all extinct, their piteous dust
  Revolves obliviously,
That I made Earth, and life, and man
  It still repenteth me.

When the hamlet hailed a birth
  Judy used to cry:
When she heard our christening mirth
  She would kneel and sigh.
She was crazed, we knew, and we
Humoured her infirmity.

When the daughters and the sons
  Gathered them to wed,
And we like-intending ones
  Danced till dawn was red,
She would rock and mutter, 'More
Comers to this stony shore.'

But I will not anthologize further. The result, though so familiar, already astonishes me by the overwhelming abundance of melancholia that it suggests. Indeed, looking back over the centuries at this long succession of wailing choirs, one begins to wonder that more of these writers did not decide, like Hardy in the end, that a gospel of tidings so ill was, even if true, better left unuttered.

Why load men's minds with more to bear
That bear already ails to spare?
  From now alway
  Till my last day
What I discern I will not say.

*   *   *

It would be interesting to know if this recurrent note of revolt against the harsh laws of life is particularly characteristic of the white races. Asia has indeed produced its own poetry of disillusion like Omar Khayyám's, or that haunting poem of Li-Po—

Lord, you offer us more wine. But do not fill our cups. I would sing

you the song of sorrow. Now comes the moment where the guests are
not so gay, when laughter falters, when the dancing-girls grow unsteady,
and the tulips let their petals fall. Now comes the one moment when the
heart speaks truth.

Lord, you have palaces, warriors invincible, scented wine—and I have
only my lovely lute that sings of bitterness at the hour when the tulips
let their petals fall.

In life we have one certainty—death. One day the mouths we kiss will
be filled with mould, and this lute that thrills beneath my fingers will
become but a perch for fowls.

The Tiger springs in the vale where once the Mang fish floated; coral
carpets the ravine where of old bloomed the violet.[1]

Hark! Out there, where the land lies white beneath the moon, hear the
monkeys lamenting as they lie on forgotten graves.

And now, Lord, fill our cups—let us empty them at a draught.

All the same, outside the West this note—perhaps it is only my
ignorance—seems relatively rarer. The literature of Arabia, Persia, or
China has plenty of tragic tales of death, cruelty, or unhappy love.
Asia has produced the pessimist resignation of Buddhism, the quietist
renunciation of Taoism. But passionate outcries of revolt against the
world seem, as a rule, much more Western. Is it that, if the Western
mind has been more rebelliously embittered by the conditions of
human life that it cannot change, this is precisely because of that very
energy, activity, and rebelliousness which have enabled it, in so many
ways, to change life's conditions? I do not know. But I should not be
surprised if there were in this an element of truth.

But however that may be, one is sometimes tempted to think that
sensitive and imaginative minds are as prone to underestimate the
amount of satisfaction existing in human life, as the insensitive and unimaginative are to underestimate its tragedies and miseries.

Apart from my children, one of the happiest-seeming people I have
known was our city rat-catcher. He was an elderly ex-gamekeeper,
apple-cheeked, hale, and young for his years; he was active, he was

---

[1] Cf. *In Memoriam*, CXXIII:

> There rolls the deep where grew the tree.
> O earth, what changes hast thou seen!
> There where the long street roars, hath been
> The stillness of the central sea.

Our beloved study of influences often grows stupid because our pedantry is
so loth to recognize that like circumstances can lead like minds to like ideas,
even where, as here, there is not the remotest possibility of 'influence'.

useful, he was interested and interesting. (How many professors can say as much?) He spent his time matching his wits against enemies that he respected and admired (I am not sure he did not even rather like them, and pity them); he told extraordinary tales of their cleverness; and when he appeared at intervals with a couple of grey bodies from my garden-shed dangling in his hand, I could see in his eye the satisfaction of a poet who has just mastered a sonnet. Maybe he had, too, a pleasanter sense of usefulness. For, after all, if no more sonnets were written, would it matter? There are more in the world already than any sane being has time for. And immortal rats would provide mankind with a much more serious problem than immortal sonnets. Anyway, my rat-catcher seemed a good deal happier than Wordsworth's Leech-gatherer. He was less lonely; and he certainly had no cause to complain that his quarry was growing scarce.[1] Similarly, one reads that among the happiest of races are—or were—the ice-bound Eskimos. It all becomes very puzzling and paradoxical.

*   *   *

Why is it, then, that we find so many writers, living in such different ages, and holding such different creeds, yet united in a pessimism that so little matches the views of ordinary men?

By 'pessimism' I do not mean what the Oxford Dictionary says it means—'the doctrine that this world is the worst possible'. For if that definition were true, pessimism would be limited to lunatics; any fool can think of ways in which life could be made far worse—suppose, for example, we all had perpetual colds in the head . . .

No doubt the 'optimism' of Leibnitz did consist in thinking this the *best* of possible worlds—that is, the best possible in the nature of things. For example, the rape of Lucrece was horrible; but only so could the Roman Republic arise, to form in due time the seed-ground for Christianity. To suppose this seems to impose curious limitations either on God's omnipotence or on God's goodness. But of course some have argued that ethical qualities are only attributable to

---

[1] Yet—so frail is human happiness at best—my poor rat-catcher has since been crippled by a car-accident, and he comes no more. The Cat has caught him—that great, brooding Cat (vaster and more mysterious than any Sphinx) which lives in my imagination as a truer symbol of Destiny than any Dove brooding on the troubled waters of the world. Human mice should not grow obsessed with the Cat; let them play out their time; but it seems to me only folly that can forget It *always*.

man, and not to God. In any case the whole theory seems merely one more of those fantastic schemes which are the stock-in-trade of philosophers.

Because 'pessimist' is the opposite of 'optimist', and 'worst' the opposite of 'best', you *can* say, then, for the sake of a childish verbal symmetry, that a pessimist believes this to be the worst of possible worlds. But since no sane person in fact believes it, there seems better reason for applying the term 'pessimist' simply to those who hold a generally sombre view of things.

Now writers may often take a more sombre view of life than common men either because they are superior and wiser, or because they are inferior and weaker, or both.

Writers may often be a superior type of human being. They may suffer more, because more finely sensitive. A philosopher would need all his philosophy to endure living in a pigsty—even in a modern and improved pigsty, highly luxurious to a pig. Again, writers may suffer from being more sympathetic. They may suffer, too, from their own solitude. Schopenhauer complained that most men were like monkeys; it only made it worse, he lamented, that from a distance they often looked so deceptively human. Or again finer minds may suffer more from the future, as well as from the present, because they foresee more clearly ills to come (which, of course, frequently fail to come). It is easy, then, for Heraclitus to be less gay than Hodge; who may be too stupid to see how black his own plight, too egoistic to see or care how black the plight of others. There was pith in Johnson's reply to the impertinent stripling who asked what the Doctor would give to be as young and gay as himself—'I could almost be content to be as foolish.'

Sometimes, on the other hand, the creators of literature make a rougher voyage of life than other men because they are in certain respects inferior. Defects of temperament may outweigh their intellectual gifts. Aristotle long ago propounded the question why genius was often melancholic. His answers do not seem very convincing. But it is not hard to find more plausible explanations than his for the sorrows of genius; such as over-sensitiveness; or over-ambition; or inward conflicts in minds too fraily balanced.

There is yet another reason—a very simple one—why literature should often seem gloomier than life. It is simply that the imagination of writers and readers alike lives on violent emotions; and the most violent emotions are those aroused by the tragic. Horace Walpole's wise aphorism that this world is a comedy to those that think, and a tragedy to those that feel, has for corollary that those who seek strong feeling incline towards tragedy. But this does not prevent authors who have piled agony on agony in their works, from living, sometimes, to a hearty old age, without showing the slightest wish to quit a world which they have perhaps spent their lives in depicting as a morass of tears. Just as an audience which has sat ravished while Desdemona was smothered, or Cordelia hanged, gropes briskly for its hats and coats, and goes placidly home to eat not a mouthful the less of supper, and to lose not a wink of sleep.

With books or plays, in fact, most of mankind are just like that Parisian populace so amusingly depicted by Marivaux:

Ce sont des émotions d'âmes que ce peuple demande; les plus fortes sont les meilleures; il cherche à vous plaindre, si on vous outrage; à s'attendrir pour vous, si on vous blesse; à frémir pour votre vie, si on la menace; voilà ses délices; et si votre ennemi n'avoit pas assez de place pour vous battre, il lui en feroit lui-même, sans en être plus mal intentionné, et lui diroit volontiers: 'Tenez, faites à votre aise, et ne nous retranchez rien du plaisir que nous avons à frémir pour ce malheureux.' . . . Cela remue son âme, qui ne fait jamais rien, qui n'a jamais rien vu, qui est toujours toute neuve.

No doubt children and the unsophisticated prefer their films and novels to end happily; but, provided that this happy goal is attained eventually, even they are ready enough to welcome almost any amount of hyperbolic terror or anguish on the way.

For these many reasons it seems understandable that creative writers should often discern, depict, and encounter in life a quite abnormal amount of gloom.

There is a further reason, which may shock bardolaters, and yet be sometimes true. Professor Hadfield has pointed out that, in applied science, the inventive brain is often in other respects by no means of the finest type. Many inventors have been only second-rate scientists, with a special, but isolated, flair for combining ideas. I suspect that the same may sometimes hold in the world of art and literature. Creative powers may go with an intellect not, in other ways, very bright. 'Ne l'écoutez-pas, monsieur', cried Lulli's irritated patron at table. 'Il n'a pas le sens commun. Il n'a que le génie.' In the human world, night-ingales can be geese.

No doubt, it has been common in the past, and still is, to look up to writers as repositories of wisdom. Arnold may talk of creative writing as 'criticism of life'; but, with certain fine exceptions, creative writers have often been too temperamental to make good critics of anything. After all, why expect dispassionate judgements from those whose main concern is with the passions? It is not so hard to understand why Plato banished poets; and why Plutarch compared their work, as a diet for young minds, to the head of the octopus—nourishing fare, but liable to bring bad dreams.

Creative writers, being sensitive and inventive, have often provided priceless evidence about life; but, being also hypersensitive and often not very intelligent, they have often been curiously incompetent at weighing and summing up that evidence. In general, then, it may be wiser to treat writers as witnesses about life, rather than judges. The world, no doubt, has long regarded many poets as philosophers; it might have been far wiser to regard many philosophers as poets. And perhaps there is less truth to be learnt about reality from poetry and fiction than from history, biography, and psychology.

*   *   *

And yet how surprisingly scanty, even so, reliable testimony on the subject of happiness remains! How rare it is to know, even with those we know best, what were the occasions, and the causes, of the happiest periods or events in their lives!

No doubt, even if people described such experiences in detail, many of their hearers—such is the diversity of tastes—would think such forms of 'happiness' sheer misery. Yet such personal confessions, if intelligent and frank, would still be of fascinating interest. But, as I say, they remain strangely and regrettably rare.

Autobiography, of course, provides a few notable exceptions. Wordsworth has described so vividly his happiness, especially as a boy among the fells, that for some, who can share his mysticism about mountains, Wordsworthianism has acquired the fervour of a religion; and for a few, like Mill, his gospel has proved salvation. Certainly I have had month on month of happiness with pack on back and mountains underfoot. I can remember an Easter morning forty years ago on Kidsty Pike, between Hawes Water and Hayes Water, when a blinding spring sun on snowy ridge beyond ridge, from Fairfield to Blencathra, brought a moment of such ecstatic intoxication that, were I a mystic, I should have called it a mystical experience. And though I cannot share Wordsworth's Nature-worship (I could as soon worship the Law of Gravity; for Nature, as I have said, were she a person, would be a *femme fatale*), I feel that he was very wise to be awake, so much more clearly than most, to the penalties men pay for too crowded, too artificial lives; to the abomination of big cities; to the health and happiness of living nearer to Nature.

> Love had he found in huts where poor men lie;
> His daily teachers had been woods and rills,
> The silence that is in the starry sky,
> The sleep that is among the lonely hills.

I have never forgotten Lord Keynes telling me how General Smuts quoted those lines to him in 1919, as they wandered, deeply depressed by the squalors of Realpolitik and treaty-intrigue, in the purlieus of Versailles.

But Wordsworth's way of life was rare and odd. Not many of us can spend our lives in a Westmorland hermitage, living on a legacy and a sinecure, and composing inspirations to be devoutly copied by three admiring females. Nor indeed would many wish to become what Wordsworth, after years of it, apparently became.

Then there is Rousseau who has no less vividly recounted the happy vagabondage of his youth, and his lotus-eating delight in drifting about the Lake of Bienne. But Rousseau is still less, for most of us, an object for prolonged imitation. He was too much of a dyspeptic and neurotic fakir.

More sympathetic by far, to me, is Rousseau's much obscurer contemporary, the charming Prince de Ligne; who really did sum up his life's happiest moments with that terse clarity one wants.

He did not know, he said, of any career happier than his, untroubled as it was by remorse, jealousy, or ambition (this last claim one may be permitted to doubt). And yet—'de vrai bonheur, je n'en ai connu que quatre jours: celui où j'ai mis pour la première fois mon uniforme, le soir de la première bataille où je me suis trouvé, le jour où l'on m'a dit pour la première fois qu'on m'aimait, et celui où je suis sorti après ma petite vérole.'

This, for once, is admirably precise; and consequently interesting. Most of us can well understand the happiness of those four occasions; but it seems a little too princely of the Prince to be able to enjoy 'real happiness' only the first time he did things; as if happiness were a sort of Goblin Market, whose fruits could never be tasted twice. Still, as he pursued the third of the above enjoyments with such indefatigable repetition that he finally died, at nearly eighty, from a cold caught at an assignation on the ramparts of Vienna, perhaps he understated his happiness. Besides, he must surely have had periods of 'vrai bonheur' from the gallant son whom he adored; even though he had to pay for it with grief for that son's early death in war.

Then there is Johnson, who being a hypochondriac, showed less, I think, than his usual sagacity on the theme of happiness. Sometimes he affirmed that man was never happy—as Pope said, 'Man never is, but always to be blest'; sometimes that man was happy only when drunk. Yet at other times he suggested, more reasonably, that it was 'the business of a wise man to be happy'; and the ultimate object of ambition to be happy at home. More specifically he described one evening spent in talk with Molly Aston as 'not happiness but rapture'. Then again, since he would have liked to spend life, had duty and religion permitted, driving in a postchaise with a pretty, conversable woman, he must surely have tasted *some* happiness on the road. Finally, it is hard to believe that he had no happiness from his beloved, grotesque Tetty and those monstrous endearments which Garrick would naughtily mimic in after-years.

Then there is Flaubert's brief report, at twenty-five, on his own few felicities (September 18, 1846)—'Les plus grands événements de ma vie ont été quelques pensées, des lectures, certains couchers de soleil à Trouville au bord de la mer, et des causeries de cinq ou six heures consécutives avec un ami qui est maintenant marié et perdu pour moi.' Terribly austere. But then Flaubert thought happiness 'une monstruosité', whose pursuit was always punished. I would far rather have been the Prince de Ligne.

Again, there is the summary of Anatole France—'Si l'on met de côté le lit des mortelles et la table où l'on s'assied avec quelques amis, mon plus grand plaisir dans la vie a été de me reciter en secret des vers de Racine.'

*　　　*　　　*

Yet such revelations, though fascinating, remain too fragmentary— glimpses of happiness, not general views of it. Human beings seem bafflingly vague about its nature, and the ways to it. Nowhere does this vagueness become clearer than in men's dreams of Heavens, Golden Ages, or Utopias.

Ah Love! could you and I with Him conspire
To grasp this sorry Scheme of Things entire,
  Would we not shatter it to bits—and then
Re-mould it nearer to the Heart's Desire!

But what *is* the heart's desire? There have been very strange ones. Men have dreamed of Heaven as an endless killing of animals in Happy Hunting Grounds—as an age-long fighting and feasting in Valhalla—as an eternal conversazione in Elysium—as an eternal siesta in Nirvana—as an eternal preoccupation with houris, or harps. Curious conceptions of bliss. Perhaps the chief interest of Heavens lies in the light they throw on the mentalities of the men who conceived them—on their pugnacity, their indolence, their sensuality, or their servility. As for streets of gold, gates of pearl, foundations of chalcedony and sardonyx, some may find them too like the garish pipe-dream of some too simple oil-magnate from the Middle West.

In fine, men do not seem very good at knowing what they really desire, or imagining what they would really enjoy, for even a few centuries at a stretch. Warier minds, indeed, have countered the misgiving that even celestial delights might pall, by exchanging eternity for timelessness. Thus their imagination takes refuge in the unimaginable—a successful evasion, for those who like it. But earthly Utopias are mostly horrid—except that their inmates are at least not expected to endure them for eternity. Golden Ages set in the past have usually been simpler—everlasting picnics, in perfect weather. One can understand their appeal to overworked peasants, like Hēsiod.

> Those were the years when, still, in Heaven Cronus reigned
> And men lived happy as Gods, with hearts that no cares constrained,
> Free from all toil and travail. Never upon them hung
> The burden of age—with hands and feet for ever young,
> They revelled and made merry, till Death, like a gentle rest,
> Ended those lives untouched of pain, in all ways blest.
> Ever the kindly cornlands, that no man toiled to till,
> Brought forth their harvests' bounty; and all men lived at will,
> Crowned with every blessing, on their own fields, quietly.[1]

This is lovely enough almost to suspend disbelief. And indeed there is no need for disbelief, if it is true that such Golden Ages are projections of the happy childhood of the individual, transferred to the childhood of the race. For then, in a sense, Golden Ages are largely true.

[1] Hesiod, *Works and Days*, 111–19; *Greek Poetry for Everyman*, p. 198.

If I were retelling the myth of Eden, I should say that in the moment when Adam and Eve tasted the Apple of Knowledge, the trees of Paradise suddenly turned sere and yellow, and its beasts, which had all been cubs or whelps or kittens, suddenly grew up, and became morose and dull. No need to drive our first parents from Eden; for in that instant it perished round them. No need to guard Paradise with a flaming sword; with the coming of understanding, Paradise had ceased to be.

And if I were remaking the myth of Heaven, I sometimes think, watching the inexhaustible zest and vitality of my children, that I should make all who entered there revert permanently to the age of seven—for then Heaven might remain Heaven for quite a long time, perhaps indefinitely. It has been said that to enter Heaven, a man must become as a little child; I am inclined to think that, lastingly to enjoy any Heaven yet invented, he must remain one.

To sum up, I doubt if any imagination can conceive the amount of pain and misery that has been suffered since life began on earth. On the other hand, imaginative minds have often underestimated the amount of simple happiness that can be got from life as it is. Lastly, it is strange how bad most human minds are, whether imaginative or not, at imagining what would make them happy—especially in Utopias and Heavens. Life can be less unhappy than many writers have imagined; but it might be less unhappy still, if men at large were not so curiously incompetent at imagining what would make them happy. Largely, it seems, they not only 'know not what they do'—they know not even what they want.

*   *   *

There is a Greek drinking-song, perhaps by Simonides, that runs—

> Health is the best that Heaven sends;
> Next, to be comely to look upon;
> Third is riches, justly won;
> Fourth, to be young among one's friends.

The first of these wishes makes the Greek world seem strangely near; the second, strangely remote. For health *is*, I still think, absolutely fundamental—a first priority; but surely this inordinate stress on good looks, as the second highest of human blessings, must to-day strike at least the male half of humanity as most peculiar. The third and fourth demands are more comprehensible. For 'riches', indeed, one might prefer to substitute 'a competence'; and even that, unless one is a miser, seems much more a condition of happiness than a direct cause of it.

For it is not clear to me that the rich are, in general, happier than men less plentifully endowed. Often they seem less happy. Evidently many of them soon exhaust satisfactory ways of enjoying their money. I have been told that a main solution of this agonizing problem is to be found in exquisite food and drink. But that may prove a solution not without physical dangers. And there are other drawbacks—the not uncommon sense of guilt about possessing opulence; the bore of managing it; the fear of losing it. Everyone knows the story of the melancholy prince whose physician prescribed for his malady the shirt of a happy man; and how, having at last, with great difficulty, found a happy man, the prince found also that the happy man had no shirt.

Perhaps men extract more enjoyment from making wealth than from spending it. But this too is a perilous pleasure; it may tend to oust all other kinds. The journal of Arnold Bennett is a vivid example. He was an honest man. But he grows tedious, and slightly disgusting, in his foolish obsession with fine food, fine clothes,[1] fine hotels, fine cars, fine yachts. Nor is one much inspired by his annual gloatings over the number of words written each year (423,800 in 1908—how bad, at that rate, a lot of them must have been!), and the money earned, down to the nearest penny (or halfpenny, for aught I know). Even the lonely beauty of the theatre at Epidaurus only inspires him to calculate the maximum takings if all its seats were sold. A commercial traveller on Parnassus. How Flaubert would have raged! Yet one must be candid: I suppose Arnold Bennett was happy, as authors go. All the same his journal does not strike me as real happiness.

Modern tendencies, in England at least, seem eliminating the extremely rich, as well as the extremely poor. In this there seems to me little to regret.

Last the Greek poet puts the joy of being young among one's friends. I have known persons who, feeling this to be a desolatingly brief blessing, tried to persuade themselves that the poet's 'to be young' could be taken in a metaphorical sense, regardless of one's calendar age. But I doubt if the Greek can here mean anything but literal youth. The poet has just stressed—even overstressed—the value of comeliness; most Greeks seem to have regarded old age with

[1] His journal contains, for example, the ineffable entry—'Beaverbrook's pyjamas second-rate.'

a realistic melancholy far removed from the rather canting com-
placency of Browning's Rabbi ben Ezra; and, after all, this is a song
for young revellers, who may well have regarded thirty as decrepitude.

Some would prefer to replace this fourth aspiration by some more
general phrase—'personal relations', or 'sympathy and affection'
(which would, of course, include the happiness that can come from
marriage and children, of which the Greek song curiously says nothing—but perhaps one can hardly expect *that* idea, either, from a
band of youths round a wine-bowl).

And many, no doubt, will complain that there are other serious
omissions. For example, there is work. But the Greek poet might have
answered: 'War and public service we all have—that goes without
saying. And we have our lands to farm. Most other forms of labour
are best left to the vulgar or the slave.' Then again, one may object
that there is nothing here about intellectual and aesthetic activities. But
again the Greek might have answered: 'What better intellectual or
aesthetic activity than is already implied, in the converse of the comely
young?' That, however, most of us would feel to be rather a limited
form of it. Finally, the Greek poet says nothing about the happiness of
religion and the next world. But there I own my sympathies are with
him, and with Confucius, who refused to concern himself with spirits,
when he knew too little of men; or to bother about death before he
even understood life.

In any case, these four lines of Greek poetry seem not a bad starting-
point for our inquiry. Only, to avoid muddle, it seems necessary first
to distinguish between the things that can be positive causes of happiness and the things that may be conditions of it. For example, a certain
calmly balanced imperturbability of temperament seems to me an
important help towards being happy. But I cannot picture it as causing
much positive happiness. Strong silent men do not give the impression
of rejoicing much in their silent strength. But life is so filled with petty
vicissitudes that a pronounced lack of imperturbability can bring very
positive unhappiness. Thus the journal of Virginia Woolf seems to me,
in spite of all her gifts, a distressing book to read, because so many of
its pages, with their anxieties, frustrations, and irritations, give the
impression of a skinless person buried to the neck in an ants' nest.
Without emotions one can have neither motive power nor happiness;
but excessive and febrile emotions seem, in the long run, to cost much
more than they give.

Again, freedom from fear is not a noticeable source of happiness; but it is an important condition of it, in a world where so many have been and are tormented by fear of want, fear of war, fear of death, fear of the next world, fear of public opinion, fear of political tyranny.

But such causes of unhappiness are so multitudinous that one would never end. My question is less ambitious. Why do many who are comparatively free from all these evils, yet fail to be happy? And what positive sources of happiness can men deliberately set out to seek?

'Simonides' seems to me essentially sound in putting first the gift of health. It is not merely that even philosophers lose much of their virtue, as Horace observed, when they have streaming colds; or, as Shakespeare echoed, when they have toothache.[1] Vitality is, in my experience, not only a precondition of most happiness, but itself one of the surest sources of it. For many, indeed, the Universe is too grim to be contemplated, let alone enjoyed, without a certain degree of intoxication. Yet most forms of intoxication are perilous. But there remains this one happy form of it that leaves no headaches—intoxication with the vital rush of the blood in one's own veins. The happiness of Wordsworth, to put it a little differently, was that he so wisely contrived to be drunk with brook-water from the fells of Westmorland. I doubt if, when all was over, Omar had got nearly as much happiness from all the grapes of Shiraz.

What else, indeed, but vitality is the main cause for the conspicuous and ubiquitous happiness of young things? If kittens and puppies, lambs and chicks and children are constantly delighted, and delightful, it is, above all, because they have a surplus of vitality—more than they strictly need, more than they know what to do with. A kitten patting a pebble or chasing a leaf, a lamb hopping and frisking with ridiculous gusto among a meadowful of stolidly chewing, dowager ewes, has solved the problem of enjoying life almost before it has experienced what life is—and probably better than it ever will again.

No doubt for human beings, even in youth, this complete lightheartedness is less easy. *Their* fears, griefs, and jealousies can commence early in childhood; and can cut deep, because they already begin to discover the hardness and complexity of life before they have acquired

---

[1] For there was never yet Philosopher,
That could endure the tooth-ake patiently,
How ever they have writ the stile of gods
And made a push at chance and sufferance.
(*Much Ado about Nothing*, V, I, 35–8)

the power and knowledge to cope with it; and so may feel themselves
impotently battling with something vast, mysterious, and cruel.
Hence small children can suffer immense miseries—the more immense
because they feel so small. Yet for the adolescent, even so, their vitality
usually comes to the rescue, with quick forgetfulness and resilient
hope. Chaucer's Squire is no fabulous being, nor Chaucer's Alisoun.
There they are by dozens, whenever I ride into Cambridge town. Life
laughs to them because they laugh at it. Not the subtlest of meta-
physics could reconcile them one-tenth as well with existence as the
mere throb and flush of twenty summers.

But afterwards? There is no elixir of life, except vitality itself. Yet, as
life goes on, vitality grows ever harder to keep. Some squander it in
frantic overwork, like Balzac or Dickens. Some waste it on diversions
far more futile—on books not worth reading, or pedantries not worth
pursuit; on stupid official functions; on dinners where the speeches are
enough to drive one to drink; on social parties where no one can hear
what anyone says, and nothing is worth hearing anyway, since people
are merely chattering what they do not mean in the least, to people for
whom they do not care twopence.[1]

The mature can no longer expect to play like spendthrifts with that
gorgeous surplus of energy which blesses youth. But not only, if one
does not overspend vitality, can one still have periods when it is a joy
in itself to be alive; but also, for mere lack of vitality, many people
seem to me to miss happiness by despairing of it when some temporary
mishap has destroyed it. Often, the process of attaining happiness
can become not unlike the process of splitting atoms; just as, in the
laboratory, the unseen target may have to be bombarded with thousands of projectiles, so, in life, happiness may need a number of
reiterated attempts. But the devitalized lack the dogged persistence to
make them. The gift of accepting the inevitable is no doubt also an
important part of happiness; but the devitalized accept as inevitable
what is not really so, and resign themselves to sit on glumly in the
hole, or rut, into which they have fallen.

---

[1] Real conversation, on the other hand, seems to me one of the keenest of
pleasures; but how rare is real conversation!

Among the personality-tests now adopted by American business, a key-ques-
tion is, I gather—'Have you enjoyed reading books as much as having company
in?' Those answering 'Yes' are black-marked as unsocial, and not 'well-rounded'.
Evidently the chances of Benjamin Franklin, or Abraham Lincoln, in the eyes of
some of their modern countrymen would have been poor indeed.

No doubt such pertinacious energy is mainly a matter of temperament; and men cannot remake their own temperaments. But it depends also, quite a lot, on physical condition. Therefore it seems to me one of the wonders of the world that men should so seldom treat their bodies with even one-tenth of the consideration they show for their cars, or their bank-balances. Yet it is a platitude that, while cars can be replaced, and bank-balances replenished, one will never (unless one believes in transmigration) find a new body.

In England, between ten and twenty, the body seems to me often to get too much attention; after twenty, very often, far too little. At school I had to play games on three afternoons a week, except every third week when we played on no fewer than four. A curious preparation for life, in which so many obtain only three or four weeks' holiday out of fifty-two.

For Mr Micawber, in theory at least, all the difference between misery and felicity lay in the difference between spending sixpence a year over or under one's income. But it is still more vital to live within one's vitality.

If I sought a symbol for happiness it would perhaps be a mountain-spring gently, but unfailingly, overflowing its basin with living water. There seems to me nothing in life more vital than to keep always this slight surplus of energy. One should always overflow.

Or again the contented hum of a car-engine on a country road, well this side of being over-driven or over-heated—that too is, for me, an emblem of happy living—a lively activity that holds reserves in hand. The quality of happiness is not *strained*.

If human energy could be bought, like electrical, I do not know on what a wise man would sooner spend his money; even if it meant something near to beggaring himself.

Nothing, indeed, seems to me more striking about the Greeks of the best period than this physical vitality which lasted often into extreme old age. Socrates was in full vigour, and made his great defence, at seventy; Isocrates died, still writing, at ninety-eight. We need not believe the story that Theophrastus expired at a hundred and seven from taking a holiday; but he does seem to have reached eighty-five, complaining that one came to the end of existence just as one was at last gaining insight into it. Aeschylus produced his *Oresteia* at sixty-seven; Sophocles his *Oedipus Coloneus* at near ninety; Euripides, his *Bacchae* at near eighty. And the comic poet Alexis is credited with two hundred and forty-five plays, and an age of a hundred and two.

It would be hard to find any counterpart to this among our Elizabethans or Jacobeans. Nash, Greene, Beaumont, and probably Peele, died in their thirties; Fletcher, at forty-six; Jonson outlived himself, and produced little of worth after his forties; even Shakespeare only reached fifty-two, and his best work was done by forty-four—after that, for me, his sun is visibly setting; even though it remains the sunset of Shakespeare.

This contrast between Greeks and Elizabethans seems hardly chance. Dirt, sack, disease, and plague probably contributed in the one case; spare diet, sun, and bodily activity in the other. Indeed, it may be no accident that Greek of the best period lacks, so far as I can recall, any special terms for the degeneracy of old age, such as our 'dotard', 'senile', or the hideously expressive 'gaga'.[1] Nor would it be easy to find in ancient biography anything like the tragic decay of Marlborough, Swift, or Ruskin, Nietzsche, Baudelaire, or Maupassant.[2]

The Middle Ages, along with numerous other fatuities, frequently encouraged the notion that it is good to be ill, and that the soul can gain by maltreating the body. The dying St Francis is said to have confessed, 'I have sinned against my brother the ass', meaning his body. He should have thought of it sooner.

It may well be mere legend that the site of Cambridge originally commended itself, as a place for spiritual learning, by its swampy unhealthiness; but an age which could call monastic lice 'the pearls of God', need hardly have found fantastic this idea of the proper site for a university.

On the other hand, whatever their theological follies, the men of the Middle Ages who did succeed in surviving must often have enjoyed a degree of vitality that any period might envy. When I consider that the author of *The Canterbury Tales*, apart from the general discomforts and insecurities of his age, had seen not only war (without ambulances or anaesthetics) and captivity, but also the Peasants' Revolt, and the Black Death (which is said to have killed more than half the English popula-

---

[1] The title of a lost comedy, Γεροντομανία ('Crazy Age' or 'Dotage') is fourth-century, and may have been specially coined by its author, Anaxandrides.

[2] Sophocles, indeed, is said to have been subjected to legal proceedings by a son who claimed that the old poet was senile. But Sophocles is supposed to have triumphantly confuted the charge by reading a chorus from the play he was writing.

tion),[1] then I am lost in admiration of a mind that could still remain, in spite of all, so sane, genial, and generous—tough without ceasing to be tender, stoic without becoming hard. By comparison our own century seems apt to be over-sorry for itself. Those have too little vitality who complain too much of life; it would taste less bitter, had they kept a better appetite.

After the fray at Swanfirth in Iceland, Snorri the Priest noted that Snorri Thorbrandson 'made little play with the cheese', and asked why.

> Snorri Thorbrandson answered that lambs found it hardest to eat when they were gagged.
> Then Snorri the Priest put his hand down the other's throat and found an arrow sticking athwart the roots of his tongue. Then Snorri the Priest took drawing-tongs and pulled out the arrow; and then Snorri Thorbrandson fell to his meat.

Such Saga characters are hardly for mere moderns to rival; but one may learn from them. There are distinct advantages in being tough.

The Renaissance, though it returned to the springs of Helicon, did not return to Roman baths. Even the Age of Reason was slow to apply reason to its health. Our eighteenth century largely over-ate and over-drank, and paid for it yelling with the gout. Even Swift, whom one tends to picture lean as Cassius, was really, as Thackeray reminds us, fat. 'His happy constitution,' writes Lady Mary Wortley Montagu of Fielding, '(even when he had, with great pains, half demolished it) made him forget everything when he was before a venison-pasty, or over a flask of champagne.' Similarly Horace Walpole, of the gentlemen of Norfolk: 'I here every day see men who are mountains of roast beef, and only seem just roughly hewn out into the outlines of the human form, like the giant-rock at Pratolino.' And indeed it is enough to recall the menus in Parson Woodforde's journal, or Boswell's alcoholic confessions.

If the foolish Boswell, instead of his heart being far away on London pavements, had hunted like Squire Western, or bestirred his lazy legs round his own countryside, he might have left some of his vapours among the mists of Loch Doon, and drowned his black moods in the Black Water of Dee. Johnson, I suspect, was seldom less unhappy than

---

[1] The Great Plague of London seems mild in comparison, if it is roughly true that it killed 60,000 out of 450,000 Londoners—less than one in seven.

when he was jogging through the Highlands; Rousseau never as care-free as in the vagabond days of his youth.

Or there is the melancholy Gray, writing to Nicholls—

And so you have a garden of your own, and you plant and transplant and are dirty and amused! Are you not ashamed of yourself? Why, I have no such thing, you monster; nor ever shall be either dirty or amused as long as I live! My gardens are in the window, like those of a Lodger up three pair of stairs in Petticoat-lane or Camomile-street, and they go to bed regularly under the same roof that I do.

But what was to stop Gray from being dirty and amused, had he but possessed as much sense as an elderly Fellow of my college, whom I remember hiring a garden somewhere in Cambridge to keep himself healthily busy? Still Gray did at least jog off occasionally to Lakes and Highlands—and his spirits rise visibly on the road.

Even in the nineteenth century, there were writers who persisted in treating their own bodies as no farmer in his senses would treat a horse—Carlyle with his overwork and blue pills, Balzac with his overwork and black coffee, Dickens with his overwork and public readings. Indeed there grew up in some quarters a notion that malady was perhaps a condition of genius. 'Notre talent! qui sait, c'est peut-être l'alliance d'une maladie de cœur et d'une maladie de foie.' So thought the Goncourts, noting the hallucinations of Flaubert and Zola; though the good sense of Taine protested. Indeed I particularly love Bourget's picture of Taine in his last years, when sickened by his studies of the rotting decadence of the *ancien régime*, going periodically to refresh himself with the sight of a specially vigorous young tree in the little square of Les Invalides—' "Allons voir cet être bien portant", me disait-il.' But the opposite view remained dear to decadents; as with that Prince Edmond de Polignac who amused Proust by observing: 'Un tel? Il ne peut pas être intelligent, il n'est pas malade.'

If Proust's Marcel had taken his stupid Albertine to the Alps with a pack, instead of dallying about Paris or Baalbec, a good deal of that eloquent misery might never have occurred; or, had it occurred (as, with her, was doubtless inevitable), would have been a good deal easier to shake off and forget—which was the only thing worth doing with it.

There is, indeed, a perpetual tendency in intellectuals to become half-disembodied spirits (apart from dinner-parties and love-affairs); and pretty poor spirits are usually the end of it. Whistler, in Paris, seeing his English fellow-students doing exercises, sneered, 'Can't you get the concierge to do that sort of thing for you?' But Whistler, often so clever, could also be an arrant fool. And this comment seems to me on a par, for folly, with Villiers de l'Isle Adam's adage that living is something one should leave to one's servants.

What a wise contrast to such artificial persons is Trollope, hunting three days a week even if he sat up all night on the outside of a coach to do it; or Scott, who could write in that noble *Journal* which is one of his finest books—'Did I ever pass unhappy years anywhere? . . . I have had unhappy days—unhappy weeks—even, on one or two occasions, unhappy months; but Fortune's finger has never been able to play a dirge on me for a quarter of a year together.' Small wonder if such a character viewed life very differently from Johnson, Goethe, Tolstoy, or Anatole France!

No doubt, this was partly a congenital cheerfulness in Scott's temperament; but his temperament remained a cheerful one precisely because he took steps to keep it so, by endless activity out of doors, planting trees, or hunting, or training with his yeomanry, or galloping about his beloved Border glens.

> December 11 (1825). A touch of the *morbus eruditorum*, to which I am as little subject as most folk, and have it less now than when young. It is a tremor of the heart, the pulsation of which becomes painfully sensible—a disposition to causeless alarm—much lassitude—and decay of vigour of mind and activity of intellect. . . . Fighting with this fiend is not always the best way to conquer him. I have always found exercise and the open air better than reasoning.

Scott's tragedy came when his sense of honour compelled him to wreck his health with overwork to pay his debts; and that tragedy only deepens sardonically when one goes to Abbotsford and sees to what an ugly chimera he sacrificed his real happiness.

But, after all, one can test such things only by personal experience. And though details of this kind remain in themselves supremely unimportant, they provide perhaps some evidence that my argument is not merely vague theory. If after five wounds, gassing, and seventeen months of hospital in the First War, I have yet never had an illness since; if I was able during the Second War to work six days a week and fifty weeks a year, from 4 p.m. to 1 or 2 a.m., in addition to Home Guard service, with only one day's absence in six years (from influenza); this good luck was, I think, mainly because between the Wars I usually spent at least one month in twelve walking, and kept a car mainly in order to walk, in addition, one day every week or fortnight, for six or seven hours, in country less depressing than the immediate outskirts of Cambridge; and because even in the Second War I managed to dig in the mornings before going down to my War Department in the afternoons. Most people, I well realize, are not so fortunately free in the disposal of their time. But that does not disprove my belief that most of those who lead intellectual lives are not particularly intelligent in the way they lead them, from not realizing that the brain easily becomes a kind of cancer to the body; and that physical condition can do more for men's happiness and usefulness than all the philosophers since Pythagoras. Valetudinarians are a curse to themselves and others; but most people seem to me not sufficiently vitality-conscious—bad stewards of their bodily energy.

I remember, years ago, hearing the late Lord Keynes remark, 'I think I have killed the exercise bug.' (That is, he had learnt to live without it. I seem to recall that Joseph Chamberlain had a similar idea.) At the time I wondered. And I wonder still if Keynes need have worked himself heroically to death in the public service during the Second War, had he adopted in earlier years a way of life less purely intellectual.

I remember this all the more because, long ago, his generosity paid for me to go with an undergraduate friend for the whole Easter vacation to Greece, only a month before my Tripos. Wildly rash it seems to me in retrospect. Yet how wise it was! It paid far better than conscientious overwork up to the eve of the examination.

So tyrannical, indeed, is the physical, so vitally important its energy, that when I merely shift from the vertical to the horizontal, and think in bed, my whole character and outlook on life often seem changed. I have come to believe that ever to think of any harassing question in bed is idiocy. One may sleep on problems; but one should never lie awake over them. Somehow the helplessness of a recumbent position, like a tortoise on its back, the numbing impotence of drowsiness, and the depressing effect of darkness, combine to make every pebble in one's path seem a rock of offence, every pismire a tiger, every pinprick a bleeding wound. Then, when one rises in the morning, back to the vertical, one wonders what all the trouble was about. The old Norseman who composed the *Hávamál* knew it all already—

An unwise man
Lies awake all night,
Worrying about everything;
He is weary
When comes the morning,
And all his woe is as it was.

'I make a point of never lying awake', said Wellington. Enviable man, to be so much his own master! I have learnt to moderate this imbecility, but not to overcome it. Another reason why one should tire the body enough in the daytime to drug that fretting mole, the mind.

'When the belly is full,' runs the Arab proverb, 'it says to the head, "Sing, fellow!"' That is not always so; the belly may get overfull. Such a proverb clearly comes from a race familiar with bellies painfully empty. Yet it remains true, I think, that when the body is in radiant health, it becomes extremely difficult for it not to infect the mind with its own sense of well-being.

But more vivid still in its expression of this simple truth which, however obvious in theory, proves in practice so far from obvious to many, is the tale in *The Arabian Nights* of Haroun-al-Raschid and his fool.

Et lorsque le Khalifat eut fini deboire, Bakloul lui dit: 'Et si, ô emir des Croyants, maintenant que tu as bu, ce verre d'eau refusait de sortir de ton corps, à cause de quelque rétention de l'urine dans ta vessie honorable, à quel prix achèterais-tu le moyen de l'en faire sortir?' Et Al-Rachid répondit: 'Par Allah, je donnerais bien, dans ce cas, tout mon empire en large et en long!' Et Bakloul, devenu bien triste soudain, dit: 'O mon seigneur, un empire qui ne pèse pas dans la balance plus qu'un verre d'eau ou qu'un jet d'urine, ne devrait pas comporter tous les soucis qu'il te donne et les guerres sanglantes qu'il nous occasionne!' Et Haroun, entendant cela, se prit à pleurer.

It is twenty years since I first read this blunt wisdom; but I have never forgotten it.

*   *   *

But there is health of mind as well as of body. Indeed it is hard, though not impossible, to have one without the other. The havoc a sick body can play with the mind is obvious; but anyone who troubles to read psychology, soon sees that a sick mind can sometimes play equal havoc with the functioning of heart, lungs, or stomach, and even distort sight, hearing, taste, or smell. Invalids have been happy; blind

men have been happy; but I doubt if much happiness can ever reach
the badly neurotic. Health of mind, however, is much more complex,
more elusive to define, more difficult to recognize.

Long before Freud, intelligent thinkers had realized that there must
be unconscious thought; but what seemed a comparatively unimportant dark cranny of the soul has now revealed itself as a labyrinthine
catacomb. It may even be that the future will come to think the discovery of the Unconscious as important as the invention of printing,
or flying, or atomic power; that the finding of this Underworld in each
of us was as epoch-making for mankind as the finding of a New World
beyond the Atlantic.

For to live without taking account of one's Unconscious is like
trying to navigate a ship without knowing what she is like below the
waterline, how many feet she draws (which turns out to be far more
than we realized), or what unseen currents may drift her off her course.
It is asking for shipwreck.

In any decision it is wise to consider the effect that the Unconscious
may be having on one's judgement; and the effect one's judgement
now may have hereafter on one's Unconscious. For each of us carries
within him, hidden in this netherworld of his own mind, Minos,
Aeacus, and Rhadamanthus, Nemesis and the Erinyes.

Unfortunately, however, though naturally, modern psychologists
have concerned themselves so much more with mental sickness, that
it is seldom easy to extract from them any clear idea of mental health—
indeed from their books one might think at times that no such thing
existed. But the type of mind that I have come most to admire is one
which wastes as little as possible of the energy it needs for battling
with the world, in battling with itself; which faces quite unshocked,
though without ceasing the needful effort to control them, the absurdities and irrationalities common to all human minds, including its
own; which neither blushes a moment for healthy desires, nor hankers
after morbid perversions; which neither over-indulges nor torments
itself; which keeps its hatreds for things, not persons, knowing that
men do not make themselves; which maintains its own individuality
unenslaved by others, yet realizes that lovelessness must find its penalty in a stifling loneliness; which carries no futile burden of guilt, no
vain regrets for the past whether happy or unhappy, preferring to use
all its energy and experience to prepare the future, however brief that
future may have become; which squanders its strength neither on

opiate daydreaming, nor on unreal hopes, nor on futile fears; which is as active as if it were building for eternity, yet resigned, as sensible men must be, to the realization that in a few years we, and all our works, shall be as if we had never been. For one who lives convinced that nothing matters which he does, becomes a slug; one who imagines that anything he performs is likely to matter prodigiously, is likely to become a pompous fool.

To picture communities as if they were individuals is common, but misleading; there is much more to be said for picturing individuals as communities—for indeed that is what they are. Each of us is legion. Better, then, freedom, toleration, and balance than self-tyranny, intestinal strife, or anarchy.

On the other hand one must admit that the mind, though it can do a good deal for the health of the body it inhabits, probably cannot do much for its own health unless it is healthy already. 'To him that hath shall be given.' A warped mentality can seldom, if ever, straighten itself. And whether it is warped or not, must depend mainly, if not wholly, on inborn temperament, upbringing, and circumstance.

The more I see of education, the less I believe in its power to improve the intelligence. It may enable certain minds not of the first order to do themselves more than justice in exams; as rats may be trained to negotiate labyrinths. But this is not increase of intelligence; and life is very different from exams.

For health of mind and character, on the other hand, upbringing seems extremely potent, both to help and to harm. The vital thing, I believe, is to grow up in a happy home (for conflicts between parents mean conflicts in the child) and in an atmosphere so warm with sympathy that few punishments are needed, beyond the sudden chill of affection temporarily withheld. 'Warm' does not mean 'stuffy'; on the contrary nothing is more vital than early training in independence. Yet this does not imply that, as in many a modern home, liberty should become licence, and democracy anarchy. No doubt time will correct such excesses of to-day, as it has corrected the opposite excesses of a century ago. Two Victorian parents come at this moment to my mind, as opposite instances of wisdom and folly. 'My father', said Lord Salisbury's schoolboy son, 'always treats me as if I were an ambassador; and I do like it so.' 'I have known boys of eight or nine years old', observed Dr Arnold, 'who did not so much as know what would happen to them after their death.' Did *he*? Words fail me to express my admiration for the first of these attitudes, or my abomination of the second.

*   *   *

But health of mind as of body needs, even if possessed, constantly to be maintained. In either case, the principle is the same—to keep stirring. Activity is difficult without health: health, without activity. One of the wisest remarks about living that I have ever read, is Alfieri's summary of his own experience—that he had always found life empty except when it was filled by both 'un degno amore' and 'qualche nobile lavoro'—'worthy love' and 'dignified work'.

This does not mean that one must be perpetually eloping with Countesses of Albany; but simply that to live on affection alone without work, or on work alone without affection, is trying to hop through life on one leg. Our natures are double—part egoist, part altruist; and both sides must be served—or one of them may die, and poison us.

Trollope, at the close of his *Autobiography*, speaks not unlike Alfieri; though not, I think, quite so wisely—'For what remains to me of life I trust for my happiness still chiefly to my work—hoping that when the power of work be over with me, God may be pleased to take me from a world in which, according to my view, there can be no joy; secondly, to the love of those who love me; and then to my books.'

Why '*secondly*, to the love of those who love me'? Surely Alfieri judged better in prizing work and affection as equally indispensable. Loveless labour is a desolate kind of life—what availed for Johnson the praise of his *Dictionary*, when he was left a melancholy widower—'till I am solitary and cannot impart it'?

But if work without love grows barren and bitter, so in the end grows love without work. That was the folly by which Antony lost the world—and, whatever Dryden says, did *not* lose it 'well'. 'Love is enough?' said Morris once, taking from the shelf his poem of that name. 'There's a lie for you, though it was I that told it! Love isn't enough in itself; love and work, yes! Work and love, yes! That's the life of a man! Why, a fellow can't even love decently unless he's got work to do, and pulls his weight in the boat.'

My only doubt with Morris, who perhaps created himself the most enviable life of any poet on record, is whether he did not work to excess. Remembering the unhappiness of those years when the beautiful Mrs Morris was too much admired by that Rossetti whom Morris had once admired so much, one wonders if he did not use overwork, at times, as a drug. When, in addition to twenty-six volumes of poetry and prose, a man sets himself to master painting, woodcuts, wallpapers, tapestries, dyeing, stained glass, furniture, printing, and politics, one cannot be surprised if his doctor diagnoses his death as due to having done as much as ten ordinary men. But if, passionate soul that he was, Morris could not always be bothered with moderation, that does not alter his essential wisdom about life.

In the quest for happiness, then, a sufficiency of activity seems vital; being itself a cause, as well as a result, of continued vitality. Few guardian angels are so effective as *le diable au corps*.

Physical differences must play a large part; but it remains amazing how this ardour of energy can sometimes resist even the decadence of age. It is enough to recall the blind Enrico Dandolo, elected Doge at eighty, leading the siege of Constantinople, and offered the crown of the Latin Empire; or Titian still vigorously painting after ninety; or Sarah Bernhardt, vowing to live to a hundred to annoy her enemies, and acting till her death at seventy-nine, even after losing a leg; or Winston Churchill taking up the weight of a six-years' struggle to save the world, at an age when most men abandon themselves to an armchair by the fire.

Most explicit of all is the Japanese Hokusai. 'From the age of six,' he says, 'I had a mania for drawing the forms of things. By the time I was fifty I had published an infinity of designs; but nothing that I produced before seventy is worth considering. At seventy-three I have learned a little about the real structure of nature, of animals, plants, birds, fishes, and insects. In consequence, when I am eighty, I shall have made more progress; at ninety I shall penetrate the mystery of things; at a hundred I shall certainly have reached a marvellous stage; and when I am a hundred and ten, everything I do—even a dot or a line—will be alive.

'Written at the age of seventy-five by me, once Hokusai, to-day Gwakio Rojin, the old man mad about drawing.'

He died, alas, at a mere eighty-nine, declaring that with another five years he would have become a great artist. But that, surely, is the way to grow old; which is simply—not to *let* oneself grow old. Activity to the last!

Johnson, idler though he could be himself, was always, and rightly, emphatic about the dangers, at any age, of vacuity. When Lady Tavistock died of grief for a husband fatally injured in a riding accident, 'she was rich,' observed Johnson, 'and wanted employment, so she cried till she lost the power of restraining her tears; putting her into a small shop, and giving her a nurse child to tend would have saved her life'. Harsh, but sound. And again there is Johnson's fulminating answer to some clerk fussing about having pilfered packthread from his employer—'Five hours of the four-and-twenty unemployed are enough for a man to go mad in; so I would advise you, sir, to study algebra. ... Your head would get less muddy, and you will leave off tormenting your neighbours about paper and packthread, while we all live together in a world that is bursting with sin and sorrow.'

Nature, men used fancifully to say, abhors a vacuum: but of human nature this is actually true. Even futile activity, whatever the Buddhist view, may be better, at least for western minds, than none at all. One of Napoleon's prisoners, Ouvrard, kept himself sane in solitary confinement by daily scattering on the floor of his cell a number of pins, and groping about till he had found them all again. It is the idle dog that is most pestered by his fleas. He would be far happier worrying a stick. We all need our sticks to worry, even if we realize at moments that they are merely dry sticks; though of course this wisdom fails if, instead of the dog worrying the stick, the stick begins to worry the dog. If the pure extravert is apt to be unintelligent, the pure introvert tends to grow broody. Life does not bear too much thinking on: the best antidote is action.

Activity, however, is not only a condition of health, and an antidote to boredom and melancholia. It can be, in itself, one of the greatest positive sources of happiness. One of the problems of our modern world is that so many unfortunate beings are forced to spend their lives on work they dislike, or would dislike if they had more sense. The ancient Greek view that much mechanical labour is unworthy of free men because it warps the body (and, they might have added, the mind) is bleak, but true. The happiest work, I think, must be creative—not in the narrow sense that we should all be painting pictures or writing odes, but in the sense that it calls on the individual for intelligent skill exerted in his own way, even if it is only growing vegetables; that it should not be the mechanical drudgery of slaves toiling at a conveyor-belt, or pouring nails down a pipe. I know an unassuming maiden lady who toils horrifying hours at coaching children in their holidays. 'But', she said to me, 'I love it.' This is partly, I dare say, maternal instinct;

but partly also because she is using a free, intelligent skill, as a sculptor carving and moulding young minds.

If I were a bricklayer, I should have no initiative of my own in laying my bricks—the architect would have settled all that; but I should at least want the fun of finding how to lay bricks as fast as they can be well laid, with that economy of effort which in a work of art we call 'grace'; but my trade union would not let me, for quite understandable, yet really lamentable reasons. And I should have to stroll wearily and listlessly about my job, like all the other bricklayers that anyone may see anywhere any day. A detestable conclusion.

The bane of our time, in short, is that instead of doing work we like, and as much of it as we healthily can, and living largely on the joy of that, we do work we dislike, and as little as possible, and expect to live only in our moments of leisure, which we try our utmost to extend. And when we get that leisure many of us spend it, not on activity, but in the lame impotence of passive spectators.

The curse of labour does not lie in labour, but in the unsatisfactory kinds of it to which all except the lucky have always been, and still are, condemned—work that distorts body or mind, that is tedious, or useless, or immoderate. To be satisfactory, indeed, it is not enough that work be of a kind that can become interesting. The human mind has a useful, yet horrible capacity for growing interested, sometimes, even in the most sterile and futile subjects. The shelves of libraries groan with books and dissertations that ought to have bored their writers too insufferably ever to get written. Ideally, work should not only be interesting to the worker; it should also not make him uninteresting to his intelligent fellow-creatures. And it should be useful not only to the doer, but to others. It is this that makes, for example, the supreme good fortune of a good doctor. Indeed it is hard for activity to seem lastingly satisfying if it serves no ends but one's own. Perhaps my happiest years were in the Second War. Those six years were laborious, anxious, often tedious; yet the need was past question; and the object of our particular efforts, we knew, was being slowly but successfully attained.

For another condition of happy activity is that it should be successful, yet not too easily successful. There should be difficulties enough to challenge brain or sinew, but difficulties that *can* be overcome; just as the happiest climate for human development is something less soft than Tahiti, less hard than Greenland. Happiness depends more on progressing and succeeding, than on being something, or possessing something. It seems likely enough that a housemaid promoted to housekeeper may feel as much satisfaction as a Foreign Secretary promoted to Prime Minister. Such things are largely relative. If the lift is going up (no matter from which floor to which)—elation; if it is going down—gloom. And so it may well be a misfortune to succeed too rapidly, or too easily. Alexander may have been beloved of the Gods in dying young—for his later life could hardly have avoided an anticlimax such as that of Charles XII. And Caesar, who had a far harder climb to success, may well have got more from life.

For most men, who are neither Caesars nor Alexanders, it is none the less usually happier to rise steadily, rather than too rapidly; to succeed constantly rather than spectacularly; to advance with a steady moderation that leaves future possibilities unexhausted; so that life itself ends before the tide of success and achievement has seriously ebbed.

The essential is always to have something in hand. In Montaigne's phrase, let death take a man still planting his cabbages. No doubt it may be necessary, with increasing age, to change and lighten one's occupations. Writers have often gone on writing too long. Painters (like Hokusai), who are happier in having work more manual and less purely mental, have sometimes fared better. But a man is a limited creature if he can do nothing but write. Let him, if he has not enough left to say, or not enough power left for saying it, find other fields. But until he comes, as we said in the First War, to 'pushing up the daisies', let him at least cultivate something or other.

No doubt, this stress on activity may strike some as febrile. There was some Indian who observed in his wisdom: 'To stand is better than to move; to sit than to stand; to lie than to sit; and to be dead than all that.' But this seems to me a dismal and detestable view of life, attributable partly to a debilitating climate. Any race that really adopted such principles would, in this aggressively competitive world, probably soon attain its wish—or its imagined wish—and become extinct indeed.

The West, at all events, has preferred energy. I remember a Turkish lady I once met who wrote, with not unjustified bitterness, that Europe had preached to the rest of mankind the turning of the other cheek, yet in practice had slapped every face it met with in the world. That reproach is true enough; though perhaps it was hardly for a Turk to make it. But, after all, from this restless activity of Europe has come most of human progress. And though in our century Europe has been losing year by year the privilege of slapping coloured faces, the knowledge Europe has learned and taught, endures and spreads.

*   *   *

Happiness, then—though not contentment (which some have thought a wiser aim; but why not aim at both?)—remains, I believe, very difficult without vigorous activity. But vigorous action, in its turn, is hardly to be had without vigorous passions. Yet thinkers and moralists have often distrusted and deprecated the passions as among the greatest enemies to happiness. Dangerous they doubtless are; yet without them there remains the other danger of becoming a bored bore. The coldest and most objective scientist would not be bothered to look through his microscope unless he were energized by some sort of feeling—whether curiosity, or ambition, or eagerness to serve his fellows. The mind of the really passionless sage would become inert as a factory with its electric current cut off. I remember a brilliant Fellow of Trinity who ended in apathetic melancholia, because he came to have no feeling except of the universal vanity of things.

'Solomon' may have said that increase of wisdom is increase of sorrow. No doubt it is often true. But equally true is Virgil's verdict that all things can grow a weariness *except* to understand—*rerum cognoscere causas*. Those who have lost even curiosity have very little left to live for; unlike the old Mercier who lived on, he said, to see what would become of Napoleon. Whatever passions age robs us of, let it spare us at least curiosity (and affection).

But, in the years before our forces fail, the most effectual type of temperament seems to me one that keeps a clear head, few dogmatic beliefs (for most human certainties are simply not rational), passionate feelings, and a no less intense self-control. Without the feelings, nothing gets done; without the judgement and the control, the wrong things get done.

Here, too, the later Churchill provides an excellent example. He was always clever, always passionately energetic. But in his earlier years he often seemed one of those forcible, yet unstable, characters that defeat themselves by an erratic lack of judgement—the sort of brilliant but dangerous mind which the English particularly distrust, in comparison with solider, more sluggish characters, like Bonar Law or Baldwin.

But at a time when most men's careers are finished, Churchill had simply matured; then came exactly the crisis that suited and needed him; and there followed six extraordinary years of emergency after emergency, where it is hard to imagine any figure in the history of war making fewer mistakes, or better repairing those that inevitably were made.

In contrast, one of the most insidious dangers of modern mass-civilization seems to me, as I have said, its tendency to exchange action for passive spectatorship. Our nineteenth-century forebears were too ready to let professional soldiers die for them; but we of the twentieth century are too ready to let professional players or entertainers live for us. Cheap fiction, picture-paper, cup-tie, cinema, wireless, television— all these trivialities take up an increasing part of our increasing leisure. All of them are ways of watching life, instead of living actively; of watching others do things instead of doing them oneself. 'The Gods alone', ran a Greek saying, 'can be spectators.'

> For they lie beside their nectar, and the bolts are hurl'd,
> Far below them in the valleys, and the clouds are lightly curl'd
> Round their golden houses, girdled with the gleaming world.

But if men grow too like such divinities of Epicurus, the result may be more Epicurean than divine. 'See the difference training makes', said Aeschylus to a fellow-poet, as they watched boxers at the Isthmian Games. 'The man who was hit, is silent. It is *the spectators* that cry out.'

I have a particular affection for that Shah of Persia who, being invited, during his stay in England, to watch the Derby, replied that he knew already that, if a number of horses ran the same way at the same time, one would run faster than the others; but that he had no desire to see which.

That twenty-two men should kick a ball for fun and exercise may be admirable; that fifty thousand others should spend the afternoon watching them do it for money, seems much more questionable. It is, I believe, wise for individuals, as for states, to balance their imports by exports. The impressions one takes in from literature or life should, for mental health and happiness, be balanced by output and activity of one's own. I have particularly noticed this truth when writing. Hobbes was probably very sound in his remark that, had he read as many books as other men, he would have known as little. Reading is often most enjoyable when one is going to use it. But there are voracious readers who resemble the all-devouring grave—author after author descends into them, yet not one living echo ever comes out again.

Indeed they might be far livelier company were they illiterate. They are like the lion's den in the fable, where multitudinous tracks entered, yet none emerged; but they are not much like lions.

Broadcasting is still more passive than reading; for the reader is at least translating black marks on paper into words. Further, broadcast talks tend to be both snippety and superficial. And television is still more passive than broadcasting—presumably it might appeal even to chimpanzees.

No doubt Aristotle and other sages have praised the contemplative life; but that meant for Aristotle, not passivity, but hard and productive thinking. I would rather make serviette-rings in an attic than soak inertly through life like a sponge.

You can of course argue that the enjoyment even of literature, art, and nature is also largely passive—and yet these are important sources of happiness. But the answer seems to me, first, that to be passive is not always bad in itself, but only in excess; secondly, that these three enjoyments yield most, not to the purely passive spectator, but to those who themselves bring a good deal of activity to bear on what they contemplate. The best books are not those which cost the reader no effort. And again the walker in lovely places gets far more from Nature than the motorist. Indeed it could be argued that the Greeks, whom it is superficial to suppose less sensitive than we to natural beauty (it is enough to read the similes of Homer), were really wiser than we, in seeing Nature's beauty as essentially a background, a scene for human action, rather than as a thing to be pored on for itself, such as it became for landscapists or Wordsworthians.

Take, for example, these pieces from the *Anthology*. Here the eternal beauty of the world is felt all the more deeply for the human activity of the brief lives that cross it—the traveller with the long road before him; the mariner making ready to put out to sea.

> Fling yourself here, O traveller, in the lush meadow-grasses
> And rest your limbs, aweary from the road that seemed so long;
> Here Zephyr's breath shall soothe you, as soughing low it passes
> Through the pines, and round you cicadas chirp their song;
> Here the shepherd of the uplands shall pipe beside the fountain
> His noontide song, where shady the plane-tree coppice grows.
> Shun for to-day the Dog-star's glare; and cross the mountain
> To-morrow. Trust the counsel that Pan himself bestows.[1]

[1] *Anth. Pal.*, XVI, 227.

With calm the seas grow purple now. No storm-winds sunder
  Roller from furrowed roller, or toss their whitened mane;
No more around the headlands the surges crash in thunder,
  Then backward flung go swirling out to the deep again.
Now the west winds are blowing, and the swallow chirps preparing
  Once more her bridal-chamber, her wattled house of straw.
Grey mariner take heart then, whether you go faring
  Past Syrtis, or the shingle of the long Sicilian shore.
Burn but a wrasse on my altar, or a gurnard red, and pray
To Priāpus, God of the Harbour, before you sail away.[1]

The road is stony, the seas are perilous; and yet what zest, what
vitality, what happiness! And if the beauty of Nature is the happier for
human activity in the foreground, human happiness is the more
radiant for the presence of Nature behind.

Now the white violet's blooming, and that lover of the showers,
  Narcissus, and the lilies that climb high up the hill,
And now, delight of lovers, spring-flower among the flowers,
  Sweet rose of Persuasion, blossoms my Zenophil.
Ah meadows, vain your laughter, in vain your shining hair:
Than all your fragrant garlands the lass I love's more fair.[2]

Without the lover's passion all the beauty of Nature might seem tantalizingly barren, like the scenery of an empty stage when the players
fail to enter; and without the beauty of Nature the passion would lose
a part of its ecstasy. Each emotion flows into and heightens the other.

Finally, these poets knew that, if all happiness must end at last in
sorrow, and at the end of all avenues rises the grey wraith of Death,
even so the sting is lessened by Nature's loveliness; facing her eternity,
man may still find some consolation in acceptance, and in the memory
of happiness that at least has been. The mountains rise only the more
majestic, in their looming loneliness, for the small grave of the hunting-
hound at their foot, with its remembrance of bygone summers in the
hills:

Although within this grave-mound thy white bones now are lying,
  Methinks, my huntress Lycas, the wild things dread thee still.
The memory of thy worth tall Pēlion keeps undying,
  And the looming peak of Ossa, and Cithaeron's lonely hill.[3]

[1] Agathias, *Anth. Pal.*, X, 14.   [2] Meleager, *Anth. Pal.*, V, 144.
[3] Simonides.

And, again, the boon to the living of the spring's living water is heightened by the presence of the dead that rests in final peace near by.

> Traveller the long way wearies, under my poplars seat thee;
> Draw near, and to my waters bow down thy thirsty head.
> And far away, hereafter, still may my memory greet thee.
> Me Simus made for Gillus, his son, that here lies dead.[1]

*   *   *

'Happiness', says an Arab proverb, 'is found between the breasts of a woman, on the back of a horse, and among the pages of books.' Love, travel, reading. Like the Greek drinking-song, this does not give the whole truth, and cannot be expected to. Indeed the first item is, I suppose, the most perilous of all forms of happiness, and often grows, like edelweiss, on a precipice. But it may serve here to introduce the wider subject of personal relations in general. With regard to these, one concrete instance may save much vague generalization. For I can think of no better example than that little-known but vivid figure, Charles-Victor de Bonstetten (1745–1832).

A child of the sombre aristocracy of Berne, he came in his early twenties to Cambridge; and readers of Gray's letters will recall how this lively little Swiss, in that port-swilling University 'où' (in Bonstetten's own words) 'aucune femme honnête ne venait égayer la vie de ces rats de livres à forme humaine', completely fascinated the melancholy poet of Pembroke, only to plunge him in deeper gloom when Bonstetten recrossed the Channel. But the special peculiarity of Bonstetten is this—that after settling down as a conscientious, though often absent-minded Swiss magistrate (he overcame the aversion of the peasants of Ticino for the potato by telling them that the King of England had these disgusting tubers every day on his royal table), he somehow succeeded in going into reverse and passing back from middle-age into a second youth. This curious miracle was occasioned by the French Revolution. For that earthquake uprooted him from his home. He wandered to Denmark, Geneva, Italy; and in the course of his exile he found the new interests, the new friendships that restored his youth.

> C'est aux approches de la soixantaine [says Sainte-Beuve], qu'il se mit décidément à rajeunir; il atteignait à soixante-dix ans sa fleur, il s'y maintenait durant une douzaine d'années, et jusqu'à quatre-vingt-deux ans et

---

[1] Nïcias of Miletus, *Anth. Pal.*, IX, 315.

même au-delà il fut dans tout son vif. L'ancien Bonstetten, celui qui avait eu cinquante ans, ne lui paraissait plus en effet que de l'histoire ancienne. Comme d'autres, en se rappelant leur temps passé, disent naturellement: *Quand j'étais jeune . . .*, lui, il disait naturellement: *Quand j'étais vieux.*

The secret of such a success seems worth knowing. What was it?

Si Bonstetten avait son secret dans cet art de ne pas vieillir qu'il pratiquait si bien, ce n'était pas seulement en apprenant toujours quelque chose, c'était aussi en aimant toujours quelqu'un. . . . Il avait un besoin positif d'aimer. Jamais il n'oubliait, mais il remplaçait vite, et remplaçait toujours: son affaire était de bien remplacer.

There is surely much to be learnt from this case of Bonstetten. He was the opposite of that old miller of Dee-side who sang so merrily, 'I care for nobody and nobody cares for me'; but I suspect the miller in question of being rather fabulous. For I much doubt the happiness of such complete lovelessness. Indeed there is a grim force in the Roman curse—'Ultimus suorum moriatur'—'Let him die the last of all his race.'

Some, of course, have doubted whether personal relationships can ever, in reality, be more than mere illusion—a saraband of shadows. Proust, who had seen so much of society, and plumbed so deeply the darker depths of passion, came to pronounce a final condemnation on the utter vanity of both: 'L'artiste qui renonce à une heure de travail pour une heure de causerie sait qu'il sacrifie une réalité pour quelque chose qui n'existe pas . . . l'erreur d'un fou qui croirait que les meubles vivent et causerait avec eux.'[1] For Proust, love itself is only valuable because its unhappiness makes us reflect more penetratingly on the impossibility of happiness. 'Nous sommes irrémédiablement seuls.'

Even the saintly and less eccentric Fénelon, two centuries earlier, found himself in the end hardly less disillusioned.

Je demande peu de presque tous les hommes; je tâche de leur rendre beaucoup et de n'en attendre rien. Je me trouve fort bien de ce marché; à cette condition je les défie à me tromper . . . j'ai appris à connaître les hommes en vieillissant, et je crois que le meilleur est de se passer d'eux sans faire l'entendu. . . . Cette rareté de bonnes gens est la honte du genre humain.

Horace Walpole is more passionate still. To the young Craufurd, protesting friendship, he replies:

[1] A nice contrast to the American view on p. 265 (footnote).

Consider my heart is not like yours, young, good, warm, sincere, and impatient to bestow itself. Mine is worn out with the baseness, treachery, and mercenariness I have met with. . . . I consider everything round me but in the light of amusement, because if I looked at it seriously I should detest it. . . . I converse with Mesdames de Mirepoix, Boufflers, and Luxembourg, that I may not love Madame du Deffand too much—and yet they do but make me love her more. But don't love me, pray don't love me. Old folks are but old women, who love their last lovers as much as they did their first. I should still be liable to believe you, and I am not at all of Madame du Deffand's opinion that one might as well be dead as not love somebody. I think one had better be dead than love anybody.

And then there is the bleak eloquence of Baudelaire—

> Que bâtir sur les cœurs est une chose sotte;
> Que tout craque, amour et beauté,
> Jusqu'à ce que l'Oubli les jette dans sa hotte
> Pour les rendre à l'Éternité.

> That to build on hearts is folly; that all things crack—
> Beauty, and Love—until we see
> Oblivion fling them all into his pack,
> To toss back to Eternity.

Proust stresses the incommunicability of the human heart; Fénelon, Walpole, and Baudelaire its corruption. One may think they exaggerate; but one must also confess, I think, that human relationships are the subject of a nauseous amount of cant. When we are told, for example, that some person was 'universally beloved', it is perhaps well to ask oneself, if one would not be the dupe of big words, how many persons ate a mouthful less for dinner the day he died. How many, indeed, do that even for their friends? And then there is that grim question—how many of the dead would be welcome if they came back to earth after five years of absence?

No doubt there are truths in life so gaunt and ghastly that it would be foolish to be obsessed by them—as well keep a skull on one's mantelpiece. On the other hand, honesty is safer and finer than self-deception; we should be able to face all truths, though we need not stare at them twelve hours a day. And one of these truths, I think, is the unreality of many human relationships; though not, luckily, of all.

It becomes a question then, for those who do not seek happiness in being 'well deceived', which relationships *can* possess a genuine reality.

There are many people who seek to have a wide circle; whether from vanity, ambition, loquacity, or a somewhat fatuous desire to be world's darlings. But those who bathe in such wide circles are apt to find them shallow. To say that 'he who has friends, has no friend' is no doubt one of those exaggerations common in epigrams; but it embodies a truth. Friendliness is, no doubt, admirable; but it is not friendship. It would not be hard to find intellectual groups which, to an often jealous and resentful outer world, seem united in serried phalanxes or close conspiracies; but to hear two members of such a group discussing a third can leave an impression of malice and *Schadenfreude* that is like ashes on the tongue.

Again there are university dons who devote themselves heroically to playing the part of Socrates with the young, and make their homes as hospitable as the tents of Arabia. This, I own, is beyond me. Talk with a purpose can be fun; but talk for talk's sake, except with a few, soon grows intolerable. The smaller the talk, the bigger the bore. Besides, I am not sure that this heroic hospitality always increases the sum of human happiness as much as it imagines. 'I must have young A to lunch', sighs old B; 'I have to go to lunch with old B', sighs young A. Charming kindliness, no doubt, on either side; but the result is often unreality. Personally, I have always preferred that my room should echo each week, at supervision, with my pupils' laughter; but that I should not invite them home in conscientious rotation to discuss the weather.

Of goodwill and kindness one can hardly imagine how the world could have too much; but too promiscuous affection is apt to be a painted surface with an undercoat of cant. When people talk of 'loving' mankind, I wish they would choose their verbs more carefully.

There is another type of relationship, fundamentally and instinctively intense, yet often mixed up with a good deal of illusion that can bring bitter disillusion—the affection of parents and children. It is often accepted now—for we are in many ways tougher-minded than our Victorian great-grandparents—that this type of affection tends naturally and inevitably to flow downward, from parents to children, more strongly than from children to parents. This hard fact, in its extremer forms, has bred some of the world's bitterest literature, like those two vitriolic lines of Beddoes—

> And feed young children with the blood of your heart
> Till they have sucked up strength enough to break it.

One thinks of Lear, and Père Goriot, and, in history, of such trage-dies as that of Henry II and his sons. No doubt such extremes are rare; no doubt such unhappy parents had partly themselves to blame; no doubt there have existed also such opposite extremes of filial piety as are typified by Antigone, or Electra, or Aeneas. But, on the whole, parents are probably wise if they do not ask or expect too much.

After all, one has thrust these poor little beings, unconsulted, into a harsh and menacing world; in compensation one should surely be prepared—as our great-grandparents too often were not—to give much and not demand overmuch in return. Then one may be lucky enough to find more than one demanded. In any case it seems senseless to be embittered if that fails to happen. Understanding between age and youth is seldom easy. And parents cannot choose their children, or children their parents, as men choose (however ill and blindly they often do it) their friends, or wives, or mistresses. Heredity remains a lottery. Cicero had for son his drunken Marcus; Marcus Aurelius begot (or thought he had) the monstrous Commodus.

Here, indeed, the pull of instinct can be terribly strong. Even the iron heart of Henry II could break over the worthless John. John was not worth it; yet some will feel a redeeming quality in the old king's unsuspected streak of tenderness. Lady Mary Wortley Montagu was far more rational about her odious offspring; of whom she writes to her separated husband—'I am sorry to trouble you on so disagreeable a subject as our son, but I received a letter from him last post.' Yet such cold rationalism seems a little repellent.

Luckily few of us have to face such predicaments. Of the real camaraderie that *can* exist between parents and children I know no example more charming than the letter of Charles de Ligne to his father from the front: 'Nous avons Sabacz, j'ai la croix. Vous sentez bien, papa, que j'ai pensé à vous en montant à l'assaut.'

The most real relationships of human beings stand built on an understanding tested and fortified by time. We can never wholly know one another—indeed we can never wholly know ourselves. But when we have reached the point where we can usually feel sure what another person will think, do, or feel, and have a deep confidence that it will not be anything we dislike or regret, we have perhaps got as far as human beings ever can. Here is surely something more solid than the hollow phantoms that all human relationships became, in theory, for Proust.

Such, for example, was the friendship between Montaigne and Étienne de la Boétie; or the marriage of Schliemann and his Sophia (to whom he so charmingly wrote, in ancient Greek, on the twenty-first anniversary of their wedding, 'I can never glorify our marriage enough ... and by Zeus I will marry you again in the next world').

The passion of lovers, on the other hand, is dangerously haunted by a special type of unreality. Here the feeling can be intense enough—often too much so; but, for that very reason, its object is particularly apt to be a phantom. When A loves B, the true state of affairs is apt to be only a ghostly (and sometimes ghastly) foursome in which real A loves B's phantom, and vice versa. Thousands of times, through the ages, men and women have died for one another, who could not, had they survived, have endured one another for twelve months. Roger Fry was no cynic, but a very lovable person; yet I have never forgotten his wry remark—'Je connais l'amour *unique*; j'en ai eu plusieurs.' There are obviously hundreds of mere infatuations for one 'marriage of true minds'. No form of intoxication is more enchanting, at least for hero and heroine, while it lasts; nor more painful as it passes off. As La Rochefoucauld noted, long before psychologists invented 'ambivalence', love of this kind is often nearer akin to hatred than to indifference.

> Too sweet is the rind, say the sages,
> Too bitter the core.

Years after their love had ended in bitterness, Louise Colet, passing Flaubert without being recognized, murmured to her daughter—'Qu'il est laid!'

Even if the hatred is avoided, one can still be aghast at the utter indifference that years of separation can scatter over a name that once set the pulses throbbing. How one feels fooled! How grey and light the ashes of old burnt-out fires! How dry and dusty the once living spring!

> Larmes du cœur par le cœur dévorées,
> Et que les yeux que les avaient pleurées,
> Ne reconnaîtront plus demain.
>
> (Musset)

> Upon a poet's page I wrote
> Of old two letters of her name;
> Part seemed she of the effulgent thought
> Whence that high singer's rapture came.

—When now I turn the leaf the same
Immortal light illumes the lay,
But from the letters of her name
The radiance has waned away.

(Hardy)

It is always perilous, in a world of chance and change, to risk one's whole heart on a single person; yet it remains, I think, *sometimes* worth the risk. No doubt it defies the warning of the Roman poet—

Nulli te facias nimis sodalem.
Gaudebis minus, et minus dolebis.[1]

It ignores the worldly wisdom of Swinburne—

Light love stands clear of thunder,
And safe from winds at sea.

Yet such warnings seem a little cowardly, and such wisdom more than a little cold. They lack that warmth of heart which is one of the most endearing of human qualities, and without which life becomes a sort of Ice Age. Better the generosity of Montrose—

He either fears his fate too much,
Or his deserts are small,
That dares not put it to the touch,
To gain or lose it all.

But any love or affection that is to be happy and lasting must generally, I think, fulfil certain conditions. First, there must be real trust. The ethics of the English may be often exasperatingly muddled; but they seem to me very sound in the very special stress they lay on 'not letting people down'. Anyone who has experienced much of life grows very distrustful on this head—he will so often have been deceived. Those are lucky who need more than the fingers of one hand to count the people in whom they can feel absolute and unquestioning faith. This unshaken confidence does not apply only to larger matters—for example that fidelity without which it is hard to imagine a perfect marriage. It applies even to trivial things like irritability—for even an angry word can brush the bloom for a moment from perfect trust.

And such moments may be remembered for far more than a moment.

[1] A friend too dear to you let no man be.
Less joy you'll find—but less of misery.

(Martial)

They laugh [writes Dorothy Osborne (whose young friends thought her ideal husband a complete chimera)] to hear me say that one unkind word would destroy all the satisfaction of my life, and that I should expect our kindness should increase every day, if it were possible, but never lessen. All this is perfect nonsense in their opinion; but I should not doubt the convincing them if I could hope I should ever be so happy as to be

Yours.

William Temple can hardly have lived up to this high standard; and 'destroy all the satisfaction of my life' is obvious hyperbole. Yet Dorothy Osborne was no fool.

The conscious mind may, and should, brush aside an instant's peevishness as the trifle it probably is; but the unconscious is less rational. There are many qualities far more blameworthy than bad temper, which are yet far less dangerous to love or friendship. The young learn this late or never; but that seems to me one of the many things they should be warned of, and seldom are.

But, of course, though trust is the rock on which intimacy must be founded to last, it is not enough. One cannot love a mere rock, however solid. The other great essential is sympathy in fundamental matters. For example, though love has laughed millions of times at barriers like the feuds of family or race, yet supposing Romeo had been a Communist, Juliet a Fascist? They might still have loved; but how long, had they survived, would that love have lasted? Even less fanatical differences can bring, sooner or later, a sword of severance.

On the other hand, one may exaggerate the importance of sympathy in matters not fundamental. I have heard of a wife telling her husband she could not love him so much because he did not love modern poetry! But I doubt if it shows much real love, or much understanding of love, to insist that one's lover love also one's smallest lap-dog.

Probably unconscious sympathy is far more important than conscious, both in producing affection and in preserving it—especially between the sexes. Elizabeth Browning was very wise in wishing Robert to love her, not for reasons he knew, but for reasons he did not know.

For similar reasons, a sound psychologist has warned those who love each other against reminiscing *excessively* even about their happy past; because memories too often hauled up into consciousness may lose the mysterious life and potency they retained in the depths of the unconscious.

Perhaps one of the greatest dangers to lasting sympathy lies in demanding and expecting too much from it. Those who ask more from life than life can give are liable in the end to get a great deal less. The youth of the earlier twentieth century, reacting with the usual excess of violence against the canting reticences of the nineteenth, often made a fetish of frankness. Like so many mistaken ideas, this was in part a fine one. In the words of Mary Coleridge (whom I am so eccentric as to find not infrequently a purer poet than her famous relative):

> We were not made for refuges of lies,
>> And false embattled bulwarks will not screen us.
> We mocked the careful shieldings of the wise,
>> And only utter truth can be between us
>
> Long suns and moons have wrought this day at length,
>> The heavens in naked majesty have told thee.
> To see me as I am, have thou the strength;
>> And even as thou art I dare behold thee.

On fundamental issues, indeed, this may be true and wise. Just as in Blake's—

> I was angry with my friend;
> I told my wrath, my wrath did end.

Yet, on the other hand, to communicate every blister received from a crumpled rose-leaf may be less helpful.

> I was moody with my friend;
> I told my mood, my mood did end;

but in the friend a corresponding black mood may have been, quite suddenly, begun—and not ended so easily.

There are times to be outspoken; times to be reserved. All varies with temperament and circumstance; only tact and common sense can decide; but, with most human beings, the times for reserve over minor grievances seem to me far commoner than many suppose. If taken in silence, an hour later such trivialities may be well forgotten.

The closest friends or lovers remain two individuals: whatever they may dream, they cannot become wholly one—or their relation would end. And so beside the romantic wisdom of Mary Coleridge there is room also for the realist wisdom of Crabbe—

> 'I speak my mind, I love the truth,' quoth he;
> Till 'twas his fate that useful truth to find,
> 'Tis sometimes wiser not to speak the mind.

Modern lovers are usually less touchy than Hardy's Angel Clare at finding that they are not the first; but though it seems generally better in such cases not to conceal the past, it may still be questioned whether it should be recounted often or in vast detail. 'Let the dead bury their dead.' The same applies also to the present. It would not be easy to find a grosser folly than the Tolstoys' habit of keeping elaborate diaries of their inmost feelings, and letting each other read them. Candour is a virtue: but loving-kindness is a still greater and more vital one. Any relation where essential truths are concealed, is hollow and unreal; but any relation where every trivial matter is blurted out, is doomed to grow inflamed and precarious.

I have known marriages where the wife would sit at lunch between husband and lover, lavishing 'Darlings' with an indiscriminating prodigality that left the onlooker bewildered as to who was really what. I have come in the end to have a horror of triangles—particularly married ones; yet they always have occurred, and always will. One cannot always even repent one's follies. And mankind will have to change past our recognition before Antony and Cleopatra, Lancelot and Guenevere, Tristram and Iseult, Paolo and Francesca, cease to wake a far warmer sympathy than the virtues of Octavia, or the faultlessness of Galahad. Man proposes; but Eros disposes. Whether, in such anguished tangles, deception or frankness causes more pain in the end, depends on temperament and circumstances; but never have I seen good come of recklessly parading such situations in public.

Reason may say, 'Where the truth is known, why pretend?' But if there is any profitable lesson to be learned from the mistakes of the eighteenth century it is, above all, this—that nothing is more irrational than to behave as if one's own mind, or those of others, were wholly rational. Human beings should never forget they are only human. Seldom will the arrogance which does forget that, escape unpunished.

Balzac said that young lovers often reminded him of an orangoutang trying to play the violin; to me they often suggest, rather, two pretty little bears playing catch with a vase of crystal.

But if a real relation between any two human beings must be built on sympathy and trust, there is another factor that seems to me often an enormous reinforcement—comradeship in a shared activity. (Once more this stress on activity in life—no doubt, I shall seem possessed by a mania for it.) Often, indeed, this is not possible. Friendship must often live only on leisure moments of talk, face to face or on paper.

But lovers who live only looking in each other's eyes may end by see-ing there less, or more, than they like.

> 'Never was there such a wooing—
> Must we always, then, be doing,
>   Strange one? Can you never rest?
> What's the world? Do you regret it?
> Face to face, we should forget it,
>   Breast to breast.'

> 'Looking in each other's faces
> Lovers learn too soon the traces,
>   Sweet, of things best undescried.
> Love that's idlest is not strongest.
> Take the road—let's take the longest,
>   Side by side.'

For the married such a common purpose lies most naturally in the building of a home, and the rearing of children. Without children, the chances of happy marriage are at least halved. But, if there are no children, there may be a partial substitute in common work, as with the Webbs.

So strong, indeed, is this tie of comradeship—or 'fellowship' as Morris called it (valuing it perhaps more than any other thing on earth) —that it can sometimes build an intense relationship between men who would otherwise find little in common—as thousands have found in the stress of war. The men of my platoon and I, in 1914–16, would have found little to say to one another in a normal world; yet, under that common stress, they became more to me than most people since.

Happy friendships are rare. Perfect marriages still rarer. But both of these are helped and fortified by a common task; and those who are not lucky enough to find any deep and intimate partnership in life may perhaps find, though even this is often hard, consolation in a wider comradeship. It is one of the maladies of our modern world, with its social divisions, class-wars, and cannibal competition, that this com-radeship is often so hard to build.

*   *   *

Finally—simple to say, but often far less simple to practise—there is gaiety of mind. Perhaps no virtue—except in the eighteenth century—has been more consistently underrated. Of four resolutions made by

Wesley in 1738, the second was: 'To labour after continual serious-ness, not willingly indulging in any the least levity of behaviour, or in laughter; no, not for a moment.' That seems to me nearly crazy. Gaiety is largely a matter of inborn disposition; but it *can* be partly acquired; and few gifts seem better worth acquiring. It may have helped to prevent Sydney Smith from becoming a bishop; but few bishops, and few monarchs, have got as much from life as Sydney Smith.

*   *   *

Vitality of mind and body; the activity to employ and maintain them; the zest and curiosity that they can animate; freedom to travel widely in nature and art, in countries of the world and countries of the mind; human affections; and the gift of gaiety—these seem to me, then, the main causes of happiness. I am surprised to find how few and simple they are.[1]

Simple they remain, even if one adds a few more principles of a negative kind, about pursuits that are seldom worth pursuing, Snarks that are apt to turn out Boojums—such as wealth, for example, which may involve so much bother to get and keep, so much responsibility to use, and comes so easily to possess its possessor, instead of being possessed by him; or power, that sweet poison, so apt to corrupt the holder, and often less pleasant to have than painful to lose; or fame, that shrill, but usually over-priced whistle, that enemy of happy privacy, bringing its queues of bores that may end by reducing a man to echo the cry—'Ceux qui viennent me voir, me font honneur, ceux qui ne viennent pas me font plaisir'; or beauty which, even were one wed to Helen herself, may keep one anxiously watching for Paris to appear. No wonder that, in Plato's Vision of Er, the wise Odysseus

---

[1] With the four wishes of the Greek poem quoted above, Sir Richard Living-stone has compared three of R. L. Stevenson's: '(1) Good health; (2) two to three hundred a year; (3) *O du lieber Gott*, friends.' Apart from the omission of the Greek desire for comeliness, they are strikingly close to those of 'Simonides'.

Dean Inge's three wishes were rather different—(1) wisdom; (2) domestic happiness; (3) the approval of my fellows. Wisdom may be a means of finding happiness, or of avoiding its reverse; but it is, as 'Solomon' thought, a dubious source for it. However, Inge might have replied that happiness was not his prime aim. Again, the approval of one's fellows seems a sandy foundation to build on; nor would one have thought Inge unduly concerned about it. Its main value, I take it, lies in this—that a sense of being useful to the world is one of the firmest sources of happiness; and public approval is *some* evidence of good service done. But, even so, how many prophets have been stoned!

chose gladly for his next incarnation the obscure life of an ordinary man. For too easily we become like ardent mushroom-hunters with an inadequate knowledge of fungi, laboriously gathering what will give the deadliest of indigestions. Perhaps the true worldly wisdom is, after all, to be unworldly.

> No fatal dreads, no fruitless vain desires,
> Low caps and court'sies to a painted wall,
> Nor heaping rotten sticks on needless fires,
> Ambitious ways to climb, nor fears to fall,
> Nor things so base do I affect at all.[1]

May it not be, then, that the broad strategy of life is indeed fairly simple, whereas it is the tactics of life that remain eternally and infernally difficult—that the general principles of living are not excessively abstruse, but their application always hard, often impossible?

Yet a walk through one of our drab industrial cities can leave one half-ashamed to talk about happiness at all. Here are so many faces that tell their story of undervitality; of overwork, or work that is drudgery, or lack of work; of boredom; of the fear of poverty, or disease, or death; of frustration and loneliness. 'Il y a horriblement de mal sur la terre.'

Christians may answer 'Why not try Christianity?' But it *has* been tried for two thousand years. They ask a lot of time. They suggest 'A change of heart'. But the kind of fundamental change suggested seems likely to need—even if ever practicable—whole centuries, or millennia. The human heart has changed, in essentials, so little through all the vicissitudes of human history since it dawned in China, Sumer, or Egypt.

Once, I have heard, Bernard Shaw came down to Cambridge to propound *his* vision of the future; and when he had ended, some solemn cleric rose up to ask, 'And on what force do you rely, Mr Shaw, to produce these beneficent changes?' And Mr Shaw, blandly smiling, answered: 'Oh, human selfishness, human selfishness.'

---

[1] Drayton. Cf. Béranger:

> Non, mes amis, non, je ne veux rien être;
> Semez ailleurs places, titres, et croix.
> Non, pour les cours Dieu ne m'a pas fait naître;
> Oiseau craintif, je fuis la glu des rois.
> Que me faut-il? Maîtresse à fine taille,
> Petit repas et joyeux entretien.
> De mon berceau près de bènir la paille,
> En me créant Dieu m'a dit: ne sois rien.

The answer may not really be quite so simple; or so cynical. But Shaw was at least more of a realist than his interlocutor. Any scheme of improvement that works, will have to depend both on human unselfishness and on human selfishness—those who look for the second to disappear would do better to resign themselves to await the Day of Judgement. Indeed human selfishness alone could work wonders of improvement, were it not for the far more calamitous havoc made by human folly.

Then the Communists set forth their remedy. But are they, in practice, very different from the old type of religious fanatic who sought Heaven by making earth a Hell? It is hard to believe it, when one has stood in some Communist capital, with its megalomaniac public buildings towering above the tight faces in the streets, and heard, as I did once, some voice of a victim newly emerged from one of their concentration camps whispering with icy conviction, 'Better a third World War, with forty million dead, than that this abomination should go on.' How much good they have done for the masses within their police-states, men will passionately dispute for years to come; but to the masses of the outside world their main gift has been a constant fear of war, and the crushing weight of sterile armaments, which nothing but their fanaticism compels.

I doubt if anyone not a crank can really offer any better alternative to the slow progress which has produced the welfare states of England and Scandinavia. This at least is free from the Fascist-Nazi folly of supposing that the individual exists for the state, instead of the state being merely a means of producing happy and healthy individuals. This at least is based on the common-sense principle that counting noses is better than breaking heads; and that a nation with some intelligence, education, and restraint, where opinions are freely discussed, does in the long run—often a very long run—sometimes choose the right course; and contrives, at least, to muddle on better than has ever proved possible by any other means, such as intelligent despots (who are likely to be followed, sooner or later, by despots unintelligent, or wicked, or both).

A flat, prosaic conclusion; yet that is nothing against its truth. But whether it is 'After us, the deluge' or 'After us, the millennium', the individual, having done his best, has the consolation, dubious perhaps, of knowing that there was little he could do to affect these vast issues, anyway. Better if poor Boswell had taken Johnson's advice to keep

Corsica out of his head, and turned his mind, instead, to giving poor Margaret Boswell some happier years. None the less, because, with all his follies and absurdities, Boswell yet loved life, and had an eye for it, he left for posterity a bequest that few have equalled. And so I end where I began, in a sense of the supreme preciousness of vitality—that vitality which can find moments of happy animation even at times that to others seem calamitous. Lady Mary Wortley Montagu is not a figure that most of us would choose to envy. Her experience led her to the grim conclusions that marriage was 'a lottery where there are (at the lowest computation) ten thousand blanks to one prize'; that 'the pursuit of pleasure will ever be attended with pain'; that 'we are no more free agents than the queen of clubs when she victoriously takes prisoner the knave of hearts'. Her own marriage failed; her son became an affliction and an ignominy; in her old age she records that for eleven years she had not dared look in her mirror. She had once called life 'a dull road'. And yet, dying, she is said to have murmured: 'It has all been very interesting; it has all been very interesting.' Even in death she kept her vital interest in the eternal strangeness of life. There are worse last words.

The Greatest Problem of To-Day

> Slowly comes a hungry people, as a lion creeping nigher,
> Glares at one that nods and winks behind a slowly dying fire,
>
> TENNYSON, *Locksley Hall*

> 'If a steady observer really looks at actual life, he will see that men never think if they can help it.'
>
> WALTER BAGEHOT

To man's future there are to-day perhaps two main dangers. One of these is ceaselessly debated, often with more heat than light. It provokes passionate emotions—often far too passionate (for what use are shrieks?)—from Guatemala to Japan, from Australia to Alaska.

The other danger is seldom mentioned. It has, indeed, called forth a certain number of books, but these are often flatly contradictory; and they are read by only a tiny fraction of the public. Indeed the whole subject is chastely avoided by the popular press; which has neither time nor space to spare for a theme so unpleasant, being preoccupied with such livelier topics as criminal violence, divorce, prostitution, homosexuality, sports-news, or television-stars.[1] In fact it seems likely that this second menace has never been heard of, even now, by the great majority of mankind.

Yet the historians of the future (assuming that there *are* historians, and a future) may reflect with some amazement that this second danger, so persistently disregarded, was still the more dangerous of the two.

It is, no doubt, rather more remote. That is to say, it is round the next corner; which, for many of us, is the same as not existing. But every day it grows. It has already caused, and is causing at this moment, suffering incalculable. It may well get rapidly worse. Strangest of all, the mass of mankind, who may well plead their utter impotence as individuals to do anything about the first menace, are themselves actively, and continuously, contributing to the second.

---

[1] Latterly this curtain of obscurantism shows signs of lifting a little—though not of course, without howls of disapproval.

The first threat, of course, is nuclear war; the second is world-overpopulation—a new Deluge, of a new kind, which *might* drown humanity in a Flood, not of water, but of themselves. We may take comfort in murmuring, like the French monarch, 'Après nous le déluge.' But we should not—especially the younger among us—feel too sure of that.

At times I have a vision of a crowd of villagers so anxiously intent on the heavings and rumblings of the mountain above them—will it erupt?—that they never notice how in smooth and sinister silence, from the far horizon behind them, there advances steadily and relentlessly the crest of a tidal wave.

World-population is not a simple subject. Read a few books about it, and you may think that at least the main facts provide firm ground: read further, and you find yourself sinking in a bog of controversy. The main trends of the past are fairly plain, though even here there are discrepant views; but these discrepancies about the past are nothing to the wide, sometimes violent, divergences about the future. The worthy Malthus is depicted by turns as a prophet unheeded, or as a plagiarizing impostor. And the statistical forecasts even of experts turn out to be highly precarious.

For example, in 1946 some American demographers suggested that the population of the United States might in 1960—then only fourteen years away—reach 153 million; and about 1990 attain a peak of 164·5 million; after which it might decline. Actually by 1955—a mere nine years later—the American population had already exceeded this peak of 164·5 million. By 1958 it had become 175 million; and some estimates expected it to reach by 1975 no less than 207–228 million; by A.D. 2000, perhaps 300 million—more, possibly, than the whole earth contained in A.D. 1. Why?

Because, for some obscure reason or reasons, the United States developed a baby-boom. Hitler and Mussolini did not find it easy, with all the powers of fanatical dictatorship, to dragoon their slave-populations into breeding much larger regiments of infantry. But apparently the Americans just came to think the ideal size of family rather larger than they had previously thought. It seems hard to judge how much this was due to increased prosperity, when the great slump was passed, and to earlier marriage; how much to mere fashion—or possibly even to a sense of national self-preservation in a dangerous world. At all events in 1948–58 the annual rate of increase was 1·7 per cent—a faster growth than even in modern India. No doubt the Americans can still feel that they have plenty of room.

Whether this sudden change is good or evil (who can say yet?),[1] it remains astonishing; and it also undermines the comforting doctrine, which is still widely put about, that nations grown highly industrialized and prosperous tend automatically to lose fertility and to stabilize their populations, or decline—so that, once the world grew a little richer throughout, the population-danger would quietly fade away, without our needing to do anything about it. (And this flattering unction, which so many now grasp at, also ignores the risk that the growth of population might prevent a country like India from reaching that minimum degree of prosperity where population-growth might start to decrease.)

Again, Raymond Pearl in 1939[2] suggested that the rate of human increase was 'rapidly slowing'—'nor does it appear that the total population of the world will ever, in its present cycle of growth at least, be double what it is at the present time.' Then Pearl put that population at a little over 2000 million; to-day, only twenty years later, some expect that figure to be, not doubled, but actually *trebled*, within the next forty years. Again, Pearl conjectured, very cautiously, that humanity might reach about A.D. 2100 a peak of 2645.5 million—and thought even that highly perilous; to-day—a hundred and forty years sooner—mankind has passed this total already (despite a second World War), and is increasing at a faster rate than ever!

Similarly in January 1950 Lord Boyd-Orr expected the world-population of 1975 to be around 3000 million; now (1959) it looks more like being 3750 million. In 1953 P. C. Putnam expected the total for A.D. 2000 to be perhaps 3900 million; now we are told that it is almost certain to reach the staggering figure of 6000–7000 million. Even estimates of existing populations have sometimes fluctuated wildly. The 1953 census purported to reveal in mainland China a total of 582 million[3]—nearly 100 million more than the estimate given by the premier, Chou-en-lai, only three years before.

But however widely such figures change, they seem always to change

---

[1] On the one hand, the United States have become the bulwark of Western freedom; and bulwarks *must* be manned. On the other, is it healthy for any nation to grow too vast?

[2] *Natural History of Population*, 1939.

[3] Plus 7·6 million in Formosa, 11·7 million elsewhere outside the Chinese mainland.

in the same direction—at each revision they grow larger and more sinister. It would be rash to overstress this tendency; but rash also to disregard it.

It remains, then, vital to remember that population-figures for any distance ahead are not prophecies, but hypotheses—at time T there will be population P, if there obtain conditions $C_1, C_2, C_3 \ldots$ If.

On the other hand, lest this provide human ostriches with the sort of sand they are always longing to lay their heads in, one must also face the figures of what actually *has* occurred in the last hundred years, still more in the last fifty; and *is* occurring now.

With this caution about the facts of the future must go an equal caution about future policies and remedies. For here the disagreements grow wider still, as individual preferences and prejudices come into play.

Sir Charles Darwin,[1] for instance, is full of sombre forebodings; yet other scientific writers on the subject remain so glib and gleeful that one's head aches with their confident crowings about the Paradise that Science is going to build us all in the century to come. (It will even, we are told, change the stars literally in their courses, and push planets into new orbits where their climates can become more agreeable!)

That these chirpy persons, with their fluorescent-lighted Heavens, feasting untold myriads on plankton-pills, may produce on the reader an effect more depressing even than the sober anxieties of Sir Charles Darwin, is here irrelevant. For that is merely an emotional reaction. And though emotion may be an essential source of energy for executing plans, it can be an unmixed nuisance in weighing them. Writers on this particular theme find it hard enough anyway to be dispassionate; for they are dealing with those highly inflammable matters—morals and sex. But, hard or no, it is necessary. I shall try, then, to remain as cold-blooded as possible; even at the risk of seeming icily callous. And if it seems also rash for a mere layman to talk on what is largely a scientific problem, I can only plead that the problem appears to me not talked about nearly enough. The dangers may be far too pressing to go on being smothered in uneasy silence. And even geese, on one famous occasion, by lifting up their voices helped to save the Capitol.

*   *   *   *

[1] *Problems of World-Population*, 1958.

Statistics are often boring; often suspect; often handy tools for special pleading. But here they are unescapable. And in broad outline most of the figures I shall give are generally agreed. Further, instead of trying to dress up the facts in flowing periods, I shall give them where possible in tabular form. This may be less elegant: it is a good deal clearer.

SUPPOSED GROWTH OF WORLD POPULATION

Date	Millions
B.C. 10,000	1^1
A.D. 1	275^1
1–700	Perhaps no growth, rather a slight decline both in Europe and in China.[2] (Death had been busy.)
1650 (beginning of rapid increase)	475
1750	695
1850	1095–1100
1900	1550
1950	2500
1975	?3750
2000	?6000–7000[3]

Not only has the growth of world-population been formidable; so also has been the acceleration in its *rate* of growth. It not only grows bigger and bigger: it also grows faster and faster.

The population of A.D. 700 may have doubled by 1650 or 1700—in 1000 years.
The population of A.D. 1650 more than doubled by 1850—in 200 years.
The population of A.D. 1850 more than doubled by 1950—in 100 years.
The population of A.D. 1950 may have doubled by 1990—in 40 years.

---

[1] Clearly all these estimates of the population before 1850 or after 1975 are very speculative indeed.

[2] In China, as in Europe, rapid increase is said to have begun about 1650. But see Ping-ti Ho, *Studies on the Population of China, 1368-1953.*

[3] 'Barring either a catastrophe, or a deterioration of social conditions for progress in health, of global proportions, a world population of between 6000 and 7000 million by the end of the century should now be expected almost as a matter of practical certainty.' (*United Nations Population Studies*, No. 28, 1958.) The sceptic may be wise still to suspend judgement. But, from such a source, the statement remains impressive.

Or, to quote another estimate:

The annual rate of growth 1850–1900 may have been ·7 per cent (doubling in about 100 years).
The annual rate of growth 1900–1950 may have been ·9 per cent (doubling in about 80 years).
The annual rate of growth may now be over 1·5 per cent (doubling in under 50 years).

We are faced with a kind of chain-explosion.

Here are some examples of recent expansion.

Europe: in 1800, 187 million; in 1940, 533 million (and 45 million had emigrated). It has been estimated that in 1940 there were in the whole world 730 million of European descent—just over one third of the human total.[1]

Ceylon: spraying with DDT reduced the death-rate by a third, from 20·4 to 13·8 per 1000, in the single year 1946–7. In 1936 it had been 37 per 1000; by 1952 it was 12. By 1956 the population was growing at a rate that would double it in 25 years or less. High death-rates can be very rapidly dealt with by modern science: but high birth-rates are a much harder matter. In 1956, Sweden (one of the few countries that treat this subject with sanity) was to help Ceylon in a 3-year plan for family control.

Java: population said to have jumped from 4·5 million in 1815 to 55 million in 1940.

India: in the sixteenth century, perhaps 100 million; in 1850, about 150 million; in 1881, 254 million; in 1931, 353 million; in 1941, 389 million; by 1966, perhaps 460 million. The population of India and Pakistan alone already exceeds that of the whole world three centuries ago.

[1] A human eruption like that convulsion of Krakatoa which scattered its dust round the globe. Other races, indeed, may be less thrilled by this triumph of the whites; but Red Indians have not, that I know, left any historians. Still our turn might come. Sometimes in the crowded streets of Cambridge or London, at moments of fantasy, I see all the faces yellow. (By A.D. 2000 there might be nearly 4000 million Asiatics—not counting those in U.S.S.R.—nearly two-thirds of the world total. A sobering prospect for Europeans and North Americans. Some may recall the dream of imperialist Japan—'We have now China. China is our steed! Far shall we ride upon her! . . . America is an immense melon, ripe for the cutting. North America will support a thousand million people: they shall be Japanese, with their slaves.')

The Indians are now increasing by perhaps six million a year. Two-thirds of the population are estimated underfed. A quarter of the children die before their first birthday; half, before their twentieth. The seriousness of the situation may be judged by a proposal that any man with two children, and with less than £13 a month, should receive a bonus of £7 if willing to be sterilized.

Singapore: in 1956 the death-rate had been lowered to 9 per thousand, while the birth-rate was 48. Annual increase—3.9 per cent (doubling the population in some 18 years).

China: total Chinese population now said to be 650 million; annual increase, 13 or even 15 million (2–3 per cent?).[1]

The attitude of the Communist government towards birth-control has been perplexingly changeable. In 1955–7 population-planning was approved; in 1958 this policy was suddenly reversed; in 1959, however, the press was again allowed to counsel family-limitation, while much seems left, in practice, to the discretion of doctors and hospitals. At one point it was reported that the government intended to stabilize the population at 800 million (if unchecked, the present rate of increase might double it in 25 years to 1300 million). But, for the present, China is still officially underpopulated. It looks as if there had been serious dissension about this matter in high quarters behind the scenes.

Taiwan (*Formosa*): increase, 1951–5, 3·7 per cent (doubling in 22–23 years).

Japan: in 1850, about 30 million; in 1920, 55 million; in 1958, 92 million. For a country so cramped this was a serious situation, and compelled drastic measures. Abortion was legalized. In 1957 there were perhaps 1,200,000 such operations, at a cost to the patient of from 1s. to 6s.; besides, possibly, not far short of a million illegal cases. Between 1947 and 1957 the birth-rate showed an astonishing drop from 33 per thousand to 17. But, since the death-rate fell almost as much, the annual rate of increase declined only from 1·3 per cent to 1·1 per cent (about 900,000 annually; which would double the popula-

[1] S. Chandrasekhar in *Population Review* (Madras) III, 2, July 1959, on the basis of the latest vital statistics (1957), gave the annual increase as some 20 million, with the prospect of a total Chinese population of 800 million by 1968.

tion in little over 60 years). Recently, however, it was hoped to reach a peak of 104 million about 1990.

Here it becomes ironic to contrast the policy of the militarist Japanese government of 1939, which had aimed at a population of 100 million by 1960; banned birth-control; set up official marriage-agencies; and urged that parents should marry three years younger, and produce at least five children.

At a Planned-parenthood Conference in Tokyo in 1955 there was even a Japanese proposal for putting a tax on all children after the third; startling at first sight, but just as rational as children's allowances in differing circumstances elsewhere.

Indeed restrictions much more drastic were reported by R. L. Stevenson from nineteenth-century Polynesia, under the pressure of population—'on Vaitupu, in the Ellices, only two children were allowed to a couple; on Nukufetau, but one. On the latter the punishment was by fine; and it is related that the fine was sometimes paid, and the child spared.'

Georgetown (British Guina): in 1945–7 the *infant* mortality was reduced by the use of DDT from 350 per thousand to 67. In consequence the population began increasing at a rate to double in seven years.

Puerto Rico: in 1800, 155,000; in 1898, when ceded by Spain to U.S.A., 820,000; in 1950, 2,200,000. In 1938 the Puerto Rican government tried giving birth-control information in nine clinics; but these were closed on orders from Washington. In 1953 the population was annually increasing by 62,000; and 60,000 were migrating to the United States, leaving the local increase at a mere 2000! But at last the wall of bigotry appears to have been breached; it was reported from Puerto Rico in 1959 that three years of experiment with women volunteers seemed, provisionally, to have revealed an effective oral contraceptive.[1]

In fine, it is estimated that in A.D. 2000 the world-population may be 6000–7000 million; in 2050, by one forecast, 12,000 million. *If* the present rate of increase continued 600 years, men would be left with one square metre each; at the rate of increase now existing on Formosa (say 3·5 per cent), there would in 350 years be one person to every square foot. Clearly all estimates for more than a few decades ahead

[1] See the article by Gregory Pincus in *Science*, 24/7/59, and R. L. Meier, *Modern Science and the Human Fertility Problem*, 1959.

306

must be largely guesswork; but at this moment the world-increase is some 125,000 a day. And yet two-thirds, or three-quarters, of the earth's inhabitants are thought to go hungry; to give them a satisfactory diet would need world-production of food to be increased by 25 per cent, with a further increase of 2 per cent each year.[1]

All these figures of growth are sufficiently astounding; but their main cause seems perfectly simple—declining mortality.

It has been Nature's simple system to balance extravagant fecundity with extravagant murder. Death has been in her hands a sort of whetstone to keep keen and clean the edges of life. There are plenty of striking examples in the vegetable and animal worlds. Thus it has been calculated (not by me!) that a pair of flies mating in April would have progeny enough, if all survived, to cover the earth by August in a layer of flies 45 feet deep;[2] that a single aphis in 300 days could produce 17,000,000,000,000,000,000,000,000,000,000 offspring; and one pair of rabbits, in four years, 1,274,840 descendants (this, indeed, seems almost moderate in comparison). One emission of a bull contains thousands of millions of spermatozoa; all, or all but one, destined to perish within a few hours. Even in man the figure is some three hundred million. The slaughter-house of existence is fantastic and wasteful past imagining.

With this natural fecundity, like a volcanic force imprisoned under a mountain, even a small escape can produce explosions; as when a few rabbits released in Australia and New Zealand, away from their natural enemies, quickly became destroying hordes, in myriads past counting. There is, indeed, a second factor also, equally difficult for the ordinary mind to grasp and get used to—the stealthy, yet staggering power of compound interest, when applied to large numbers or long periods. For instance, an annual increase of 1·3 per cent sounds at first hearing a very moderate fertility; yet in some 50 years it could turn a population of 2,500,000,000 into one of 5,000,000,000. A 3½ per cent increase doubles a population in a mere 20 years, and multiplies it tenfold in 67. There could be no more vivid vindication of Dr Johnson's stress on the illuminating value of arithmetic But the ordinary man still finds the true situation incredibly hard to realize.

Many find it also too horrid to realize. Indeed it recalls that unbearable episode in Hardy's novel where Jude's eldest boy hangs first the

[1] See Colin Bertram, *Adam's Brood*, 1959.
[2] R. A. Piddington, *The Limits of Mankind* (1956).

younger children, then himself, with the scribbled note—'Done because we are too menny'.
But mental cowardice will not help.

*　　　*　　　*

This predicament, then, of the human race is mainly the work of medical science. Man has merely disturbed the ancient balance of Life and Death. One is reminded of that Greek legend which told how the wise physician Asclepius, son of Apollo, came by his skill even to raise the dead—so that Zeus, to preserve the fabric of the world, had to blast the rash healer with a thunderbolt.

'True enough,' replied an Indian farmer to remarks about the past benefits of British rule, 'yet what is all that but putting a spoke in Nature's wheel? In old days war, plague, famine kept the population within manageable bounds.'[1] Nature's remedy might one day be a return to increased mortality. But that could take forms far from pleasant. Those who talk of 'trusting Providence' should at least bear in mind some of the things that Providence has permitted.

*　　　*　　　*

Any population must either increase, diminish, or remain the same. Each, under certain conditions, can become undesirable or dangerous. Under the Roman Empire, Italy came to have too few people: to-day it has too many.

Stability is obviously undesirable in a population either too small, or too big (as that of the world may well be to-day). Thus it has been suggested that the population of Great Britain, now *comparatively* stabilized,[2] is yet far too large—overcrowded in peace, and hopelessly vulnerable in war; so that half its inhabitants ought to be transferred to other parts of the Commonwealth. For instance:

	Present population		Population proposed	
Great Britain	50 millions		25 millions	
Canada	13	,,	25	,,
Australia	8	,,	15	,,
White Africa	$2\frac{3}{4}$	,,	5	,,
New Zealand	$1\frac{1}{2}$	,,	5[3]	,,

[1] J. Chartres Molony, 'Population Problems', in *Contemporary Review*, 1948. Under British rule from 1857 to 1947 the Indian population doubled; but the average peasant's holding dwindled. From 1927 to 1947, with increased growth of population, the level of living is said definitely to have declined.
[2] It is at present increasing by about 2 million every decade.
[3] See F. Hoyle, *Decade of Decision*, 1953.

That England would be pleasanter if less populous, many may agree; but many may also doubt whether a mass-migration on this titanic scale could be carried through, even by the ruthlessness of an Assyrian king.

On the other hand we have seen in our time how the *comparative* stability of French population, with its slow increase, weakened France in the face of Germany. (For this reason, since 1920, France has opposed legal obstacles to birth-control.) A like danger may hereafter confront Western Europe from the proliferation of less advanced peoples elsewhere, especially in Asia and Latin America.

In any case, stability is a very difficult fence to sit balanced on. Populations tend either to grow or to lessen. But depopulation too has obvious perils. First, politically. The growing tendency to prefer two children in a family to six brought in the thirties gloomy, though mistaken, calculations of an England and Wales reduced perhaps by A.D. 2035 to 4·5 million. It looked for a time—and the anxiety, though it proved then a mare's nest, might recur—as if some West-European nations like England and Sweden might need, for survival, precisely the opposite policy to that required in many other parts of the world— an increase, instead of a decrease, in births.

But the recent recovery of birth-rates in the United States and other advanced countries (which may, of course, be only temporary) shows how difficult are any such predictions. After all, as Wilhelm Busch so tersely put it:

> Vater *werden* ist nicht schwer;
> Vater *sein* dagegen, *sehr*.
>
> *Become* a father—easy done:
> What is hard is *being* one.

With liberal family-allowances to make parenthood less 'hard', and a sense of national self-preservation to stress the need, a lot can sometimes be effected to restore fertility. Still such declines seem sometimes to have gone disastrously far—one may recall Plutarch's melancholy picture of the Greece he lived in (c. 100 A.D.) which, he says, could no longer raise from its whole territory the three thousand hoplites that the single small city of Megara sent to face the Persians at Plataea in 479 B.C.; or the disappearance of its sturdy peasantry from Roman Italy in the face of slave-labour, giant estates, and cheap foreign corn; or the depopulation of the Scottish Highlands. And then there is the exceptional case of Eire, reduced by famine, then by migration and late marriage, from 6½ million in 1848 to less than three to-day. Some Irishmen now think their country underpopulated. Who can say? It might be wiser to be at least thankful that they are now far more comfortable and less congested than their forefathers a century since, or the people of India now.

Secondly, there is an economic risk with a falling population, of increased unemployment. Also the population goes on ageing.[1]

Thirdly, there is a eugenic danger. When the size of families comes to be planned (as in England, seemingly, since about 1880), such planning is more likely to be done by the more prosperous and the more prudent. Obviously if the less intelligent produce more children, more and more children tend to be less intelligent. (And tests *seem* to indicate that this is actually the case.) It is a kind of *un*natural selection; as if a poultry-keeper were to breed from his worse layers. He would get fewer and fewer eggs. It has been suggested that from this cause the average Intelligence Quotient is tending to drop two points a generation. One may feel doubt: but it is hard not to feel concern.

This danger may be accentuated in a Welfare State, which enables every boy with brains to rise to a higher level, where he tends to have fewer children. The more efficiently the cream is thus separated, the thinner the milk that remains below. The nation may grow stupider because its cleverer members have fewer children; the masses may grow stupider because their cleverer members are continually siphoned off. And by an ironic paradox this relative deterioration of the masses would be largely due to the efforts of their own leaders to improve their opportunities. (I have heard of an able person from a poor home remarking that *he* was certainly not going to help undermine the middle-class, just when he had managed to climb into it.)

Here, however, time may work a cure, by levelling out the difference in fertility between richer and poorer. Yet there would still remain that other similar menace of the higher birth-rate of the less developed countries. *That* difference seems far more difficult to whittle down. At present the technologically advanced peoples do form more than a third of mankind; by A.D. 2000 they might have sunk to a fifth—though doubtless technology will by then have spread far among races still undeveloped to-day.

[1] Cf. the German gibe during the last war—'Why are all French Generals aged 70?'—'Because all the generals of 75 are dead.'

But it is *over*population that seems far the greatest peril of the present world.

And yet, though the statistics may appear a very sinister writing on the wall, and the ghost of Malthus rises again in far grimmer shape than that gentle and genial cleric ever assumed in his lifetime, it must be frankly admitted that a number of clever scientific minds remain, as already mentioned, imperturbably optimistic, and roll out breezy books on roughly the following lines.

'Overpopulation? Sheer nonsense! Trust Science. Food? We shall make nothing of the miracle of feeding the five thousand millions. R. L. Meier in 1956 suggested we could cope with *fifty* thousand million; though that might mean urbanizing all the flat spaces of the earth.[1] For, as the Devil once suggested doing, we really *can* turn stones into bread.

'Malthus was an old croaker. As everybody knows, he argued that populations, whether of men or rabbits, unless checked by want and disease, grow by geometrical progression, like compound interest or a snowball; and since food-supplies cannot keep up this pace, the feckless creatures tend to breed to the limit of subsistence—would quickly eat up the moon itself, were they upon it, and it made of green cheese. Yet at the end of the century and a half since Mathus wrote, the white races, though vastly multiplied, live far better than they did at the beginning. Malthus forgot one vital point—that men are more inventive than rabbits. But we *are*.

'The secret is—power. From sunlight and sea, from wind and water, Science will produce more energy than we know how to use. Above all there is nuclear power—especially when we have beaten the hydrogen-bomb into something more efficient than a billion ploughshares.

'With all this power at our elbows, we can re-create the earth. As the Russians are already doing, we can alter mountain-ranges and reverse the flow of rivers. We can afforest wildernesses, and make deserts like the Sahara blossom better than any rose. We can multiply the earth's fertility with new fertilizers, new varieties of crop, new pesticides.

'Again, you now waste most of the food-value in plants, by eating only their fruit, or seeds, or roots. But we can process sugars and proteins from leaves, grass, and woody residues. Further, we can

[1] R. L. Meier, *Science and Economic Development* (1956), p. 141.

cultivate plants more efficient in their photo-synthesis, such as algae—particularly *chlorella*, a green water-weed of incredible fecundity. A mere million acres of *chlorella* could produce half the protein needed by the present world-population. And fuel as well.

'Then there are all sorts of food, eaten by some human beings, though disdained by the rest—locusts, grasshoppers, termites, sugar-ants, bees, aphids, silkworms, spiders, the eggs of water-bugs.

'But these, of course, are mere flea-bites. We can extract plankton—minute forms of organic life—on a vast scale from the oceans. If it can nourish whales, then, properly treated, it can nourish us. Indeed we can create artificial whales—atomic submarines—to sweep up and process the stuff.

'But Science can do more than all this. It can free us from the tyranny of *natural* foodstuffs, animal and vegetable, altogether. The nutrition of the future can be largely synthetic—made in factories. Already in the Second War the Germans produced fats from hydro-genated coal. We can get sugar from coal or sawdust; fat from mineral oil; and so on. Cornfields, ricefields, pastures are gross waste of space; they will be replaced by the compactness of the automated factory. Then it will be the laboratory that blossoms; and just as synthetic dyes have replaced madder or indigo, and synthetic fabrics are replacing natural silk or wool, so synthetic foods, synthetically flavoured, will make obsolete the beasts and fruits of the field.

'And then raw materials? Fears about the exhaustion of natural reserves in fuels, metals, and so on are likewise mere bogeys. No doubt the human race has long been living on the accumulated capital of past aeons—coal, oil, rich ores and deposits—with the blind reck-lessness of a rake's progress. And but for Science we should now face a ruinous reckoning. But, with skill and energy enough, we shall simply find access to sources less accessible and so, till now, unprofitable. We can get our carbon from limestone, sulphur from gypsum, metals from the earth's igneous rocks—or, still better perhaps, from the infinite abysses of the sea. Fraudulent speculators in the past have floated schemes for extracting gold from sea-water, which merely floated away with the investors' gold. But fundamentally the idea was sound enough. The metals *are* there—it is merely a matter of technique. The quantities in a cubic metre of sea-water may be almost unimaginably small; but our power to extract them will have become unimaginably great.

Again, we can employ new substitutes, such as titanium for iron: we can create new materials, such as plastics.

'Further, we shall abolish a great deal of the needless local scarcities that now exist, by improving transport out of recognition, so that whatever is wanted flows wherever it is wanted, freely and at once.

'Finally, there is space. When we have turned this old world upside down, we need not weep like Alexander for new ones to conquer. They are there waiting in the sky. And our rockets will conquer them.

> The World was all before them, where to choose
> Thir place of rest, and Providence thir guide.

So Milton, of the first man and woman with Paradise behind them. But modern man has Paradise, if he chooses, before him; not merely this world to choose from, but the Universe; and for his guide, not Providence, but Science.

'Only, of course, this is going to take multitudes of scientists and engineers. At present rates of production, for example, the United States will have by A.D. 2000 some 3,300,000 of them; but they may well require far more. If that country has now one scientist or engineer in two hundred persons, by 1980 the need may be for one in every ninety; by 2000, for one in every forty. It may be necessary to attract them by special privileges and advantages; to catch them still earlier in life; and to swell their numbers by drawing on the largely still virgin field of women.'

*   *   *

Some readers may find all this fantastic. Perhaps it is. I do not know. But we should remember that many of the fantastic-seeming dreams, and nightmares, of H. G. Wells have in our time come true—only too true. And there is nothing here that has not been seriously suggested by scientific writers within the last ten years. One of them spoke of these 'sanguinary hopes'. He meant, of course, 'sanguine'; but others may feel that 'sanguinary' might be really the better word. I do not know. Some may be thrilled by these prospects; some, appalled. I own that I shudder. But I comfort myself with the thought that, if such a world does come, I shall not be there; and that if such a world does come, those who live in it may, after all, be conditioned to like it. If so, I should not easily be conditioned to like *them*. But that is beside the point. It is not a matter, now, of being emotional; but of trying to weigh coldly three main questions:

(1) Can we thus solve the problem of a portentously increasing world-population?

(2) If we can thus solve it, do we want to?

(3) Is there any possible, and preferable, alternative?

*   *   *

(1) Is it possible to find a solution on these lines—a vast extension of science to cope with a vast extension of population?

One can believe that many of the schemes suggested may be physically possible[1] (whether or no they would be economically possible), *given sufficient time*. In these three words may lie the whole crux. Will sufficient time be given? Or will the flood rise faster than the dams? Does not such optimism underrate the resistances to be overcome, and overcome quickly? For there are both the resistances of people, and the resistances of things.

First, the resistances of things. Builders of new worlds in the clouds may forget that though scientists have become wizards, they have not yet become gods: these hopeful programmes may not allow sufficiently for the snags, hitches, and drawbacks into which a hurried scientific revolution, on this scale, might run. We are, for example, still baffled after years of research, not only by cancer, but by the common cold. We may recall a certain British scheme for growing groundnuts on a most magnificent scale—with results far from magnificent. The Comet was a triumph of engineering; yet tiny cracks in fatigued metal brought disaster after disaster. To remedy these defects cost enormous expense and delay.

Nature, again, is apt to turn Nemesis whenever men tamper too rashly. We have seen forest-felling, over-grazing, and over-cultivation bring erosion and dust-bowls that can send the slowly accumulated topsoil of centuries soaring skyward on one windy day. We have seen rabbits grow resistant to myxomatosis; bacteria to antibiotics. We can produce nuclear power; but we cannot tell yet what effects we may also produce from the radioactivity we are so rashly pouring into earth,

---

[1] One may doubt, however, if space-travel can help the population problem. It is a little hard at this stage to see what purpose, apart from science and adventure, could be served by journeys to heavenly bodies either infernally hot or infernally cold, and often with no atmosphere, or a poisonous one, full of carbon dioxide, ammonia, or methane. As for the starry spaces, since we can hardly hope to travel faster than light, most of the universe seems safely beyond the reach of our insatiable species.

sea, and air. One would have thought, then, that it might be only prudent for these scientific planners of a wholesale revolution in human life to allow a little more than most of them do for the unpredictable and the unforeseen.

*   *   *

Secondly, there is the problem of human resistances. We are faced with a swarming multitude of nearly three thousand million souls, fast increasing every day. They are largely illiterate, uneducated, full of prejudices, traditions, and emotions. Two-thirds of them, or even three-quarters, are estimated to be underfed; as against half before the last war. To feed them properly, even for the moment, would need, it is said, a 25 per cent increase in world food-supplies. It seems, then, a little optimistic to believe that, in the comparatively short time that may be available, they could be steered through a scientific revolution on the colossal scale suggested, requiring immense amounts of capital; of organization; of power to compel or persuade on one side, and of patient acquiescence on the other. Hopeful scientists are a little apt to write as if they were already living in a world-state run by a scientific dictatorship; forgetting that mankind is divided into scores of nations so diverse, and so jealous of their independence, that even in enlightened Western Europe even an obvious benefit like freeing trade encounters obstacles and delays without end.

In the world to-day the differences in wealth between nations have become as striking as they ever were between individuals. The average citizen of the United States, for example, consumes nearly twice as many food-calories, 70 times as much energy, 100 times as much steel, as the average Indian; produces nearly 100 times as much; and has more than twice the expectation of life. Indeed the United States, with 6 per cent of the world's population, enjoys 50 per cent of the goods produced. In the process it also uses up 50 per cent of the world-supply of the main minerals; the other advanced countries use another 45 per cent; leaving 5 per cent for the rest of mankind. One can hardly expect Indians, Chinese, and the rest to regard this state of affairs with much satisfaction; or to tolerate it one moment longer than they must. At the gate of Dives sit now many Lazaruses.

Doubtless, then, it is right and wise that the richer peoples should aid the poorer. Actually no nation in history has ever been as generous in this way as the United States. And very little thanks they have earned;

partly because gratitude, rare enough between individuals, is almost non-existent between nations; partly because Asia has now become rather like an English eighteenth-century constituency with rival candidates—U.S.A. and U.S.S.R.—bribing and counter-bribing for support. But bribery wins small thanks.

In any case there are stringent limits to international philanthropy by governments. The masses in Europe and America would react violently against policies that started reducing their own living-standards noticeably nearer to those of Indian peasants. And there remains only too much force in the argument that aid to backward nations with high birth-rates may merely encourage them to breed up to the new limits of subsistence, so that their last state is only worse than their first; that it would be, in the Chinese phrase, 'pelting a stray dog with dumplings'.

On the other hand, the hungry masses of Asia and Africa can hardly be expected to see things so. The bigger and hungrier they become, the more chance of their turning for salvation to Communism, with its drastic drive for getting things done; and therefore the greater the risk of war and the hydrogen-bomb. The bomb, of course, might solve the problem of population; and thereafter mankind might have learnt its lesson. But the lesson would be too hideous; and at its end there might be no learners left. 'What is wanted,' wrote T. E. Lawrence, 'is a new master species with birth-control for us, to end the human race in fifty years—and then a clear field for some cleaner mammal. I suppose it must be a mammal?' But that seems the nightmare-language of despair.

For overpopulated peoples, however, Marxism has the extra appeal that it flatly denies Malthusianism. Marx detested Malthus as one who shifted the blame for poverty and unemployment from wicked capitalist to improvident worker. And Marxists still argue that a Communist state has no cause to fear overpopulation—not, at least, on economic grounds. Even if Russia's two hundred million, Mr Khrushchev has said, were increased by a further two hundred million, that would be a trivial matter.[1]

---

[1] Feb. 7, 1955. 'Bourgeois ideologists have adopted cannibal theories, among them that of overpopulation. They debate how to lower the birth-rate, to diminish population-growth. With us, comrades, the problem is quite different. If, to the 200 million that we are, were added 200 million more, that would be little.' So talked also Hitler, and Mussolini, and the militarists of Japan.

No doubt Malthus failed to foresee a good many new factors—the revolutions brought by science to both industry and agriculture; the opening of vast virgin lands, with a vast flow of emigration to them, and of food from them; the effects of improved transport, and of birth-control (which he apparently thought wicked).[1] But Malthus may have been premature rather than wrong. To-day the virgin lands are occupied; and even if the Red Flag now waved over Tokio and New Delhi, Japan and India would still be dangerously overcrowded. Even Communist China seems driven now to hesitant consideration of birth-control.

Meanwhile over half mankind lives in non-Russian Asia; and all but 2 per cent of these in countries that are undernourished.[2] One cannot be surprised if in the coming decades they prefer to believe, with Marxism, that their sufferings are unnecessary; and that the magic remedy is to liquidate both the capitalist classes and the capitalist nations. The scientific optimists, therefore, had better be quick. The pressure of humanity accumulates as dangerously as fire-damp in a mine.

It has indeed been hoped that fertility might fall of itself with growing prosperity, as in Western Europe; but in prosperous U.S.A. and Canada the rate of increase has recently bounded up. It has been hoped that fertility might fall of itself with growing density, as with fruit-flies. (*Drosophila melanogaster*, if crowded in bottles, being a nervous and sensitive little creature, gets rattled by too much 'togetherness', and becomes less fecund.[3]) But it seems hard to draw much comfort from this little insect either, while a country as badly overpopulated as India still goes on increasing by six million a year. No doubt at *some* degree of overcrowding human beings might lose fertility, like the flies; but it looks as if the degree of overcrowding required might be perfectly hellish. Long before that point was reached a human population might well grow dangerously desperate. Indeed it seems highly

---

[1] Malthus mentions, indeed, that 'in the wildness of speculation it has been suggested (of course more in jest than in earnest) that Europe ought to grow its corn in America, and devote itself solely to manufactures and commerce.' But this he rejected as desperately risky. Perhaps, in the *long* run, it is.

[2] PEP., *World Population and World Resources* (1955), p. 25. (One of the best discussions of the whole subject.)

[3] See Raymond Pearl, 'The Influence of density of population upon egg-production in *Drosophila melanogaster*' in *Journal of Experimental Zoology*, lxiii (1932), 57–84.

precarious to draw such analogies between flies and men. As was long ago sagely observed by Pope:

> Why has not man a microscopic eye?
> For this plain reason—man is not a fly.[1]

* * *

Be this as it may, the whole population-question may now perhaps be admitted to deserve *some* thought. The scientific optimists seem to me a little overconfident. They may be able to work, some day, the wonders they promise. We can judge better when they have worked them. But meanwhile one may ask why most of them are so ardent about scientific increase in world-supplies, yet so chilly about scientific limits for world-population. Why not work for both simultaneously? Why not attack the problem from both ends at once?

Well-being depends on the number of mouths as much as on the size of the pudding. Why concentrate *wholly* on enlarging the pudding —especially when so much of it is, as yet, pie in the sky? One begins to suspect in some of these optimists an illogical and psychological resistance to population-planning in itself.

The essential issue is nothing abstruse. If some simple labourer already has difficulty in supporting fifteen children, hungry, ragged, and shoeless, it seems hardly the height of good sense to say—'Go ahead! Have fifteen more. Just see how ingenious we shall be in showing you how to support them all!' It might be less Micawberish to

---

[1] One minor effect of this growing overpopulation can be seen already in our own streets. Just as Puerto Ricans pour into the United States, so West Indians have poured into England; not because of the allurement of the English climate, but because the West Indies have over-bred, and are over-breeding. Persons of liberal principles are shocked if one views this influx with misgiving. But principles, however liberal, are no substitute for common sense. It is not a question of racial superiorities; it is merely a question whether racial hotch-potches are really desirable. Philanthropists may beam genial blessings on the prospect of a human race mixed ultimately into a coffee-coloured cocktail; but the advantages of that are far from certain. Meanwhile, in the immediate future, it may be a posterity of unhappy half-breeds that pays. We do not know enough about the eugenic side. But we do know what colour-problems and racial tensions have cost in America, Africa, and elsewhere. Instead of recklessly creating them in our own midst, it might be wiser to make immigration rather less facile, and to give generously towards improving conditions in the West Indies, while also spreading there the essential knowledge of family-planning. It has been said, 'L'Angleterre se portugalise'. That might become true.

slow down this foolish philoprogenitiveness—who wants thirty children anyway?—until one is a little surer of feeding and clothing the family as it is.

Let the scientific optimists, then, pursue their grandiose schemes for bringing us abundance—all luck to them! But why not try as well to introduce a little reason into human multiplication? Actually, the amount of time, money, and brains now spent on research into methods of controlling births is grotesquely minute compared with the amount of all three devoted to research on methods of exterminating by the million those already born. A pleasantly ironic paradox. Is it not time for a little less prudery, and a little more prudence?

*   *   *

There is a further point. Even if scientific virtuosity should solve at vast expense (and who pays?) the problem of supporting six or twelve thousand million people on this earth whose resources are already dangerously ransacked, that solution must be not only attained, but also maintained. Yet the more elaborate, artificial, and complicated our world-system becomes, the greater must be its fragility and insecurity. Of that we have a small-scale example here in England. Because we can no longer live from our own soil, twice in thirty years we were brought by submarine blockade far nearer to total ruin than we had ever been in our more self-supporting days, when we faced Louis XIV or Napoleon. 'It was', the Duke said to Creevey, of Waterloo, 'a damned nice thing—the nearest run thing that ever you saw in your life.' But the thing was run nearer still to destruction in 1917 and 1942. Even in peace we remain most precariously placed, as a world's workshop that might one day find itself out of work. In the same way, and on a far greater scale, a world-structure too elaborately scientific, if once disrupted by war, revolution, natural cataclysm, or disastrous epidemic, might collapse into a chaos not easily rebuilt. The peasant living on his own ground is a good deal more secure; even after national disaster his fields are still there; he may still fall on his feet, and not have far to fall. That is more than St Simeon Stylites could hope for, when he got nearer Heaven by perching on top of a seventy-foot column. It is not without risk that modern societies imitate St Simeon. Some thinkers have conceived of future humanity going back to an agrarian life. But if populations like ours tried going back to the land, a good many millions must first lie under it. The more populous the world, and the more intricate its structure, the greater must be its fundamental insecurity —like a skyscraper in a land of earthquakes.

*   *   *

In any case, even if the world contrives, with endless effort, expenditure, and risk, to support five, ten, twenty thousand million, what then? If only for want of space, the mad game of multiplication must still be stopped somewhere. And if it must be stopped sooner or later, why not sooner? Because we hope it will stop of itself? It may. But it might do that dangerously late. There was once, says the Roman poet, a simple rustic who stood waiting on a river-bank for the river to finish rolling by. One day it would. But a good deal too late for *him*. There was once, says Chinese wisdom, another rustic, who burst himself trying to run away from his shadow. It would have been simpler for him to walk into a wood.

One possible outcome of the present muddle might be a growth of pressure in South-east Asia to the point of general collapse—a consequent extension of the Communist net, whether Chinese or Russian, over most of the area—then a drastic arrest of this feckless multiplication by the usual ruthless methods of totalitarian dictatorship, with a rigid population-plan and savage penalties for unpermitted parenthood. That might be a solution of sort; but it could easily become a hideous one, and full of danger for the West. However it would only be one more repetition of the lesson taught, for the hundredth time, by Hitler—that those who will not face unpleasant facts often find themselves faced in the end with facts more unpleasant still.

*   *   *

(2) Even supposing we could support a vastly increased world-population, do we really want to?

This seems to me a not unimportant question. Yet I have hardly ever seen it even mentioned. Most writers on the subject seem to assume that *if* by filling men's bellies with 'the green mantle of the standing pool', sweetened by synthetic sugar made from sawdust, the globe can somehow be made to sustain *x* billions, then there is no more need to worry, and all is well. But is it? Are all these billions desirable, even could they be permanently feasted on champagne and caviar? Do we really want the earth turned into a human ant-heap, conurbanized or suburbanized from Calais to Vladivostok, with its wild nature disfigured and defiled, and the individual feeling himself more and more an impotent drop in a vast, but perhaps far from pacific, ocean of humanity?

One's answer may largely depend—let us own it—on personal temperament. But that need not prevent this problem of values from being rationally discussed.

* * *

Both psychologically and politically, it may be suspected that man is seldom at his best in large masses. Even at social parties, or at meetings, the amount of intelligence shown seems often to vary inversely with the numbers present. Herd-instinct in human beings is usually debased or misguided instinct. For full development even the humble cabbage likes elbow-room; the average gardener constantly tends to defeat himself by greedily planting his seeds too close; and England is full of neglected spinneys and copses with miserable little trees all stunting one another. In fine, the worth of human beings, like the worth of paper-money, can be quickly cheapened by over-production. When the devils massed in Pandemonium, they reduced themselves to the size of pigmies; much the same can happen to men in giant communities. The individual citizen of a super-state comes to feel himself a mere drop in the ocean; and, feeling impotent, he grows irresponsible. What is he but, as Po Chu-i put it, 'a single grain of rice falling into the Great Barn'? What matters ultimately in life is states of mind—and the states of mind of individuals, not of mobs.

Greek thought (which is often worth weighing still) felt all this intensely. Barbarians, they considered, might swarm in tribes and hordes and nations—Scythians, Thracians, Medes: but the good life required a city-state. Thus Plato in his *Laws* fixed the ideal number of adult male citizens at a mere 5040—an eighth of the size of his own Athens. And that number, he said, must not grow. With women and children, aliens and slaves, this suggests a total community of under 100,000—something like the size of Cambridge.

Aristotle went further still. To him even Plato's 5040 seemed excessive. His ideal city was still smaller; and its numbers, he insisted, must be controlled, when necessary, by abortion, at an early stage before sensation was reached. Clearly a most wicked man!

The population, then, both of Greek Utopias and of actual Greek cities, may strike us as absurdly small. Yet if each individual was to live the full, many-sided life of a free citizen in a closely unified state, it was quite logical that Greek thinkers should thus envisage communities small enough for all their members to know one another, and for a single speaker to address them all. The Greeks would have thought our 'villes tentaculaires' as monstrous as dramas running to a thousand pages, or ships a hundred miles long.

For a few centuries such city-states as these sometimes worked wonders, and made a chapter of brilliance unsurpassed in human history. But, of course, history was against them. For all their dazzling individualism, such communities were too tiny to endure. A nation-state, Macedon, became too strong for them; and so a very different, Hellenistic Greece arose, centred round the giant-city of Alexandria. But the quality was gone.

Rome in her turn began as a city-state; and was morally at her finest before what had been a city swelled into a world-empire. Though Rome grew greater, Romans, on the whole, did not. One may wonder if that far smaller Rome which withstood Gaul and Carthaginian, might not have resisted Goth and Vandal also more toughly than did that vast imperium which sprawled from the Euphrates to the Tyne.

To-day, at all events, our most admiring memories of antiquity look back, not to the Macedon of Alexander, or to the Rome of the Caesars, so much as to those cities of Hellas before them, where men left great works, and great thoughts, 'to a *little* clan'.

So too in history since then—again and again, great things and striking characters have come from small communities, like the Iceland of the Sagas, or the cities of medieval and Renaissance Italy, or that Elizabethan England which had perhaps only a tenth of our present population. Even to-day some of the smallest states in the world, like those of Scandinavia, or Switzerland, still lead in progress and enlightenment. Small communities may grow at times parochial, like Ibsen's Norway; but vast ones can become as stupid and unwieldy as a dinosaur.

As with super-states, so with super-cities—they are tremendous, but odious—cancers of civilization. One may dream of a time when posterity will say in horror, 'Would you believe it!—a million of them would pig together in the same town!'; and regard us with the same incredulous disgust as *we* feel for medieval habits of sleeping six in a bed, or for medieval schools where a big boy would lie one way, and two smaller ones the other way, with their feet beside his head. The terrible Mongols of Genghiz Khan held that men shut themselves up in cities, as silkworms shut themselves up in cocoons — simply to die. That idea may not be wholly wrong.

Others, I realize, will disagree with all this. I was struck recently by an undergraduate's letter in the magazine of a provincial university, protesting against the idea 'that man exists for the cultivation of his individuality and reason.' 'Modern Society,' cried this satisfied youth, 'is conurbanised man; a mass controlled by a specialized and centralized bureaucracy. To view such a Society with the lethargic idealism of an 18th Century Rationalist is cawing in Cloudcuckooland. We *are* centralized; we *are* specialized; we *are* conurbanised; and the co-ordinating factor of all is Organization. Bewail the denial of Individuality; bewail the modern moron and his lack of Reason; but modern Society is geared to the speed of a mass-production line, not to the decentralized beauty of contemplating the infinite while making rush mats.'

An interesting letter. Very modern—despite its archaic passion for capital letters. The writer is young, and youth is often a rebel; yet he is anti-rebellious. He belongs to a university, and universities (despite the meaning of the word) have been strongholds of individualism; yet he is anti-individualist. Is this the real voice of the future—the harbinger of termite-man? I do not know. But it illustrates, though one should not, of course, take it too seriously, what I distrust and dislike in the mind of Megalopolis. I do not spend much time in contemplating the infinite; I have not the least wish to make rush mats. But I like individuals, and I detest masses.

About the optimum population, say, for England there would, of course, be a vast diversity of opinions. Even the optimum population economically—that is, what would produce the maximum average income—remains beyond even economists to determine. For the situation is continually changing. What, for example, will be the effects of automation? But standards of living are not everything (although to listen to some people to-day one might think so). Many will feel that England would be a far pleasanter and healthier place to live in—were it not for power politics—if there were far fewer of us. Those who want ocular demonstration of this have only to glance at traffic-blocks a hundred miles long. And worse things are yet to come. Indeed, we approach the ironic situation where everyone will possess a car capable of sixty miles an hour and, in consequence, for a large part of the time no one will be able to drive at more than six. That in its turn will lead to burying yet more of England's green fields under asphalt and tarmac—a lamentable remedy. But there are far more important considerations than car-space. It may well be destructive to men's souls to be cut off from all contact with wild Nature, and reduced to a few anaemic geraniums in a window-box—if that. For the commercial mind, which now rules so much of the 'civilized' world, Nature is merely something to be raped and ravaged for two pennyworth of profit; but Nature, though she takes her time, can take also bitter revenges.

A hundred and fifty years ago England was a country of beauty unsurpassed—seldom grandiose, or titanic, but the perfection of its own quieter kind. Jane Austen was no Dorothy Wordsworth or Emily Brontë; she distrusted poetry; but she too felt that quality in her eighteenth-century way—'It was a sweet view—sweet to the eye and to the mind, English verdure, English culture, English comfort, seen under a sun bright without being oppressive.' In many places to-day we have replaced all that with unsurpassed hideousness. Ribbon-building, arterial roads, oil-refineries, nuclear power-stations, tank-ranges, missile-ranges, conurbations, caravans, holiday-camps— all make their contributions. And to our remaining 'beauty-spots' we crowd in such hordes that the beauty vanishes, and only spots, and hordes, remain.

So it goes on, far and wide, in the world of to-day. I remember the London editor of an 'intellectual' weekly who snorted at population-planning—'*I* believe in life'. But in spite of this pretty little sentiment is mere multiplication so valuable?[1] Man, it appears, has multiplied more than any other mammal with the possible exception of the rat— not a very pleasing rival in this odd pre-eminence. And 'believers in life' seem apt to care little enough about the other kinds of life that man in his reckless proliferation elbows off this planet for ever. Some may prefer to phrases about 'belief in life' Schweitzer's words about having '*respect* for life'. Our lack of that has exterminated whole species like great auk, dodo, and moa; within three decades, North America is said to have massacred no less than sixty million bison,

---

[1] I have never forgotten the shrewd mother-wit of a Swiss guide in the Faulhorn hut many years ago. His countrymen, he said, had come to prefer a few children *with* shoes to more without. He saw no virtue in simple multi-plication—'Das können die Tiere auch machen'—'Even animals can do *that*!'

sometimes even by the expeditious method of driving whole herds over precipices. Maybe, Wilfrid Blunt exaggerated, with the passionate vehemence of a poet:

> And Thou hast clean forgot the fair great beasts of yore,
> The mammoth, aurochs, elk, sea-lion, cave-bear, boar,
> Which fell before his hand, each one of them than he
> Nobler and mightier far, undone by treachery.

Maybe in the scale of the world's troubles such matters as the extinction of a few animals are only minor. But this process, which we call 'progress', is all part of that frantic self-assertion of *homo sapiens* which in the end impoverishes himself. Indeed I have sometimes an eccentric notion that the earth would be a better, certainly a more beautiful, place if three-quarters of mankind were painlessly turned, like nymphs in Ovid, into trees.

Since, then, human quality seems more important than human quantity, individuals than masses; and since mean and ugly surroundings tend to breed mean and ugly souls; I take the highly unpopular and eccentric view that, even if it is possible to support a much greater world-population, it might still be desirable, on the contrary, to make it much smaller. Posterity might gain, for example, if the present numbers of mankind slowly dropped by, say, two-thirds. Now the full depth of my iniquity stands exposed.

*   *   *

As things are, of course, anything of the kind remains wildly improbable. What might be psychologically and aesthetically desirable, remains politically too perilous. If nations cannot agree even about limiting their armaments, how should they hope to agree about limiting their populations—their factory-fodder and their cannon-fodder? They must pile up babies as they pile up bombs. For in a world of power-politics, the anarchy of an international jungle, the big creatures tend to devour the small (as with Hungary and Tibet).

Long ago Holland declined because her power was built on too small a base; now Western Europe, failing to unite, remains overshadowed by U.S.A. and U.S.S.R. If all the British emigrants to America had gone instead to Canada, Australia, and New Zealand, the British Commonwealth might carry far more weight to-day; if the British Empire had not split in 1776, or if the English-speaking races reunited now, Anglo-Saxondom might be a good deal more secure. And though there are already two hundred million Russians, one can conceive a time when the U.S.S.R. might crave admission to N.A.T.O. against the menace of, say, eight hundred million Chinese. In 1944, besides making lavish children's allowances, the Soviet Government took to encouraging its women with 'the Order of the Glory of Motherhood' for seven to nine offspring, and 'the Order of Mother Heroine' for ten. As Emerson put it, translating Béranger:

> 'Tis heavy odds
> Against the gods
> When they will match with myrmidons,
> With spawning, spawning myrmidons.
> Our turn to-day! We take command,
> Jove gives the globe into the hand
> Of myrmidons, of myrmidons.[1]

Therefore, till there is world-control of war, there can hardly be world-control of population.

On the other hand, without control of population, abolition of armaments seems vain. Men are never wholly disarmed while they have fists and teeth, sticks and stones. And how, to take but one instance, could a disarmed Australia and New Zealand, with a disarmed United States and United Kingdom powerless to help, resist being swamped by overcrowded Asiatics? Should they resign themselves? Try persuading them! And even if they did resign themselves, they would soon be overpopulated in their turn.

There is, on the other side, some faint hope that overpopulation might prove damaging to national efficiency, and that the shrewder states might come in time to see this. Already the force of circumstances has driven governments to act more intelligently in India and Japan— in Japan with *some* success. There are other smaller countries where the same could occur. It is not true, then, that *nothing* can be done; even in the world as it is.

*   *   *

(3) Remedies? It is hard to see any but a concentrated drive for population-planning. But to this there remain the most formidable obstacles—practical, scientific, and psychological.

---

[1] Zeus provided subjects for his son Aeacus by turning ants (Greek '*myrmēkes*') into men; whence their tribal name of Myrmidons.

One great practical difficulty is the time-lag. The 125,000 persons added each day to the earth's myriads are likely, for the most part, to remain here another half-century, and to produce more offspring of their own. Even the drastic measures taken during the last decade in Japan are not expected to bring the growth of her population to a stop for another thirty years.

Secondly, apart from other practical difficulties like finance, organization, education, there is the scientific difficulty of devising a contraceptive cheap and simple enough to be used by largely illiterate and backward millions. Even if research can eventually produce an effective oral antidote ('the Pill') such as is now reported from Puerto Rico, years of experiment and experience will be needed to establish that it is both effective, and harmless for a lifetime; enormous organization and outlay will be needed also to distribute it through the world.

Thirdly (and perhaps the most obstinate of all) there are the psychological obstructions—improvidence, incompetence, conservatism, bigotry, conscientious objections. Population-planning is denounced as against Nature, or against the will of God, or against the will of Marx. Some conscientious objections deserve respect; but it becomes a little hard to keep patience with the ancient parrot-cry 'Unnatural!' All civilization is 'unnatural'. To be purely 'natural' we must perch nude in trees. Progress has come by taming Nature, with prudent respect for her terrible power of striking back. The Spanish Inquisition objected to the rocks in the Tagus being blasted, on the ground that if God had wished the Tagus navigable, He would have made it so. In the early eighteenth century there were Scottish ministers who denounced farmers for fanning their grain to winnow it, as defiers of God who makes the wind blow 'where it listeth'. Our forefathers denounced sanitation and vaccination as thwarting Providence. Even within living memory there were men who opposed the use of anaesthetics for women in childbirth, as if some Heavenly Shylock were being defrauded of his due of pain.

But it does not appear that Providence is much disposed to favour the improvident, or to help those who will not use their wits to help others and themselves. Ibsen's Pastor Manders was too pious to insure an orphanage devoted to God's work. It burnt.

To those who think, on the contrary, that the basic principle of all morals is never to inflict avoidable suffering, mental or physical, on any being, human or non-human, especially on the helpless, nothing will seem more immoral than pitching unwanted children into an overcrowded world. Not to be born is no hardship: to be born only too often *is*. One can hardly picture the unborn crying (except in Butler's Erewhon)—'Why was I never born!' But plenty besides Job and Swift have cursed the day they were.

Sex and religion are topics that can excite the most raving human prejudices. When the two combine, dispassionate judgement becomes difficult indeed. In the West, especially, the physical side of healthy human love has for long periods aroused an absurd and obsessional sense of guilt; so that even the Apple of the Fall was long taken by many to symbolize the passions of the flesh (though with ironic misogyny St Thomas Aquinas argued that Eve could not have been intended simply for a companion, because in that case it would have been more rational to provide Adam with another man).

Obviously it can be bad to become a slave to sex. But to what is it *not* bad to become a slave? Though there exist plenty of gluttons and drunkards, few to-day would argue that it is therefore wicked to enjoy food and drink for their own sakes, or to take more than a bare subsistence of bread and water. Locusts and wild honey are out of fashion. Yet population-planning is still regarded in many quarters as if it were incitement to a world orgy. And so Puerto Rican clinics could be closed on orders from Washington; in 1916 Margaret Sanger was imprisoned for opening one in Brooklyn; contraceptive measures are still banned in Connecticut by a law eighty years old, whose legality was unanimously upheld by the state's Supreme Court in December 1959; and American women in Japan are said to have successfully protested to General MacArthur against any steps in the direction of population-control. (These good ladies must have been singularly edified by what the Japanese have done since.) Similarly Gandhi condemned family-planning, except by abstinence. (But then Gandhi apparently had scruples even about killing plague-infected rats.)

No doubt a lot of this opposition comes, like Gandhi's, from genuine idealism; so does a great deal of the worst harm done in the world. Idealists can be the very devil. But when one considers the blind indifference that some—I repeat, *some*—of these pillars of society seem to feel about the consequences which their prudish obstructiveness can cause in terms of human unhappiness, one may be reminded of the cocotte once taken by Baudelaire to the Louvre—'Louise Villedieu, putain à cinq francs, qui m'accompagnant une fois au Louvre, où elle n'était jamais allée, se mit à rougir, à se couvrir le visage, et me tirant à chaque instant par la manche, me demandait devant les statues et les tableaux, comment on pouvait étaler publiquement de pareilles indécences.'

One may wonder, too, why what is now generally accepted as right and proper for the royal families of Europe should be withheld as improper from the proletariat of east and west.

The Church of Rome itself, slower than most to accept innovation, has at least recognized that a problem of population exists. After all, Rome is in Italy. So Rome has sanctioned one method of avoiding conception—that of choosing the infertile periods in the monthly cycle. There is only one unfortunate drawback – that the 'safe' period is quite unsafe. It cannot be relied on. But it is hard to believe that, in face of the mounting danger, sane men, having once admitted the avoidance of conception to be permissible in principle, can continue indefinitely to insist on this crudely materialistic distinction between one method and another; so that it would remain lawful to juggle with the calendar, but unlawful, say, to swallow a pill. No doubt there exists a calculation that Catholics can be induced to out-breed heretics (as is happening in Holland); but such local gains might be dearly paid for in the world at large. For a long time men can be persuaded to go on doing what is clean contrary to their own interests, and to the interests of those they care for; but in the end, as the truth percolates, such folly grows more difficult. The Church of England has in this way moved to some extent with the facts. The Lambeth Conferences of 1908 and 1920 condemned birth-control; that of 1930 was grudgingly permissive; that of 1958, more benevolent. In November 1959 the Archbishop of York described population-planning as 'inevitable and right'.

How men think and feel about this matter in Asia, one of the most vital areas, remains hard to tell. One does not hear of opposition in Japan to the government's drastic steps; in 1950 it was reported that, in six major Japanese cities, 75 per cent of men favoured population-planning; and in rural areas, 64 per cent. Buddhists in Ceylon, though they object to taking life, are apparently not opposed to preventing it. And Islam in this matter seems to have no strong views.

On the other hand a senior Indian official has written: 'Why will the villager not respond? For the same reason that he does not respond to scores of other piecemeal blandishments, from the composting of manures to domestic hygiene. He suffers from a profound listlessness of spirit, sunk into a state of utter hopelessness, in a perpetual twilight of the senses. . . . Reproduction becomes an animal function, a proliferation which leads as much to death as to life.' That seems natural enough, in the appalling circumstances. Besides, even for the peasant not sunk in apathy, children can be set to work in early youth on the family land, and may provide the only social insurance for the parents' old age. On the other hand, a survey among women in Baroda (1950) showed 70–82 per cent in favour of family-limitation.[1] Sir Malcolm Darling, who has devoted tireless patience and energy to talking with the people of India, records how, after the last war, the younger of two Moslems he met maintained birth-control not to be contrary to Islam, though the older denied this, with the old savage argument—'God knows how to weed them out. Are there not plague and war?'; and, again, how a Sikh once quoted to him the ancient maxim of Guru Govind Singh (1675–1708)—'Too many children—Hell'. And not long ago Mr Nehru himself (hardly a cynical materialist) could say in public: 'We should be a far more advanced nation if our population were about half what it is.' It seems, then, not impossible that prejudice and obscurantism in this matter may be, paradoxically enough, often less strong among the 'backward' races than in the 'enlightened' West.[2]

*　　　*　　　*

If the problem is to be solved—and solved against time—much must depend on the will of governments to face the facts; much on the ability of science to find a method cheap and safe enough; much perhaps on help from the richer countries. But much also—probably far more —depends on the individual human being, and his power to realize his own plight. Hence the need for constant and frank discussion, instead of leaving the subject, as now, ostrichized in a conspiracy of uneasy

[1] See H. Belshaw, *Population Growth and Levels of Consumption* (1956) pp. 33, 36, 42.

[2] As shown, for example, in a recent letter to the *Guardian* from an indignant person who, after the usual hackneyed misstatements that food-supplies could easily be made adequate, that higher standards of living can be reliably counted on to reduce fertility, and that the less developed races have widespread religious objections to planning population, concluded 'as a Christian (a Roman Catholic) I know that it is wrong.' With all the politeness I could muster, I wrote inquiring on precisely what passages of the Gospel this 'knowledge' was founded; and why he condemned oral contraceptives before (so far as I know) Rome itself has pronounced on this particular point. But perhaps such questions were too improper for the *Guardian*: I was not printed.

silence; and the need for patient and tireless propaganda against man's reckless propagation.

This spread of understanding may prove hard; it may prove too little and too late. Yet it seems puzzling that it *should* be so hard; puzzling above all, that the women of the world should for untold generations have so often allowed themselves to be turned into breeding-machines—their adult lives burdened, weakened, and shortened by successions of pregnancies at excessively close intervals, largely from the mere crude egoism of the male. One thinks, for example, of poor Anne Donne, dead at thirty-two in childbirth—her twelfth in fourteen years—having married a poet of perhaps more piety than pity; and of the millions of other women victimized like Tolstoy's Countess, by husbands with all his possessiveness and none of his genius. This is not a topic on which one would expect to quote Jane Austen, of all people—a woman often as conventional as she was clever. Yet one may be struck by all the allusions even in *her* letters to acquaintances dead in childbirth, or worn out by child-bearing; till at times she is goaded into comments of considerable acidity.

Feb. 2nd, 1817. 'Good Mrs. Deedes!—I hope she will get the better of this Marianne, & then I w^d recommend to her & Mr. Deedes the simple regimen of separate rooms.'

March 23rd, 1817 (of Anne Austen). 'Poor Animal, she will be worn out before she is thirty.—I am very sorry for her.—Mrs Clement too is in that way again. I am quite tired of so many Children. Mrs Rann has a 13th.'[1]

It may be recalled how the heroine of Aristophanes' *Lysistrata* mobilized the women of Greece to end the suicidal war that was ruining all their cities, by a strike of wives. That was only a poet's fantasy. In actual fact that war dragged on till it had ruined Athens, and fatally weakened all Hellas. But one can imagine Aristophanes calling to-day, in many parts of the world, for a similar strike of mothers, to check the ruinous overcrowding of the earth. It is no use crying 'Individualists of the world, unite!' For individualists are usually hopeless at uniting. But there might be something in the cry 'Women of the world, unite!' For it is they, could they but see it, who pay most

[1] Cf. Mme de Sévigné to her son-in-law, who, she thought, was wrecking her daughter's health: 'Il paraît bien que vous ne savez ce que c'est que d'accoucher. . . . Pourvu que je ne trouve point une femme grosse, et toujours grosse, et encore grosse.' (18/10/1671).

heavily, and most immediately. Griselda has been far too patient. Is it really so exorbitant to suggest that parents should be content with three children apiece, to the vast advantage of the world, the children, and themselves? In a 1951 Census Report an Indian Registrar-General could define 'childbirth to a mother who has already given birth to three or more children of whom at least one is alive' as 'improvident maternity'.[1] Not all would go so far as that. But the striking thing is that even a Registrar-General can now go so far.[2]

Yet I cannot pretend to much optimism. Nothing perhaps could better illustrate the fecklessness of humanity than the statistics of abortion—vast, where it is legalized; vast, even where it is not. Here are millions every year willing to undergo an operation dangerous, painful, and repugnant, rather than use common caution (though it would be rash to assume that we are always wiser in other ways ourselves). Still, even if one is not very hopeful, there is no harm—on the contrary—in dreaming sometimes about what the future *could* be, provided one does not expect one's dreams to be quickly, or accurately, or even approximately fulfilled. History is full of forecasts grotesquely false; yet a few have come amazingly true. And surely it is more intelligent to think, in some measure, about the future, than to drift blindly towards one heeds not what. No doubt it is pleasantly ironic to reflect that Socrates in Plato should discuss at vast length how to govern a state, when, if tradition speaks true, he could not govern even his own wife; and should propound how to make a whole community virtuous, when he could not instil a drop of sweet reasonableness into his own Xanthippe. But, for all that, Plato's *Republic* has had both influence and prescience. So why should men not indulge sometimes in fantasies of the future, as they would have it be?

My own dream, then, is of a world far emptier than ours, with plenty of wild nature; as different from our over-urbanized countries as the Swiss National Park among the peaks of Val Cluoza from the cruel and crowded cages of old-time Zoos, with unhappy captives pacing eternally behind their bars. There Science would serve to lessen drudgery, not to multiply it; to make the world fairer and freer, not

---

[1] Such 'improvident maternity' was estimated to account for 40–45 per cent of total births.

[2] Very little has been done, however, to mend matters; Warren S. Thompson (*Population and Progress in the Far East*, 1959) estimates that effective population-control would cost 25 times the amount now spent by India on family-planning!

more squalid and oppressive. There would be an aristocracy of human beings, and a proletariat of machines. For machines are immune from weariness or boredom; like those metal slaves that Homer's Hephaestus made to serve in his hall on Olympus.

Such a world would still be subject to chance and change. It could still progress. (Too many Utopias have been imagined static, as if anything human could ever hope to escape from time.) It would still be subject to those human troubles and sorrows which are also unescapable; but not burdened, as we are, with multitudes of other troubles wholly needless and avoidable. William Morris dreamed regretfully of a medieval London 'small, and white, and clean'. One may doubt if medieval London was ever very clean at close quarters. But at least its river, and its countryside were. And such a London as Morris's could be imagined in the far future, as centre of a happier England, with its natural loveliness revived.

THE HAPPY ISLES

They dwell in cities; yet the woods toss round them,
    Isleing the white walls of each little town
In gulfs of green. Still marvelling to have found them,
    Their roads dance off again by dene and down,
        Or furzed heaths bracken-brown.
  The badger shuffles by the lone wayside;
Far through unsullied forests their silent pylons stride.

Around their teeming tilth, wild Nature's beauty.
    There even men have cast their chains away.
Steel are their only slaves—in carefree duty,
    Bright-fanged, deft-fingered, their machines all day
        Purr twinkling at their play.
  Yet hands have won again their happy skill
To body in stone and metal the dreams each dreams at will.

Warm fellowship; though still Fate stands beside them.
    Few sorrows; save the Death that waits for all,
Or Love's unkindness. Days so full betide them,
    They hearken not the Past's cold-haunting call,
        Nor brood what shall befall.
  Yet their brows knit at dismal tales of yore—
Of our maggot-swarming cities, our want, and waste, and war.

White wings in the infinite height of their blue sky-way,
  (Man, the unresting, is a wanderer still)
Yet now, not Death, but Life flings there its highway—
  Peace in their Heaven, on their earth good will.
    There from the stars to kill
  No man-made meteors shriek; beneath that sun,
In that fair world uncrowded, room for everyone.

No strange land this, far from our Europe's prison;
  No phantom coast beyond the sunset's flames.
Yon rolling forest is the Weald, rerisen,
    Two thousand years still living in its names;
    Yon stainless stream, the Thames.
  This is no island washed by faery seas—
Only our own, as it might be, in far-off centuries.[1]

This may, no doubt, be merely one of those lying dreams that come, says Virgil, through the Ivory Gate; and can live only in an ivory tower. Destiny has probably very different things in store. But it may take a good deal of thought to prevent their being things much less pleasant, in this revolutionary crisis that now seems sweeping down, so swiftly and silently, upon mankind.

It is said that in the Rome of the second century B.C. that unpleasant person, Cato the Elder, convinced of his country's danger, took to ending all his speeches in the Senate with the sentence, however irrelevant it might be to the matter in hand, 'Ceterum censeo delendam esse Carthaginem'—'But I hold that Carthage should be destroyed'. In the same way I begin to feel that, whatever one writes, and whatever one writes on, one really ought to add 'Ceterum censeo delendam esse propaginem'—'But I hold that human multiplication should be stopped'. However, few modern writers are likely to do that; or to be listened to, if they did.

Still if any man, or woman, of good will has time, money, or energy to spare, I do not know what good cause they could better serve than this. They might, of course, be mistaken—in issues so vast and complex anyone can be mistaken. But I doubt it. They might fail to produce the slightest effect. Success in a field so difficult can never be assured; it can only be deserved. Human blindness is so unlimited that, having floundered within thirty years into two cataclysmic wars, it may easily

[1] *From Many Times and Lands*, p. 317.

flounder now into a world-disaster beside which those two world-wars were child's play. The human race would doubtless survive even that. The human race is terribly tough. But it might be at a frightful cost, in suffering and degradation. It is in the hope, however uncertain, of averting this that every intelligent person should at least give thought to what has now become, I believe, the most pressing problem in the world.